Together these readings, and the comments that introduce them, explore not only what exists in our schools today, but what is possible, even desirable, for tomorrow. As such, they are pertinent reading for anyone who cares about the quality of our children's education and the future of our schools.

DONALD A. READ, Professor and Chairman of Health Education at Worcester State College, has been on innovator in humanistic approaches to teaching in health and sexuality. He is the author/co-author of eight books including *The Concept of Health, Creative Teaching in Health* and *Health and Modern Man,* as well as a number of articles on health and education.

SIDNEY B. SIMON is Professor of Humanistic Education at the University of Massachusetts, where he has been instrumental in developing humanistic education studies. He has written over 100 articles on the subject and is also the author of several books, including *Values Teaching* and *Values Clarification.*

Edited by

Donald A. Read / *Worcester State College*

Sidney B. Simon / *University of Massachusetts*

HUMANISTIC EDUCATION SOURCEBOOK

with an introduction by Don Hamachek

PRENTICE-HALL, INC. / *Englewood Cliffs, New Jersey*

Library of Congress Cataloging in Publication Data

READ, DONALD A. comp.
  Humanistic Education sourcebook

  Includes bibliographies.
  1. Education, Humanistic—Addresses, essays,
lectures. I. Simon, Sidney B., joint comp. II. Title.
LC1011.R38   370.11'2   74-23501
ISBN 0-13-447714-6
ISBN 0-13-447706-5 pbk.

© 1975 by PRENTICE-HALL, INC., Englewood Cliffs, New Jersey

Printed in the United States of America

10 9 8 7 6 5 4 3 2 1

PRENTICE-HALL INTERNATIONAL, INC., *London*
PRENTICE-HALL OF AUSTRALIA, PTY. LTD., *Sydney*
PRENTICE-HALL OF CANADA, LTD., *Toronto*
PRENTICE-HALL OF INDIA PRIVATE LIMITED, *New Delhi*
PRENTICE-HALL OF JAPAN, INC., *Tokyo*

This book is dedicated to the beautiful humanistic teachers of all kinds who are struggling to make schools better for people and better than the schools they themselves knew when they were younger, and who see in the humanistic education movement the ways to do just that.

Contents

Introduction   vi

From the Editors   vii

1 / On the Facilitation of Learning

The Interpersonal Relationship in the
Facilitation of Learning
        Carl R. Rogers   3

2 / Bringing Together Ideas and Feelings in Learning

Psychological Education
        Alfred S. Alschuler   23
Learning to Feel—Feeling to Learn: Prologue
        Harold C. Lyon, Jr.   33
Bringing Together Ideas and Feelings in Learning
        Carl R. Rogers   39
What Is "Confluent Education"?
        George Isaac Brown   50
Humanistic Education
        Alfred S. Alschuler   62
Values and Valuing
        Louis E. Raths, Merrill Harmin, and
        Sidney B. Simon   72
Laboratory Training in Planned Change
        Dorothy Mial   82
Humanistic Goals of Education ✓
        Arthur W. Combs   91

Affect and Learning
  Gerald Weinstein and Mario D. Fantini   *101*

Sensitivity Education
  Stephen M. Corey and Elinor K. Corey   *113*

"To Get Beyond the Words . . ."
  Harold C. Wells   *118*

The Human Side of Learning
  Arthur W. Combs   *123*

3 / The Teacher as Psychologist

The Teacher as Psychologist
  Arthur T. Jersild   *133*

The Boundary Line Between Education
and Psychotherapy
  Rudolf Ekstein   *136*

Education and Therapy
  Walter M. Lifton   *143*

Teaching Emotional Education in the Classroom
  Albert Ellis   *155*

4 / Sensitivity Education: Problems and Promise

Confrontation Techniques—A Two-Sided Coin
  Leonard Blank, Gloria B. Gottsegen, and
  Monroe G. Gottsegen   *165*

Sensitivity Training and Education: A Critique
  Clifford H. Edwards   *173*

Sensitivity Training: Salvation or Conspiracy?
  Thomas W. Wiggins   *179*

Critique of Sensitivity Training
  Milton K. Reimer   *184*

Encounter Groups ". . . May Loom as a Potential
Source of Salvation"
  John D. Black   *188*

Sensitivity Education: Problems and Promise
  Arthur W. Combs   *192*

Encountering What?
        John R. Silber   *196*
The Limits of Social Education ✓
        Joseph Junell   *201*
Irrationalism and the New Reformism
        Mary Anne Raywid   *211*
Differentiating Affective Concerns
        Morton Alpren   *219*
Encounter Groups and Brainwashing
        William R. Coulson   *224*

5 / "I Learn by Going Where I Have to Go."

Human Relations Training for Elementary
School Principals
        Terry A. Thomas   *241*
The Personal Approach to Good Teaching
        Arthur W. Combs   *249*
Helping Teachers Improve Classroom Group Processes
        Richard A. Schmuck   *262*
Sensitivity Training: The Affective Dimension
of Inservice Training
        Raymond L. Jerrems   *293*
Sensitivity: A Superintendent's View
        James A. Kimple   *303*

6 / Teaching with Feeling

Notes on Teaching for Personal and Social Growth:
Positive Focus
        Robert C. Hawley   *311*
Sensitivity Modules
        Howard Kirschenbaum   *315*
Guidelines for Sensitivity Training in Your School
        Larry J. Krafft and Leland W. Howe   *321*
Health—The Affective Approach
        Orvis A. Harrelson   *325*

Letting Go: Emotion in the Classroom
    Kent Owen   329

Educational Applications of Humanistic Psychology
    Dennis Romig and Charles C. Cleland   333

Free Expression Through Movement
    Edith A. Buchanan and
    Deanna Stirling Hanson   345

The Structure of Affect in the Art Curriculum
    David W. Ecker   353

Humanism: Capstone of an Educated Person
    Stephen N. Stivers, L. Gerald Buchan,
    C. Robert Dettloff, and Donald C. Orlich   363

7 / We Learn Through Experience and Experiencing

Self-Science Education: The Trumpet
    Gerald Weinstein   373

Human Development in the Classroom
    Uvaldo H. Palomares and Terri Rubini   383

Value Clarification
    Sidney B. Simon and Sara Massey   388

Depth Unfoldment Experience: A Method
for Creating Interpersonal Closeness
    Herbert A. Otto   391

How to Help Students Learn to Think . . . About
Themselves
    Merrill Harmin and Sidney B. Simon   400

Sociodrama in the Classroom—
A Different Approach to Learning
    T. J. Michels and Nolan C. Hatcher   409

Developing Sexual Awareness: A Humanistic Approach
    Donald A. Read   415

Role Playing in the Classroom
    Mark Chesler and Robert Fox   421

The Come Alive Classroom: Personal Approaches to
Good Teaching in Health
    Donald A. Read   433

Let's Be an Ice Cream Machine!
Creative Dramatics
  Gary A. Davis, Charles J. Helfert,
  and Gloria R. Shapiro   *439*
Simulation Games as Method
  Virginia M. Rogers and Audrey H. Goodloe *451*
Communication Grows in a "Magic Circle" ✓
  William Lefkowitz   *457*
Self-Concept: A Critical Dimension
in Teaching and Learning
  John T. Canfield and Harold C. Wells   *460*

Directory of Organizations and Periodicals on
Alternative Education   *469*

"Just A Few" Additional Readings   *479*

Introduction

The idea—indeed, the spirit—of humanistic education is finally emerging from its shaky, fledgling early years into a mature ideational construct and conceptual framework for understanding and improving educational practices. It is an idea which still has some growing to do, particularly in the area of coordinating its subjective hopes and dreams with objective facts and reality. That is why I am pleased to see this book come along at this point in time. This is a coordination book: it organizes under a single cover a multitude of readings in an effort to pull together and coordinate the vast field of empirical and clinical literature devoted to humanistic education.

The editors have titled this *Humanistic Education Sourcebook* because that is, in fact, what it is—a source of ideas and points of view about how a humanistic emphasis can be operationalized in a school setting. There is nothing magical about a humanistic approach to education. It takes as much hard work, planning, preparation, and dedication to be a good "humanistic" teacher as it does to be any other kind of teacher. Teaching and learning from a humanistic framework does not mean that teachers play amateur psychologists or that thinking and knowing take second chair to feeling and perceiving. Humanistic education begins with the assumption, however, that teaching is first and foremost a relationship between teacher and student which includes *human* behavior, *human* meanings, and *human* understandings that grow out of uniquely *human* experiences. In this context, a student's (and a teacher's) feelings and perceptions are not *more* important than thinking and knowing, but, rather, *as* important in the total educational program.

Since "sensitivity training" is sometimes erroneously confused with humanistic education, I think you should know that this is not a book about sensitivity training. Humanistic education is a broad conceptual approach to the educational process and sensitivity "experiences" are simply one of many possibilities built into a humanistically-oriented curriculum. Unfortunately, the concept of sensitivity training has been badly contaminated by persons who, because of lack of background in psychology and supervised clinical training, unwittingly set up emotionally damaging experiences for some sensitivity group participants because they don't know what to do with feelings once these feelings are in the open. This volume does not advocate indiscriminate use of sensitivity training. But, among other things, it will expose you to several excellent discussions related to the pros and cons of sensitivity experiences that may help you appreciate and respect the potential for good and ill inherent in them.

Curriculum content is a top priority in an educational system. So, too, is the human content. This volume will help you put both in their proper perspective.

Don E. Hamachek
Michigan State University

From the Editors

We had some very strong feelings about this book. We had feelings that such a book was needed. It was to be a real resource for those people who were into humanistic education or for those who were moving towards making their work increasingly human-centered.

We had feelings that teachers there in the "eye of the storm" would welcome the comfort inherent in holding between the same two covers a rich vein of ideas from pioneers in humanistic education such as Rogers, Combs, Weinstein, Otto, and others. We had strong feelings that future teachers would be nourished and challenged by reading these inspiring words and learning more about the concepts and techniques of this exciting phenomenon we call humanistic education.

It is our hope that with the readings and commentaries that follow, teachers, administrators, counselors, personnel workers, and students will reexamine their own attitudes concerning the teaching-learning situation. We hope it will cause teachers of all stripes to consider and examine other learning alternatives.

The *Humanistic Education Sourcebook* is designed for use in a variety of curricula and methods. It will prove useful in curriculum development, curriculum theory and practice, and general methods courses at both the elementary and secondary levels. Because of its present-future orientation, some educators will use it as their basic text for a course. Others may find it a helpful supplement to books oriented toward more traditional ideas and theories.

We are hopeful that this *Humanistic Education Sourcebook* will be widely used in in-service programs for experienced teachers, or placed in the first day packet of materials delivered to the neophyte teacher.

We feel we have collected together many of the significant efforts of a number of the leading authors. In different ways, they dig into the various issues facing this discipline we call humanistic education. We hope that these readings and commentaries create a viable sounding board and perhaps a linkage between the emerging forces in this field of education.

This collection, of course, is not meant to be exhaustive. Instead, these readings represent a sample of *what is* and *what can be*. The literature is expanding rapidly. It is an exciting and dynamic thrust in education. We cherish our own involvement in that evolution, and we welcome your involvement in it, too.

Now that we are at the end, we would like to thank some special people. Thanks to Lois Jones for reading, inquiring, and commenting on the final manuscript. Thanks to Jack Canfield for suggesting, and then writing, a final entry for this book with his associate Harold Wells. Thanks to Don Hamachek for contributing his beautiful introduction to this book. And special thanks to all the authors sharing their words, their hopes, and their wellspring of insights with all of us.

Donald A. Read and Sidney B. Simon
Amherst, Massachusetts

1 / On the Facilitation of Learning

Here then is a goal to which I can give myself wholeheartedly. I see the facilitation of learning as the aim of education, the way in which we might develop the learning man, the way in which we can learn to live as individuals in process. I see the facilitation of learning as the function which may hold constructive, tentative, changing, process answers to some of the deepest perplexities which beset man today.

But do we know how to achieve this new goal in education, or is it a will-of-the-wisp which sometimes occurs, sometimes fails to occur, and thus offers little real hope? My answer is that we possess a very considerable knowledge of the conditions which encourage self-initiated, significant, experiental, "gut-level" learning by the whole person. We do not frequently see these conditions put into effect because they mean a real revolution in our approach to education and revolutions are not for the timid. But we do find examples of this revolution in action.

—Carl R. Rogers

The Interpersonal Relationship
in the Facilitation of Learning

Carl R. Rogers

I wish to begin this paper with a statement which may seem surprising to some and perhaps offensive to others. It is simply this: Teaching, in my estimation, is a vastly overrated function.

Having made such a statement, I scurry to the dictionary to see if I really mean what I say. Teaching means "to instruct." Personally I am not much interested in instructing another. "To impart knowledge or skill." My reaction is, why not be more efficient, using a book or programmed learning? "To make to know." Here my hackles rise. I have no wish to *make* anyone know something. "To show, guide, direct." As I see it, too many people have been shown, guided, directed. So I come to the conclusion that I *do* mean what I said. Teaching is, for me, a relatively unimportant and vastly overvalued activity.

But there is more in my attitude than this. I have a negative reaction to teaching. Why? I think it is because it raises all the wrong questions. As soon as we focus on teaching, the question arises, what shall we teach? What, from our superior vantage point, does the other person need to know? This raises the ridiculous question of coverage. What shall the course cover? (Here I am acutely aware of the fact that "to cover" means both "to take in" and "to conceal from view," and I believe that most courses admirably achieve both these aims.) This notion of coverage is based on the assumption that what is taught is what is learned; what is presented is what is assimilated. I know of no assumption so obviously untrue. One does not need research to provide evidence that this is false. One needs only to talk with a few students.

Carl R. Rogers, "The Interpersonal Relationship in the Facilitation of Learning," in *Humanizing Education: The Person in the Process,* Robert R. Leeper, editor. Washington, D.C.: Association for Supervision and Curriculum Development, 1967, pp. 1–18. Reprinted with permission of the Association for Supervision and Curriculum Development and Carl R. Rogers. Copyright © 1967 by the Association for Supervision and Curriculum Development.

But I ask myself, "Am I so prejudiced against teaching that I find no situation in which it is worthwhile?" I immediately think of my experience in Australia only a few months ago. I became much interested in the Australian aborigine. Here is a group which for more than 20,000 years has managed to live and exist in a desolate environment in which a modern man would perish within a few days. The secret of his survival has been teaching. He has passed on to the young every shred of knowledge about how to find water, about how to track game, about how to kill the kangaroo, about how to find his way through the trackless desert. Such knowledge is conveyed to the young as being *the* way to behave, and any innovation is frowned upon. It is clear that teaching has provided him the way to survive in a hostile and relatively unchanging environment.

Now I am closer to the nub of the question which excites me. Teaching and the imparting of knowledge make sense in an unchanging environment. This is why it has been an unquestioned function for centuries. But if there is one truth about modern man, it is that he lives in an environment which is *continually changing*. The one thing I can be sure of is that the physics which is taught to the present day student will be outdated in a decade. The teaching in psychology will certainly be out of date in 20 years. The so-called "facts of history" depend very largely upon the current mood and temper of the culture. Chemistry, biology, genetics, sociology, are in such flux that a firm statement made today will almost certainly be modified by the time the student gets around to using the knowledge.

We are, in my view, faced with an entirely new situation in education where the goal of education, if we are to survive, is the *facilitation of change and learning*. The only man who is educated is the man who has learned how to learn; the man who has learned how to adapt and change; the man who has realized that no knowledge is secure, that only the process of *seeking* knowledge gives a basis for security. Changingness, a reliance on *process* rather than upon static knowledge, is the only thing that makes any sense as a goal for education in the modern world.

So now with some relief I turn to an activity, a purpose, which really warms me—the *facilitation of learning*. When I have been able to transform a group—and here I mean all the members of a group, myself included—into a community of *learners,* then the excitement has been almost beyond belief. To free curiosity; to permit individuals to go charging off in new directions dictated by their own interests; to unleash curiosity; to open everything to questioning and exploration; to recognize that everything is in process of change—here is an experience I can never forget. I cannot always achieve it in groups with which I am associated but when it is partially or largely achieved then it becomes a never-to-be-forgotten group experience. Out of such a context arise true students, real learners, creative scientists and scholars and practitioners, the kind of individuals who can live in a delicate but ever-changing balance between what is presently known and the flowing, moving, altering, problems and facts of the future.

Here then is a goal to which I can give myself wholeheartedly. I see the facilitation of learning as the aim of education, the way in which we might develop the learning man, the way in which we can learn to live as individuals in process. I see the facilitation of learning as the function which may hold constructive, tentative, changing, process answers to some of the deepest perplexities which beset man today.

But do we know how to achieve this new goal in education, or is it a will-of-the-wisp which sometimes occurs, sometimes fails to occur, and thus offers little real hope? My answer is that we possess a very considerable knowledge of the conditions which encourage self-initiated, significant, experiential, "gut-level" learning by the whole person. We do not frequently see these conditions put into effect because they mean a real revolution in our approach to education and revolutions are not for the timid. But we do find examples of this revolution in action.

We know—and I will briefly describe some of the evidence—that the initiation of such learning rests not upon the teaching skills of the leader, not upon his scholarly knowledge of the field, not upon his curricular planning, not upon his use of audio-visual aids, not upon the programmed learning he utilizes, not upon his lectures and presentations, not upon an abundance of books, though each of these might at one time or another be utilized as an important resource. No, the facilitation of significant learning rests upon certain attitudinal qualities which exist in the personal *relationship* between the facilitator and the learner.

We came upon such findings first in the field of psychotherapy, but increasingly there is evidence which shows that these findings apply in the classroom as well. We find it easier to think that the intensive relationship between therapist and client might possess these qualities, but we are also finding that they may exist in the countless interpersonal interactions (as many as 1,000 per day, as Jackson [1966] has shown) between the teacher and his pupils.

What are these qualities, these attitudes, which facilitate learning? Let me describe them very briefly, drawing illustrations from the teaching field.

REALNESS IN THE FACILITATOR OF LEARNING

Perhaps the most basic of these essential attitudes is realness or genuineness. When the facilitator is a real person, being what he is, entering into a relationship with the learner without presenting a front or a facade, he is much more likely to be effective. This means that the feelings which he is experiencing are available to him, available to his awareness, that he is able to live these feelings, be them, and able to communicate them if appropriate. It means that he comes into a direct personal encounter with the learner, meeting him on a person-to-person basis. It means that he is *being* himself, not denying himself.

Seen from this point of view it is suggested that the teacher can be a real person in his relationship with his students. He can be enthusiastic, he can be bored, he can be interested in students, he can be angry, he can be sensitive and sympathetic. Because he accepts these feelings as his own he has no need to impose them on his students. He can like or dislike a student product without implying that it is objectively good or bad or that the student is good or bad. He is simply expressing a feeling for the product, a feeling which exists within himself. Thus, he is a person to his students, not a faceless embodiment of a curricular requirement nor a sterile tube through which knowledge is passed from one generation to the next.

It is obvious that this attitudinal set, found to be effective in psychotherapy, is sharply in contrast with the tendency of most teachers to show themselves to their pupils simply as roles. It is quite customary for teachers rather consciously to put on the mask, the role, the facade, of being a teacher, and to wear this facade all day removing it only when they have left the school at night.

But not all teachers are like this. Take Sylvia Ashton-Warner, who took resistant, supposedly slow-learning primary school Maori children in New Zealand, and let them develop their own reading vocabulary. Each child could request one word—whatever word he wished—each day, and she would print it on a card and give it to him. "Kiss," "ghost," "bomb," "tiger," "fight," "love," "daddy"—these are samples. Soon they were building sentences, which they could also keep. "He'll get a licking." "Pussy's frightened." The children simply never forgot these self-initiated learnings. Yet it is not my purpose to tell you of her methods. I want instead to give you a glimpse of her attitude, of the passionate realness which must have been as evident to her tiny pupils as to her readers. An editor asked her some questions and she responded: " 'A few cool facts' you asked me for. . . . I don't know that there's a cool fact in me, or anything else cool for that matter, on this particular subject. I've got only hot long facts on the matter of Creative Teaching, scorching both the page and me" (Ashton-Warner, 1963, p. 26).

Here is no sterile facade. Here is a vital *person,* with convictions, with feelings. It is her transparent realness which was, I am sure, one of the elements that made her an exciting facilitator of learning. She does not fit into some neat educational formula. She *is,* and students grow by being in contact with someone who really is.

Take another very different person, Barbara Shiel, also doing exciting work facilitating learning in sixth graders.[1] She gave them a great deal of responsible freedom, and I will mention some of the reactions of her students later. But here is an example of the way she shared herself with her pupils—not just sharing feelings of sweetness and light, but anger and frustration. She had made art materials freely available, and students often used these in creative ways, but the room frequently looked like a picture of chaos. Here is her report of her feelings and what she did with them.

> I find it (still) maddening to live with the mess—with a capital M! No one seems to care except me. Finally, one day I told the children . . . that I am a neat, orderly person by nature and that the mess was driving me to distraction. Did they have a solution? It was suggested they could have volunteers to clean up. . . . I said it didn't seem fair to me to have the same people clean up all the time for others—but it *would* solve it for me. "Well, some people *like* to clean," they replied. So that's the way it is (Shiel, 1966).

I hope this example puts some lively meaning into the phrases I used earlier, that the facilitator "is able to live these feelings, be them, and able to communicate them if appropriate." I have chosen an example of negative feelings, because I think it is more difficult for most of us to visualize what this would mean. In this instance, Miss Shiel is taking the risk of being transparent in her angry frustrations about the mess. And what happens? The same thing which, in my experience, nearly always happens. These young people accept and respect her feelings, take them into account, and work out a novel solution which none of us, I believe, would have suggested in advance. Miss Shiel wisely comments, "I used to get upset and feel guilty when I became angry—I finally realized the children could accept *my* feelings, too. And it is important for them to know when they've 'pushed me.' I have limits, too" (Shiel, 1966).

Just to show that positive feelings, when they are real, are equally effective, let me quote briefly a college student's reaction, in a different course. ". . . Your sense of humor in the class was cheering; we all felt relaxed because you showed us your human self, not a mechanical teacher image. I feel as if I have more understanding and faith in my teachers now. . . . I feel closer to the students too." Another says, ". . . You conducted the class on a personal level and therefore in my mind I was able to formulate a picture of you as a person and not as merely a walking textbook." Or another student in the same course,

---

[1] For a more extended account of Miss Shiel's initial attempts, see Rogers, 1966a. Her later experience is described in Shiel, 1966.

> . . . It wasn't as if there was a teacher in the class, but rather someone whom we could trust and identify as a "sharer." You were so perceptive and sensitive to our thoughts, and this made it all the more "authentic" for me. It was an "authentic" *experience,* not just a class (Bull, 1966).

I trust I am making it clear that to be real is not always easy, nor is it achieved all at once, but it is basic to the person who wants to become that revolutionary individual, a facilitator of learning.

PRIZING, ACCEPTANCE, TRUST

There is another attitude which stands out in those who are successful in facilitating learning. I have observed this attitude. I have experienced it. Yet, it is hard to know what term to put to it so I shall use several. I think of it as prizing the learner, prizing his feelings, his opinions, his person. It is a caring for the learner, but a non-possessive caring. It is an acceptance of this other individual as a separate person, having worth in his own right. It is a basic trust—a belief that this other person is somehow fundamentally trustworthy.

Whether we call it prizing, acceptance, trust, or by some other term, it shows up in a variety of observable ways. The facilitator who has a considerable degree of this attitude can be fully acceptant of the fear and hesitation of the student as he approaches a new problem as well as acceptant of the pupil's satisfaction in achievement. Such a teacher can accept the student's occasional apathy, his erratic desires to explore byroads of knowledge, as well as his disciplined efforts to achieve major goals. He can accept personal feelings which both disturb and promote learning—rivalry with a sibling, hatred of authority, concern about personal adequacy. What we are describing is a prizing of the learner as an imperfect human being with many feelings, many potentialities. The facilitator's prizing or acceptance of the learner is an operational expression of his essential confidence and trust in the capacity of the human organism.

I would like to give some examples of this attitude from the classroom situation. Here any teacher statements would be properly suspect, since many of us would like to feel we hold such attitudes, and might have a biased perception of our qualities. But let me indicate how this attitude of prizing, of accepting, of trusting, appears to the student who is fortunate enough to experience it.

Here is a statement from a college student in a class with Morey Appell.

> Your way of being with us is a revelation to me. In your class I feel important, mature, and capable of doing things on my own. I want to

think for myself and this need cannot be accomplished through textbooks and lectures alone, but through living. I think you see me as a person with real feelings and needs, an individual. What I say and do are significant expressions from me, and you recognize this (Appell, 1959).

One of Miss Shiel's sixth graders expresses much more briefly her misspelled appreciation of this attitude, "You are a wounderful teacher, period ! ! !"

College students in a class with Dr. Patricia Bull describe not only these prizing, trusting attitudes, but the effect these have had on their other interactions.

> . . . I feel that I can say things to you that I can't say to other professors . . . Never before have I been so aware of the other students or their personalities. I have never had so much interaction in a college classroom with my classmates. The climate of the classroom has had a very profound effect on me . . . the free atmosphere for discussion affected me . . . the general atmosphere of a particular session affected me. There have been many times when I have carried the discussion out of the class with me and thought about it for a long time.

> . . . I still feel close to you, as though there were some tacit understanding between us, almost a conspiracy. This adds to the in-class participation on my part because I feel that at least one person in the group will react, even when I am not sure of the others. It does not matter really whether your reaction is positive or negative, it just *is*. Thank you.

> . . . I appreciate the respect and concern you have for others, including myself. . . . As a result of my experience in class, plus the influence of my readings, I sincerely believe that the student-centered teaching method does provide an ideal framework for learning; not just for the accumulation of facts, but more important, for learning about ourselves in relation to others. . . . When I think back to my shallow awareness in September compared to the depth of my insights now, I know that this course has offered me a learning experience of great value which I couldn't have acquired in any other way.

> . . . Very few teachers would attempt this method because they would feel that they would lose the students' respect. On the contrary. You gained our respect, through your ability to speak to us on our level, instead of ten miles above us. With the complete lack of communication we see in this school, it was a wonderful experience to see people listening to each other and really communicating on an adult, intelligent level. More classes should afford us this experience (Bull, 1966).

As you might expect, college students are often suspicious that these seeming attitudes are phony. One of Dr. Bull's students writes:

> . . . Rather than observe my classmates for the first few weeks, I concentrated my observations on you, Dr. Bull. I tried to figure out your

motivations and purposes. I was convinced that you were a hypocrite. . . . I did change my opinion, however. You are not a hypocrite, by any means. . . . I do wish the course could continue. "Let each become all he is capable of being." . . . Perhaps my most disturbing question, which relates to this course is: When will we stop hiding things from ourselves and our contemporaries? (Bull, 1966).

I am sure these examples are more than enough to show that the facilitator who cares, who prizes, who trusts the learner, creates a climate for learning so different from the ordinary classroom that any resemblance is, as they say, "purely coincidental."

EMPATHIC UNDERSTANDING

A further element which establishes a climate for self-initiated, experiential learning is empathic understanding. When the teacher has the ability to understand the student's reactions from the inside, has a sensitive awareness of the way the process of education and learning seems *to the student,* then again the likelihood of significant learning is increased.

This kind of understanding is sharply different from the usual evaluative understanding, which follows the pattern of, "I understand what is wrong with you." When there is a sensitive empathy, however, the reaction in the learner follows something of this pattern, "At last someone understands how it feels and seems to be *me* without wanting to analyze me or judge me. Now I can blossom and grow and learn."

This attitude of standing in the other's shoes, of viewing the world through the student's eyes, is almost unheard of in the classroom. One could listen to thousands of ordinary classroom interactions without coming across one instance of clearly communicated, sensitively accurate, empathic understanding. But it has a tremendously releasing effect when it occurs.

Let me take an illustration from Virginia Axline, dealing with a second grade boy. Jay, age 7, had been aggressive, a trouble maker, slow of speech and learning. Because of his "cussing" he was taken to the principal, who paddled him, unknown to Miss Axline. During a free work period, he fashioned a man of clay, very carefully, down to a hat and a handkerchief in his pocket. "Who is that?" asked Miss Axline. "Dunno," replied Jay. "Maybe it is the principal. He has a handkerchief in his pocket like that." Jay glared at the clay figure. "Yes," he said. Then he began to tear the head off and looked up and smiled. Miss Axline said, "You sometimes feel like twisting his head off, don't you? You get so mad at him." Jay tore off one arm, another, then beat the figure to a pulp with his fists. Another boy, with the perception of the young, explained,

"Jay is mad at Mr. X because he licked him this noon." "Then you must feel lots better now," Miss Axline commented. Jay grinned and began to rebuild Mr. X. (Adapted from Axline, 1944.)

The other examples I have cited also indicate how deeply appreciative students feel when they are simply *understood*—not evaluated, not judged, simply understood from their *own* point of view, not the teacher's. If any teacher set herself the task of endeavoring to make one non-evaluative, acceptant, empathic response per day to a pupil's demonstrated or verbalized feeling, I believe he would discover the potency of this currently almost nonexistent kind of understanding.

Let me wind up this portion of my remarks by saying that when a facilitator creates, even to a modest degree, a classroom climate characterized by such realness, prizing, and empathy, he discovers that he has inaugurated an educational revolution. Learning of a different quality, proceeding at a different pace, with a greater degree of pervasiveness, occurs. Feelings—positive and negative, confused—become a part of the classroom experience. Learning becomes life, and a very vital life at that. The student is on his way, sometimes excitedy, sometimes reluctantly, to becoming a learning, changing being.

THE EVIDENCE

Already I can hear the mutterings of some of my so-called "hard-headed" colleagues. "A very pretty picture—very touching. But these are all self-reports." (As if there were any other type of expression! But that's another issue.) They ask, "Where is the evidence? How do you know?" I would like to turn to this evidence. It is not overwhelming, but it is consistent. It is not perfect, but it is suggestive.

First of all, in the field of psychotherapy, Barrett-Lennard (1962) developed an instrument whereby he could measure these attitudinal qualities: genuineness or congruence, prizing or positive regard, empathy or understanding. This instrument was given to both client and therapist, so that we have the perception of the relationship both by the therapist and by the client whom he is trying to help. To state some of the findings very briefly it may be said that those clients who eventually showed more therapeutic change as measured by various instruments, perceived *more* of these qualities in their relationship with the therapist than did those who eventually showed less change. It is also significant that this difference in perceived relationships was evident as early as the fifth interview, and predicted later change or lack of change in therapy. Furthermore, it was found that the *client's* perception of the relationship, his experience of it, was a better predictor of ultimate outcome than was the perception of the relationship by the therapist. Barrett-Lennard's original study has been amplified and generally confirmed by other studies.

So we may say, cautiously, and with qualifications which would be too cumbersome for the present paper, that if, in therapy, the client perceives his therapist as real and genuine, as one who likes, prizes, and empathically understands him, self-learning and therapeutic change are facilitated.

Now another thread of evidence, this time related more closely to education. Emmerling (1961) found that when high school teachers were asked to identify the problems they regarded as most urgent, they could be divided into two groups. Those who regarded their most serious problems, for example, as "Helping children think for themselves and be independent"; "Getting students to participate"; "Learning new ways of helping students develop their maximum potential"; "Helping students express individual needs and interests"; fell into what he called the "open" or "positively oriented" group. When Barrett-Lennard's Relationship Inventory was administered to the students of these teachers, it was found that they were perceived as significantly more real, more acceptant, more empathic than the other group of teachers whom I shall now describe.

The second category of teachers were those who tended to see their most urgent problems in negative terms, and in terms of student deficiencies and inabilities. For them the urgent problems were such as these: "Trying to teach children who don't even have the ability to follow directions"; "Teaching children who lack a desire to learn"; "Students who are not able to do the work required for their grade"; "Getting the children to listen." It probably will be no surprise that when the students of these teachers filled out the Relationship Inventory they saw their teachers as exhibiting relatively little of genuineness, of acceptance and trust, or of empathic understanding.

Hence we may say that the teacher whose orientation is toward releasing the student's potential exhibits a high degree of these attitudinal qualities which facilitate learning. The teacher whose orientation is toward the shortcomings of his students exhibits much less of these qualities.

A small pilot study by Bills (1961, 1966) extends the significance of these findings. A group of eight teachers was selected, four of them rated as adequate and effective by their superiors, and also showing this more positive orientation to their problems. The other four were rated as inadequate teachers and also had a more negative orientation to their problems, as described above. The students of these teachers were then asked to fill out the Barrett-Lennard Relationship Inventory, giving their perception of their teacher's relationship to them. This made the students very happy. Those who saw their relationship with the teacher as good were happy to describe this relationship. Those who had an unfavorable relationship were pleased to have, for the first time, an opportunity to specify the ways in which the relationship was unsatisfactory.

The more effective teachers were rated higher in every attitude measured by the Inventory: they were seen as more real, as having a higher level of regard for their students, were less conditional or judgmental in their attitudes, showed more empathic understanding. Without going into the details of the study it may be illuminating to mention that the total scores summing these attitudes vary sharply. For example, the relationships of a group of clients with their therapists, as perceived by the clients, received an average score of 108. The four most adequate high school teachers as seen by their students, received a score of 60. The four less adequate teachers received a score of 34. The lowest rated teacher received an average score of 2 from her students on the Relationship Inventory.

This small study certainly suggests that the teacher regarded as effective displays in her attitudes those qualities I have described as facilitative of learning, while the inadequate teacher shows little of these qualities.

Approaching the problem from a different angle, Schmuck (1963) has shown that in classrooms where pupils perceive their teachers as understanding them, there is likely to be a more diffuse liking structure among the pupils. This means that where the teacher is empathic, there are not a few students strongly liked and a few strongly disliked, but liking and affection are more evenly diffused throughout the group. In a later study he has shown that among students who are highly involved in their classroom peer group, "significant relationships exist between actual liking status on the one hand and utilization of abilities, attitude toward self, and attitude toward school on the other hand" (1966, p. 357–58). This seems to lend confirmation to the other evidence by indicating that in an understanding classroom climate every student tends to feel liked by all the others, to have a more positive attitude toward himself and toward school. If he is highly involved with his peer group (and this appears probable in such a classroom climate), he also tends to utilize his abilities more fully in his school achievement.

But you may still ask, does the student actually *learn* more where these attitudes are present? Here an interesting study of third graders by Aspy (1965) helps to round out the suggestive evidence. He worked in six third-grade classes. The teachers tape-recorded two full weeks of their interaction with their students in the periods devoted to the teaching of reading. These recordings were done two months apart so as to obtain an adequate sampling of the teacher's interactions with her pupils. Four-minute segments of these recordings were randomly selected for rating. Three raters, working independently and "blind," rated each segment for the degree of congruence or genuineness shown by the teacher, the degree of her prizing or unconditional positive regard, and the degree of her empathic understanding.

The Reading Achievement Tests (Stanford Achievement) were used as the criterion. Again, omitting some of the details of a carefully and rigorously controlled study, it may be said that the children in the three classes with the highest degree of the attitudes described above showed a significantly greater gain in reading achievement than those students in the three classes with a lesser degree of these qualities.

So we may say, with a certain degree of assurance, that the attitudes I have endeavored to describe are not only effective in facilitating a deeper learning and understanding of self in a relationship such as psychotherapy, but that these attitudes characterize teachers who are regarded as effective teachers, and that the students of these teachers learn more, even of a conventional curriculum, than do students of teachers who are lacking in these attitudes.

I am pleased that such evidence is accumulating. It may help to justify the revolution in education for which I am obviously hoping. But the most striking learnings of students exposed to such a climate are by no means restricted to greater achievement in the three R's. The significant learnings are the more personal ones—independence, self-initiated and responsible learning; release of creativity, a tendency to become more of a person. I can only illustrate this by picking, almost at random, statements from students whose teachers have endeavored to create a climate of trust, of prizing, of realness, of understanding, and above all, of freedom.

Again I must quote from Sylvia Ashton-Warner one of the central effects of such a climate.

> . . . The drive is no longer the teacher's, but the children's own. . . . The teacher is at last with the stream and not against it, the stream of children's inexorable creativeness (Ashton-Warner, p. 93).

If you need verification of this, listen to a few of Dr. Bull's sophomore students. The first two are mid-semester comments.

> . . . This course is proving to be a vital and profound experience for me. . . . This unique learning situation is giving me a whole new conception of just what learning is. . . . I am experiencing a real growth in this atmosphere of constructive freedom. . . . The whole experience is very challenging. . . .

> . . . I feel that the course has been of great value to me. . . . I'm glad to have had this experience because it has made me think. . . . I've never been so personally involved with a course before, especially *outside* the classroom. It's been frustrating, rewarding, enjoyable and tiring!

The other comments are from the end of the course.

> . . . This course is not ending with the close of the semester for me, but continuing. . . . I don't know of any greater benefit which can be gained from a course than this desire for further knowledge. . . .

> . . . I feel as though this type of class situation has stimulated me more in making me realize where my responsibilities lie, especially as far as doing required work on my own. I no longer feel as though a test date is the criterion for reading a book. I feel as though my future work will be done for what *I* will get out of it, not just for a test mark.

> . . . I have enjoyed the experience of being in this course. I guess that any dissatisfaction I feel at this point is a disappointment in myself, for not having taken full advantage of the opportunities the course offered.

> . . . I think that now I am acutely aware of the breakdown in communications that does exist in our society from seeing what happened in our class. . . . I've grown immensely. I know that I am a different person than I was when I came into that class. . . . It has done a great deal in helping me understand myself better. . . . Thank you for contributing to my growth.

> . . . My idea of education has been to gain information from the teacher by attending lectures. The emphasis and focus were on the teacher. . . . One of the biggest changes that I experienced in this class was my outlook on education. Learning is something more than a grade on a report card. No one can measure what you have learned because it's a personal thing. I was very confused between learning and memorization. I could memorize very well, but I doubt if I ever learned as much as I could have. I believe my attitude toward learning has changed from a grade-centered outlook to a more personal one.

> . . . I have learned a lot more about myself and adolescents in general. . . . I also gained more confidence in myself and my study habits by realizing that I could learn by myself without a teacher leading me by the hand. I have also learned a lot by listening to my classmates and evaluating their opinions and thoughts. . . . This course has proved to be a most meaningful and worthwhile experience. . . . (Bull, 1966).

If you wish to know what this type of course seems like to a sixth grader, let me give you a sampling of the reactions of Miss Shiel's youngsters, misspellings and all.

> . . . I feel that I am learning self ability. I am learning not only school work but I am learning that you can learn on your own as well as someone can teach you.

> . . . I have a little trouble in Social Studies finding things to do. I have a hard time working the exact amount of time. Sometimes I talk to much.

. . . My parents don't understand the program. My mother say's it will give me a responsibility and it will let me go at my own speed.

. . . I like this plan because thire is a lot of freedom. I also learn more this way than the other way you don't have to wate for others you can go at your on speed rate it also takes a lot of responsibility (Shiel, 1966).

Or let me take two more, from Dr. Appell's graduate class.

. . . I have been thinking about what happened through this experience. The only conclusion I come to is that if I try to measure what is going on, or what I was at the beginning, I have got to know what I was when I started—and I don't. . . . So many things I did and feel are just lost . . . scrambled up inside. . . . They don't seem to come out in a nice little pattern or organization I can say or write. . . . There are so many things left unsaid. I know I have only scratched the surface, I guess. I can feel so many things almost ready to come out . . . maybe that's enough. *It seems all kinds of things have so much more meaning now than ever before.* . . . This experience has had meaning, has done things to me and I am not sure how much or how far just yet. I think I am going to be a better me in the fall. *That's one thing I think I am sure of* (Appell, 1963).

. . . You follow no plan, yet I'm learning. Since the term began I seem to feel more alive, more real to myself. I enjoy being alone as well as with other people. My relationships with children and other adults are becoming more emotional and involved. Eating an orange last week, I peeled the skin off each separate orange section and liked it better with the transparent shell off. It was jucier and fresher tasting that way. I began to think, that's how I feel sometimes, without a transparent wall around me, really communicating my feelings. I feel that I'm growing, how much, I don't know. I'm thinking, considering, pondering and learning (Appell, 1959).

I can't read these student statements—6th grade, college, graduate level—without my eyes growing moist. Here are teachers, risking themselves, *being* themselves, *trusting* their students, adventuring into the existential unknown, taking the subjective leap. And what happens? Exciting, incredible *human* events. You can sense persons being created, learnings being initiated, future citizens rising to meet the challenge of unknown worlds. If only one teacher out of one hundred dared to risk, dared to be, dared to trust, dared to understand, we would have an infusion of a living spirit into education which would, in my estimation, be priceless.

I have heard scientists at leading schools of science, and scholars in leading universities, arguing that it is absurd to try to encourage all students to be creative—we need hosts of mediocre technicians and workers and if a few creative scientists and artists and leaders emerge, that will be enough. That may be enough for them. It may be enough to suit you. I want to go on record as saying it is *not* enough to suit me. When I realize the incredible potential in the ordinary student, I want to try to release it. We are working hard to release the incredible energy in the atom and the nucleus of the atom. If we do not devote equal energy— yes, and equal money—to the release of the potential of the individual person, then the enormous discrepancy between our level of physical energy resources and human energy resources will doom us to a deserved and universal destruction.

I'm sorry I can't be coolly scientific about this. The issue is too urgent. I can only be passionate in my statement that people count, that interpersonal relationships *are* important, that we know something about releasing human potential, that we could learn much more, and that unless we give strong positive attention to the human interpersonal side of our educational dilemma, our civilization is on its way down the drain. Better courses, better curricula, better coverage, better teaching machines, will never resolve our dilemma in a basic way. Only persons, acting like persons in their relationships with their students can even begin to make a dent on this most urgent problem of modern education.

I cannot, of course, stop here in a professional lecture. An academic lecture should be calm, factual, scholarly, critical, preferably devoid of any personal beliefs, completely devoid of passion. (This is one of the reasons I left university life, but that is a completely different story) I cannot fully fulfill these requirements for a professional lecture, but let me at least try to state, somewhat more calmly and soberly, what I have said with such feeling and passion.

I have said that it is most unfortunate that educators and the public think about, and focus on, *teaching*. It leads them into a host of questions which are either irrelevant or absurd so far as real education is concerned.

I have said that if we focused on the facilitation of *learning*—how, why, and when the student learns, and how learning seems and feels from the inside, we might be on a much more profitable track.

I have said that we have some knowledge, and could gain more, about the conditions which facilitate learning, and that one of the most important of these conditions is the attitudinal quality of the interpersonal relationship between facilitator and learner. (There are other conditions, too, which I have tried to spell out elsewhere [Rogers, 1966b]).

Those attitudes which appear effective in promoting learning can be described. First of all is a transparent realness in the facilitator, a willingness to be a person, to be and to live the feelings and thoughts of the moment. When this realness includes a prizing, a caring, a trust and respect for the learner, the climate for learning is enhanced. When it includes a sensitive and accurate empathic listening, then indeed a freeing climate, stimulative of self-initiated learning and growth, exists.

I have tried to make plain that individuals who hold such attitudes, and are bold enough to act on them, do not simply modify classroom methods—they revolutionize them. They perform almost none of the functions of teachers. It is no longer accurate to call them teachers. They are catalyzers, facilitators, giving freedom and life and the opportunity to learn, to students.

I have brought in the cumulating research evidence which suggests that individuals who hold such attitudes are regarded as effective in the classroom; that the problems which concern them have to do with the release of potential, not the deficiencies of their students; that they seem to create classroom situations in which there are not admired children and disliked children, but in which affection and liking are a part of the life of every child; that in classrooms approaching such a psychological climate, children learn more of the conventional subjects.

But I have intentionally gone beyond the empirical findings to try to take you into the inner life of the student—elementary, college, and graduate—who is fortunate enough to live and learn in such an interpersonal relationship with a facilitator, in order to let you see what learning feels like when it is free, self-initiated and spontaneous. I have tried to indicate how it even changes the student-student relationship—making it more aware, more caring, more sensitive, as well as increasing the self-related learning of significant material.

Throughout my paper I have tried to indicate that if we are to have citizens who can live constructively in this kaleidoscopically changing world, we can *only* have them if we are willing for them to become self-starting, self-initiating learners. Finally, it has been my purpose to show that this kind of learner develops best, so far as we now know, in a growth-promoting, facilitative, relationship with a *person*.

REFERENCES

APPELL, M. L. "Selected Student Reactions to Student-centered Courses." Mimeographed manuscript, 1959.

APPELL, M. L. "Self-understanding for the Guidance Counselor." *Personnel and Guidance Journal* 42(2): 143–48; October 1963.

ASHTON-WARNER, S. *Teacher.* New York: Simon and Schuster, 1963.

ASPY, D. N. "A Study of Three Facilitative Conditions and Their Relationship to the Achievement of Third Grade Students." Unpublished Ed.D. dissertation, University of Kentucky, 1965.

AXLINE, VIRGINIA M. "Morale on the School Front." *Journal of Educational Research* 38: 521–33; 1944.

BARRETT-LENNARD, G. T. "Dimensions of Therapist Response as Causal Factors in Therapeutic Change." *Psychological Monographs,* 76, 1962. (Whole No. 562.)

BILLS, R. E. Personal correspondence, 1961, 1966.

BULL, PATRICIA. Student reactions, Fall 1965. State University College, Cortland, New York. Mimeographed manuscripts, 1966.

EMMERLING, F. C. "A Study of the Relationships Between Personality Characteristics of Classroom Teachers and Pupil Perceptions." Unpublished Ph.D. dissertation, Auburn University, Auburn, Alabama, 1961.

JACKSON, P. W. "The Student's World." University of Chicago. Mimeographed, 1966.

ROGERS, C. R. "To Facilitate Learning." In: Malcolm Provus, editor. NEA Handbook for Teachers, *Innovations for Time To Teach.* Washington, D.C.: Department of Classroom Teachers, NEA, 1966a.

ROGERS, C. R. "The Facilitation of Significant Learning." In: L. Siegel, editor. *Contemporary Theories of Instruction.* San Francisco, California: Chandler Publishing Co., 1966b.

SCHMUCK, R. "Some Aspects of Classroom Social Climate." *Psychology in the Schools* 3: 59–65; 1966.

SCHMUCK, R. "Some Relationships of Peer Liking Patterns in the Classroom to Pupil Attitudes and Achievement." *The School Review* 71: 337–59; 1963.

SHIEL, BARBARA J. "Evaluation: A Self-directed Curriculum, 1965." Mimeographed, 1966.

2 / Bringing Together Ideas and Feelings in Learning

We get closer to what I'm speaking of in a human relations group where a person first has a deeply moving experience of relating to another, and then attends a general session where the process of the encounter group is discussed. "Oh," he says to himself, ". . . that's what I've just been through." The affective-experiential and the cognitive have been brought close together in time, and each is tied to the other. So if I were to attempt a crude definition of what it means to learn as a whole person, I would say that it involves learning of a unified sort, at the cognitive, feeling, and gut level, but with a clear awareness of its different aspects. I suspect that in its purest form this occurs rarely, but perhaps learning experiences can still be judged by their closeness or remoteness to this general definition.
—Carl R. Rogers

Psychological Education

Alfred S. Alschuler

At the joint frontier of psychology and education, a new movement is emerging that attempts to promote psychological growth directly through educational courses. Currently there are psychological education courses designed to increase achievement motivation, awareness and excitement, creative thinking, interpersonal sensitivity, joy, self-reliance, self-esteem, self-understanding, self-actualization, moral development, identity, non-verbal communication, body awareness, value clarity, meditative processes and other aspects of ideal eupsychian adult functioning. Although most of these courses have been developed and offered in other settings such as industrial training programs, Peace Corps training and private educational institutes, some of these courses have been taught experimentally in public schools. Psychological educators who have been working independently are beginning to meet together to foster mutual collaboration. In fact, the first conference on "Affective Education" was held in August, 1968 in Sausalito, California, under the sponsorship of the American Association of Humanistic Psychology and Esalen Institute. New centers of psychological education are emerging that offer these courses to the general public. The most well known organizations are Esalen Institute in Big Sur, California; National Training Laboratories in Bethel, Maine; Western Behavioral Sciences Institute in La Jolla, California; and Outward Bound, Inc., in Andover, Massachusetts. A number of large research and development projects have been funded to introduce this type of education into schools. Cooperative Program of Education Development (COPED), sponsored by National Training Laboratories and the National Education Association, is one project. Others are: the Achievement Motivation Development Project, sponsored by The Office of Education; foundation grants to Western Behavioral Science Institute to introduce "basic encounter" techniques into a school system; a grant to Esalen Institute to support

This paper was written pursuant to the Contract 0-8-071231-1747 with the Office of Education, U.S. Department of Health, Education and Welfare, under the provisions of the Cooperative Research Program.

23

the introduction of sensitivity training in elementary, junior and senior high schools. This effort, coupled with recent publicity in the popular press, undoubtedly will increase the demand from students and parents for these courses. Because psychological education is clearly gaining momentum, it is important to examine carefully the goals of this movement.

GOALS OF PSYCHOLOGICAL EDUCATION

In psychological education, the course procedures are the best clues to the course goals since it is through these procedures that the desired psychological states are fostered in the course. For example, Outward Bound courses attempt to promote "self-reliance" (Katz & Kolb, 1968). Most of the course exercises ask students to engage in physically difficult tasks like scaling a cliff or swimming 50 yards underwater in one breath. Outward Bound courses usually end with a solo survival experience in the wilderness in which the trainee lives off the land. Procedurally, "self-reliance" is defined as mastering these challenging physical tasks. Similarly, it is possible to identify the goals of other psychological education courses by focusing on their procedures. When this is done, four common eupsychian goals emerge quite clearly.

First, most courses contain procedures to develop a constructive dialogue with one's own fantasy life. In Synectics training, a creativity course, students are asked to "make the strange familiar" by fantasizing themselves inside a strange object or to "make the familiar strange" by fantasizing about a common object (Gordon, 1961; Prince, 1969). In other creativity courses, remote associations are encouraged in order to attain a new, useful and creative perspective on some problem (Allen, 1962; Brown, 1964; Crawford, 1964; Parnes & Harding, 1962; deMille, 1967; Olten, 1966; Osborn, 1963; Uraneck, 1963; Whiting, 1958). In other psychological education courses, students are taken on guided tours of day dreams and night dreams and on fantasy trips into their own body (Assagioli, 1965; Perls, Hefferline & Goodman, 1965; Schutz, 1968). In achievement motivation courses, students are encouraged to fantasize about doing things exceptionally well and are taught how to differentiate between achievement imagery and ordinary task imagery. Subsequently, these achievement images are tied to reality through careful planning and projects (Alschuler, 1967; Kolb, 1965; McClelland, 1965). These eupsychian procedures often bring previously ignored aspects of one's personality into awareness. Usually this is a joyful, enhancing experience in contrast with psychoanalytic dream analysis and free association, which are oriented to uncover unconscious conflicts. The implication of these procedures is that most adults neither make constructive use of their fantasy life nor remember how to enjoy fantasy in a childlike, healthy way.

A second set of common procedures involves nonverbal exercises, such as silent theater improvisations, free-expression dance movements, meditation, the exaggeration of spontaneous body movements and a wide variety of games. Often it is easier to understand psychological concepts when they are learned motorically rather than simply comprehended intellectually. For example, in achievement motivation courses, the concept of "moderate risk taking" is taught through a darts game in which the student must bid on his performance and only "wins" when he makes his bid. A very low bid earns few points while a very high bid is nearly impossible to make. Subsequently, the game experience is generalized to other life situations. In sensitivity training and encounter groups, nonverbal exercises are used to increase channels of communication. Some personal feelings can be expressed more effectively in motions than in words. Other times nonverbal activities are used because they increase one's expressive vocabulary and are simply joyful experiences. As with constructive fantasizing, proponents of these methods believe that this type of expression, communication and learning is underdeveloped in most people (Boocock and Schild, 1968; Borton, 1968; Leonard, 1968; McClelland, 1965; Moore, 1960; Murphy, 1967; Newberg, undated; Perls, Hefferline & Goodman, 1965; Ruesch & Kees, 1956; Schutz, 1968; Spolin, 1963).

A third set of typical procedures focuses on developing and exploring individuals' emotional responses to the world. In most courses, how people feel is considered more important than what they think about things. Without emotional experiences ranging from laughter and exhilaration to tears and fear, the instructor is likely to consider the course a failure. For example, if an adolescent is scaling a cliff in an Outward Bound course and does not feel any fear, he probably will not increase his self-confidence through his accomplishment. Similarly, techniques in sensitivity training foster intense emotional confrontation among group members. Trainees are encouraged to express their feelings openly and honestly. For example, members learn to recognize their anger and to resolve it maturely, rather than allowing it to create continued inner turmoil. In achievement motivation courses, strong group feelings are developed to help support the individual in whatever he chooses to do well. In all of these courses, a shared belief exists that emotion increases meaningful learning and that the capacity for the full range of affective responses is a crucial human potentiality often underdeveloped in adults. As a result, a wide range of techniques to enhance affect have been created (Borton, 1966, 1967, 1968; Bradford, 1964; Gunther, 1968; Leonard, 1968; Litwin, 1966; Malamud, 1965; Otto, 1966, 1967, 1967a, 1968; Peterson, undated; Schutz, 1968; Yablonsky, 1967).

A fourth characteristic set of procedures emphasizes the importance of living fully and intensely "here and now." The emphasis takes many forms. In Gestalt awareness training, the goal is philosophically explicit (Perls, Hefferline & Goodman, 1965). In most courses, it is subtle and implicit. Usually psychological education courses are held in retreat settings that cut people off from past obligations and future commitments for brief periods of time. The isolated settings dramatize the "here-and-now" opportunities. Generally, little emphasis is placed on future "homework" or past personal history as an explanation of behavior. An example of a long term program involving communal living is Synanon, a total environment program for addicts, which promotes self-reliance and "self-actualization" and in the process cures addiction. Synanon requires the addict to stop taking drugs immediately upon entering the program. Other "bad" behavior that stands in the way of self-actualization is pointed out as it occurs. Historical explanations for bad behavior are considered excuses and are not tolerated (Yablonsky, 1967). In other psychological education programs, the games, exercises, and group processes are model opportunities to discover and explore new behavior. Most of these courses consider references to the past and future as avoidance of the present opportunity.

These four eupsychian states have some similarity to psychoanalytic therapy. The critical moment of growth in psychoanalysis occurs in the cure of the transference neurosis. The "patient" has an intense emotional realization of how he has transferred his childhood irrational fantasies to the here-and-now therapeutic context. He acts out his neurosis in the therapeutic relationship. The new awareness stemming from the catharsis allows the patient to change in meaningful ways first in the therapeutic relationship and then outside. These same elements exist in most psychological education courses, but they are transformed. Students discover the creative power of their fantasy life, not the destructive aspects of unconsciously motivated fantasy. Highly sensitive, understanding communication is experienced by attending to nonverbal cues, whereas in psychoanalysis, behavioral tics and "acting out" are probed for their neurotic messages. Intense affect is more often ecstatic than angry and unhappy as in traditional psychoanalytic experiences. In both types of change procedure, the assumption is made that long-term change results from the changes that occur in the here-and-now relationship.

The goals and content of these courses differ from existing academic and vocational courses in several important ways. Psychological knowledge is experiential knowledge in contrast with academic knowledge (mathematics, science, history) that is appropriately abstract. Psychological knowledge is firmly rooted in the person's affect, fantasy, and actions, and is not merely deposited in the student's internal data bank. This is the difference between knowing about the revolutions of 1848 and experiencing the anxiety and uncertainty of changing a life style quickly, as when a parent dies or when one has an accident. It is the difference between knowing probability statistics and taking action when the odds are 50:50 for success. Obviously, psychological knowledge is as important for a student's repertoire as his academic knowledge or vocational skills.

There are also some similarities in psychological, academic and vocational goals. As in foreign languages, science, history and mathematics, psychological education courses teach a new vocabulary and pattern of thought. Like vocational courses and athletics, psychological education courses teach new action skills through exercises, games, role plays, etc. And, like psychotherapy, psychological education is concerned with affect. These statements are straightforward and unremarkable. But, consider for a moment how many courses attempt to promote a synthesis of all three. Typical high school curricula are divided into academic "thought" courses and vocational "action" courses (typing, shorthand, auto mechanics, etc.). It is not possible to divide psychological knowledge into separate compartments. For example, interpersonal sensitivity is a way of thinking, feeling and acting in on-going relationships with other people. Psychological education courses attempt to create and enhance this synthesis within the course itself in order to foster its occurrence outside and after the course.

Psychological education courses aim for long-term life changes, not short-term gains in mastery. It can be said that psychological education attempts to increase long-term "operant" behavior as well as "respondent" behavior. Operant behavior is voluntary, seemingly spontaneous and certainly not required by the situation. What a person does with his leisure time is an indication of his operant behavior since it stems from stable internal cues and needs few external cues to come forth. Respondent behavior, whether it is affective, cognitive or motoric requires external cues and incentives before it will occur, just as an examination question brings forth respondent knowledge that otherwise probably would not have been demonstrated.

In practice, most school learning calls for respondent behavior: multiple choice and true-false questions, reading assigned chapters solving a given set of mathematical problems correctly, or writing an essay to a prescribed theme. Interestingly, respondent measures of learning do not predict long-term operant behavior very well; perhaps because when school is over there are very few people who follow a person around defining the problems, presenting test questions and evaluating the response (Mc-Clelland, 1967; McClelland, *et al.*, 1958). Success and fulfillment in work, marriage, interpersonal relations and leisure time result more from operant than respondent behavior. Educational theorists have begun to draw attention to the importance of teaching that results in operant, voluntary, internalized student behavior (Bloom, 1956; Kranthwohl, *et al.*, 1956). However, the key academic and vocational success criteria very likely will continue to be end-of-semester tests, standardized achievement tests, and other short-term respondent measures that fail to predict what the student will remember later and whether he will choose spontaneously to use what he learned.

The goals of psychological education courses will probably change in the future as a result of many influences. As in the past, some new courses will no doubt be developed for specific institutional needs. For example, industry was one of the chief financial supporters for courses in creativity training because it wanted to increase the patenting output of research scientists. Recently the Peace Corps has commissioned the development of self-assessment workshops to replace the pychiatric, illness-oriented diagnosis that has existed in Peace Corps training programs. By extrapolation it is easy to envision other new courses: identity formation courses for Outward Bound adolescents; individuation courses for elderly men and women; training in the "helping relationship" for parents, supervisors, teachers and coaches. Although these courses could have different problem foci, most likely they would include the enhancement of fantasy, affect, and nonverbal communication in intense course experiences that develop eupsychian capacities.

RESEARCH QUESTIONS

It is currently possible to identify several important research questions: Do psychological education courses have significantly greater long-term impact than other forms of therapy and education? If so, what makes the courses more effective? Very little long-term outcome research on these courses exists at present.

One prototype research effort has been conducted and illustrates how outcome research can lead to the development of psychological education as a discipline. McClelland and Winter (1969) studied the 3-year impact of a series of achievement motivation courses given to adult businessmen. McClelland and Winter's principal finding demonstrated that achievement motivation training stimulated greater entrepreneurial activity than normal maturation and more than other current types of executive training programs. (Effectiveness was measured in terms of promotions, pay raises, major new investments, etc.) However, the course was effective only for those men who were in a position to take initiative on their job; they had appropriate entrepreneurial opportunities. This raises many new questions about similar existing psychological education courses. Do students only show change and growth in the training settings where the opportunities for growth are accentuated? Should initial diagnoses be made in order to accept only those trainees whose life situations afford continued opportunities to develop what they have learned? Should psychological educators also assume some responsibility for changing the institutions and settings that promote or inhibit growth outside of the course? Should psychological educators take responsibility for restructuring academic and vocational courses to provide clear opportunities for initiative, responsibility, achievement motivation, interpersonal sensitivity, and creativity? What is the long-term effect on motivation, creatvity, and sensitivity if only new opportunities are provided?

McClelland and Winter also present evidence identifying what course factors are responsible for the long-term changes. Of the many achievement motivation courses they studied, the most effective courses included: (1) procedures that taught the thought and action characteristics of people with high achievement motivation; (2) procedures that provided affective and cognitive supports for whatever change the person desired; and (3) procedures that focused on making careful long-term plans. Often the latter is absent from other psychological education courses in which the here-and-now emphasis and the diffuse nature of the long-term goals seem to preclude this type of goal setting (Campbell & Dunnette, 1968). Current exceptions are some creativity training programs in industry that have proved highly effective in generating new inventions (Parnes, 1967). As in achievement motivation training, the long-term goals are always clearly in mind during the course. In these cases, the combination of here-and-now course excitement and commitment to long-term goals seem to be necessary for maximum effectiveness.

There are many difficulties in doing the valuable type of long-term outcome research conducted by McClelland and Winter. What educator can wait 3 years to find out which inputs he should use in his next course? The feedback loop is too long. Design and control problems in "change" research are extreme. Operant outcome criteria are particularly difficult to measure and the research is expensive. A critical breakthrough in facilitating this type of research would consist of identifying those changes during or just after the course that predicted long-term growth. This would shorten the feedback loop and quicken research progress. A search for these short-term predictors raises an important theoretical question. Do the desired eupsychian states simply increase in frequency after the course is over, or do basic transformations take place much as children move from concrete to formal operational thinking over a period of years? If the desired eupsychian states are reached through basic transformations, then the course experiences probably would not bear a one-to-one correspondence to the desired long-term outcome. This developmental approach would require a basic shift in the short-term, here-and-now course goals.

CONCLUSION

Developmental theories can be as important to the creation and evaluation of psychological education courses as are better descriptions of eupsychian states. For example, Jung argues that "individuation" occurs as conscious and unconscious functions are developed and synthesized; i.e., perceiving through sensation and intuition and evaluating through affect and analysis (Jung, 1959; Progoff, 1953). When these four functions are equally well developed, mandala symbols from the collective unconscious begin to emerge in dreams and creative art work indicating the unique unity the person has attained. There is a well-validated diagnostic test that measures the relative development of these four functions. Appropriate psychological education courses could be given to enhance those functions that were least developed. If successful, and if Jung was correct, mandala symbols should emerge more frequently in fantasy productions.

In general, there is the possibility of developmental theory providing a framework for the proper sequencing of psychological education courses to maximize psychological growth during the entire life cycle.

REFERENCES

ALLEN, M. S. *Morphological Creativity*. Englewood Cliffs, N.J.: Prentice-Hall, 1962.

ALLPORT, G. "The Mature Personality." Chap. 12 in *Pattern and Growth in Personality*. New York: Holt, Rinehart & Winston, 1961.

ALSCHULER, A. S. "The Achievement Motivation Development Project: A Summary and Review." Harvard Research and Development Center, Harvard Graduate School of Education, 1967. Available through Publications Office, Longfellow Hall, Appian Way, Cambridge, Mass. 02138.

BLOOM, B., ed. *Taxonomy of Educational Objectives, Handbook I: Cognitive Domain*. New York: David McKay Co., 1956.

BORTON, T. "Reaching the Culturally Deprived." *Saturday Review*, 19 February 1966, pp. 77–78+.

BRADFORD, L. P., GIBB, J. & BENNE, K., eds. *T-Group Theory and Laboratory*

Method: Innovation in Re-Education. New York: John Wiley & Sons, 1964.

BROWN, G. "An Experiment in the Teaching of Creativity." *School Review* 72, 4 (1964): 437–450.

COLEMAN, J. S. *Equality of Educational Opportunity.* United States Office of Education, OE 38001, 1966.

ERIKSON, E. "Identity and the Life Cycle." *Psychological Issues* 1, 1 (1959): 1–171.

FEATHERSTONE, J. "Teaching Children to Think." *The New Republic* (September 1967): 15–19.

FLANAGAN, J. "Functional Education for the Seventies." *Phi Delta Kappan* (September 1967): 27–33.

FREUD, S. *The Problems of Lay Analysis.* New York: Brentano's, 1927.

GORDON, W. J. J. *Synectics: The Development of Creative Capacity.* New York: Harper & Row, 1961.

HOWARD, J. "Inhibitions Thrown to the Gentle Winds." *Life,* 12 July 1968, pp. 48–65.

JAHODA, M. *Current Concepts of Positive Mental Health.* New York: Basic Books, 1958.

JUNG, C. G. *Archetypes and the Collective Unconscious.* New York: Pantheon Books, 1959. (Section 6).

KATZ, R. & KOLB, D. "Outward Bound and Education for Personal Growth." Mimeographed paper available from David Kolb, Sloan School of Management, Massachusetts Institute of Technology, Cambridge, Mass.

KOLB, D. A. "Achievement Motivation Training for Under-Achieving High School Boys." *Journal of Personality and Social Psychology* (December 1965); 2, 6, 783–792.

KRANTHWOHL, D. R., BLOOM, B. & MASIA, B. *Taxonomy of Educational Objectives, Handbook II: Affective Domain.* New York: Donald McKay Co., 1956.

LITWIN, G. "Organizational Climate." 1966. Film available through the Audio-Visual Department, Harvard Business School, Soldiers Field Road, Boston, Mass. 02163.

MASLOW, A. H. *Toward a Psychology of Being.* Princeton, N.J.: D. Van Nostrand Co., 1962.

McCLELLAND, D. C. "Achievement Motivation Can Be Developed." *Harvard Business Review* (November 1965), 43, 6–8+.

————. "Measuring Behavioral Objectives in the 1970s." Speech given at the Air Force Education Seminar, Aerospace Education Conference, Washington, D.C., 4 September 1967.

McCLELLAND, D. C., BALDWIN, S. L., BRONFENBRENNER, V. & STRODTBACK, F. L. *Talent and Society.* Princeton, N.J.: D. Van Nostrand Co., 1958.

McClelland, D. D. & Winter, D. G. *Motivating Economic Achievement.* New York: Free Press, 1969.

Moore, S. *The Stanislavski Method.* New York: Viking Press, 1960.

Murphy, M. "Esalen, Where It's At." *Psychology Today* (December 1967).

Newberg, N. "Meditative Process." Multilith paper available from author at Office of Affective Development, Philadelphia Public School Building, 21st and Parkway, Philadelphia, Pa.

Olton, R. M. "A Self-Instructional Program for the Development of Productive Thinking in Fifth and Sixth Grade Children." In *First Seminar on Productive Thinking in Education,* edited by F. E. Williams. St. Paul, Minn.: Creativity and National Schools Project, Macalester College, 1966.

Osborn, A. D. *Applied Imagination.* New York: Scribners, 1963.

Parnes, S. "Methods and Educational Programs for Stimulating Creativity: A Representative List." In Parnes, S. *Creative Behavior Guidebook.* New York: Scribners, 1967. In *Journal of Creative Behavior* (Winter 1968): 1, 2, 71–75.

Parnes, S. & Harding, H. F., eds. *Source Book for Creative Thinking.* New York: Charles Scribner's Sons, 1962.

Perls, F. S., Hefferline, R. F. & Goodman, P. *Gestalt Therapy: Excitement and Growth in the Human Personality.* New York: Dell, 1965.

Piaget, J. *Psychology of Intelligence.* Paterson, N.J.: Littlefield, Adams & Co., 1960.

Progoff, I. *Jung's Psychology and Its Social Meaning.* New York: Grove Press, 1953, chap. 6, "Dreams and the Integration of the Psyche."

Ruesch, J. & Kees, W. *Non-Verbal Communication.* Berkeley, Calif.: University of California Press, 1956.

Schutz, W. *Joy.* New York: Grove Press, 1968.

Spolin, V. *Improvisation for the Theater.* Evanston, Ill.: Northwestern University Press, 1963.

Uraneck, W. O. "Creative Thinking Workbook." 1963. Available from the author, 56 Turning Mill Road, Lexington, Mass. 02173.

Whiting, C. S. *Creative Thinking.* New York: Reinhold Publishing Corp., 1958.

Wolpe, J. & Lazarus, A. *Behavior Therapy Techniques.* Long Island City, N.Y.: Pergamon Press, 1967.

Yablonsky, L. *The Tunnel Back: Synanon.* New York: Macmillan, 1965.

Yeomans, E. "Education for Initiative and Responsibility." 1967. Available from the National Association of Independent Schools, 4 Liberty Square, Boston, Mass.

Zilboorg, G. & Henry, G. W. *A History of Medical Psychology.* New York: W. W. Norton & Sons, 1941.

Learning to Feel—
Feeling to Learn

Harold C. Lyon, Jr.

I am writing this book in an attempt to share with others what has become one of the most exciting and important discoveries in my life: that learning can be enjoyable when one learns to feel and then goes on to feel to learn. Nonsense? Perhaps, until one experiences what I'm talking about. My biggest fear in writing this book (purely verbal expression by necessity) is that I will lose much of the feeling that I might convey if we sat down together to actually discuss and experience rather than read about the things I am trying to share.

Recognizing that much feeling will be lost in writing rather than in sharing experiences in person, I have chosen to use several descriptions of experiences by others—especially students from whom I think we as teachers have a great deal to learn—or prescriptions or recipes for experiences which you may try with your own students or children. If I can get you to take that step—experiencing and feeling some of these things for yourself—then I know I will have accomplished my purpose. You will be hooked! You won't be able to return to the emptiness of the purely intellectual classroom once you have felt the charged atmosphere and warmth of the humanistic classroom—an environment where feelings are integrated with intellectual content. So in this book I have attempted to concentrate on the first step—getting you to want to try these things yourself and presenting some things you might try, knowing that if you do you will probably go far beyond this book in developing your own individual techniques. In a way this book is meant to be a launching pad, a catalyst, a stimulator, or a fuse.

Humanistic Education, the integration of cognitive learning with affective learning, is a natural outgrowth of Humanistic or Third Force psychology which has grown in large part as a reaction against the fact

Harold C. Lyon, Jr., *Learning to Feel—Feeling to Learn.* Columbus, Ohio: Charles E. Merrill Publishing Company, 1971, pp. 3–9.

that the more academic psychologies (Behavioristic and Freudian) seem inadequate in dealing with the higher nature or humanness of man. We can see the influence of the Behaviorists in most of our schools today as we watch teachers trying to shape students according to the academic goals of the teacher and frequently ignoring the actualization or growth of the individual.

I am not advocating that the classroom become primarily a therapeutic "couch" for children, though there should be some therapeutic things happening. I'm not advancing a set of therapeutic procedures for teachers to use, though dealing with feelings can be therapeutic. I am not advocating that teachers become amateur psychoanalysts or that they replace counselors or school psychologists, though perhaps in a humanistic school, counselors and psychologists might be freer from the rush of overwhelming anxiety problems that prevent them from helping normal children find their own productive and fulfilling place in this world. Most teachers are not professionally or legally qualified to perform the function of psychoanalyst, though some research has shown that perhaps we shouldn't be as timid about this as we have been. The argument has been that therapy should be attempted only by a professional with a Ph.D. or an MD. According to Carl Rogers:

> There is solid evidence that this is a mistaken view. An outstanding example is the work of Rioch [1] showing that selected housewives can be given training in a year's time which enables them to carry on therapy with disturbed individuals—therapy which in its quality is indistinguishable from the work of experienced professionals.[2]

So, in spite of the fact that I am not pushing for teachers to become amateur psychoanalysts, there is ample room and a great need for a bold move by educators and teachers toward the affective realm.

What this book is trying to say is that isolating cognitive learning from affective learning is a mistake—a mistake, the impact of which we are feeling on campuses and in classrooms all over the country. It's a mistake which has created a large number of intellectual "half-men," brilliantly developed, perhaps, on the intellectual end of the continuum, but severely lacking on the feeling or affective end. Most of the activities students enjoy about school are those highly charged with feelings and emotions and which have absolutely nothing to do with the curriculum; in fact they are usually classroom taboos. I'm talking about what we have

---

[1] Margaret J. Rioch, E. Elkes, A. A. Flint, B. S. Usdansky, R. G. Newman, & E. Sibler, "NIMH pilot study in training mental health counselors." *American Journal of Orthopsychiatry* 33, 1963: 678–689.

[2] Carl Rogers, *Freedom to Learn* (Columbus, Ohio: Charles E. Merrill Publishing Company), p. 319.

labeled as extracurricular activities. I'm talking about boy-girl relationships, love-making, protests, social causes, dances, rock music, cars, and really getting to know someone.

I'm not advocating that we should all gravitate to the affective end of this continuum, shedding all our inhibitions as a few unfortunate businessmen have done after visiting Esalen or Bethel, Maine. They quickly found that their bosses didn't appreciate being honestly and openly called the "sons of bitches" they were felt to be. The better therapists and group leaders at such institutions as Esalen and the National Training Labs at Bethel, Maine, though admitting that the chief drawback to such group experiences is the lack of a mechanism for effective follow-up, are careful to make it clear to participants that the healthiest place for someone to be is somewhere between the two extremes of this continuum. Society is not ready for the purely "affective" human being. There are some of these hyper-open individuals around, and most suffer from the severe frustration that's bound to result from dealing with a world that is largely closed and "up-tight." One of the few courses of action open to these people is to withdraw from society into their own fantasy worlds or communes. The healthy individual in the 1970's hopefully will be somewhere in the middle ground with, perhaps, a few clear and wide open channels with one's husband or wife, or a few close friends. He or she will be able to deal with feelings and intellectual matters.

Nor is this book advocating that teachers become such totally open individuals that their classes are "T-groups." It does advocate an integration of the intellectual atmosphere *with* feelings in the classroom. It is proposing that we begin to accept students, teachers, parents, and friends as being more than intellectual beings. It advocates that we begin to look upon people as whole human beings who have feelings—feelings which directly influence their intellectual growth.

Such a practice can replace our old ideas of teaching with the joy of discovery. Anyone who has watched a class of fifth graders transform a classroom from utter chaos into one buzzing with children discovering things, after having been allowed to evolve their own rules for behavior, has discovered the lesson of "allowing" rather than "making." For instance, a child who feels a need to ask for his own word—a particular gut feeling word of anger, joy, or fear that is gripping him that day—and has it written for him in his own word book, discovers the word instantaneously and most likely never forgets. To him, writing and reading become a natural extension of speech as he discovers what he is actually trying to tell. How much more effective it is to facilitate a child's own discovery of words through integration of his own feelings than it is to force inane "Dick and Janisms" on him day after day!

A student who has discovered something significant needs no instructor-assigned grade as a measure of his accomplishment. He deeply feels the accomplishment immediately, and that's the best reward possible.

Humanistic education, the integration of cognitive learning and affective experience, is present in many forms. It's really a name for a practice that a few of those rare human teachers have been practicing for generations.

A pertinent example of "humanistic education" and the results it can produce was made vividly clear to me while serving as a consultant to the White House Task Force on the Education of the Gifted. The Task Force members toured various institutions of higher education throughout the country in an attempt to pinpoint what it is that makes certain gifted individuals realize their high potential while so many others fall short. This enlightening encounter took place while visiting the U. S. Military Academy at West Point to see how the military treats its gifted. The Social Science Department at West Point, under the leadership of General George A. Lincoln (later Director in the Nixon Administration Office of Emergency Preparedness), has always been a hotbed of gifted individuals. At the time of our visit, I believe they had at least eight Rhodes Scholars on the Social Science Faculty plus a number of other extremely gifted and distinguished young officers. The Task Force visiting team arranged to meet with a group of about twelve of these officers, including such notables as Peter Dawkins, the Rhodes Scholar—All American football player whose picture appeared on the covers of *Life, Newsweek,* and *Time* several times before he reached the age of 25. Harold Gores, one of the Task Force members, put the following question to the group: "To what predominant factor, if any, do you attribute your exceptional success and achievement?" To me, the fascinating thing was that almost every one of them had the same answer. In each of their lives some one or two individuals had built an unusual relationship with them, either in their latter few years of high school or at West Point. In most cases the individuals had been either teachers or athletic coaches. They had put social or military status aside and had built a more intimate relationship than tradition dictated, pushing and encouraging the students as individuals to step out and achieve far more than the students thought they were capable of doing. In other words, a humanistic bond was developed between two people. The fascinating part of it was that about four of these officers named the same one or two instructors without knowing that this was the case. If we could only identify what these special teachers have that others do not and pay attention to this in our teacher training institutions, we might be on the way to a break-through. Ironically enough, Colonels Bob Gard and Ab Greenleaf, both of whom had later served as military assistants to the Secretary of Defense, were two of the inspirational instructors mentioned by several of the young officers and were also two very personable officers whom I recalled as being exceptional. In most of the cases described, the push and encouragement to stand on tiptoe had come personally, but in a particular area of endeavor such as academics, debating, or athletics, rather than in general vague encouragement. There are many different kinds of humanistic education stories, but this serves as an example of the far-reaching effects humanistic education can have.

The idea of giving students as many tastes of success as is possible has great application to the classroom, especially in a child's very early years. The teachers who have cared to celebrate a child's tiniest achievements and to encourage his feelings have the power to transform their classrooms into humanistic ones in which children bloom rather than wilt. Robert Rosenthal's research on teacher expectations provides some indication of this.[3]

Although Robert Thorndike has shown that the conclusions reached by Rosenthal's study are inadequately supported by data, there is little doubt that the theory being tested is a correct one.[4] Rosenthal set out to test the hypothesis that, rather than disadvantaged children doing poorly because they came from disadvantaged families, they really do poorly because teachers expect them to do so. He and his colleagues divided rats into two groups at random, giving them to two different groups of people. They instructed both groups to teach their rats to run a maze. However, the first group was told that their rats would learn the maze quickly because they came from good genetic backgrounds. The second group was told that their rats would learn very slowly, if at all, because they were of poor genetic background. The first group's rats learned the maze much more quickly and better than those from the group which had low expectations for their rats. They then took the experiment into the classroom. They told the teachers from a school district that they were going to administer a new validated test which would accurately predict which students would progress rapidly during the coming year (the test was actually an I.Q. test in disguise). A few weeks after the testing, they visited each teacher and casually mentioned the names of several children who had scored as "rapid achievers." (The names were actually chosen at random.) At the end of the year, the children mentioned during the visit had surpassed the others significantly in all subjects. The reason? The teachers had expected them to do well, and hence worked with them, believed in them, and encouraged them. A humanistic relationship had been contrived and it worked!

A similar experiment has been conducted with Mexican–American

---

[3] Robert Rosenthal and Lenore F. Jacobson, "Teacher Expectations for the Disadvantaged," *The Scientific American*, no. 4 (April, 1968), pp. 19–23.

[4] Robert L. Thorndike, Book Review of Rosenthal and Jacobson's *Pygmalion in the classroom*, *American Educational Research Journal* 8, no. 4 (November, 1968), pp. 708–711.

children in Arizona which also adds to the evidence that children will tend to perform better if the teacher expects this of them. Mexican–American children who the teachers identified as special achievers did far better under those conditions than when in control groups.

Les Rollins, former Assistant Dean of Harvard Graduate School of Business, has spent his lifetime identifying young leaders talent and attempting to determine what it is that makes a young person succeed. He feels that the crucial years for setting a pattern of success, mediocrity, or failure come early in life, but that the individual's pattern can be and frequently is set *firmly* in the last few years of high school and the first few years of college. The bigger the taste of success achieved in these years, the greater the chances of later success. A teacher who puts feeling into his or her work has a far greater chance of giving students tastes of success than the impersonal or entirely cognitive teacher who stands officially behind status authority rather than natural authority.

When a torpedo shoots at a submarine, the servo-mechanism in the torpedo cranks in feedback causing the torpedo to change course, locking in on the submarine as its goal. Humans have a similar mechanism in them which can lock in on either success or failure as a goal. The more early "success experiences," the more likely that success becomes an individual's goal. When the "success oriented" individual progresses through life and approaches one of the many obstacles or by-paths leading to failure, he consciously (and often unconsciously) increases his energy and effort to get over the obstacle or by-path and stay on the path to success, his goal. The pessimist, who has made failure his goal, on the other hand, comes to one of these by-paths, takes it, fails, and says, "I failed. I knew I would!" Accordingly, it seems vital for us to allow, to inject, or even to contrive, as many success experiences in our children's and student's lives as we are able. The human teacher who has learned to feel, and hence uses feelings in his teaching, has at his or her disposal so many of the attributes helpful for giving "success experiences" to others.

I hope that the chapters which follow will stimulate you to make your own personal, joyful discovery of what it can mean to deal with students as human beings and to appreciate their feelings which abound within the classroom.

Bringing Together Ideas and Feelings in Learning

Carl R. Rogers

I have given a great deal of thought as to how ideas and feelings can be melded into one experience in the learning process. If I were to get technical (which I will do only for a moment), I would say that these remarks are about bringing together the cognitive and the affective-experiental. Though that last is a clumsy hyphenated word, it does seem to catch my meaning—that this kind of learning is a visceral, as well as an emotional and intellectual, type of experience. What do I mean by this? Let me try to illustrate by a trivial but personal example.

For years I have been trying to grow two golden-leaved shrubs at either side of the entrance to my driveway. At long last they are thriving. But the other day I was in a hurry. I backed quickly down the driveway, swung the wheel, hit something, and stopped the car. To my horror the rear wheel had gone right over the center of one of the shrubs. My physiological reaction was extreme, as though my whole body was reacting to what I had done. As I surveyed the damage, calling myself names it would not be proper to put in print, I found myself repeating the sentence, "Don't turn the wheel until you're out in the street. Don't turn the wheel until you're out in the street."

Now that was *learning*. It had its cognitive element, which even a five-year-old could have grasped. It certainly had its feelings components —several of them. And it had the gut-level quality of experiential learning. All of me had learned a lesson which I will not soon forget, and that is the sort of thing I wish to discuss. Of course, this kind of learning does not need to be negative in character. It can also be the warm, physical glow that comes from sharing so many interests with a new acquaintance that you realize, "I'm on the way to making a new friend."

Let me give some additional dimensions to this idea. In the first

This article is based on the address which Dr. Rogers gave at the 1971 Library-College conference in San Francisco, California.

39

place, it should be understood I am not talking about a professor lecturing in a situation where all the affective-experiential meanings exist outside of what is ostensibly going on. By this I mean a situation in which the professor is anxiously asking himself, "Can I make this last for fifty minutes?" and his students—who are experiencing equal anxiety—sit and wonder, "Do you suppose he'll ask this junk on the final exam?" Clearly, all these affective-experiential aspects are divorced from whatever cognitive elements are in the lecture itself.

In the second place, it should be equally clear that I do not mean a passionate intellectual argument between two professors. In this case both the affective and the cognitive *are* found in the same experience, but they run in totally different directions, for the mind of each is saying, "My abstractions are more logical than your abstractions," while the feelings are saying, "I'll beat you down, if it's the last thing I do!" The trouble is, unfortunately, that the speakers are aware only of their cognitive processes.

We get closer to what I'm speaking of in a human relations group where a person first has a deeply moving experience of relating to another, and then attends a general session where the process of the encounter group is discussed. "Oh," he says to himself, ". . . that's what I've just been through." The affective-experiential and the cognitive have been brought close together in time, and each is tied to the other. So if I were to attempt a crude definition of what it means to learn as a whole person, I would say that it involves learning of a *unified* sort, at the cognitive, feeling, and gut level, but with a clear awareness of its different aspects. I suspect that in its purest form this occurs rarely, but perhaps learning experiences can still be judged by their closeness or remoteness to this general definition.

THE CURRENT SITUATION

Each year I become more pessimistic about what is going on in educational institutions. They have focused so intently on the cognitive, and have limited themselves so completely to "education from the neck up," that this narrowness is resulting in serious social consequences. Not long ago Columbia University brought together trustees, administrators, students, and faculty members for a weekend workshop whose purpose was to close the communications gap. It made some progress, but not much. Toward the end, one student—addressing himself to the faculty— said: "I don't know if our two worlds can ever meet. Our world has feelings in it." This same sentiment was voiced by another student who said, "What I discovered was that a whole man is comprised of mind, heart, soul, and muscle. What I discovered about the faculty, for the most part, is that it is men comprised of mind." [1]

Some years ago Archibald MacLeish stated the problem another way when he said, "We do not feel our knowledge. Nothing could better illustrate the flaw at the heart of our civilization. . . . Knowledge without feeling is not knowledge and can lead only to public irresponsibility and indifference, and conceivably to ruin." [2] As a consequence of this over-stress on the cognitive, and of the avoidance of any feeling connected with it, most of the excitement has gone out of education. Fortunately, there is one redeeming feature, and this is that no one can take the excitement out of learning.

I have days when I think educational institutions at all levels are doomed. I also have moments when it seems that if we could only do away with state-required curricula, compulsory attendance, tenured professors, hours of lectures, grades, degrees, and all that, perhaps everybody could move outside the stifling hallowed walls and learning could flourish on its own. Suppose every educational institution, from kindergarden through even the most prestigious graduate school, were to close tomorrow. What a delightful situation that would be. Parents, children, adolescents, and young people—perhaps even a few faculty members—would feel free to devise situations in which they could *learn!* Because of this feeling millions of people would be asking the same question—"Is there anything I want to learn?" and if so, "How can I invent the means to tackle the job?"

THE CONDITIONS FOR INTELLECTUAL AND AFFECTIVE LEARNING

There are some experiences in my professional life that I remember vividly. One of these experiences occurred in a plush-seated auditorium at the University of Michigan during the 1956–57 academic year. I was talking to a highly sophisticated audience, and I was advancing a new and quite tentative theory as to what conditions were necessary before one-to-one psychotherapy could produce change in individuals. During the course of this talk I challenged almost all the sacred cows in the therapeutic world. I said, though not openly, that effectiveness in therapy is not a question of whether the therapist has been psychoanalyzed, or

---

[1] Harold C. Lyons, Jr., *Learning to Feel—Feeling to Learn,* (Columbus, Ohio: Charles E. Merrill Publishing Co., 1971), p. 26.

[2] James Reston, "The Forgotten Factor," *New York Times,* November 29, 1970, Part IV, p. 11.

has a knowledge of personality theory, or possesses expertise in diagnosis, or even has a thorough acquaintance with therapeutic techniques. I also said that effectiveness in therapy depends on *attitudes,* and I even had the nerve to define what I thought those attitudes were.

It wasn't a very popular talk. Because I had anticipated the reaction. I took pains to see that this was one of the most closely reasoned, carefully stated presentations I ever gave. I am still proud of it, and, though it was not popular, it has sparked more research than any talk I have ever given. As a result, I became bolder and postulated that these same attitudinal changes would promote any whole-person learning—that they would hold for the classroom as well as the therapist's office. This hypothesis also sparked research, but before I comment on such studies, let me describe these attitudinal conditions as they relate to education. They are attitudes which, in my judgment, characterize a facilitator of learning.

REALNESS IN THE FACILITATOR OF LEARNING

Perhaps the most important of these attitudes is realness or genuineness. When the facilitator is a real person, when he enters into a relationship with the learner without presenting a front or facade, he is more likely to be effective. This means that the feeings he is experiencing are available to him, and that he is able to live these feelings, be them, and communicate them if appropriate. It means that he has a direct personal encounter with the learner. It means he is *being* himself, not denying himself. He is *present* to the student.

PRIZING, ACCEPTANCE, TRUST

There is another attitude which stands out in those who are successful at facilitating learning. I have observed this attitude. I have experienced it. Yet, it is hard to know what term describes it, so I shall use several. I think of it as prizing the learner; prizing his feelings, his opinions, and his person. It is a caring for the learner, but a non-possessive caring. It is an acceptance of this other individual as a separate person, having worth in his own right. It is a basic trust—a belief that this other person is trustworthy. The facilitator who is imbued with this attitude can accept the fear and hesitation of the student as he approaches a new problem. Such a teacher can also accept the student's occasional apathy, his desire to explore by-roads of knowledge, and his disciplined efforts to achieve major goals.

EMPATHIC UNDERSTANDING

Another element which establishes a climate for self-initiated, experiential learning is empathic understanding. When a teacher has the ability to understand a student's reactions from the inside, and has an awareness of the way education and learning seems to the student, then the likelihood of learning is significantly increased. This kind of understanding is quite different from such evaluative comments as, "I understand what has gone wrong with you." When there is sensitive empathy the teacher has a feeling of viewing the world through his student's eyes, and the learner's reaction is likely to be, "At least someone understands how it feels to be me without wanting to analyze or judge me. Now I can blossom and grow and learn."

There is still a further condition for learning by the whole person. Specifically, the student must to some extent perceive that these attitudinal elements exist in the teacher. Students are even more suspicious than therapy clients, mainly because the former have been "conned" for so long that they think a "real" teacher is simply exhibiting a new brand of phoniness. Therefore, the teacher who prizes a student in non-judgmental ways is certain to arouse disbelief. Yet, it is the same empathic response which finally convinces the student that this is not only different, but that it can be an entirely new experience.

WHAT ARE THE PERSONAL RESULTS?

Dr. "X" is a high-school teacher who is a living example of what happens when a person manifests these attitudes. She seems to be without pretense, facade, or defensiveness; and you can't talk with her for five minutes without realizing that she thinks high-school students are the greatest. The way she moves sensitively and empathically into the feelings of her students is uncanny. Her courses are entitled Psychology, Human Relations, etc., but they would be better labeled Learning Experiences. The boys and girls discuss anything which concerns them—drugs, family problems, sex, pregnancy, contraception, abortion, the draft, the grading system—literally any topic. They have learned to trust her, and the level of self-disclosure is amazing

At this point you may be saying, "O.K., O.K., perhaps they do get help in their personal adjustment, but is there any content?" There is indeed. Miss "X" is a tremendous reader, and her enthusiasm for books is contagious. Some of the students are classed as slow learners, but they are reading Buber and Kierkegaard, Fromm, Slater, and Holt. People tell Miss "X" that these books are far too advanced for high-school students, but she laughs and says that these young people love to be challenged. The students also choose the films they want to see, plan community trips, and prepare individualized projects. In short, they are excited, personally involved learners.

WHAT ARE THE RESEARCH RESULTS?

In a 1959 study of therapist-client relationships, Barrett-Lennard found that those clients who eventually showed more therapeutic change perceived more of these conditions at the time of the fifth interview than did those who eventually showed less change.[3] I feel certain this finding would hold in the classroom as well. If so, it would mean that if we went to a classroom during the first five days of the school year and measured the attitudes that exist in the teacher, and as they were perceived by the students, we could predict which classrooms would contain learners, and which would contain prisoners. In other words, to the degree that these attitudes were held and perceived, we could know which classrooms would have students who learned by the whole person. We could also know which classrooms would contain passive, restless, and rebellious students, with little but rote learning going on.

The research which has tried to discover whether relationships exist between attitudinal conditions and various elements of the learning process has come about largely through the efforts of David Aspy. Among other things, Dr. Aspy has found that levels of interpersonal conditions can be measured with reasonable objectivity, and that these levels are significantly related to gains in reading achievement among third graders.[4] Furthermore, attitudinal conditions were found to be related to grade-point average,[5] to cognitive growth,[6, 7, 8] to an increase in creative interest and

[3] G. T. Barrett-Lennard, "Dimensions of Therapist Response as Causal Factors in Therapeutic Change," *Psychological Monographs*, LXXVI (Whole no. 562, 1962).

[4] David N. Aspy, *A Study of Three Facilitative Conditions and Their Relationships to the Achievement of Third Grade Students* (Ann Arbor, Mich.: University Microfilms, 1969).

[5] Robert R. Carkhuff and Bernard G. Berenson, *Beyond Counseling and Therapy* (New York: Holt, Rinehart and Winston, Inc., 1967), p. 10.

[6] David N. Aspy, "Counseling and Education," in *The Counselor's Contribution to Facilitative Processes*, ed. by Robert R. Carkhuff (Urbana, Ill.: Parkinson, 1967).

[7] David N. Aspy, "The Effect of Teacher-Offered Conditions of Empathy, Positive Regard, and Congruence upon Student Achievement," *Florida Journal of Educational Research*, XI (January, 1969), pp. 39–48.

[8] Charles G. Truax and Robert R. Carkhuff, *Toward Effective Counseling and Psychotherapy: Training and Practice* (Chicago: Aldine Publishing Co., 1967), p. 116.

productivity,[9] to levels of cognitive thinking, and to the amount of student-initiated talk.[10]   Finally, Schmuck found that attitudes were related to a diffusion of liking and trust in the classroom, which in turn was related to better utilization of student abilities and confidence in oneself.[11]

From this a teacher might conclude that it pays to be personal and human in the classroom.   Moreover, it would seem that this payoff is not only in such things as grades and reading achievement, but is also present in such elusive characteristics as creativity, liking for others, and self-confidence.   One exciting aspect of these findings is that they should enable us to select teaching personnel who possess those interpersonal qualities which have been shown to be facilitative of whole-person learning.[12]   In a nut-shell, these findings have implications for a positive, unified learning by the whole person as well as genuine meaning for the training of teachers.

IMPLICATIONS FOR TEACHER TRAINING

If, then, we decide to have learning which combines the cognitive and the affective-experiential—the intellectual and the gut-level—and if we know with a modest degree of accuracy the interpersonal conditions which produce that kind of learning, what is the next step? Clearly, it is to make a change in the way we train our teachers. This, of course, will not be easy to do, for most teacher-training institutions are bastions of tradition, and as such they stress only cognitive learning and the methods by which it can be achieved. They are past masters at providing an atmosphere which says, "Don't do as I do. Do as I say." Is it possible to effect change in such institutions?

Before we answer this, let us first ask another question, namely, "Is it possible to develop interpersonal qualities in student-teachers or anyone else preparing for the education field?" I believe the answer is definitely, "Yes." In the first place, we have already seen that it would be possible to select candidates who exhibit realness, prizing, and empathic understanding in their relationships. In the second place, it is becoming increasingly clear that such attitudes can be developed. I, myself, have seen

[9] Samuel F. Moon, "Teaching the Self," *Improving College and University Teaching,* XIV (Autumn, 1966), pp. 213–229.

[10] David N. Aspy and F. N. Roebuck, *An Investigation of the Relationship Between Student Levels of Cognitive Functioning and the Teacher's Classroom Behavior* (Study at the University of Florida, 1970). In press.

[11] Richard Schmuck, "Some Aspects of Classroom Social Climate," *Psychology in the Schools,* III (January, 1966), pp. 59–65.

[12] David N. Aspy, "Supervisors, Your Levels of Humanness May Make a Difference," submitted to *Educational Leadership,* 1971.

them develop in counselors-in-training, and I know of no reason why the same could not happen with in-service teacher-trainees.

I am bold and brash enough to say that if I were given a free hand, and if I had the energy and the funds, I could introduce such ferment into schools of education that within one year they would be revolutionized in a positive way. Since this must sound extremely arrogant, I would like to state as precisely as I can how I would go about the task. Needless to say, much of the plan might change as obstacles were encountered and as the participants desired to move in somewhat different directions.

First, I would enlist the aid of many skilled facilitators who are familiar with small-group processes. Then, since it is necessary to begin somewhere, I would indicate that task-oriented groups should be formed in each institution to consider the topic, "How can this school help the whole person learn?" In a general meeting I would explain that the purpose of these groups is not only to learn *about* the topics, but that the participants are to learn as whole persons. In other words, it is not a purely cognitive experience. No doubt this would turn away a great many, for people are fearful of getting personally and experientially involved in learning. Suppose only a small percentage volunteered. That would not concern me.

I would then have three weeks of intensive group experiences devoted to cognitive and experiental elements. This would be followed by back-up sessions with each small group on a weekly basis, and a weekend session three months later. At this time all participants could discuss any problems they have met, all the changes they have seen, and the steps they want to take in bringing about further change. Obviously, the choice of facilitators would be important, but again we have both objective measures and subjective guidelines for selecting persons with the needed qualities.[13] If this program were to be initiated in teacher-training institutions, one precondition would have to be clear. This condition is that no one would be discharged because of dissent from on-going practices in the institution, or because of innovative practices in the classroom.

CHANGE AND TURBULENCE

On the basis of experience, I feel certain that the process I have described would at first polarize both faculty members and their students. Because of this it would create turbulence within the institution, but I happen to believe that such turbulence would be constructive.

[13] Aspy, 1971.

Traditionalists would be angry at the innovators, and vice versa. Sacred cows would be questioned. But student teachers, and even their professors, would start thinking, and as a result they would learn and grow.

One probable outcome of this ferment would be a "free university" type of teacher-training institution in which the students would form their own curricula, participate in the facilitation of learning, and find other means of evaluation than grades. And what would this student do as a new teacher in his own classroom? Most importantly he would simply *be* the attitudes I have already described, and because of this fact new participatory methods would emerge. For those who might need extra guidance, however, Lyon's new book, *Learning to Feel—Feeling to Learn,*[14] would help immensely, for it is full of practical ideas on implementing such a concept.

THE FERMENT OF CONTINUING CHANGE

These, then, would be some of the steps for initiating change in teacher education. I feel certain that within one year there would be many people in teacher-training institutions who learned as whole persons, and who were eager to have their students learn in the same fashion. It would be like an infusion of yeast into a lump of dough. The numbers involved might be small but the pervasive effect would be enormous. You may well ask, "How can I be so sure of all this?" I am sure because I have with my own eyes seen it happen twice. The first time was when the Immaculate Heart system of Los Angeles moved toward self-directed change as a result of taking this idea seriously. The second time I saw this happen was when an inner-city school in Louisville, Kentucky, responded to a program founded on the importance of attitudes.[15] In both instances the initial polarization seemed unfortunate, but out of it grew a new and confident sense of direction.

An example of this spirit may be seen in the following letter that I received from a professor at Immaculate Heart College:

> We are working on a self-initiated and self-directed program in teacher education. We had a fantastically exciting weekend workshop here recently. Students, faculty, and administration, 75 in all, brainstormed in a most creative and productive way. The outcome is that students now immerse themselves in schools all over the city observing classes, sittting in on faculty meetings, interviewing teachers, students, and administra-

[14] Lyon.
[15] W. A. Dickenson, *et al.,* "A Humanistic Program for Change in a Large Inner-City School System," *Journal of Humanistic Psychology,* X (Fall, 1970), pp. 111–120.

tors. Our students will then describe what they need to know, to experience, to do, in order to teach. They will then gather faculty and other students around them to assist in accomplishing their own goals.

The lessons from this are several. The professor, who was a regular faculty member at the beginning of our Immaculate Heart project, was deeply affected by the encounter-group experience, and as a result she took further training in leadership techniques and group dynamics. In time she became open to her students and was able to implement several new ideas. While all this was going on, she became so influential in the college that she was placed in charge of a teacher training program. All this development took place because she had learned as a whole person, and this letter gives evidence of the way in which she is encouraging future teachers to incorporate both the cognitive and the affective-experiential into their learning.

As usual, when given the chance to be self-directing—that is, when trusted to learn—students work harder than anyone has a right to demand of them. There can be little doubt that they in turn will provide a similar opportunity for *their* students to learn to feel, and feel to learn. This is the exciting, pervasive ferment occasioned when an individual has a chance to learn as a whole person.

CONCLUSION

From all this I conclude that we already have the theoretical knowledge, the practical methods, and the day-by-day skills with which to change the educational system. We know how to bring together, in one experience, the intellectual learning, the range of personal emotions, and the basic physiological impact, all of which constitute significant learning by the whole person. We also know how to develop student teachers into agents for this sort of change. This being the case, there is only one question left, and that is, do we have the will to utilize this know-how for humanizing our educational institutions? That is the question we all must answer.

SELECTED REFERENCES

ASPY, DAVID N. "Counseling and Education." *The Counselor's Contribution to Facilitative Processes.* Edited by Robert R. Carkhuff. Urbana, Ill.: Parkinson, 1967.

ASPY, DAVID N. "The Effect of Teacher-Offered Conditions of Empathy, Positive Regard, and Congruence upon Student Achievement." *Florida Journal of Educational Research,* XI (January, 1969), 39–48.

ASPY, DAVID N. *A Study of Three Facilitative Conditions and Their Relationships to the Achievement of Third Grade Students.* Ann Arbor, Mich.: University Microfilms, 1969.

ASPY, DAVID N. "Supervisors, Your Levels of Humanness May Make a Difference." Submitted to *Educational Leadership,* 1971.

ASPY, DAVID N., and ROEBUCK, F. N. *An Investigation of the Relationship between Student Levels of Cognitive Functioning and the Teacher's Classroom Behavior.* Study at the University of Florida, 1970. (In press.)

ASPY, DAVID N., and ROEBUCK, F. N. *The Necessity for Facilitative Interpersonal Conditions in Teaching.* Gainesville: University of Florida. (Unpublished manuscript.)

BARRETT-LENNARD, G. T. "Dimensions of Therapist Response as Causal Factors in Therapeutic Change." *Psychological Monographs,* LXXVI (Whole no. 562, 1962).

BLANK, LEONARD, GOTTSEGEN, GLORIA B., and GOTTSEGEN, MONROE G. *Confrontation, Encounters in Self and Interpersonal Awareness.* New York: Macmillan Co., 1971.

CARKHUFF, ROBERT R., and BERENSON, BERNARD G. *Beyond Counseling and Therapy.* New York: Holt, Rinehart and Winston, Inc., 1967.

DICKENSON, W. A., *et al.* "A Humanistic Program for Change in a Large Inner-City School System." *Journal of Humanistic Psychology,* X (Fall, 1970), 111–120.

LYON, HAROLD C., JR. *Learning to Feel—Feeling to Learn.* Columbus, Ohio: Charles E. Merrill Publishing Co., 1971.

MOON, SAMUEL F. "Teaching the Self." *Improving College and University Teaching,* XIV (Autumn, 1966), 213–229.

RESTON, JAMES. "The Forgotten Factor." *New York Times,* November 29, 1971, Part IV, 11.

ROGERS, CARL R. "The Necessary and Sufficient Conditions of Therapeutic Personality Change." *Journal of Consulting Psychology,* XXI (April, 1957), 95–103.

ROGERS, CARL R. *Freedom to Learn.* Columbus, Ohio: Charles E. Merrill Publishing Co., 1969.

ROGERS, CARL R. *Carl Rogers on Encounter Groups.* New York: Harper & Row, 1970.

SCHMUCK, RICHARD. "Some Aspects of Classroom Social Climate." *Psychology in the Schools,* III (January, 1966), 59–65.

TRUAX, CHARLES B., and CARKHUFF, ROBERT R. *Toward Effective Counseling and Psychotherapy.* Chicago: Aldine Publishing Co., 1967.

What Is "Confluent Education"?

George Isaac Brown

What is "confluent education"?

At home, first graders watch a Jacques Cousteau television special on turtles. They see the frigate birds eat most of the eggs the turtles lay. The next day in class their teacher has them play the roles of turtles and frigate birds. They not only "do" this but also talk about how they feel as they do it. And they talk about similar feelings they've had in other situations. They write stories and learn to read and to spell new words. Can first graders understand tragedy? Can they experience tragedy as part of the condition of nature and life? Can they be the stronger for this? And can they learn "readin', 'ritin', and 'rithmetic" as well as they would in a conventional lesson—perhaps better?

This incident and these questions are part of what this book is about.

Confluent education is the term for the integration or flowing together of the *affective* and *cognitive* elements in individual and group learning—sometimes called humanistic or psychological education.

Affective refers to the feeling or emotional aspect of experience and learning. How a child or adult feels about wanting to learn, how he feels as he learns, and what he feels after he has learned are included in the affective domain.

Cognitive refers to the activity of the mind in knowing an object, to intellectual functioning. What an individual learns and the intellectual process of learning it would fall within the cognitive domain—unless what is learned is an attitude or value, which would be affective learning.

It should be apparent that there is no intellectual learning without some sort of feeling, and there are no feelings without the mind's being somehow involved.

As an example of how the cognitive and affective dimensions can be related, the diagram below demonstrates one way in which the approach of confluent education can be applied to the study of Columbus's discovery of America.

George Isaac Brown, *Human Teaching for Human Learning: An Introduction to Confluent Education.* New York: The Viking Press, 1971, Copyright © 1971 by George Isaac Brown.

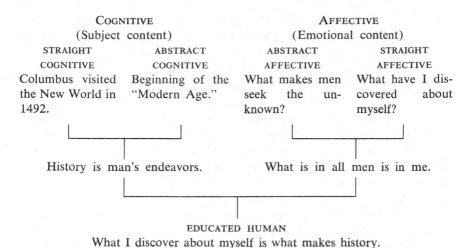

COGNITIVE		AFFECTIVE	
(Subject content)		(Emotional content)	
STRAIGHT COGNITIVE	ABSTRACT COGNITIVE	ABSTRACT AFFECTIVE	STRAIGHT AFFECTIVE
Columbus visited the New World in 1492.	Beginning of the "Modern Age."	What makes men seek the unknown?	What have I discovered about myself?

History is man's endeavors.   What is in all men is in me.

EDUCATED HUMAN
What I discover about myself is what makes history.

There has been an ebb and flow of movements in American education, all ostensibly concerned with the improvement of learning. Sometimes these have focused on the child, as in the progressive-education movement under the influence of Dewey. At other times the emphasis has been on subject matter, as in the area of science and mathematics during the Sputnik era.

Throughout all this—and probably since the beginning of teaching—whether student- or subject matter-oriented or possessing some combination of both, the authentic teacher has endeavored to reach that perfect point in teaching where what the student encounters as new learning in the classroom is like Baby Bear's porridge—neither too hot nor too cold. Sometimes consciously, sometimes subconsciously, the teacher has tried to structure his teaching so that the material to be learned is not too easy—thus boring—and not too hard—thus discouraging—but just challenging enough to be exciting and at a level of difficulty that will enable the student, with a reasonable application of energy, to cope with it and succeed.

As any teacher worth his chalk will tell you, this is not easy to do, especially with a large class of students. However, it is almost impossible when a teacher's methods and curriculum are bounded by limits that ignore the student as a *feeling-thinking* human being.

After World War II, the problem of high-school dropouts and so-called "disadvantaged" students dramatically awakened the educational establishment to the obvious fact that what it had been doing for students as a whole did not work for these individuals. The initial response was to give them stiffer doses of the same stuff, and that didn't work, either. Necessarily, then, some educators began to devise different approaches. They began to consider the affective along with the cognitive dimension of learning. They were somewhat handicapped, however, because techniques for teaching in the affective domain were scarcely available. Not until recently has the bridge been made between what workers in humanistic psychology and Esalen-type activities were doing and the needs of these educators. Unfortunately still prevalent is the attitude that the disadvantaged child is more different from than like other students, and thus that what we do with the disadvantaged child and how we do it is probably not relevant to other students. Portions of this book will demonstrate that such an attitude has little basis in reality. For many educators, the dropouts and the disadvantaged were probably the first major indications of the need for work in the affective dimension of learning.

There are other emerging areas of concern.

At the time of this writing there continues a growing schism between young people and those they consider "the establishment." This schism and other intergroup conflicts are marked by an increasing number of incidents of violence. Violence is a primitive response. A primitive response in a socialized person is often a "last" response, used when all else has seemed to fail. When a breakdown in communication is complete, those involved are so frustrated that violence may well break out, especially when the issues are *felt* to have deep personal relevance.

This situation is another example of the need for affective learning and confluent education. Attempts at communication solely on a rational level are bound to fail when the issues involved have personal relevance for the participants. Personal relevance connotes an affective dimension; people feel and value as well as think about the position they hold. Denying or ignoring the existence of feelings in communication is like building a house without a foundation or framework. Furthermore, the primitive response of violence finds its source in feelings of impotence. An educational system can strongly influence feelings in the direction of either potency or impotence. If the system initiates or promulgates feelings of failure, low self-esteem, or self-depreciation, it can easily contribute to feelings of impotence. On the other hand, if an educational system is alert to the student as an affective organism, to how his "affectivity" relates to his cognitive experience and ultimately to his behavior as a whole person, and if the system has methods and a curriculum that deal with the evident and subtle needs of the individual student, it can do something constructive about diminishing violent response. This would seem an obviously crucial investment.

Violence, as it erupts on college and school campuses, is one of the more visible agonies of education. The sources of this violence are undoubtedly complex. But there are two factors that are often overlooked. Feeling impotent is one. For example, the ghetto black confronts the subculture of the university or the school and finds it alien, rejecting, and frustrating, offering him no immediate way to learn how to cope. This experience is overlaid on years of deprivation and so-called failure. It is no wonder that his cumulative feeling of impotence erupts in violence. The second factor is that this student is joined or supported by those who have been classified as "successful" within society and the educational establishment. These allies have been promised by the establishment, explicitly and implicitly, certain real and magical satisfactions that are "automatically" to follow academic success. Instead, these favored students find their achievement empty of personal meaning, answers to the basic questions many young people have: Who am I? What am I doing here? And they find "plastics," as in the film *The Graduate,* an irrelevant answer. Yet the problem of student violence is only one manifestation of what seems to be a widespread social condition.

Acts of aggression, hate, and violence perpetrated by individuals, groups, and nations become more frequent and increasingly generalized. Feelings of isolation, alienation, frustration, and impotence, along with the the loss of identity and purpose, at the least touch most of us; they surround many of us. A breakdown of law, an increase in disorder, a disintegration of the sense of community or tribe, and the erosion of marriage and family as a meaningful societal unit leave us personally void and socially empty.

And these conditions are so much with us that we apparently become inured to them. Moreover, we seem to numb ourselves to the sources of the conditions. We feel helpless and often hopeless as to what can be done about all this. Obviously, in terms of treatment, there are not enough psychiatrists and psychologists available even if there were a way to induce people in need to seek help. This is compounded by a situation in which a large segment of our citizenry, out of fear, skepticism, prejudice, distrust, or ignorance, refuse to have anything to do with anything that smacks of psychology. An extreme example is the person whose lack of confidence in the professional manifests itself in the kind of rugged individualism that not only applies to his own problems but is also insisted upon as the one problem-solving approach for everybody else.

There are undoubtedly many reasons for the prodigious disintegration now so much with us. The mess is complex and, like a decomposing heap of garbage, is compounded of many ingredients. Let us look at one of the major ingredients.

The greatest potential for change and significant improvement in our individual predicaments and in our dilemma as a society lies in the school. It is the one institution in Western civilization outside the family that most profoundly affects the human condition. It is also the institution that, though resistant, is the most practical in which to innovate. Up to this point, with certain exceptions because of the dedication and skill of some teachers and administrators, schools at best have had a vacuous influence on their students. At worst, however, schools can create a hell on earth and an attitude of personal despair for some of those constrained within. Once a student is categorized and classified, it is psychologically and practically almost impossible for him to break out of his category. Once branded "slow" or a "failure," he is immutably branded.

The above condition is a dramatic and obvious one. Even more pervasive, however, for both success and failure in our educational system, is the subtle yet typical pedagogical aberration in which overconfidence in and overstress on the intellect as the exclusive way of knowing produces generations befogged in illusion and fantasy, generations critically out of touch with the only reality available to them—the reality of each moment. This will be elaborated on a bit later in this chapter.

If schools can be significantly changed—elementary through university—we can ameliorate the deleterious effects of education and contribute substantially toward improving the human condition—a contribution the schools are uniquely in a position to make.

What would be the nature of this change? A proliferation of Summerhills—sensitivity training in each classroom—therapy for all—a daily quota of ecstasy?

No.

What is proposed here is common sense, is something we've "known" about for some time, is possible within the present educational establishment, and although possibly eventually leading to considerable modification in school organization and curriculum, can be readily instituted in schools as they are now. "Readily" could be from five to ten years, for a very good beginning—a time period no longer than that of curriculum reforms like the new math.

The change would be simply to be aware that thinking is accompanied by feeling and vice versa, and to begin to take advantage of the fact.

Such a change could mean the difference between a sick society and and a healthy one. A sick society at best muddles along, fumbling with patchwork stanching and binding up of its wounds, and while burying its mistakes increases the variety but not the meaning of its funeral orations and rites. A sick society at worst could totally turn on itself in a blazing neocrophilic orgy of self-destruction. A healthy society learns from its mistakes and allows its members to grow toward authenticity, communication, and productivity. It makes available a continuing choice between the tranquillity of reflection and the excitement and gratification of individual and group creative endeavor no matter what the focus of the creativity.

History has recorded the place and problems of change and innovation in education as they relate to Western culture. There are a number of examples of Western man's attempt to thrust both the emerging dimensions of knowledge and the process of knowing into educational practices: In reaction to the vocational emphasis of the Sophists, Socrates stressed the pursuit of virtue; Alcuin, at the direction of Charlemagne, attempted to restore the learning of Greece and Rome; Scholasticism focused on Aristotle; the rise of the physical sciences challenged classical literature and theological speculation; Pestalozzi, Froebel, and others aroused interest in the "natural" development of human powers; in America, Dewey and Kilpatrick contributed "learning as doing"; and recently education has been enriched by the application of such technological development as television, programmed learning, and so on.

We are now at a new threshold. Simultaneously emerging in our time are a number of approaches to the extension of human consciousness and the realization of human potential. Some are dangerous, some are irresponsible, and some are exciting, holding great promise. There are a variety of exploratory practices and theories that can be grouped under the taxonomic umbrella of humanistic psychology. These have been the largest resource for work in the new area of confluent education.

To reiterate, confluent education describes a philosophy and a process of teaching and learning in which the affective domain and the cognitive domain flow together, like two streams merging into one river, and are thus integrated in individual and group learning. The term "affective," as we stated earlier, refers to the feeling or emotional aspect of experience and learning. And the more familiar "cognitive" refers to the activity of the mind in knowing an object—to intellectual functioning. Schools have focused almost exclusively on cognitive learning.

One hears much about relevance today. How, then, do we know when something is relevant? It is relevant when it is personally meaningful, when we have feelings about it, whatever "it" may be. There has been concern in the educational establishment for motivating learners, but this is usually only fancy wrapping on the package. If the contents of the package are not something the learner can feel about, real learning will not take place. We must attend not only to that which motivates but to that which *sustains* as well.

The position of most educators at all levels is that the primary function of schools is to teach the learner to be intellectually competent. The position is described by those who hold it as realistic, hardheaded, and a number of other fine-sounding things. Our belief is that this position is instead most unrealistic and illusionary. Oh, yes, it would greatly simplify matters if we could somehow isolate intellectual experience from emotional experience, but at the moment this is possible only in textbooks and experimental designs. The cold, hard, stubborn reality is that whenever one learns intellectually, there is an inseparable accompanying emotional dimension. The relationship between intellect and affect is indestructibly symbiotic. And instead of trying to deny this, it is time we made good use of the relationship. Indeed, the purest, highest form of abstract thinking is coupled with congruent feelings on the part of the thinker, even in the grossest sense of pleasure, boredom, or pain. Or, as Michael Polanyi has observed, it is the passion of the scholar that makes for truly great scholarship.

The more of reality a person has available to him, the more effective he becomes in work, in play, and in love. What has happened to most of us is that we have learned to continually substitute fantasies for reality. This is aggravated by the fact that we share many of these fantasies; that is, they are socially reinforced. This is a large and complex area. But here is a somewhat oversimplified description of how the substitution of fantasy for reality can occur.

As children, we are unable to separate the acts we do from the feelings or impulses that accompany them. When we are punished for a naughty act, we also assign the punishment to the feelings that precipitated and sustained the act. What we feel is thus as bad as what we do. As we become socialized or learn to behave in acceptable ways, we not only restrain our "bad" acts but also repress our "bad" feelings. There are a number of psychological mechanisms that enable us to do this, but whatever the means we use, we are forced to deaden ourselves. We must deny feeling. The more we deaden our bad feelings, the more we deaden all feeling, for apparently we have no way of selecting for elimination only those unacceptable feelings. The deadening is an over-all process. As the process of deadening persists, we lose touch to the extent that we are no longer aware of what we really do feel. We eventually reach a point where we have little choice about how we behave, for, deprived of feelings to tell us what we want or don't want, we react primitively, compulsively, ritualistically. It is not surprising, then, that without access to their feelings a large number of people really do not know what they want.

We do not suggest as an ideal the hedonistic, anarchistic individual who expresses his feelings no matter what, where, when, or who. This sort of person is as "out of it" as the one who has no feelings. A healthy individual has a mind and uses it—not to deny the existence of feelings but to differentiate how, when, and with whom it is appropriate to express feelings spontaneously from occasions when one must wait. When he chooses to postpone or control the *expression* of his feelings, however, he does not at the same time deny to himself that *they exist*.

The denial of the existence of genuine feelings has three unfortunate effects, which are related. These are the replacement of real feelings by pseudo-feelings—feelings we *think* we have—the fear of change, and the substitution of fantasy and illusion for reality.

An outgrowth of our struggle to keep certain feelings from emerging into consciousness is the preservation of our precious self-concept. We experience ourselves in certain ways and struggle mightily to preserve that status quo. Change is a threat, for if we open ourselves to new experience and thus allow for change to occur, we must in that opening give up control. That is precisely what we have steeled ourselves against for many years.

One way we avoid change is by creating with our minds imaginary catastrophes that might happen if we were to move into the unknown of new experience. We terrify ourselves, or at least think we are terrified. And in order to stay the way we are or the way we conceive ourselves to be we dissipate huge amounts of psychic energy in manipulating our environment—especially other persons in our personal universe—so that it will respond to us in terms of our self-concept. We believe we "need" others to support, to judge, to punish, to advise, to order, to do an infinite number of things for us that we ostensibly cannot do for ourselves. We are thus out of touch with our own strength and resources. We all do need others. But it is absurd and wasteful to believe that we need others to do things we are perfectly capable of doing ourselves—to refuse to take responsibility for ourselves and for what we do or could do. We imagine both what some people will do to us and what others must do for us. In each case this is an illusion that accompanies the fantasy of our own limitations.

The obvious waste of living in fantasy in contrast to reality is illustrated by the story of the student who finally got a date with a girl he had been hotly pursuing for two months. He had an exam the next day, so he made the date for nine o'clock, planning to study from seven until nine. He sat down to study, and instead, for two hours, thought about what he was going to do on the date. Then he went out with the girl, and spent the rest of the evening worrying about the exam for which he had not studied.

This example may seem of minor significance. But if we magnify it by how often and how much we keep ourselves out of the present by either hanging on to the past or anticipating the future, the enormity of this waste becomes readily apparent. The only reality we can experience is the reality of the moment. All else is fantasy, something we create for ourselves. We grow and mature through reality experiences. False alternatives merely reinforce our status quo, help keep us stuck.

We have touched on the need for change and growth for the individual. This need is just as important for a society. When the evolving flow of change is impeded, the result is much like what follows the continued damming of a river. Pressure accumulates, and if it is not relieved the dam will eventually burst and destroy everything in the river's path.

Heraclitus, an early Greek philosopher, described the nature of the universe as in constant flux—like the flowing of a stream, always changing. Parmenides, another philosopher, antithetically held that the universe contains absolutes. But even if we were to agree with Parmenides, we would still be confronted with the necessity of searching for these absolutes. Searching is a process, and process makes for change.

Another way to put it is as Tancredi does in Lampedusa's novel, *The Leopard,* when he says to the Prince, "If we want things to stay as they are, things will have to change."

When we total individual resistance to change, we approximate societal resistance to change. When we add to the description of the process of resisting change the prevalent use of clichés, masks, roles, and games, we find it hard not to become discouraged and overwhelmed about our future as a society. In addition, our solutions to these problems are usually utopian in form. Utopias are a hangup. Because of the imperfection of our process of socialization, where we seem either to oversocialize, without sufficient counterbalancing experiences (as in therapy), or to undersocialize, without sufficient recognition of the needs and rights of others (which thus end up frustrated and pillaged, and require expensive policing or remedial work), the chances of realizing a utopia seem minuscule at best. Furthermore, because of the uniqueness or idiosyncratic nature of each individual, an over-all, continuing, harmonious socialization process seems highly unlikely for a long time to come. And this would seem to negate the probability of the harmonious society, the utopian dream. What we can do instead of soothing ourselves with this dream, however, is to concentrate our thoughts and energies on the process of growth itself, especially within the social institutions over which ostensibly we do have some control.

What about that control? The shaping of an institution is obviously in the hands of the shapers. And if the shapers themselves are in a sense misshapen, then they will tend to create the institution in their own image. If we have learned well the lessons of denial, distortion, and repression of genuine feelings, it would seem to follow that our institutions will reflect these avoidances in their structure, goals, and operation. This is especially true of the social institution we call "school" and "university." We have developed clever and elaborate rationales for the avoidances. Furthermore, these rationales are blessed with the sanctity of tradition. And tradition quickly and subtly becomes equated with "truth." Thus, as a people, we are on a merry-go-round of avoidance reinforcement. Tickets are hawked by distinguished leaders, who are tacitly supported by a large chorus, some of whom nod their heads in placid agrement while some stand dumbly, humbly confused, perhaps not even caring.

The leaders and followers are not to be condemned, however, for— to paraphrase a certain distinguished teacher—they know no other way. And that, unfortunately, is very true.

So how can we break the chain, get off the merry-go-round, so that we can move on—if not in a straight line, at least in a healthy direction— so that change will begin to become possible?

Most of the content of the curriculum in our classrooms originally had its source in human experience. When that live experience was transmuted into what was hoped would be a more efficient ordering of the curriculum, its vitality was usually lost. The educator, when justifying the transmutation, would argue, for example, that it was not possible for each student to learn the history of mankind by re-experiencing all the events on which it was based, or, for another example, that there was not time for the student himself to complete the sequence of mathematical frustrations followed by the excitement of insight that successive mathematicians throughout time had experience, which gave mathematics a body of knowledge.

Instead, educators, by compressing and organizing knowledge in all areas of the curriculum, have created in the classroom what Paul Tillich has called the fatal pedagogical error—"To throw answers like stones at the heads of those who have not yet asked the questions." Not only has this reinforced and compounded the pathological condition of unfeeling that we have already described, but it has also had a significant negative effect on cognitive learning itself.

Yet because much of the curriculum is founded on human experience, human dimensions can be reintroduced into classroom learning. And this is where there is hope. The aspect of what and how the learner feels can be integrated with what schools believe he should know. This integration can not only increase his desire to know but also assure that his continuing learning will be a rich, meaningful, and emotionally healthful personal experience.

For a long time we have known the importance of personal involvement in learning. Educational psychologists have, however, expressed this negatively: "If learning has no personal meaning, it will not change behavior." Seldom has the converse been stated: "If we add an emotional dimension to learning, the learner will become personally involved and, as a consequence, there will be change in the learner's behavior."

Only recently have we had knowledge of and experience with ways of incorporating the emotional dimension into learning in the classroom. The work of individuals like Maslow, Rogers, and Perls and of institutions like Esalen, the N.T.L. group, Synanon, and mental-health organizations has provided oases in the impoverished dustlands of education. And the courage and foresight of officers in bodies like the Ford Foundation have given encouragement and support to our work in this area. This book will describe some of this work.

You will see that there is much that remains to be done. There are the problems of training a large number of teachers; of further developing materials, lessons, and teaching units in the various subject areas; of implementing these approaches for use by the educational establishment as a whole. There is the problem of community education, for communities are exercising control on what goes on in schools. This holds both threat and promise—threat because unless people understand what confluent education is really about they could be alienated by its innovative nature, and promise because there is so much dissatisfaction in the community with the way things are in schools today.

We need training centers, curriculum-development projects, research (both empirical and clinical), and organizations for coordination and dissemination of what we learn.

What is proposed would require an initial national expenditure of millions, leading perhaps to billions, of dollars. It is not difficult to imagine this growing eventually to a national budget larger than that for defense. This might include not only the renovation of our own educational system but also foreign aid in confluent education. The emotional-educational needs of other societies are probably as great as our own, though the need is obviously greater in some than in others. There is no society within our knowledge that is not in dramatic need of emotional education. This could be our greatest investment ever in world peace.

Semanticists and others have been pleading for years for international communication beyond conventional verbalized intellectualism, where symbols erect a thick semitranslucent screen between nations and the persons who represent and compose them.

Until we learn to respond in authentic ways to one another in our private lives, in our work, or in our political confrontations, we shall continue to ride the absurd carrousel of repeating over and over the same wasteful, destructive mistakes.

This is not inevitable.

We can learn. Man is capable of growth and maturity. But he must have a place and an opportunity. And of our social institutions the educational system, at least, must change its ways and become a major contributor toward that end. It can do that by recognizing the importance of affective or emotional learning as a primary educational function. Administrators and teachers must become cognizant of how the integration of affective learning with cognitive learning benefits both domains.

Fra Giovanni, in 1513, said: "The gloom of the world is but a shadow. Behind it, yet within reach, is joy. There is a radiance and glory in the darkness could we but see, and to see we have only to look. I beseech you to look!"

So let us take a beginning look.

Humanistic Education

Alfred S. Alschuler

In the Symposium, Alcibiades praised Socrates by saying, "He is exactly like the busts of (the god) Silenus which are set up in the statuaries' shops, holding pipes and flutes in their mouths; they open in the middle and have images of gods inside them. When I opened him (Socrates) and looked within at his serious purpose, I saw divine and golden images of such fascinating beauty that I was ready to do in a moment whatever Socrates commanded." Silenus was a minor Greek diety, a follower of Dionysus, disconcertedly homely, and nearly human. Usually he was seen drunk, sitting precariously on the back of an ass, yet he was reknown for the unsurpassed wisdom and knowledge of past and future that emerged, as with Socrates, in any dialogue. Silenus was a popular god, for he symbolized the universal desire to be discovered and valued for one's inner virtues. All of us want to be a Silenus and to have our Alcibiades. "His words are ridiculous when you first hear them," continues Alcibiades, "but he who opens the bust and sees what is within will find that they are the only words which have a meaning in them, and also the most divine, abounding in fair images of virtue and extending to the whole duty of a good and honorable man." As Humanistic Educators, we are Alcibiades for our students, opening them up, discovering their inner virtues and drawing forth (literally, 'educating") the "good and honorable man."

Only a small number of events in a lifetime radically change the way a person lives—a deeply religious experience, getting married or divorced, having a child, the death of parents, involvement in a serious accident. These dramatic, singular events transform a person's outlook, relation to others and view of himself. By comparison, daily learning experiences in school are undramatic, regularized and designed to promote steady, small increments in external knowledge rather than rapid changes in motives, values and relationships. Obviously we do not want to create regular apocalyptic events that drastically change students' personal lives. However, the ultimate teaching goal of Humanistic Education is to develop effective strategies and human technology for educating inner strengths as profoundly as these rare life-changing events.

UNIQUELY HUMAN LEARNING

Inchoate work in Humanistic Education exists. Scattered across the United States a handful of individuals working in isolated independence have created programmatic approaches to the discovery and enhancement of inner strengths. These Humanistic Education courses respond directly to previously unanswered student questions about setting goals, clarifying values, forming identity, increasing their sense of personal efficacy and having more satisfying relationships with others. The array of humanistic education courses include training in: achievement motivation, awareness and excitement, creative thinking, interpersonal sensitivity, affiliation motivation, joy, self reliance, self esteem, self assessment, self renewal, self actualization, self understanding, strength training, development of moral reasoning, value clarification, body awareness, meditative processes and other aspects of ideal adult functioning.* The variety of virtuous sounding titles testifies to the extent of developmental efforts underway, and also reflects the absence of a definitive description of ideal end states. In spite of this diversity, most of these courses share four general goals, in addition to their unique and specific emphases.

First, most courses attempt to develop a person's *imagination* by using procedures that encourage a constructive dialogue with one's fantasy life. In Synectics training, a creativity course, students are asked to "make the strange familiar" by fantasizing themselves inside a strange object, or to "make the familiar strange" by fantasizing about a common object. In other creativity courses, remote associations are encouraged in order to attain a new, useful and creative perspective on some problem. In other courses, students are taken on guided tours of day dreams and night dreams and on fantasy trips into their own body. In achievement motivation courses, students are encouraged to fantasize about doing things excep-

---

* Descriptions of a number of these courses along with a comprehensive bibliography are contained in *New Directions in Psychological Education*, A. S. Alschuler, *Educational Opportunities Forum*, whole issue, January, 1970, State Education Department, Albany, New York. The three most well developed sets of curriculum materials exist for: 1) *Teaching Achievement Motivation*, by A. Alschuler, D. Tabor, J. McIntyre, Education Ventures, Inc., Middletown, Connecticut, 1970; 2) "Urban Affairs and Communications," T. Borton and N. Newberg, specialists in Humanistic Education, Philadelphia Board of Education Building, Philadelphia, Pa.; 3) "Value Clarification," see *Values and Teaching*, L. Raths, M. Harmon, S. Simon, Columbus, Ohio: Charles Merrill Books, 1966.

tionally well and are taught how to differentiate between achievement imagery and plain old task imagery. Later in the course, these achievement images are tied to reality through careful planning and projects. These procedures often bring previously ignored aspects of one's personality into awareness. Usually this is a joyful, enhancing experience in contrast to psychoanalytic dream analysis and free association, which are oriented to uncovering unconscious conflicts. The implication is that most adults don't make constructive use of their fantasy life and have forgotten how to enjoy fantasy in a childlike but healthy way.

Second, most courses try to develop better *communication skills* by using non-verbal exercises, such as silent theater improvisations, free expression dance movements, meditation, the exaggeration of spontaneous body movements and a wide variety of games. In sensitivity training and encounter groups, non-verbal exercises are used to increase channels of communication. Some personal feelings can be expressed more effectively in motions than in words. Other times, dance and theater improvisations are used because they increase one's expressive vocabulary and are simply joyful experiences. As with constructive fantasizing, proponents of these methods believe that this type of expression, communication and learning is underdeveloped in most people.

A third goal common to these courses is to develop and explore individuals' *emotional responses* to the world. In most courses, how people feel is considered more important than what they think about things. Without these emotional experiences, ranging from laughter and exhilaration to tears and fear, the teacher is likely to consider the course a failure. For example, if an adolescent is scaling a cliff in an Outward Bound course and does not feel any fear, he will not increase his self confidence through his accomplishment. In Achievement Motivation courses, strong group feelings are developed to help support the individual in whatever he chooses to do well. In all of these courses, there is a shared belief that affect increases meaningful learning and that the capacity for the full range of affective responses is a crucial human potentiality often underdeveloped in adults. As a result, a wide range of techniques to enhance affect have been created.†

A fourth goal emphasizes the importance of *living fully and intensely* "here and now." The emphasis takes many forms. In Gestalt awareness training, the goal is philosophically explicit. In most courses, it is subtle and implicit. Usually courses are held in retreat settings which cut people off from past obligations and future commitments for brief periods of time.

† *Human Relations Education: A Guidebook to Learning Activities,* prepared by the Human Relations Project of Western New York, reprinted by the University of the State of New York, the State Education Department, Curriculum Development Center, Albany, New York, 1969.

The isolated resort settings dramatize the "here and now" opportunities. In general there is little emphasis on future "homework" or past personal history as an explanation for behavior. A vivid example is Synanon, a total environment program for drug addicts, which promotes "self actualization," and in the process cures addiction. Synanon requires the addict to kick drugs immediately upon entering the program. Other "bad" behavior which stands in the way of self actualization is pointed out as it occurs. Historical explanations for bad behavior are considered excuses and are not tolerated. In other Humanistic Education programs, the games, exercises, group process, etc., are model opportunities to explore, discover and try out new behavior here and now. The assumption is that if a person can't change "here and now," where the conditions for growth are optimal, he is not likely to continue growing outside and after the course.

The existing procedures for developing new thinking, action and feelings in the "here and now" constitute human methods for educating inner strengths. These methods make it possible to create, without trauma, the sequence of uniquely human learning that occurs during and after rare, dramatic, life-changing events.

In most of these naturally occurring events there is a strong focus of attention on what is happening "here and now." Whether it is a mother's labor during birth, the taking of marriage vows, the shock of realizing your arm is broken, or the ecstasy of a religious vision, the intensity of the experience crowds out familiar reactions. One characteristic that sets these experiences apart is the simultaneous intensity of radically new thoughts, actions and feelings. Usually these experiences break established relationships, as when a parent dies. Often they disrupt habitual patterns of living, or dissolve longtime beliefs. Whether the experience is revelatory or traumatic in nature, it breaks basic continuities in a person's life. After the peak of the experience has passed, there is a period of some confusion and puzzlement, during which the person attempts to make sense out of what happened and to establish meaningful new continuities. This attempt takes many forms, from conversation with friends to meditation and prayer. Even if the experience is never fully understood, in time the consequences become clearer—how relationships are altered, what goals and values are different, and what new behaviors occur. After a while these changes seem more familiar and practiced. For example, new roles become less confusing. As the newness of being a parent wears off, the role becomes an integral part of a person's life, with its own rich set of relationships, behaviors and meanings. Similarly, in time, the traumatic loss of a loved one results in new relationships, behaviors and meanings that we internalize in our way of living.

This sequence of learning can be conceptualized as a six-step process and used as a guideline in planning Humanistic Education courses and sequencing existing humanistic procedures.

1. Focus attention on what is happening here and now by creating moderate novelty that is slightly different from what is expected.
2. Provide an intense, integrated experience of the desired new thoughts, actions and feelings.
3. Help the person make sense out of his experience by attempting to conceptualize what happened.
4. Relate the experience to the person's values, goals, behavior and relationships with others.
5. Stabilize the new thought, action and feelings through practice.
6. Internalize the changes.

This teaching strategy is not simply a heuristic device. A considerable amount of support for the validity of these guidelines exists in the theoretical and empirical research literature on personality change.‡

This strategy indicates a number of ways that Humanistic Education differs from more traditional academic training. The most effective way to proceed through this learning sequence is to set aside a large block of time, often as long as a week or more, in a special location for a concentrated workshop. The untypical setting helps create moderate novelty, reduces distractions and helps focus attention on the new experiences. The concentrated time period is needed to allow the participants to follow new thoughts, to try out new behavior and to stick with their feelings to a natural conclusion. *Emotions,* in contrast to *thoughts,* tend to be non-reversible and difficult to stop quickly at the end of a 45-minute class period. This inhibits the expression of feelings, just as longer time periods encourage the expression of feelings. In this sense, Humanistic Education is experience based and inductive, in contrast to academic learning—which tends to be more abstract, logical and deductive.

A less obvious difference is the integration and simultaneous development of thoughts, feelings and actions. Learning achievement motivation, for example, involves developing a specific cognitive pattern of planning, a special type of excitement and a set of related action strategies. Most normal learning situations differ by rewarding expertise as a "thinker" in academic courses, or as a doer in physical courses like vocational educa-

‡ The most relevant summaries of this literature can be found in D. C. McClelland, "Toward a Theory of Motive Acquisition," *American Psychologist,* May, 1965; D. C. McClelland and D. G. Winter, *Motivating Economic Achievement,* Free Press, 1969; Campbell, J., Dunnette, M., "Effectiveness of T-Group Experience in Managerial Training and Development," *Psychological Bulletin,* August, 1968, pp. 73-104.

tion or athletics. This makes it especially difficult for teachers to be concerned in practice with educating the "whole child." However, there is some justification for the way schooling fragments human functioning into component parts. It does prepare students for adult lives in which separate role performances are played out in many directions. Just as students move from class to class during the day, adults move from role to role. We work in one place, have our intimate, loving relationships in another place, and usually travel to still other places for recreation. In each role adults are known for a narrow set of behaviors, just as students are known by their teachers as a math student, or typing student and rarely as a complex, many-sided individual. Experience-based learning integrates human functioning in the service of balanced maturation.

The art and technology of Humanistic Education, in large part, lies in the creation of productive learning experiences. Only the outlines of this technology are clear at this time. Teachers must be insightful diagnosticians of children's experience, so that moderately novel situations can be created. These situations bridge the gap between where the child is and where he can be. Thus, teachers must know a wide range of Humanistic Education procedures and be knowledgeable about the goals of human development. This expertise allows them to help students conceptualize, relate and apply their new experiential knowledge. Few learning experiences require extensive hardware and materials. Most procedures involve the person in relation to his own body, feelings and imagination or in relation to his environment and other people. A comprehensive source book of humanistic methods would be useful, but ultimately each teacher must adapt and sequence these methods to create the course of learning, i.e., the curriculum. In this sense, curriculum innovation is constant, and Humanistic Educators need to become adept at improvising sequences of learning that lead to internalization.

Compared to typical school goals, Humanistic Education courses aim for long-term internalization, not short-term gains in mastery. More precisely, these courses attempt to increase "operant" behavior as well as respondent behavior. Operant behavior is voluntary, seemingly spontaneous and certainly not required by the situation. What a person does with his leisure time is an indication of his operant behavior. Respondent behavior requires external cues and incentives before it will occur, just as an examination question brings forth respondent knowledge that otherwise probably would not have been demonstrated. In practice, most school learning calls for respondent behavior: multiple choice and true-false questions, reading assigned chapters, solving a given set of mathematics problems correctly, or writing an essay to a prescribed theme. To be most meaningful to a student, Humanistic Education must result in operant, internalized behavior, since after the course is over there will not be anyone to follow him around defining the problems, presenting the alternatives, guiding the response and evaluating the results. Paradoxically, the most important thing to do in helping a person develop long-term operant behavior is to stop doing anything. Support must be gradually transferred from external sources to the person's own inner resources. The problem is to leave on time—not too soon, because guidance is needed in the early phases, and not too late because that retards essential self reliance. At the present time, staging perfectly timed exits is an art in need of becoming a technology.

HUMANIZING SCHOOLS

Educating the "good and honorable man" is a ubiquitous aim of schooling. The problem is not the legitimacy of humanistic goals for public education, but how to translate these goals fully into practice. Specifically, it is unethical to develop students' ability to relate more warmly and directly their achievement motivation, their capacity for creative thinking through Humanistic Education courses, and then send them back into normal classrooms where these processes are not functional. For example, many Humanistic Education courses teach people how to develop collaborative and trusting relationships. Only in schools are there so few structured opportunities for practicing team-work and cooperation. From the humanistic point of view, the way people learn is just as important as what they learn. Ideally, there should be at least as much variety in the teaching-learning process within a single school as exists outside and after school, where students are variously required, ordered, coached, coaxed, persuaded, led, followed, threatened, promised, lectured, questioned, joined, challenged and left alone. Compared to this handsome array of naturally occurring learning processes, the typical range within a school is embarrassingly narrow. As Humanistic Education courses are introduced in schools, corresponding new processes should be available in regular courses in order for students to *practice what they have learned.*

How students learn is determined in large part by the rules of the implicit learning game and the teacher's leadership style. Both rules and leadership styles can be modified easily, although these methods of changing the processes of learning generally are not used. One of the first errors made by teachers who decide to increase the number of alternative learning processes is to decrease the number of rules and amount of teacher leadership, because this seems to decrease authoritarianism while increasing the possibility of many types of student initiative and learning styles. The key to a systematic variation in learning processes, however, is not how many rules and directions, but *what kind.* For example, such highly rule-governed activities as baseball and square dancing are non-authoritarian, and stimulate specific human processes. A variety of desired learning processes can be aroused by changing the rules which govern the nature of the scoring system, the type of obstacles to success and how decisions about strategy and tactics are made.§ Implementing a variety of "learning games" requires of teachers great flexibility and repertoire of personal styles; they must have actualized many of the "divine and golden images" with themselves.

Just as it is unethical to develop inner strengths in students and put them into classrooms with a narrow range of legitimate learning styles, so too is it unethical to expect this flexibility within teachers or among a school faculty in a school that does not encourage, support and reward this variety. Ultimately, the administrative style, rules and rewards in a whole school must implement a pluralistic philosophy of education. The task of humanizing schools is, of necessity, multi-leveled and wholistic.

The technology of planned change in schools is just now emerging. As recently as 1965 there was only one book devoted exclusively to the problem. Since then, the Office of Education and the National Training Laboratories have sponsored a large-scale investigation of how to increase innovation in teaching, learning and human relations at all levels in school systems—The Cooperative Project for Educational Development (COPED). The results of COPED suggest a four-phased strategy for maximizing the likelihood of effectively introducing Humanistic Education in a school. ||

1. *Selection*
   The top administrator and other key decision makers should be committed in principle to innovation in advance of specific training programs. Representatives from all groups within the school should be eligible for the special training programs.

2. *Diagnosis*
   Organizational strengths and weaknesses need to be assessed. This can be done most effectively through interviews with potential participants prior to the major change efforts. Information is obtained on such factors as the reward system, rules, communi-

§ For a complete explication of this position see "The Effects of Classroom Structure on Motivation and Performance," A. S. Alschuler, *Educational Technology,* August, 1969, and "Motivation in the Classroom," Chapter 3 in *Teaching Achievement Motivation,* A. Alschuler, D. Tabor, J. McIntyre, Education Ventures, Inc., Middletown, Connecticut, 1970.

|| Based on a private conversation with Dr. Gale G. Lake, Director of COPED and editor of the *COPED, Final Report,* April, 1970, ERIC Files, U.S. Office of Education, Division of Research.

cation patterns, current school issues and individual goals. Often it helps if these data are shared with the school system in a "diagnostic workshop." The purpose of this collaborative meeting is to further clarify the problem and place priorities on the goals of change.

3. *Introductory Training*

A training program is designed to meet the defined needs. This workshop introduces the members of the school to relevant aspects of Humanistic Education. The workshop follows the six-step sequence described earlier. During the final phase, the school is encouraged to select an ongoing "change management team" with representatives from all groups in the school.

4. *Follow Through*

After the initial training the aim is to build into the school system a permanent team of self sufficient change management experts and well-trained Humanistic Educators. The "change management team" coordinates this development, and conscientiously supports the introduction of Humanistic Education. These changes can be accomplished through internal task forces, additional specialized training or a variety of organizational development services from outside consultants. To start the "follow through," the team is encouraged to implement a high visibility project likely to succeed.

This strategy for change differs markedly from traditional approaches through graduate school teacher education and curriculum reform. It more closely resembles the creation of a Research and Development group within a corporation. This comparison highlights the fact that businesses often spend as much as 10–15% of their budget on R & D activities whereas the typical corresponding allocation by schools is less than 1%. The absence of this strong coordinating group in school vitiates the effectiveness of "new curricula" and restricts the influence of well-trained new teachers. The creation of an effective change management team coordinates and internalizes curriculum innovation within the school.

Although the existence of this coordinating group does facilitate changes in the character of schooling, it does not guarantee perfect guidance towards ultimate human goals. For instance, some teachers make humanistic methods ends in themselves. The use of game simulations and role playing, ipso facto, is considered good, Creativity training courses are endorsed whether or not the problems to be solved are meaningful. Courses in Theater Improvisation are introduced to develop non-verbal behavior independent of significant personal relationships and goals. As a result, these courses and methods often fail precisely in what they are trying to accomplish. Strenghtening imagination simply becomes bizarre fantasizing; a narrow focus on feelings leads to misunderstanding; exclusive attention to non-verbal communication stimulates anti-intellectual distrust of rational, goal-directed behavior.

Major advances in Humanistic Education are not likely to come simply from the proliferation of methods, training, teacher-curriculum-developers or the creation of self-renewing schools, although each of these tasks are worthy. We need guiding visions of the "good and honorable man" and utopian models for the places where we live. Human abilities are strengthened, integrated, balanced and given meaning only in the pursuit of these goals. The essentially heuristic value of these unattainable ideals is conveyed in the word "Utopia," a pun made by Thomas More on "Eutopia" (good place) and "Outopia" (no place). In the last century, over 200 utopian communities were started—and none has survived. The longest-lived utopian communities are those which face the question of life and death daily (kibbutzem, Synanon) or which surround a single charismatic leader (Ashrams with their gurus) or those which share an ultimate faith (Amish, Oneida). In the United States, most of us no longest-lived utopian communities are those which face the question of who command our sympathy by their stand against those public figures who would be our gurus. Ultimate faith is being replaced by immediate action concerns against visible injustice and for personal pleasure. This is reflected in our schools, where pluralistic demands for innovation often mask the loss of an ultimate sense of mission.

The consequences of this value crisis are to leave key ethical questions unanswered for all types of education: What kind of teaching and subject matter is in the best interest of students? Who is to decide? How? How do you know when a teacher is competent? How do you know when teaching is effective, ineffective or negative? Choices about what new curricula to develop, how to train teachers, what kinds of learning outcomes to assess and how best to humanize schooling depend on answers to these ethical questions. Obviously, there is no single set of definitive conclusions; but, instead, there is the opportunity for all educators to engage in a uniquely human search for values. The continuing attempt to discover "divine and golden images" and to draw forth the "good and honorable man" is the mission of Humanistic Education.

Values and Valuing

Louis E. Raths, Merrill Harmin,
and Sidney B. Simon

Persons have experiences; they grow and learn. Out of experiences may come certain general guides to behavior. These guides tend to give direction to life and may be called values. Our values show what we tend to do with our limited time and energy.

Since we see values as growing from a person's experiences, we would expect that different experiences would give rise to different values and that any one person's values would be modified as his experiences accumulate and change. A person in the Antarctic would not be expected to have the same values as a person in Chicago. And a person who has an important change in patterns of experience might be expected to modify his values. Values may not be static if one's relationships to his world are not static. As guides to behavior, values evolve and mature as experiences evolve and mature.

Moreover, because values are a part of living, they operate in very complex circumstances and usually involve more than simple extremes of right and wrong, good or bad, true or false. The conditions under which behavior is guided, in which values work, typically involve conflicting demands, a weighing and a balancing, and finally an action that reflects a multitude of forces. Thus values seldom function in a pure and abstract form. Complicated judgments are involved and what is really valued is reflected in the outcome of life as it is finally lived.

We therefore see values as constantly being related to the experiences that shape them and test them. They are not, for any one person, so much hard and fast verities as they are the results of hammering out a style of life in a certain set of surroundings. After a sufficient amount of hammering, certain patterns of evaluating and behaving tend to develop.

Louis E. Raths, Merrill Harmin, and Sidney B. Simon, *Values and Teaching*, chap. 3. Columbus, Ohio: Charles E. Merrill Publishing Company, 1966. For information about current values clarification materials or a series of nation-wide training workshops, contact Values Associates, Box 43, Amherst, Mass. 01002.

Certain things are treated as right, or desirable, or worthy. These tend to become our values.

In this book we shall be less concerned with the particular value outcomes of any one person's experiences than we will with the process that he uses to obtain his values. Because life is different through time and space, we cannot be certain what experiences any one person will have. We therefore cannot be certain what values, what style of life, would be most suitable for any person. We do, however, have some ideas about what *processes* might be most effective for obtaining values. These ideas grow from the assumption that whatever values one obtains should work as effectively as possible to relate one to his world in a satisfying and intelligent way.

From this assumption comes what we call the *process of valuing*. A look at this process may make clear how we define a value. Unless something satisfies *all* seven of the criteria noted below, we do not call it a value. In other words, for a value to result, all of the following seven requirements must apply. Collectively, they describe the process of valuing.

1. *Choosing freely.* If something is in fact to guide one's life whether or not authority is watching, it must be a result of free choice. If there is coercion, the result is not likely to stay with one for long, especially when out of the range of the source of that coercion. Values must be freely selected if they are to be really valued by the individual.

2. *Choosing from among alternatives.* This definition of values is concerned with things that are chosen by the individual and, obviously, there can be no choice if there are no alternatives from which to choose. It makes no sense, for example, to say that one values eating. One really has no choice in the matter. What one may value is certain types of food or certain forms of eating, but not eating itself. We must all obtain nourishment to exist; there is no room for decision. Only when a choice is possible, when there is more than one alternative from which to choose, do we say a value can result.

3. *Choosing after thoughtful consideration of the consequences of each alternative.* Impulsive or thoughtless choices do not lead to values as we define them. For something intelligently and meaningfully to guide one's life, it must emerge from a weighing and an understanding. Only when the consequences of each of the alternatives are clearly understood can one make intelligent choices. There is an important cognitive factor here. A value can emerge only with thoughtful consideration of the range of the alternatives and consequences in a choice.

4. *Prizing and cherishing.* When we value something, it has a positive tone. We prize it, cherish it, esteem it, respect it, hold it dear. We

are happy with our values. A choice, even when we have made it freely and thoughtfully, may be a choice we are not happy to make. We may choose to fight in a war, but be sorry circumstances make that choice reasonable. In our definition, values flow from choices that we are glad to make. We prize and cherish the guides to life that we call values.

5. *Affirming.* When we have chosen something freely, after consideration of the alternatives, and when we are proud of our choice, glad to be associated with it, we are likely to affirm that choice when asked about it. We are willing to publicly affirm our values. We may even be willing to champion them. If we are ashamed of a choice, if we would not make our position known when appropriately asked, we would not be dealing with values but something else.

6. *Acting upon choices.* Where we have a value, it shows up in aspects of our living. We may do some reading about things we value. We are likely to form friendships or to be in organizations in ways that nourish our values. We may spend money on a choice we value. We budget time or energy for our values. In short, for a value to be present, life itself must be affected. Nothing can be a value that does not, in fact, give direction to actual living. The person who talks about something but never does anything about it is dealing with something other than a value.

7. *Repeating.* Where something reaches the stage of a value, it is very likely to reappear on a number of occasions in the life of the person who holds it. It shows up in several different situations, at several different times. We would not think of something that appeared once in a life and never again as a value. Values tend to have a persistency, tend to make a pattern in a life.

To review this definition, we see values as based on three processes: choosing, prizing, and acting.

CHOOSING: (1) freely
(2) from alternatives
(3) after thoughtful consideration of the consequences of each alternative

PRIZING: (4) cherishing, being happy with the choice
(5) willing to affirm the choice publicly

ACTING: (6) doing something with the choice
(7) repeatedly, in some pattern of life

Those processes collectively define valuing. Results of the valuing process are called values.

The reader might pause for a moment and apply the seven criteria for a value to one of his hobbies, be it sewing, skiing or hi-fi. Is it prized, freely and thoughtfully chosen from alternatives, acted upon, repeated, and publicly known? If so, one might say that you *value* that hobby.

VALUE INDICATORS

Obviously not everything is a value, nor need it be. We also have purposes, aspirations, beliefs, and many other things that may not meet all seven of those criteria. However values often do grow from our purposes, aspirations, beliefs, and so on. Let us briefly discuss some things that could indicate the presence of a value but that are different from values. We call these expressions which approach values, but which do not meet all of the criteria, *value indicators*.

1. *Goals or purposes.* To have purposes gives direction to life. If the purpose is important to us, we cherish it and we organize our life in ways by which we can achieve the purpose. This doesn't mean that every stated purpose is a value. Instead, we should think of a stated purpose as a potential value or a value indicator. If, in our presence, a child should state a purpose, it is, until we inquire further, merely a stated purpose— and we have an opportunity to pursue with him whether or not he prizes it, has freely chosen it, has wanted it for some time, and is willing to do what is necessary to achieve it. Some stated purposes are dropped when these processes are applied. The child finds out that what he said is not what he really wants. He might have had what amounts to a passing interest in the idea, but even brief examination often results in depreciation of the stated purpose. Thus a purpose *may* be a value, but, on the other hand, it may not be.

2. *Aspirations.* We sometimes indicate a purpose that is remote in terms of accomplishment. It is not something that we wish or expect to accomplish today or tomorrow, or within a week or sometimes even a month. The statement of such an aspiration frequently points to the possibility of something that is valued. We shall not know if it is truly a value until we have asked questions which relate to the seven criteria which have been mentioned. When the responses are consistent with those criteria, we can say that we have touched a value.

3. *Attitudes.* Sometimes we give indications that we may have values by expressing attitudes. We say that we are *for* something or *against* something. It is not always a sound practice to infer that such a statement represents a value. Is it really cherished? Has some consideration been given to alternatives? Does it come up again and again?

Is it related to the life activities of the person who expresses it? Unless these criteria are met, it may be just so many words. That is, it may just be an attitude and not a value.

4. *Interests.* Very often you hear people say that they are interested in something. Care should be taken, however, in concluding that this means that a value is present. Very often when we say we are interested, we mean little more than that we would like to talk about it or to listen to someone talk about it, or that we might like to read a little more in that area. It isn't a combination of the criteria which have been proposed. It may be a bit more than a passing fancy, but very frequently it does not work out to be a value.

5. *Feelings.* Our personalities are also expressed through our feelings and through statements about how we feel. Our feelings are sometimes hurt. Sometimes we feel outraged. On other occasions we are glad, sad, depressed, excited; and we experience dozens of other feelings. We cannot always say that a value is present. In terms of a definition of a value, our feelings may be responses which are dissipated by very brief reflection. We should have to ask a number of questions in order to find out if the feeling reflects an underlying value.

6. *Beliefs and convictions.* When we hear someone state what he believes, it is all too easy to accept the statement as a value. A man may believe that there should be discrimination with respect to race, but he may be ashamed of that belief. He may not prize holding it. Moreover, upon examination, he may have doubts about the truth or goodness of his belief. It is the examined belief, the cherished belief, the freely chosen belief, and the belief that pervades life that rises to the stature of a value. The verbal statement provides a pointer, but it is only through careful examination that we get to know whether it represents a value.

7. *Activities.* We sometimes say about a figure in public life, "That's what he says, but what does he do?" We seem to be saying that not until a person does something do we have some idea of what he values. With values, as with others things, actions speak louder than words. Of course, it isn't true that every thing we do represents our values. For example, we are pretty sure that going to church does not necessarily mean a commitment to religion. One may go to church for many reasons. One may go often and regularly to bridge parties, all the while wishing that he didn't have to go. One may do a certain kind of work every day without having chosen that work or prizing it very much. In other words, just by observing what people do, we are unable to determine if values are present. We have to know if the individual prizes what he is doing, if he has chosen to do

what he is doing, and if it constitutes a pattern in his life, etc. All by themselves, activities do not tell us enough, but they may indicate a value.

8. *Worries, problems, obstacles.* We hear individuals talk about worries that they have, or problems that they have, and we sometimes infer from the context that we know the values that are involved. Here again we may be giving undue importance to verbal statements. If we were to ask questions bearing upon the seven criteria which have been proposed, we might find out that nothing of great importance is involved; that the statement represented "a conversation piece." Many of us talk a good deal, and we may mention problems or worries only as ways of entering into a conversation. Examining the worry or the problem may reveal that something *is* deeply prized, that a belief *is* being blocked, that one's life *is* being disturbed, and under these circumstances we can be more confident with the judgment that a value is involved.

We have explained something about eight categories of behavior which have a significant relationship to valuing. There is no implication that other categories of behavior may not be just as important. However, these eight categories—goals and purposes, aspirations, feelings, interests, beliefs and convictions, attitudes, activities, and worries—are often revealed in the classroom. We believe it is important that opportunities for revealing these become a vital part of teaching, for the next step—as will be discussed in later chapters—is for the teacher to help those children who choose to do so to raise these value "indicators" to the level of values, that is, to the level on which all seven of the valuing processes operate.

We now want to turn our attention to one of the value processes that seems to have particular importance in our work with children growing up in this confused and complex world, the process of choosing.

THE CRUCIAL CRITERION OF CHOICE

Because we see choosing as crucial to the process of valuing, it may be useful at this point to expand on the conditions that must exist if a choice is really to be made.

The idea of choosing suggests the notion of alternatives. One chooses something from a group of things. If there is only one possibility, we cannot make a choice and, according to our definition, we cannot have a value in that area. Yet so often we eliminate all but one alternative or we restrict alternatives available to children. For example, we say to a child that he must either sit silently in his chair or stay after school. Or we ask, "Wouldn't you like to learn your multiplication table, John?" If we restrict alternatives, so that the child's preferred choice is not among them, we cannot say that his choice represents a value. It is common practice to give children either-or choices, both of which may be undesirable from his standpoint, then wonder why he does not value his own behavior.

Unless we open up decisions, and include alternatives that a child might really prefer, we may only give the illusion of choice, at least in terms of this value theory. Values must grow from thoughtful, prized choices made from sufficient alternatives.

When we take the lead in presenting alternatives to children, we should also take some care in seeing to it that *the alternatives have meaning* for them. A student may be familiar with only one of the possible choices and may not be aware of what the others involve. We can discover this by asking questions; and if he doesn't know what other choices could mean, we can help him to understand them better. It is useless, therefore, to ask a young child to make choices from among alternatives he doesn't understand, and it is inaccurate to *think* a choice has been made when, for example, a child selects democracy over autocracy without much understanding of either.

We should also help children to see the probable *consequences of a choice* and find out if they are willing to accept the consequences which may follow. Where a child has put himself on record as willing to take the consequences, the situation has been clarified, and his choice has some meaning. Without such an understanding of and acceptance of the consequences, we can hardly call the choice meaningful.

Also there is the idea that the child needs to be really *free to choose*. If for many reasons we don't want him to choose a particular alternative, like setting fire to the house, we should let him know that this is not within the realm of choice. We should not try to fool him into thinking that he is a free agent and then disappoint him when we refuse to honor his choice. We should be clear and forceful when we deny choices. Otherwise we subvert the faith of the child in the very process of deciding and choosing. But when we are concerned with values, we must be willing to give the child his freedom to choose. In short, we are saying that a coerced choice is no choice at all. It is not likely that values will evolve from a choice imbued with threat or bribery, for example. A condition of choosing that the value theory suggests is freedom to choose. One important implication for teachers is the diminution of the punishment and reward systems so widely used in schools. Choices cannot be considered sufficiently free if each one is to be weighed, approved or disapproved, or graded by someone in charge.

Does this mean that the whole world should be open for choice and that we should respect a child's choice no matter what it is? Most teachers, in the light of policies suggested by a school board or school administrators, make quite clear to students that there are areas where choice is not possible. One of these relates to life itself. We do not allow children to engage in activities which might result in serious danger. This is almost always directly stated and carried out without exception. We say to children that in matters like this they cannot choose, that their behavior is restricted; and the reason we give is that the consequences of an unwise choice are not tolerable or that the alternatives can probably not be well enough understood to make a choice meaningful.

Many of us are also against vulgarity in many forms. Profane language, obscene behavior, filth, and dirtiness are matters on which many of us take a stand. We may indicate to children that they may not engage in things of this kind; that the policies for which we stand do not allow such things to go on; that deviations from our standard bother us too much to be tolerated. When an individual reveals this kind of behavior, we may directly intervene and, perhaps privately, talk with the student. Thus may some teachers want to restrict choices in areas that are important to adults.

In almost every culture and in many communities there are areas which are sometimes called "hot" or "very delicate." In some communities it may be matters pertaining to religious issues; in some other communities it may be matters relating to political issues; sex is frequently such an issue. Where these so-called hot issues are matters of civil rights, rights which belong to all individuals, teachers may wish to challenge restrictions or taboos. It is good policy, however, to do this on a professional level, working among colleagues first, and not to take up things with children in a public way which may be against public policy. It is usually wiser to make attempts to clarify public policy and to modify it before involving the children in affairs that might be extremely embarrassing and extremely provoking. Whether children should be encouraged to reflect and choose in a controversial area is not the point. They *must* reflect and choose if values are to emerge. The question is one of what teachers might do first in communities which frown upon opening certain issues.

In summary, we are saying that if children—or adults, for that matter—are to develop values, they must develop them out of personal choices. We are also saying that these choices, if they are possibly to lead to values, must involve alternatives which (1) include ones that are prized by the chooser; (2) have meaning to the chooser, as when the consequences of each are clearly understood; and (3) are freely available for selection.

THE PERSONAL NATURE OF VALUES

The point has been made that our values tend to be a product of our experiences. They are not just a matter of true or false. One can not go to an encyclopedia or to a textbook for values. The definition that has been given makes this clear. One has to prize for himself, choose for himself, integrate choices into the pattern of his own life. Information as such doesn't convey this quality of values. Values come out of the flux of life itself.

This means that we are dealing with an area that isn't a matter of proof or consensus. It is a matter of experience. So, if a child says that he likes something, it does not seem appropriate for an older person to say, "You shouldn't like that." Or, if a child should say, "I am interested in that," it does not seem quite right for an older person to say to him, "You shouldn't be interested in things like that." If these things have grown out of a child's experience, they are consistent with his life. When we ask him to deny his own life, we are in effect asking him to be a hypocrite. We seem to be saying in an indirect way, "Yes, this is what your life has taught you, but you shouldn't say so. You should pretend that you had a different life." What are we doing to children when we put them into positions like this? Are we helping them to develop values or are we in effect saying that life is a fraud and that one should learn to live like a fraud very early in life?

We have an alternative approach to values, and this will be presented in the following chapters. For now, it is important to note that our definition of values and valuing leads to a conception of these words that is highly personal. It follows that if we are to respect a person's life, we must respect his experience and his right to help in examining it for values.

As a matter of fact, in a society like ours, governed by our Constitution, teachers might well see themselves as obliged to support the idea that every individual is entitled to the views that he has and to the values that he holds, especially where these have been examined and affirmed. Is this not the cornerstone of what we mean by a free society? As teachers, then, we need to be clear that we cannot dictate to children what their values should be since we cannot also dictate what their environments should be and what experiences they will have. We may be authoritative in those areas that deal with truth and falsity. In areas involving aspirations, purposes, attitudes, interests, beliefs, etc., we may raise questions, but we cannot "lay down the law" about what a child's values should be. By definition and by social right, then, values are personal things.

As a matter of cold fact, in the great majority of instances, we really don't know what values an individual child has. We are apt to make inferences which go beyond the available data and to attribute values to children which they do not hold. We probably will be better off if we assume in almost every case that we really don't know. If we are interested in knowing, we might well initiate a process of investigation and inquiry, and more attention will be given to this notion later.

One last point needs to be made before we go on. Some people, when they travel, seem to be much more interested in the motels or hotels at which they stop than in the experiences which they have along the way. Some other people are much more interested in the road than the inn. In what has been said thus far, the reader may see that we associate ourselves with the latter group. We are interested in the processes that are going on. We are not much interested in identifying the values which children hold. We are much more interested in the process because we believe that in a world that is changing as rapidly as ours, each child must develop habits of examining his purposes, aspirations, attitudes, feelings, etc., if he is to find the most intelligent relationship between his life and the surrounding world, and if he is to make a contribution to the creation of a better world.

The development of values is a personal and life-long process. It is not something that is completed by early adulthood. As the world changes, as we change, and as we strive to change the world again, we have many decisions to make and we should be learning how to make these decisions. We should be learning how to value. It is this process that we believe needs to be carried on in the classrooms, and it is at least partly through this process that we think children will learn about themselves and about how to make some sense out of the buzzing confusion of the society around them.

Laboratory Training
in Planned Change

Dorothy Mial

At a time when burgeoning laboratory or "sensitivity" training programs are sometimes caught in a cross fire between overly enthusiastic advocates and overly fearful critics, it may be helpful to stop the action long enough to assess contributions and to look at legitimate concerns. Otherwise, a good and useful educational innovation may be done in by uncritical lovers, on the one hand, and unloving critics, on the other—to borrow John Gardner's description of the dilemma of social institutions in general.

No program survives and grows unless there is need to nurture it. With laboratory training now used in business and industry, in government, in community organizations, as well as in education, what are the needs that keep it alive? More specifically, what needs in elementary education have led to an increasing use of laboratory methods in leadership and organizational development programs?

In 1959, the first training laboratory designed especially for educational leaders was conducted by the National Training Laboratories and cosponsored by the National Association of Elementary School Principals. The program was designed for the principal as an agent and manager of change. Now, 12 years later, the principal's job seems even more complex. The head of anything as complex as a school set in today's changing community needs knowledge and technical competence, but he also needs a high degree of skill and sensitivity in responding to the human problems and potentialities inherent in any school system. The absence of such skill in the principal and his staff is signaled loud and clear through distorted perceptions, miscommunication, underuse of resources, and failure to innovate in response to new demands. An overarching need is to get people with a common concern for better education connected up in ways that foster collaborative problem solving. From more militant teachers, parents, students, blacks, people's boards, and from the traditionally powerless, voices clamoring for more influence over education grow louder and more insistent. They need to be heard and responded to in ways that tap new sources of creativity.

The principal faced with this challenge is in a tough spot. Potentially, he links the school to the community, the faculty to the board, the central office to the faculty, in Rensis Likert's terminology, he is a "linking pen." At the interface between key subgroups, he can facilitate growth or block it. He is a major factor in how innovative teachers in a building, how understanding parents, and how supportive central offices are likely to be. In the process of all this, he can grow personally and professionally, or he can be caught in the crunch. Like most of us, the principal generally *knows* better than he *does*. Laboratory training offers methods aimed at helping people in difficult roles use knowledge to improve practice.

A HISTORICAL NOTE

The origins of laboratory training are traced generally to Kurt Lewin's experimental work in group dynamics; specifically, to a conference of community leaders called in 1946 by the Connecticut Interracial Commission. The conference was an experiment in new ways of teaching individual and group skills that enable people to live and work together productively. Half by accident and half by plan, its staff and participants discovered the learning potential of an initially unstructured group, in which the content for learning is the processes by which members build a group that can work together, where each member learns about his own behavior and the behavior of the other members. The T-group was born and was destined to become an important element in laboratory education. People who had been operating in the dark about the impact of their behavior found in the T-group a way to learn how they came across, or—to put it more formally—to see the consequences of their modes of relating and communicating.

The group of scientists who worked with Lewin organized the NTL Institute in 1947 as the focal agency of their work. The Institute was under the auspices of the NEA's Adult Education Service and was originally named the National Training Laboratory in Group Development. It became the National Training Laboratories, a Division of the National Education Association, in 1962. In 1967, it became an independent, nonprofit corporation associated with the NEA. The expanding group of scientists, most of them located at universities across the country, became known as the "NTL Network." Today, NTL Institute is one of many organizations providing services based on laboratory method, and the several hundred scientists associated directly with NTL represent only a fraction of those offering such services.

Over the past 20 years, laboratory training his moved from a major emphasis on programs for individuals, generally strangers to each other, to a major emphasis on team training or "in-house" programs designed for entire faculties or staff groups. *Organizational development* has come to be the term describing programs whose target for change is the organization of the system and whose goal is to develop internal resources for continuing develpment.

In another direction, programs designated by terms like *personal growth, human potential, self-discovery* have also multiplied. Though benefits to the organization may spill over through released potential and freer access to personal resources, the contract in such programs is with the individual, not the organization.

Thus, there have been many applications and many spin-offs of laboratory training, but a number of the directions were set at the beginning: the assumption that learning is an experience-based matter, that optimal learning results when there is a blend of knowing, feeling, acting, and valuing; the emphasis on here-and-now behavior, but also on attempting to understand it in the light of knowledge and theory; a continuing effort to link scientific knowledge with practic; the invention of experimental designs for learning; and a continuing preoccupation with what one needs to learn in order to manage change effectively. The current focus on sensitivity training has grown out of increasing recognition that much of the work people do—the time spent in committees, in classes, in staff conferences—is unproductive because of human impediments to open communication and collaboration. Anyone who questions the reality of this problem might reflect for a few minutes on his own experience during the past 48 hours.

STRATEGIES FOR CHANGE

Richard Schmuck and Philip Runkel of the Center for the Advancement of the Study of Educational Administration in Oregon suggest in *Organizational Training for a School Faculty* [1] that two strategies are available when customary educational practices become inadequte to cope with massive changes in the community. One is to invent or adapt models that may respond more readily to new demands—the community school, for example. The other is to improve the organizational problem-solving capability of existing schools. Either strategy can be effective. Each demands that the people involved develop skills in teamwork, in utilization of resources, in communication within the school and the community.

Schmuck and others have demonstrated that strong use of laboratory training methods to increase problem-solving capability can lead to changes if facilitated by new norms that sanction new modes of behavior.

In other cases, "start-up" training programs for the entire staff of a new school have helped anticipate or prevent customary problems. In South Brunswick, New Jersey, James Kimple, superintendent; Fred Nadler, principal of an experimental middle school and Robert Chasnoff, a professor at Newark State College and NTL trainer and consultant, describe such an approach in reports to the U.S. Office of Education under a Title III project.[2] Here, laboratory methods were used in an extensive organizational development effort that began with the faculty of the new school and spread throughout the system.

In the Oregon program, the design included analysis of ongoing group processes of the faculty, practice of new modes of behavior before actually using them in daily work, and the use of the school as its own laboratory for learning and change. Groups were used in ways very different from the classical T-group:

> Personal development was not our target. We did not attempt to improve the interpersonal functioning of individuals directly; when this occurred, it was incidental. Our targets were the faculty as a whole and several subgroups in it. We sought to increase the effectiveness of groups as task-oriented entities. We tried to teach subgroups within the school and the faculty as a whole to function more effectively as working bodies carrying out specific tasks in that particular job setting.[3]

Training involved the entire staff—secretaries, the head cook, the head custodial staff, as well as all the faculty and the administrators. Sizes and membership of subgroups were rotated to ensure maximum interaction among all participants.

There were concrete observable changes in the behavior of faculty and administration. Teachers used approaches in the classroom that had been tried out first in the training program. The Principal's Advisory Committee became a more powerful force, with decision-making prerogatives. The turnover rate in the experimental school was 3 percent, in contrast with 10 to 16 percent in comparable schools. Faculty meetings were initiated by faculty members and ran smoothly, with strong participation. The principal's interpersonal relationships with staff were noticeably improved. Incidentally, he requested and was granted funds to attend an NTL Educators' Laboratory to increase his own leadership skills. Finally, a new job—vice-principal for curriculum—was created at the experimental school and became a model for similar posts in other schools. The job was defined as consultant on interpersonal relationships to task groups, as liaison between groups, and as supporter for curricular efforts.

The South Brunswick program combined intensive human relations training with a summer laboratory school that freed the staff from the usual parent, pupil, teacher, administrator, and student teacher assumptions about what school should be. Thus freed, teachers demonstrated great resourcefulness in solving teaching and learning problems and in inventing fresh approaches to freshly seen realities. The effectiveness of the program was evaluated in terms of the number of changes in classroom practices; the reduction of complaints; greatly increased and more enthusiastic participation by teachers in the practice teacher program; the extension of the practice teaching program for the first time to a full semester, when the teams of experienced and inexperienced teachers that were formed during the summer continued to work together; the new perceptions of parents as partners in the educational process; the wider practice of giving and receiving help among faculty; the increased use of consultants and more frequent professional discussions among teachers; and finally, the more frequent use of the administrator as a resource. An additional significant change was the linkage established between the school systems and the Newark State College teacher training program.

These two approaches to change have been cited at some length to indicate the transformation in recent years in the application of laboratory education methods. Though there are clear interpersonal and even intrapersonal learnings—without which organizational development can always be blocked—these two applications are a far cry from training groups of individuals who do not expect to work together after the training.

Today, individuals may still sign up for personal growth experiences in which they can try out new behavior with strangers. This can be a rich and rewarding experience. When participants return home to help organize "OD" programs within the system or to encourage team participation in future laboratories, it often becomes an important first step in organizational development. But the individually centered program is not promoted as a major strategy for reaching organizational objectives. An important development in laboratory training today is the staff's assumption of more responsibility for helping participants make the transfer from learning to practice. A major means of achieving this goal is the development of programs that combine learning about self and relationships with others with guided application to workaday tasks.

GUIDELINES FOR USE OF LABORATORY TRAINING

Laboratory training is a powerful invention. Its apparent relevance to the solution of human relationship problems in a wide range of settings has led to increasing demand for it. And this, in turn, leads to a need for guidelines to protect both prospective clients and the developing profession of applied behavioral science. With this need in mind, NTL Institute has published "Standards for the Use of Laboratory Method," which may be useful to school administrators and boards of education who want to safeguard the use of laboratory method in inservice training programs.*

NTL has also sought to safeguard both the discipline and its clients by developing effective professional programs for trainers and consultants, with the help of grants over recent years from the U.S. Office of Education, the National Institute for Mental Health, and the Ford Foundation. Another significant measure to protect both the public and the emerging profession of applied behavioral science is the creation of a new international professional accrediting association. At present, the "NTL Network" of trainers is recognized as the closest thing to an accredited group of trainers.

Points related to staff selection and qualifications are particularly important and are quoted below:

STANDARDS FOR LABORATORY TRAINERS AND CONSULTANTS

1. NTL Institute endorses the Ethical Standards of the American Psychological Association and urges its members to guide their conduct accordingly.

2. In relationships with individual clients and client groups, persons representing NTL Institute are expected to discuss candidly and fully goals, risks, limitations, and anticipated outcomes of any program under consideration.

3. NTL Institute trainers and consultants are expected to endorse the purposes and values and adhere to the standards presented in this article.

4. NTL Institute trainers and consultants are expected to have mastered the following skills:

   Ability to conduct a small group and provide individual consultation, using the theory and techniques of laboratory method.

   Ability to articulate theory and to direct a variety of learning experiences for small and large groups and for organizations.

   Ability to recognize their own behavior styles and personal needs and to deal with them productively in the performance of their professional roles.

* Copies can be ordered from NTL Institute at NEA headquarters.

Ability to recognize symptoms of serious psychological stress and to make responsible decisions when such problems arise.

5. NTL Institute trainers and consultants are expected to have a strong theoretical foundation. This ordinarily implies graduate work in a behavioral science discipline or equivalent experience in the field.

6. NTL Institute trainers and consultants are expected to complete the following training experiences:

Participation in at least one NTL Institute Basic Human Relations Laboratory.

Supervised co-training with senior staff members.

Participation on laboratory staff with experienced trainers in programs for a variety of client groups.

Participation in an NTL Institute or university program specifically designed to train trainers.

(Note: Basic human relations laboratories, executive development programs, and similar beginning-level programs are designed to help participants be more effective in personal and job roles, not to become trainers. No capabilities as a T-group trainer or consultant should be assumed as a result of participation in one or more basic laboratories or short-term experiences.)

7. NTL Institute trainers and consultants are expected to continually evaluate their own work, to seek individual growth experiences, and to contribute to the evaluation and development of the art and science of training and consultation.

GUIDELINES FOR EVALUATING COMPETENCE

The following questions are suggested as an approach to evaluating groups or individuals offering services using laboratory method and its derivatives:

How do the education and training of staff members compare with the standards listed in this article?

Are the services and programs regularly evaluated, and is evidence of such evaluations available?

What controls and standards does the group utilize to assure adherence to ethics?

Is the staff able and willing to articulate the rationale for the methods and content it utilizes?

Does the group have experience in working with similar clients?

Those who pioneered laboratory training in human relations and created NTL in 1947 saw themselves as motivated by a strong social purpose—the application of behavioral science to human problems encountered in working and living together. Laboratory training has been called "a process in search of a problem," but today there is no doubt that the problem is calling for the process. The problem is a general failure to make full use of the resources that are available to cope with incredibly complex problems.

The concepts, processes, and methods that laboratory training represents can contribute significantly—perhaps uniquely—to work on the following kinds of problems:

Alienation between young people and adults, between school and community, between races.

Young people who are not developing their potential.

The cleavage between teachers and administrators at a time when team work is desperately needed.

The failure to link school and community in vitally needed social efforts.

The tendency, under pressure to innovate, to rely on gimmicks and tinkering when drastic overhauling and new goals are needed.

The general inadequate effort to apply what behavioral science has learned—about change, about learning, about organizations, and about communities—to problems of education.

We do not know what man's relation to man will be a generation from now; we can only glimpse the possibilities. They may be catastrophically worse. They may be more satisfying, more collaborative, more growth producing. Carl Rogers, writing in the *Journal of Applied Behavioral Science,*[4] published by NTL, suggests that the greatest problem before us may be neither the hydrogen bomb nor the population explosion but how much change the human being can accept, absorb, and assimilate, and how fast. To encourage optimism, Rogers cites the ability of the Western democratic cultures "to respond appropriately—at the last cliff-hanging moment—to those trends which challenge their survival and the magnetic attraction of the experience of change, growth, fulfillment"—even when growth entails pain.

Laboratory training assumes both the need for change and the potential for growth and improvement for the individual as a person and in his professional role, for the organization, and for education itself.

FOOTNOTES

1. Schmuck, Richard, and Runkel, Philip. *Organizational Training for a School Faculty.* Eugene, Ore.: Center for Advanced Study of Educational Administration, 1970. (Mimeographed)
2. U.S. Office of Education. Reports of South Brunswick Township, Project No. 67-03566-0, 1967–68.
3. See footnote 1.
4. Rogers, Carl R. "Interpersonal Relationships: U.S.A. 2000." *Journal of Applied Behavioral Science* 4: 265–80; July/August/September 1968.

ADDITIONAL READINGS

BENNE, K. D., BENNIS, W., and CHIN, R., editors. *The Planning of Change.* New York: Holt, Rinehart & Winston, 1961.

BRADFORD, L. P., GIBB, J. R., and BENNE, K. D., editors. *T-Group Theory and Laboratory Method: Innovation in Re-Education.* New York: John Wiley & Sons, 1964.

LIKERT, R. *New Patterns of Management.* New York: McGraw-Hill Book Co., 1961.

SCHEIN, E. H., and BENNIS, W. G. *Personal and Organizational Change Through Group Methods: The Laboratory Approach.* New York: John Wiley & Sons, 1965.

SCHMUCK, R. A., RUNKEL, P., and LANGMEYER, D. *Theory to Guide Organizational Training in Schools.* Eugene, Ore.: Center for the Advanced Study of Educational Administration, 1969.

WATSON, G. *Concepts for Social Change.* Washington, D.C.: NTL Institute for Applied Behavioral Science, 1967.

WATSON, G. *Change in School System.* Washington, D.C.: NTL Institute for Applied Behavioral Science, 1967.

Humanistic Goals of Education

Arthur W. Combs

SELF-ACTUALIZATION—PRIMARY GOAL OF EDUCATION

Modern education must produce far more than persons with cognitive skills. It must produce *humane* individuals, persons who can be relied upon to pull their own weight in our society, who can be counted upon to behave responsibly and cooperatively. We need good citizens, free of prejudice, concerned about their fellow citizens, loving, caring fathers and mothers, persons of goodwill whose values and purposes are positive, feeling persons with wants and desires likely to motivate them toward positive interactions. These are the things that make us human. Without them we are automatons, fair game for whatever crowd-swaying, stimulus-manipulating demagogue comes down the pike. The humane qualities are absolutely essential to our way of life—far more important, even, than the learning of reading, for example. We can live with a bad reader; a bigot is a danger to everyone.

Social scientists in recent years have given increasing thought to the problem of self-actualization. "What," they ask, "does it mean for a person to be truly operating at the fullest extent of his possibilities?" The answers they find to these questions are helping us to understand what self-actualizing persons are like and how it is possible to produce them. These studies are in many ways among the most exciting currently occurring on the psychological scene. To this point, four basic qualities seem to be central to the dynamics of such personalities. Self-actualizing persons are:

1. Well informed.

Arthur W. Combs, *Educational Accountability: Beyond Behavioral Objectives.* Washington, D.C.: Association for Supervision and Curriculum Development, 1972. Reprinted with permission of the Association for Supervison and Curriculum Development and Arthur W. Combs. Copyright © 1972 by the Association for Supervision and Curriculum Development.

2. Possessed of positive self-concepts

3. Open to their experience, and

4. Possessed of deep feelings of identification with others.

Informed educators have taken their cues from this work.

Self-actualization is not just a nice idea—whatever we decide is the nature of the fully functioning, self-actualizing person must also be the goal of education, as of every other institution for human welfare. The production of such persons is, after all, what it is all about. In 1962 one group of educators tackled the problem of trying to define what the basic principles of self-actualization might mean for education. This work has been published in the ASCD 1962 Yearbook entitled *Perceiving, Behaving, Becoming,*[1] a volume which is among the most popular in educational history and which, though it is now ten years old, continues to be an educational best seller.

The authors of this book began with a series of papers by four outstanding psychologists who defined the nature of self-actualization. From that beginning the educators asked, "If these things are so, what does this mean for education?"

In the course of their examination they found innumerable aspects in the current educational scene which actually prevent the development of healthy personalities. They were also led in their discussions to point the way toward new objectives for education more likely to achieve the production of self-actualizing persons than those to which we have been accustomed.

Many people believe that there is no place in our educational structure for "affective" concerns. They ask, "Do you want education for intellect or adjustment?" As though it were necessary for us to make a choice between the production of smart psychotics and well-adjusted dopes! Affective, healing aspects of behavior are not something separate and apart from cognition. Modern psychologists tell us that affect or feeling is simply an artifact of the degree of personal relevance of the event perceived. We have no feeling about that which is of no concern to us. The greater the degree of personal relevance, the greater is the degree of feeling or affect or emotion which is likely to be experienced by the behaver. The attempt to rule out the humane aspects of life from the classroom is thus to make the classroom sterile. If affect has to do with relevance, then we are either going to have affective education or none at all. If the humane qualities we expect of education are important, they must be given their proper

---

[1] A. W. Combs, editor. *Perceiving, Behaving, Becoming: A New Focus for Education.* ASCD 1962 Yearbook. Washington, D.C.: Association for Supervision and Curriculum Development, 1962.

place in the perspective we take on accountability. We cannot afford to be so preoccupied with the cognitive, behavioral aspects that we later find we have "thrown out the baby with the bath water."

Unfortunately, humane qualities are already relegated in our public schools to "general" objectives—which means they are generally ignored—while teachers concentrate their efforts on what they are going to be evaluated on. English teachers concentrate on English, coaches concentrade on winning football games, science teachers concentrate on getting students into national science competition, and elementary teachers are evaluated on how well children learn to read, write, and figure. But no one evaluates teachers on whether their students are becoming good citizens, learning to care for each other, work together, etc. Everyone knows that people tend to do those things they are being evaluated for. Indeed, it is an understanding of this fact that has brought about the pressures for accountability. If humane qualities are to be achieved, such qualities must be given front rank in importance and schools must be held accountable for their nurture.

If the four qualities of self-actualization previously mentioned are accurate, we need much more than behavioral objectives as criteria for their achievement. Such questions as a positive self-concept, openness to experience, and identification do not lend themselves to behavioral measurement. Aspects of self-actualization can be assessed, but rarely in precise behavioral terms. Indeed, the attempt to do so may even impede their effectual development. The humane qualities we seek in education, such as positive self-concepts, feelings of identification, responsibility, openness to experience, adaptability, creativity, effective human relationships are, like any other behavior, outcomes of *personal meaning;* and it is here that we need to look for answers to our problems of accountability.

THE ASSESSMENT OF PERSONAL MEANING

To deal effectively with the internal qualities of personal meaning and the humane objectives of education, a new approach is needed. Called for is a psychology that differs from the limited concepts available to us in the various forms of S-R psychology with which we traditionally have lived. What is needed is a humanistic psychology expressly designed to deal with the human aspects of personality and behavior, a psychology which does not ignore the student's belief systems but makes them central to its concerns. Fortunately, such a psychology is already with us.

The past 30 years have seen the appearance of "humanistic" psychology on the American scene. This approach has a holistic character capable of dealing quite directly with many of the more general objectives of education.[2] Psychologists attached to this new frame of reference call themselves by many names: self psychologists, transactionalists, existentialists, phenomenologists, perceptualists, and the like. By whatever name, however, these psychologists are concerned with more than the specific, precisely designed behaviors of individuals. They are deeply concerned with questions of values, human goals and aspirations, feelings, attitudes, hopes, meaning, and perceptions of self and the world. These are the qualities which make us human, and it is because of these concerns that this point of view has come to be known as the humanistic approach. Humanistic approaches to psychology, it should be clearly understood, do not deny the tenets of behavioral approaches. Quite the contrary, they include such approaches, but extend beyond them to deal with more holistic matters not readily treated in the older behavioral system. This is precisely what is needed in modern approaches to educational accountability.

The viewpoint of this booklet is that behavioral objectives provide too narrow a basis for proper assessment of educational outcomes, and our concepts of accountability must be expanded if they are properly to match the broadest goals and requirements for our educational system. Humanistic approaches to psychological thought provide us with theoretical guidelines to effective practice consistent with these broader goals. It is high time that these new conceptions be made an integral part of the training of educators and given wide dissemination throughout the profession. This booklet is not the proper vehicle for a detailed description of the humanistic position. Interested readers may find an introduction to this position in the work of such writers [3] as Carl R. Rogers, Abraham Maslow, Arthur W. Combs, Earl Kelley, Gordon Allport, and William Purkey.

What is needed now is a systematic attempt to give principles and contributions of humanistic psychology wider understanding at every level of our educational structure. This is a point of view specifically designed to deal with the problems of personal meaning. As a consequence it is able to provide important guidelines for thinking about our broader objec-

[2] A. W. Combs, D. L. Avila, and W. W. Purkey. *Helping Relationships: Basic Concepts for the Helping Professions.* Boston: Allyn and Bacon, Inc., 1971.

[3] Some sample titles are: C. R. Rogers. *Freedom To Learn.* Columbus, Ohio: Charles E. Merrill Publishing Company, 1969; A. H. Maslow. *Motivation and Personality.* New York: Harper & Row, Publishers, 1954; A. W. Combs and D. Syngg. *Individual Behavior: A Perceptual Approach to Behavior.* New York: Harper & Row, Publishers, 1959; E. C. Kelley. *Education for What Is Real.* New York: Harper & Row, Publishers, 1947; G. W. Allport. *Personality and Social Encounter.* Boston: Beacon Press, 1964; W. W. Purkey. *Self Concept and School Achievement.* Englewood Cliffs, New Jersey: Prentice-Hall, Inc., 1970.

tives, for finding better ways to achieve them, and for assessing whether or not our educational processes have truly achieved their objectives.

If behavior is symptom and meaning is cause, then if we could somehow assess meaning we would not need to be so concerned about measurement of behavior. Meanings, however, lie inside persons and, at first glance, it would seem impossible to assess them. It is true that meanings cannot be observed directly, but neither can electricity, and we have managed to measure that pretty effectively by inference. The same thing works for personal meaning. While meanings cannot be read directly, they can be inferred by a process of "reading behavior backward." If it is true that behavior is the product of perception, then it should be possible to observe a person's behavior and infer the nature of the perceptions which produced it.

Actually, this is what all of us do in interpreting the behavior of those who are important to us. In our research at the University of Florida on the helping professions, we find it also the approach to students, patients, and clients which distinguishes effective counselors, teachers, nurses, professors, and Episcopal priests from ineffective ones.[4] Such inferences are not made by seeking one-to-one concomitants. The process calls for a holistic rather than an atomistic approach to understanding human behavior. Instead of cataloging specific behaviors, the observer uses himself as an observation instrument and observes all he can by immersing himself in the situation. By a continuous process of observing, inferring, and testing his inferences over and over, he is able in time to arrive at accurate understandings of the peculiar meanings producing the behavior in the persons he is observing. Meanings can be assessed.

The problem is not one of learning to do something entirely new. It is a matter of learning to do what all of us already do occasionally with persons who are important to us. We have little trouble being sensitive to and interpretive of meanings existing for those above us in the hierarchy, such as principals, supervisors, and superintendents. What is needed now is to learn to do these things more often, more precisely, and in more disciplined fashion with persons in positions subservient to us, such as students. These are skills that can be learned. Indeed, many fine teachers already have them.

The assessment of meaning has an additional advantage. If focuses the attention of educators on the causes of behavior directly. The attempt to catalog behaviors with too great specificity may actually take us further and further away from the basic meanings producing them. Assessing outcomes through global behavior is likely to be somewhat closer to the

---

[4] Combs, *Florida Studies in the Helping Professions, op. cit.*

basic causes of behavior but may still be far less exact than we might desire. As a matter of fact, too much attention to the observation of specific behavior can seriously interfere with understanding the causes of behavior, by concentrating attention on symptoms rather than causes. Like hundreds of other teachers of "Human Growth and Development," I used to send my young teachers-in-training to observe the behavior of a child in the classroom, insisting that they should record precisely what the child did from moment to moment. These instructions were intended to discipline the student into being a careful observer.

This is still standard practice in many colleges of education. Unfortunately, what it does is to concentrate the student's attention on the behavior of the child instead of on the causes of that behavior. In recent years I have found it more helpful to send students into a classroom, not to observe it, but to participate in it. They are instructed to "get the feel" of the classroom. "See if you can figure out how the child is thinking and feeling about himself, his classmates, his teachers, the work of the school. See if you can figure out his purposes, what he is trying to do, then tell me what you saw that made you think your inference was accurate." This procedure concentrates the student's attention on making and supporting inferences about the causes of children's behavior rather than on simply observing the symptoms. I find that since we have adopted this system my students have become far more effective than previously.

If such procedures for assessing meaning seem imprecise and vague as we have described them here, they need not be. It is quite possible to make inferences with high degrees of accuracy and reliability by application of the usual tests for scientific credibility already mentioned in this booklet.[5] Inferential techniques are already widely used in psychological research, especially in the study of such personal meanings as attitudes, beliefs, self-concept, and purposes. The assessment of meaning outcomes of education can be made with whatever degrees of precision is desired, from informal observation to highly controlled and systematized procedures.

The exploration of highly personal meaning, of course, does not lend itself well to study by standardized techniques. There are, however, procedures in fairly wide use for the assessment of meanings of a more general sort. With a comparatively small diversion of funds and human talent currently assigned to behavioral approaches to the problem, many more could be developed within a comparatively short time. If the heart of learning is the personal discovery of meaning, the proper assessment of educational outcomes should be the most accurate possible understanding of the personal meanings being produced by the system. Use of behavioral objectives is a highly inaccurate approach to that problem. If the goals

[5] Allport, *The Use of Personal Documents in Psychological Science, op. cit.*

of accountability are to be achieved, we are going to have to find ways of assessing personal meaning more accurately and simply.

Traditional psychologists of S-R, behavioristic persuasion are often aghast at inferential procedures which seem to them to be grossly unscientific and subjective. Their commitment to the behavioristic approach to psychology makes it impossible for them to accept inferential techniques, even though these have long since been adopted in many of the physical sciences for solution to some of their knottiest problems. The formulation of inferences *can* be made highly accurate by use of the very same techniques as those used in any of the other sciences.

The attempt to approach accountability through assessment of personal meanings is not only likely to be more effective, it has additional advantages of great practical value in the classroom. This approach is far simpler for teachers to manage than are highly specific lists of behavioral objectives, because with such an approach there are fewer concepts to master. Attention can be given to basic principles rather than to limitless details. The teacher preoccupied with manipulating behavior is likely to find himself dealing with classroom problems through various forms of reward and punishment, or such controlling devices as force, coercion, exhortation, or bribery. Such approaches are very likely to produce their own resistance in the students whose behavior he is attempting to change. It is a part of our American heritage to resist being managed, and it should not surprise us if such techniques call forth in students ingenious and creative devices for sabotaging the system.

The teacher who is concerned about personal meanings of students is much more likely to find that his relationships with students are warmer and more human. Human aspects are not rejected but actively sought and appreciated. Empathic teachers, honestly concerned with understanding how students think, feel, and perceive are far more likely than other teachers to be liked by their students, have less problems with motivation and discipline, find themselves more successful in carrying out their assigned tasks—to say nothing of being more relaxed and happy on the job.

A major objection to inferential approaches to the study of behavior proposed by behavior modification-performance criterion advocates is that inferences can only be made from behavior, and thus this approach is no different from the goals they seek. "We are willing," they say, "that you should make inferences about behavior if you wish, but what is the point? Why not simply observe behavior?" Of course it is true that humanists must begin their studies of student behavior from careful observation of it. Every psychologist, no matter what his allegiance, must begin from that base. A major point of this discussion, however, is that sole reliance on observation of behavior is but a symptomatic approach to assessing outcomes of teaching. Approaching accountability in that fashion thus concentrates attention on the wrong dynamic, and the attempt endlessly to catalog specific desired behaviors creates an unnecessary and complicating detour for understanding.

The holistic-inferential approach to assessment offers a much more direct and efficient approach to the causes of behavior. It does not attempt to itemize all behavior or gather it up in great masses. Instead, it uses the observer himself as an effective screen for observing those aspects of behavior providing the most efficient clues to the causes he is seeking to understand.

An analogy from mathematics may help us to understand these two different approaches. Arithmetic is a system of mathematics especially designed to deal with countable events, things which can be directly observed in units at a very primitive level. Algebra, on the other hand, is a more advanced system of mathematics designed to deal with unknown numbers, events which must be inferred. Some mathematical problems can be dealt with quite simply by ordinary arithmetic. Others can be approached much more efficiently through the techniques of algebra, which make it possible to deal with matters which cannot be immediately designated. There are even some problems which cannot be dealt with except in algebraic terms. Holistic-inferential approaches to understanding behavior are like algebra. They make it possible for us to move quickly and efficiently to vital understandings without the plodding necessities imposed by behavioral objectives approaches. Like algebra, also, the holistic-inferential approaches do not deny the validity or usefulness of more atomistic approaches. They include them—and extend beyond them.

Precise answers to the assessment of personal meaning extend considerably beyond the scope of this booklet. Many techniques have already been worked out, either informally over the years by persons engaging in the various helping professions or, more recently, in the work of humanistically oriented psychologists. Since a great many persons today believe the problem is important, almost certainly we should be able to make tremendous strides in this form of assessment in the future. The immediate need is to go to work on a three-pronged effort directed toward:

1. *Making meaning important.* Since people only do what seems important to them, the first step in improving our capabilities for the assessment of meaning is to regard it as an important question. This calls for encouraging teachers, principals, supervisors, administrators, and everyone else engaged in the educational effort to understand that their inferences are important and helping them at every level to sharpen their skills in this regard. This will not be an easy task in view of the current preoccupation with strictly behavioral approaches to educational problems. The extraordinary pressures being placed on educators everywhere to emphasize such

objectives leave little room for much concern with the development of skill in the assessment of personal meaning. A major first step in the encouragement of attention to personal meaning will, therefore, need to be the development of a more adequate perspective on assessment problems and deceleration of the current tallyho for behavioral objectives, behavioral modification, and performance-based criteria.

Beyond that, educators at every level of operation need to be encouraged to experiment with the assessment of personal meaning and to sharpen their own skills toward these ends. As we have previously stated, the process of inference is a matter of reading behavior backward, and this is a process that all of us naturally use in dealing with people who are important to us. The problem for people on the firing line is to learn to do this more often, more systematically, and more effectively in their professional roles.

2. *Collection and evaluation of already existing techniques.* People have been making inferences about other people since time immemorial. As a consequence, we already have in existence ways of assessing personal meaning of an informal character accumulated through the experience of persons in helping professions over generations. A serious attempt should be mounted to gather these, assess their effectiveness, and make them more readily available to others throughout the profession.

In addition to such informal techniques, psychologists, sociologists, anthropologists, and others in the social sciences have developed an ever increasing number of more formal techniques over the past 30 or 40 years for assessing human attitudes, values, beliefs, and perceptions of self and the world. There is, for example, a very large literature on projective techniques and the use of personal documents for assessing personal meaning. Such studies need to be exhumed from wherever they are burried in the literature, examined and assessed, and made more widely available to persons who are interested in measuring personal meaning in more formal terms.

3. *The development of new techniques.* Vast sums of money are currently being poured into the effort to improve America's schools by the application of behavioral objectives approaches to assessment and by the injection of industrial techniques into every aspect of our educational effort. These tremendous capital outlays are matched by vast expenditures of human energies focused on behavioral approaches to educational accountability. We have already mentioned how this preoccupation can actually inhibit or destroy the search for viable alternatives to educational assessment.

Most of our financial and human resources are currently focused on doing more of what we already know very well how to do. What is badly needed now is the diversion of very large chunks of these financial and human resources to the exploration of problems we have so far sorely neglected. A redistribution to concentrate efforts on the study of personal meanings and their assessment in educational settings would provide education with enormous dividends within a comparatively short time.

Affect and Learning

Gerald Weinstein and Mario D. Fantini

In seeking a point of departure for innovation and reform, two of the major questions educators confront are "What content is most meaningful to youngsters?" and "How can we teach it most effectively?"

The emphasis in education has long been on the means: How can control of the class be achieved and maintained? How can the teacher make contact with the children? And, especially, how does one teach them a particular subject?

Under the impetus of Sputnik, the pendulum of education swung from a long-term preoccupation with methods of teaching to an intense interest in content. The chief result was the curriculum-reform movement of the past decade. The recent recognition of our failure to teach poor, minority-group children, however, has begun to fuse these two interests. Increasingly, educators are realizing that how one goes about teaching is very closely related to what one tries to teach. Experience with the socio-economically different pupil has made it dramatically clear that no teaching procedure can be effective if the content is of little interest to the class.

LEARNING AND BEHAVIOR

The discrepancy between the behavior of individuals in society and what they have learned, or at least what the schools purport to teach, suggests the need for examination of education's chosen channel for changing or affecting behavior. Traditionally, this channel has been subject matter per se—the courses offered, the curriculum taught, the academic disciplines. A discrepancy exists between subject matter and behavior because the behavioral objectives of education have become submerged, if not obliterated, by narrow subject-matter objectives, which include

Gerald Weinstein and Mario D. Fantini, eds., *Toward Humanistic Education: A Curriculum of Affect.* New York: Praeger Publishers, Inc., chap. 2. © 1970 by the Ford Foundation. Reprinted by permission.

nothing about the student's behavior and his relations with others. John Goodlad has stated this predicament clearly.

> Little effort has been made to determine the ultimate aims of schooling and the respective contribution each discipline can make to them. Instead, the objectives of schooling have become the composite of the objectives set for each subject. . . . The goals of today's schools do not extend beyond those subjects that have succeeded in establishing themselves in the curriculum.[1]

In most schools today, curriculum is based more on the requirement of the various subject disciplines than on other needs. Rarely is curriculum designed to help the student deal in personal terms with the problems of human conduct.

How can we account for this gap between educational practices and the professed aims of American education? One possible explanation is that the ultimate aims of education are so complex that the practitioner can readily identify only the more immediate objectives of the subject matter. Although a broad-range goal of teaching literature may be to help the child know himself better by developing an understanding of the ways in which man has responded to his experiences in all periods, somehow few literature courses go beyond the immediate objectives of teaching the child to understand plot, character, and theme. Even in some of the more experimental curriculum guides, specific objectives of units read "To enable the student to identify the basic elements of tragedy," or "To enable the student to describe the rhetorical sense implied in a work of literature." [2]

It is easier to teach toward such specific objectives and, more generally, to recognize and deal with the child's need to know how to read, write, compute, and to have some knowledge of his environment than it is to recognize and deal with his need for a satisfying self-definition, for constuctive relationships with others, and for some control over what happens to him. The first set of needs is given the overwhelming emphasis in our educational system.

The proper study of curriculum begins with a statement of educational objectives. Let ours be made clear: Education in a free society should have a broad human focus, which is best served by educational objectives resting on a personal and interpersonal base and dealing with students' concerns. This belief rests on philosophical and moral grounds, but it also has plainly practical implications in terms of the price a society pays for negative social behavior—crime, discrimination, tensions, and, ultimately, widespread pathology.

[1] *The Changing School Curriculum* (New York: Georgian Press, 1966), p. 92.
[2] *The Detroit Lakes Plan: An Experiment in Curriculum* (Detroit Lakes, Minn.: 1966), from the section on "Approaches to Literature."

Many educators, decision makers, and citizens do not agree. They feel that it is either impossible or inappropriate for the schools to assume responsibility for a curriculum with an ultimately humanitarian goal. This does not mean that they are oblivious to the human condition. It may mean that they feel that the school's legitimate business involves no more than the impartation of knowledge and skills and that humanitarian objectives are the responsibility of other institutions in society.

The Elementary School Teaching Project proceeded on the assumption that the broad objectives of American education must include the preparation of students to engage in constructive personal and social behavior. We believe that existing practice is not affecting behavior adequately. We also believe that in today's complex, precarious world a society has little choice but to pursue the path toward humanitarian behavior. Otherwise, no matter, how successful its educational system is in teaching the specific stuff of subject matter, the society is likely to decline and decay. The ultimate purpose of this report, therefore, is to search for paths to greater consonance between education and the way in which people might or should behave.

THE NEED FOR RELEVANCE

Poor, mainly urban, mainly minority-group students—the crisis clientele—particularly and poignantly spotlight the widespread failure of education to lead students toward the behavior our society considers desirable. But the problems that confront this group so acutely afflict other groups as well.

One of the most glaring deficiencies in education is lack of contact with the learner. "School is phony—it has nothing to do with life like we know it. The people we read about are all one way—all good or all bad—and so are the things that happen to them." This verdict is typical of the "disadvantaged," but is it so different from the attitude of other groups?

"It all starts in the first grade," states a Harvard freshman from a well-to-do background.

> There we are treated to a candy-cane world where all the children in the textbooks are white tots living in suburbia with a dog running around the lawn. When suburban kids find out about the slums, they're apt to get skeptical. When slum kids are taught about a world that has nothing to do with the world in which they live, they have to do the same.[3]

Many teachers and administrators who work with the disadvantaged are hungry for ways to make contact with their pupils, to make education

[3] Steven Kelman, "You Force Kids to Rebel," *Saturday Evening Post* (Nov. 19, 1966), p. 12.

more meaningful to them. They flock to workshops, institutes, and special training sessions. There they learn a great deal about the nature of the "culturally deprived child," but little about how to meet his needs. One teacher told us,

> I understand my children better now, but I still don't know what to do with them. For example, I learned that one third of my children probably come from broken homes and that this poses severe problems for the growing child. Now that I know this fact, what do I do to teach them better? How is my understanding related to what I'm expected to teach them in social studies, math, science, and the rest?

Most of the instructional prescriptions that have been offered for dealing with students with learning problems take the form of such rudimentary, isolated practices as using "hip" language, role-playing, and stories based on pupils' experiences. The teacher at first finds these practices exciting, but they are of limited utility. He is still left with standard content and methodology, which he senses are not making contact with the learner.

Similarly, attempts to improve standard content—the work of the Biological Sciences Curriculum Study, the Physical Science Study Committee, Educational Services Incorporated, and other contemporary curriculum-reform agencies—have done much to make the process and curriculum structure more significant in terms of academic subjects, but they have not touched the core of the problem: to make the content more *personally* meaningful, especially for the poor, minority-group child.

The current prescriptions fail to make contact, we believe, because they lack intrinsic relevance for many children, and for poor children in particular. To see what is relevant, and how relevance may be achieved, let us examine some causes of irrelevance in education.

1. Failure to match teaching procedures to children's *learning styles.*

The current literature on lower-class children indicates that they learn best in situations that are nonverbal, concrete, inductive, and kinesthetic. If teachers can develop and use techniques geared specifically to the way children learn best, the teaching will bear a degree of relevance no matter what is being taught. Relevance, then, depends in part on *how* one teaches.

2. The use of material that is outside or poorly related to the learner's *knowledge* of his physical realm of experience.

Teaching that relates to an urban child's neighborhood or city, for example, is more relevant to him, and therefore more likely to engage his interest, than teaching exclusively about suburban life or foreign countries. Relevance, then, depends in part on *what* is taught.

3. The use of teaching materials and methods that ignore the learner's *feelings.*

The learner's feelings about his experiences may serve to involve him more deeply in content. For instance, a unit on the city policeman may appear to be relevant because it falls within the experience of urban pupils. But if the learner has a fear of policemen, the selection of such a subject may actually inhibit his learning unless his fears are identified and addressed at the outset. The reasons for tension between police and community residents must be dealt with, beginning perhaps with incidents in the pupils' experience and proceeding more deeply into the role assigned to the police and the work and concerns of individual policemen. In short, contact must be made with the subject matter on the human level.

In order to achieve relevance at the level of students' feelings, the teacher must determine their attitudes about a given subject before moving them into a more analytical or cognitive realm. Later, the teacher may ask the learner to account for particular feelings, to help him begin to analyze them. A skillful teacher can use the learner's feelings about his experiences to lead him into an awareness of his deeper concerns, a step toward the next level of relevance.

4. The use of teaching content that ignores the *concerns* of the learners.

Concerns involve feelings and emotions more deeply than at the third level of relevance. Concerns are the most persistent, pervasive threads of underlying uneasiness the learners have about themselves and their relation to the world. Concerns always engage feelings, but feelings do not always involve corners. For example, a person may have an immediate, spontaneous reaction to another person or experience intense emotion in listening to an orchestral performance without having a concern about either the person or the orchestra. Feeling anger at having one's toe stepped on would be an immediate feeling; anger at hearing criticism of a group to which one belongs represents a feeling so deep-rooted that it probably reflects a concern. Relevance is achieved on this fourth level if the teacher attempts to deal with fundamental questions that people frequently ask themselves, such as "Who am I?" "How do I fit into the scheme of things?" "Why do I feel the way I do?" "Is there something wrong with me?" "Do they think I'm any good?"

Effective teaching utilizes all four levels of relevance. Educators are beginning to adapt their teaching to the first two levels—pupils' learning styles and experiences. What they are not meeting adequately are the third and fourth levels, which constitute the affective domain. Instead of helping children to deal with the questions they ask themselves, the school asks children, "What do we mean by the Common Market?" "How are animals and people different?" They ignore the child's most persistent question: "What does it have to do with *me?*" But unless there is a connection between the knowledge placed before the child and his experiential and emotional framework, the knowledge he gains will matter little to him and will not be likely to contribute to the behavioral aims of education.

It is our general hypothesis that relevance is that which connects the affective, or feeling, aspects and the cognitive, or conceptualizing, aspects of learning. We believe, further, that a better linkage between the affective domain—the learner's concerns—and the practices of the school would reduce the discrepancy between learning and behavior.

AFFECT AND COGNITION

Educators generally define cognition as the act of processing perceived information and developing higher orders of abstraction and conceptualization. Sterling M. McMurrin, former U.S. Commissioner of Education, defines the cognitive and affective functions of teaching as follows:

> The cognitive function of instruction is directed to the achievement and communication of knowledge, both the factual knowledge of the sciences and the formal relationships of logic and mathematics—knowledge as both specific data and generalized structure. It is discipline in the ways of knowing, involving perception, the inductive, deductive, and intuitive processes, and the techniques of analysis and generalization. It involves both the immediate grasp of sensory objects and the abstractive processes by which the intellect contructs its ideas and fashions its ideals.
>
> The affective function of instruction pertains to the practical life—to the emotions, the passions, the dispositions, the motives, the moral and esthetic sensibilities, the capacity for feeling, concern, attachment or detachment, sympathy, empathy, and appreciation.[4]

But how does the relation between the cognitive and affective functions affect motivation and learning? Affect is not only intense feeling or emotion; it is also an expression of the basic forces that direct and control behavior. In the affective domain "the most influential controls are to be found." That domain "contains the forces that determine the nature of an individual's life and ultimately the life of an entire people."[5] Many of these forces, such as the inner need for a positive self-concept, power, connectedness, and so on, have been made more salient by the current focus on the rights and status of minority groups. These are the intrinsic drives that motivate behavior.

In urging that the teacher vigorously explore the affective domain we are not asserting its primacy over cognition or erecting a wall between

[4] "What Tasks for the Schools?" *Saturday Review* (Jan. 14, 1967), p. 41.

[5] David R. Krathwohl, Benjamin S. Bloom, and Bertram B. Masia, *Taxonomy of Educational Objectives* (New York: David McKay, 1956), p. 91.

cognition and affect. Indeed, cognitive learning is a natural way of becoming more capable of dealing with one's inner needs. The more analytic the person, the more means he presumably has available for dealing with his feelings and concerns. Consequently, cognitive machinery should link inner needs to the environment and provide the organism with means of coping with the requirements of the environment.

As Dr. George I. Brown suggests

> . . . it might help to talk about "harmony between affect and cognition in the sense that within the on-going growth of the individual, often the affective domain has become anesthetized, or feelings can be going in a different direction from the cognitive knowing: The intent is to get a harmony between the two so that they both go in the same direction.[6]

But the educational system does not foster harmony between affect and cognition; it usually emphasizes cognition at the expense of affect.

The reasons are both operational and policy-based. It is less demanding to teach for cognitive than for affective objectives, and it is far less difficult to grade student achievement in the cognitive realm. A more fundamental reason, however, is the prevalent feeling that the student's beliefs, attitudes, feelings, and concerns are private and should not be dealt with in the school. As Krathwohl has remarked

> Our own society has fluctuated as to the affective objectives it will permit the school to develop. Political and social forces are constantly at work, pressing the schools for some affective objectives and just as constantly placing restrictions on the school with regard to others. The play of these forces has, in many instances, made teachers and school administrators wary of expressing these objectives and all too frequently has led school staffs to retreat to the somewhat less dangerous cognitive domain.[7]

For these reasons, the school severely restricts attempts to link cognition and affect to the use of such elements as play, classroom climate, readiness, teacher-pupil interaction, and motivation as means of encouraging the learner to accept prescribed content. For example, a young child who appears to be emotionally unready to read is not forced into a structured reading program but is placed in a "reading readiness" program, which capitalizes on his interests as a way of facilitating his learning of content. Similarly, the teacher may use children's fear of doctors as a basis for developing a unit on "Our Community Friends—the Doctor, Dentist, and Nurse." Popular music or current slang may be used to introduce a unit on poetry. In these examples, fear or slang is not regarded as

[6] From a letter to the authors by George I. Brown, Professor of Education, University of California, Santa Barbara, May 12, 1967.

[7] Krathwohl *et al., op. cit.,* p. 90.

content worthy of attention in itself; rather, it is used as a "hook" for the institutionalized cognitive content—the subject matter. All instructional roads seem to lead to cognition as the end product. But, as we have noted, cognition makes scant contribution to the broader behavioral objectives of education.

> . . . our preference for approaching affective achievement through the attainment of cognitive objectives tends to focus attention on these cognitive goals as ends in themselves without our determining whether they are actually serving as means to an affective end.[8]

Today cognitive processes and content are riding the peak of the educational wave. Cognitive development is equated with mastery of institutionally prescribed content, with "understanding of" or "knowledge about" a variety of *academic* subjects, rather than understanding or knowledge of how these subjects can serve the needs of the student. The entire machinery of the school, including its reward system, reflects this stance; grades, promotion, recognition, and so on are based on the degree of mastery of the cognitive. In fact, the operational definition of learning used in the school is a cognitive definition. The classical notion of learning as a "change in behavior" is commonly interpreted by our schools to mean a change in cognitive behavior, measured by paper-and-pencil tests and verbalization. Catalogues and research reports from many schools of education indicate that this emphasis on change in cognitive behavior is reinforced by much of the teaching in educational psychology and research in learning.

Yet, as we noted at the outset, cognitive understanding does not guarantee behavior in harmony with the understanding. Studies of the relationship between academic achievement and performance in later life point to the same conclusion. Holland and Richards conclude from their own and earlier investigations that "studies of academic and non-academic potential and achievement have little relationship to other kinds of non-academic potential and socially important performance.[9]

Why does the cognitive orientation not affect behavior directly? In that it encourages (or requires) the individual to reconstruct reality symbolically or abstractly, cognition is removed from the real and disconnected from the feeling level of learning. Dewey described the experiential level of learning as follows.

> To "learn from experience" is to make a backward and forward connection between what we do to things and what we enjoy or suffer from

---

[8] *Ibid.,* p. 57.

[9] John L. Holland and James M. Richards, Jr., "Academic and Non-Academic Accomplishment: Correlated or Uncorrelated?" *ACT Research Reports,* No. 2 (April 1965), p. 20. See also Krathwohl *et al., op. cit.,* p. 20.

things in consequence. Under such conditions, doing becomes a trying; an experiment with the world to find out what it is like; the undergoing becomes instructions—discovery of the connection of things. . . . Experience is primarily an active-passive affair; it is not primarily cognitive.[10]

The pervasive emphasis on cognition and its separation from affect poses a threat to our society in that our educational institutions may produce cold, detached individuals, uncommitted to humanitarian goals. Certainly, a modern society cannot function without ever increasing orders of cognitive knowledge. Yet knowledge per se does not necessarily lead to desirable behavior. Knowledge can generate feeling, but it is feeling that generates action. For example, we may know all about injustice to minorities in our society, but until we feel strongly about it we will take little action. A link to the affective, or emotional, world of the learner is therefore necessary. *Unless knowledge is related to an affective state in the learner, the likelihood that it will influence behavior is limited.*

Yet, as we have noted, the spiral is usually reversed: The areas of affect are prescribed—often severely limited and narrowly defined—by the cognitive, in order to serve the cognitive. With the affective in this subordinate position, it is unlikely, or at best coincidental, that knowledge will influence behavior.

THE AFFECTIVE AS RELEVANT CONTENT

Concerns, wants, interests, fears, anxieties, joys, and other emotions and reactions to the world contain the seeds of "motivation." Dealing with the child's inner concerns constitutes recognition of, and respect for, him. By validating his experiences and feelings, we tell the child, in essence, that he *does* know something. Probably this is the most important factor in linking relevant content with self-concept. For when the teacher indicates to the child in effect that the experience he brings with him has nothing to do with the "worthwhile" knowledge that the school intends to set before him, he is, without realizing it, telling the child in effect that *he* is worthless, for he *is* his experience.

It is not surprising that when teachers do talk about the real problems students are facing, there is a marked change in attentiveness. At such times the teacher generally thinks, "We're digressing, let's get back to work." Suppose that several students interrupt a social studies lesson to tell of a fight they saw on the subway between a policeman and a young boy. They

---

[10] John Dewey, *Democracy and Education* (New York: Macmillan, 1964), p. 140. (Originally published in 1916.)

say that the boy, who had tried to break away, was slapped several times. They think this is unfair and wouldn't like it to happen to them. A social studies lesson could be given great relevance if the teacher treated this experience not as a digression but as legitimate content in its own right. Information about the city's system of law enforcement would become personally meaningful if it could be tied directly to the incident and to the students' own concerns about powerlessness.

The reason students' motivation is higher during such "digressions" than during regular lessons is that they can relate what they are learning cognitively to their own concerns. Moreover, their subsequent behavior is more likely to be affected directly by the learning that takes place. Relevance, then, becomes a matter of functionally linking extrinsic curricula to basic intrinsic concerns and feelings.

Our observations lead us to the conclusion that schools ignore the affective domain as content and instead assume that students will be motivated to learn an extrinsic body of content if enough pressure is placed upon them. Although many pupils make the adjustment, some educators are beginning to question whether the costs are not excessive. For one thing, many learners who adjust to the pressure end up regarding formal education as an exercise to be tolerated or a system to be beaten. For another, the pressure to adjust and succeed, exerted especially by parents, often produces emotional tensions in students that result in antisocial behavior in adolescence or later in life. In either case, learning is too often regarded, even by students who are adept at adjusting to the pressures, as forced and unnatural. And, finally, it is the "disadvantaged" who are least likely to have the environmental and psychic resources with which to adjust.

THE THREE-TIER CURRICULUM

The model for an affective curriculum suggested in Chapter III is only one approach to the problems of content relevance and behavioral dissonance. It is advanced as a means of redressing an imbalance—of filling vital areas that the traditional educational system has ignored—rather than as a replacement for all areas of curriculum. Its place in a total school curriculum may be illustrated by visualizing the school in terms of three tiers, or curricular modes.[11]

[11] We are indebted to Dr. Bruce R. Joyce for his insight in describing a school with three curricular modes, in *Restructuring Elementary Education: A Multiple Learning Systems Approach* (New York: Teachers College, Columbia University, 1966), p. 4. For a more detailed account of this organizational pattern, see Mario D. Fantini and Gerald Weinstein, *Making Urban Schools Work* (New York: Holt, Reinhart & Winston, 1968).

One tier is comprised of reading, computation, and writing skills, among others; basic. information in the social studies, science, language, and other disciplines; and major concepts of specific disciplines—the generally acknowledged essential building blocks for the intellectual development of the child. This tier serves as an information and skills-retrieval base. It is also the mode that lends itself best to individually paced, materials-centered, and automated instruction. Most current discussion of individualized and programmed instruction is directed to this tier.

The second tier, or curricular mode, consists of drawing latent talents and abilities from the learner. Joyce terms this the idiosyncratic or "personal discovery" tier. Like the first tier, it is highly individualized, and it calls for the development of individual creativity and the exploration of interests—everything from learning to play a tuba to working on a research project of a student's own design to writing a play.

The third tier may be thought of as a group-inquiry curriculum. It consists mainly of societal issues and problems that are related to the self and an exploration of self and others—not in the sense of individual emotional problems but in terms of the thread of *commonality* that runs through these personal issues. Exploration of a common concern—world hunger, pollution, racial injustice—should lead to individual self-examination in terms of the effects of a common issue on oneself and the possible courses of action in dealing with the issue. Inherent in this tier is the development of the individual's own personality, his skill in interpersonal relations, and the awareness skills of identifying, articulating, and evaluating his own feelings, concerns, and opinions and comparing them with those of others in a group. It is here that the curriculum of concerns would fit most readily. Although the affective may be used in any of the tiers to facilitate connection to the learning process, it is in this third tier, and possibly in the second tier, that it can become fully developed content in its own right.

In a school using all three curricular modes effectively, none would be isolated; each would overlap and interlock with the others. For example, the group-inquiry tier could not function adequately without dipping into the basic skills-and-information tier.[12]

Reading, writing, and oral expression—that is, the communications skills generally—are important as means of self-discovery and development of interests (the second tier), and for exploration of societal issues (the third tier). Mathematics, history, economics, and science—virtually all subject matter—are functionally necessary at various points throughout the curriculum. As Joyce explains, "Each of these curricular modes has advantages for some educational purposes and severe limitations for others.

---

[12] Joyce, *op. cit.,* p. 3.

Blended together in proper proportions, they can achieve a far greater and a more balanced educational result than can any one of them taken alone." [13]   We recommend a curriculum of concerns as an ingredient to be blended with other curricular modes, not as a "wall-to-wall curriculum."

To summarize, then, our present educational system gives highest priority to cognitive content and regards other content areas merely as instruments for getting to prescribed cognitive content.   The prevailing assumption is that by mastering cognitive content, the individual learns to behave appropriately as a citizen in an open society.   We question the validity of this assumption that extrinsic subject matter alone can lead to humanitarian behavior—that is, whether the cognitive man is necessarily the humanitarian man.

Our proposal is to reverse the direction of the prevailing cognitive emphasis.   We suggest that knowledge alone does not adequately produce the behavior necessary to such a society.   The chances of affecting behavior will be greater if the learner's feelings and concerns are recognized and made to direct the cognition that logically should follow and if cognition is used to help the learner cope with his concerns.

For the so-called disadvantaged in particular, but for all children generally, we believe that the affective realm contains intrinsic forces for motivation and, consequently, may have greater impact on behavior and on realizing human potential.   We regard cognition and affect as complementary, not contradictory, forces.   They have not played balanced roles in education because affect has received such meager recognition, experimentation, and practice.   Krathwohl and his colleagues refer to the affective domain as a Pandora's box: "To keep the 'box' closed is to deny the existence of the powerful motivational forces that shape the life of each of us.   To look the other way is to avoid coming to terms with the real." [14]

Affect can serve not only to revivify elements of the old subject matter but also, and primarily, to open vistas for new subject matter.

Chapter III focuses on the development of an analytic instructional model that may enable teachers to work in the affective realm and thereby generate more relevant content and procedures.   We suggest that a curriculum based on the children's concerns not only will be more relevant but also will be a step toward answering the problems of human conduct.

[13] *Ibid.*
[14] Krathwohl *et al., op. cit.,* p. 91.

Sensitivity Education

Stephen M. Corey and Elinor K. Corey

What is sensitivity education all about?

Sensitivity education helps people become more *aware* of, more *sensitive* to, what happens as they react to one another, especially in face-to-face situations. It helps men and women and boys and girls perceive what they do to one another, and to themselves, in the give and take of face-to-face communication.

When sensitivity education is successful, more of these interaction events, hopefully, are taken into account. People get in closer touch with themselves and with the others they live and work with.

Is there a difference between sensitivity education and sensitivity training?

Not much, if any. Many school people seem to dislike the implications of the word "training" and associate it with less important activities.

The expression sensitivity education suggests two things that sensitivity training may not. First, the setting for sensitivity education is more apt to be in formal institutions of education—schools or colleges. Second, attempts to increase sensitivity represent a continuous and pervasive emphasis rather than being intensive and focal as is usually the case in sensitivity training.

Isn't there great variation in what is done and called sensitivity education?

Yes, the procedures vary greatly. No one seems to have arrived at the final answer as to how increased sensitivity can best be brought about. The central purpose of all sensitivity education, though, is to help people become more aware of what happens when there is face-to-face interaction.

113

This is the case even when other expressions are used, such as encounter groups or T-groups.

Should high priority be placed on including more sensitivity education in the schools?

It is hard to imagine anything more important at the present time than the improvement of human relations, and that is what successful sensitivity education furthers. Our material wealth is unbelievable but we often seem to be in the Dark Ages in our human relationships. The evidence of our inability to sense, and subsequently to do enough about, the horrible and terrifying effects people have on one another is heartbreaking. Sensitivity education is needed in large amounts and throughout our lifetime.

Why is the term "laboratory" used so often in discussions of sensitivity education or sensitivity training?

The word "laboratory" calls attention to the fact that sensitivity education is most apt to be furthered in a setting in which people are actively reacting to one another rather than by reading about such interactions and discussing what has been read. This means a laboratory rather than an academic setting. Historically, all aspects of human relations training have tended to be academic. It was believed that if relevant information was learned and certain slogans were accepted and repeated, human relations sensitivity as an aspect of improved human relations would almost automatically take place.

What is the most important single thing a teacher might do to further sensitivity in the classroom?

The first essential step is to try to create a classroom climate that encourages boys and girls to report and discuss the way they are feeling about themselves and one another and their teacher. Usually these expressions of feelings are discouraged and punished.

When did sensitivity education in the sense of this discussion get started?

Unusual individual teachers have for a long time helped boys and girls become more aware of themselves and of one another. As a so-called "movement," however, the National Training Laboratory in Group Development got under way more than 20 years ago and its influence has been great. This Laboratory, along with the numerous training activities developed later at Esalen in northern California, are often cited as being most influential in the spread of sensitivity education or training ideas and practices.

Many people talk about sensitivity training as if it were a kind of therapy. Is it?

Most of the meaningful interactions between two or more people probably have therapeutic potential. This is most apt to be true if the interactions are relatively frank and their effects are reported and considered immediately and thoughtfully. There may be some difference in therapeutic implications between sensitivity education undertaken primarily to enable people to work together better and that undertaken primarily to further their personal development.

The National Training Laboratory started out with emphasis on the former. Esalen activities have more to do with personal growth and are probably more consistently therapeutic.

What is the reason for the rather recent surge of interest in sensitivity education?

There are probably many reasons. One is that many people who have had some of it report that they were benefited. Another important reason, undoubtedly, is our serious and increasing concern and worry about the quality of modern human life—our worry about the effect of the total environment, including other people, on the quality of human existence.

Does sensitivity education require a group context?

In the sense in which the words are used here, yes. In order for human relations events to occur, so that there can be practice in perceiving them, people must actively interact. This requires at least two people, face-to-face. The worth of these interactions for sensitivity education is greatly enhanced if the members of the group within which they take place try to observe certain ground rules.

What are some of these sensitivity education ground rules?

One calls attention to the desirability of reporting frankly the feelings and thoughts that the interactions provoke. And they must be reported in the "here and now," so to speak, because doing so greatly helps the group members understand interrelationships among human interaction events. Another ground rule discourages long explanations and references to personal biography. Confrontation is favored. Politeness and evasiveness and sparring are discouraged. The point to most of these rules, whether they are explicit or implicit, is that they further the honest reporting and discussing of human relations events *as they take place*. Only when they are so reported are they available for study, and only when their context has been shared can they be helpfully examined and understood.

Is sensitivity education beneficial to very young children?

There is no lower or upper age limit for some form of sensitivity education. Children in nursery schools have been helped to become more aware of the effects of their interpersonal behavior on other children and on themselves. They can be helped to keep in closer touch with the way they feel about and perceive what other people do to them and what they do to other people.

Most sensitivity training seems to be quite intensive, like a course or subject. Is this the case for sensitivity education?

Sensitivity education or training can either be intensive and focal or continuous and undertaken to implement some larger purpose. All school experience should represent continuous sensitivity education in the sense that it exploits opportunities to further constructive human relationships. Doing so is the central purpose for sensitivity education. Any "subject matter" will be better learned in a classroom that is a good laboratory for human relations. To try to teach arithmetic or chemistry or whatever to groups of children and pay no attention to the effects they are having on one another and their feelings about their teacher is to be blind to important influences on learning.

Why do discussions of sensitivity education so often get heated?

Sensitivity education has much to do with the emotions and increased candor in their expression. This troubles many people because the culture most of us have learned almost forces us to inhibit or disguise our feelings. People who have benefited from sensitivity education are apt to be more candid. This stirs things up.

Are not some people violently opposed to the whole idea of sensitivity training or sensitivity education?

They certainly are. We have not yet learned to deal with human relationships in general very objectively. Claims for sensitivity education often get pretty wild as do the objections. The kind of candor that characterizes sensitivity training groups threatens many people. Some have reported particular sensitivity training experiences as devastating, and these reports circulate and get exaggerated. When anyone is relatively unaware of his emotions, and of those of others, he is apt to believe that the emotions are not very important. Anyone who is grown up, some critics say, should be able to handle his emotions. Education to this end wastes time.

Do people who advocate sensitivity education have common values or a common life style?

They would appear to be a pretty heterogenous lot from the point of view of life style. A majority, though, seem to be much concerned with getting as much pleasure as is possible from the "here and now" and from human relationships in general. This, when and if it is recognized, arouses conflict with what many of us have been taught to believe about the inevitability and wholesome disciplinary value of suffering and pain and the postponement of pleasure and the hazards in its quest.

What might ·be a good way to learn more about sensitivity education?

Try to get in a sensitivity education or sensitivity training group with other knowledgeable and responsible people. Try in your everyday work to increase your perceptions of the effects people are having on one another. You probably would be surprised at the cues you have overlooked. Try to make more visible to your pupils or students what they are doing to one another as they interact in class. Forget, for a while, any evaluation of these effects. Just try to see them and check their correctness. Try, too, to make more visible the effects you have on the young people and the effect they have on you. This could be a good start toward sensitivity education.

"To Get Beyond the Words . . ."

Harold C. Wells

It is called by a variety of names, sensitivity training, the T-group method, sensitivity education, encounter groups, and many more, and it is coming on like an old-fashioned Fourth of July. The fireworks have just begun in scattered locations, but before this day is done the heavens over our land will have seen a mystical magical show of multicolored pyrotechnics! It is likely that a good many of the participants and even some of the spectators will get burned or at least singed in the process. It is going to be something to see—but you really ought to be in on the action—that is a greater risk, of course—but that is also the name of this game.

What the above-named phenomenon is, is no easier to describe than to name. Yet there are some identifiable elements in the educational use of this technique:

1. *Feelings*—Sensitivity training deals with the "right now" feelings of learners: what their feelings are, the true expression of them, and learning how to cope with them. The inner world of the learner as well as his relationships become subject matter.

2. *Values and Attitudes*—Opportunities for value examination are created or seized, options are compared and contrasted, and deliberate value choices are made and acted upon.

3. *Concerns*—The concerns of learners are treated with the same respect as the concerns of teachers and others. All concerns are legitimate in these programs, not just those related to "school work."

4. *Process*—This kind of education focuses on the processes with which an individual may deal with his feelings, values, attitudes, concerns.

Harold C. Wells, "To Get Beyond Words . . . ," *Educational Leadership*, December 1970, pp. 241–44. Reprinted with permission of the Association for Supervision and Curriculum Development and Harold C. Wells. Copyright © 1970 by the Association for Supervision and Curriculum Development.

118

5. *Self-Actualization*—The common broad goal of these programs is full humanness; not "the educated man," not "normality," but the best that man can become, the fully alive, authentic, "becoming" person.

In summary, sensitivity training as used in the schools legitimatizes the current feelings, values, attitudes, and concerns of learners and helps them develop methods for successfully managing these life forces as they move toward full humanness.

SENSITIVITY TRAINING IN THE SCHOOLS

Educators have been very active participants in the encounter group movement. Many thousands of school people have experienced sensitivity training. Most of them have probably undertaken this training as private citizens. However, both pre- and in-service teacher training designs have begun to incorporate sensitivity training as at least one module.

The first, and perhaps most obvious, result of so many educators being in T-groups is that a lot of "turned-on" teachers have returned from a weekend group and have tried techniques on students that they found meaningful in the lab. These fired-up teachers have often ended up just fired! They are the ones providing the fireworks alluded to earlier.

Creating headlines is not an inevitable result, of course. Many manage to bootleg training devices into the classroom, and some precious few have been successful in getting administration approval for voluntary guidance groups or elective classes built around a "human relations" theme.

One such teacher is Alice Louise Elliott. She "taught" six elective classes made up of from 25 to 40 students with IQ's ranging from 85 to 160, in the 10th, 11th, and 12th grades. The classes were a unique blend of General Semantics training and encounter groups. General Semantics has been defined as "the study of the relationships between language and behavior, between words and their consequences." The encounter group format enabled students to acquire an understanding of the principles of General Semantics in an experiential setting. They discussed such questions as, "What are the implications of 'I-thou relationships'?" "Do people need people? For what? When?" "Is man his choices?"—and the more direct question, "How is it with you at this moment?"

For measurement of results, Elliott relied principally on self-report instruments. She states,

Results show important gains for students in learning to listen, to delay signal responses, and to delay reactions of anger which resulted in less alienation and more empathy with their fellow students, teachers, and parents. They also reported being more honest with themselves and others by learning to communicate better. They increased their sense of humor and decreased their feelings of prejudice. They were more trusting of selves, less phony and artificial, more fully functioning, and more independent in thought and behavior.[1]

Besides the "bootleggers" and a few "Alice Elliott-type" teachers around, there is a second very significant trend which owes a great deal to the sensitivity training movement: affective education curricula. Most of the efforts in this direction have been designed as supplements to the regular school program. They include group development techniques, devices for examining student values and attitudes, techniques for developing self-esteem, and processes for recognizing and coping with one's feelings. Representative of this new emphasis is the work of Bessell and Palomares of the Human Development Training Institute in San Diego. In their elementary school program the children are seated in a "magic circle" and the teacher guides them in discussion of such concepts as "What gives us a good feeling?" and actual experiences in the concept.

Perhaps a brief description of a single activity from Philadelphia's Affective Education Project will give the reader a better feel for the process concerns of workers in this field and also the extent to which they have been able to integrate cognitive, affective, and psychomotor learnings.

> "Students interlock fingers of the right hand with thumbs free, and are told to imagine that they are their thumbs expressing their personalities. They are to meet their partners and write poems about the experience." (Borton then has them write poems and examine other poetry which is concerned with human relationships.)
>
> His lesson continues: "Experiment with new ways of meeting the same person's thumb. See how many ways you can develop. Change partners. Do you enjoy any of these other patterns of behavior? Pick one (your original if you like) and try shaking hands the same way. Try talking the same way.
>
> "After class, try acting the same way for a few minutes. If you like this new way of relating, practice it and live it." [2]

---

[1] Alice Louise Elliott. "Fostering the Self-Actualizing of High School Students Through General Semantics Training in Encounter Groups." Unpublished doctoral dissertation, United States International University, May 1969.

[2] Terry Borton. *Reach, Touch, and Teach.* New York: McGraw-Hill Book Company, 1970, pp. 100–101.

WHAT RESEARCH SAYS ABOUT
SENSITIVITY TRAINING

We do not really have data beyond the teacher-student "I like it!" variety. Many competent people, scholars and practitioners, are beginning the search for evidence. It is my conviction, however, that precise designs and measurement over extended periods of time have not been characteristic of this (or any other) movement in education. Nor should this surprise or dismay us for we are dealing with a rather new emphasis in the profession and we are approaching it with our customary enthusiasm, faith, and sincerity. And that is all right too, just as long as we begin to specify our goals, tighten our designs, and sharpen our instruments, which we are doing.

WHAT ARE THE DANGERS?

One of the dangers is that there are too many people worrying about the dangers! The persistent concern over psychotic episodes stemming from adult encounter groups has not been warranted on the basis of our experience. That is not to say that the concerns are not realistic when we are dealing with 7- to 17-year-olds. They are, and I for one do not want my own children subjected to *encounter group* experience without my having a great deal to say about the structure of the experience and the leader of the group, and perhaps not even then!

On the other hand, the almost out-of-hand rejection of any educational program that purports to deal with the feelings, concerns, and values of learners is absurd. When this climate prevails, as it does in our country, by and large, any sensible, defensible application or modification of either encounter groups (à la Elliott) or the more structured activities described by Terry Borton is immediately suspect in the minds of insecure administrators and "uptight" parents. And that is a tragedy, for it is precisely those kinds of thoughtful applications of sensitivity training that can help us respond to the enormous problems of our schools and society.

This is not to say that we all ought to rush into the pond without testing the water. Any conscientious professional has to be concerned that we do not psychologically damage children by putting them in situations where their defenses are lowered to the extent that they become vulnerable to an unwitting attack by another group member. Protection from this sort of thing is a function of capable leadership and intelligent learning experience design.

WHAT CAN WE EXPECT NOW?

So, one of the things we can look for is the development of teacher leadership capable of designing and conducting long-range growth experiences for students of all ages in the affective area. These will probably minimize the encounter group format. Where encounter groups are used they will no doubt have some cognitive forms as a basic part of their structure, as Elliott has shown.

They will probably also be limited to high school age groups or older, be led by well-trained professionals, the goals and techniques to be used will be explicitly stated in advance, those techniques used will not include body contact activities, and participation will include many opportunities for cognitive consideration of what it all means. Designs will begin with behavioral goals and will provide for all of the elements mentioned earlier, including pupil feelings, values, and concerns. They will also emphasize students' strengths and successes rather than weaknesses. They will provide for trying out new behaviors in a safe setting and for encouragement to follow up those trials with risk-taking ventures in the larger society.

Finally, it seems likely that we can expect a considerable amount of experimentation with "group-building" processes.

In conclusion, let me make a plea for a pluralistic educational system. In every school building in America we need some "turned-on" teachers who have a vision of what man can become and who have the insight, enthusiasm, and competence to help the rest of us examine our work in relation to these humanistic goals. They must have the strength and self-assurance to be iconoclastic, for we have a faltering society and a school system in serious trouble, and we can ill afford to be complacent about our present situation.

Your job and mine is to cherish and protect those who see life through different eyes, who operate from different premises and different value systems. We must sit with them, feel with them, experience with them, get beyond the *words*. For it is the words that hold us back. Words like "sensitivity training," "encounter groups," "feelings and concerns" are frightening to many people—just as are "freedom," "love," and "peace"! The only way we can achieve understanding—and progress—is to get beyond the words to the activities, events, and behaviors the words stand for!

The Human Side of Learning

Arthur W. Combs

Anyone who doesn't know that education is in deep trouble must have been hiding somewhere for the last fifteen years. Somehow we have lost touch with the times, so we find young people opting out, copping out, and dropping out of the system. The processes of education have become concerned with nonhuman questions, and the system is dehumanizing to the people in it. Earl Kelley once said, "We've got this marvelous school system with beautiful buildings and a magnificent curriculum and these great teachers and these marvelous administrators, and then, damn it all, the parents send us the wrong kids."

For a number of generations now, we have been dealing with learning from a false premise. Most of us are familiar with Pavlov's famous experiment conditioning a dog to respond to a bell. The principles he established then are the ones we still use to deal with the problems of learning in our schools today. But Pavlov's system depended on: 1) separating his dogs from all other dogs, which made the learning process an isolated event; 2) typing his dogs down so that they could only do precisely what he had in mind, a technique not very feasible for most elementary teachers; 3) completely removing the dogs from all other possible sources of stimuli, a hard thing to do in a classroom.

This point of view has taught us to deal with the problem of learning as a question of stimulus and response, to be understood in terms of input and output. Currently it finds its latest expression in behavioral objectives, performance based criteria for learning that systematically demand that you: Establish your objectives in behavioral terms; set up the machinery to accomplish them; and then test whether or not you have achieved them. Such an approach seems straightforward, businesslike, and logical; and that's what is wrong with it. I quote from Earl Kelley again, who once said, "Logic is often only a systematic way of arriving at the wrong answers!"

I'm not opposed to behavioral objectives. Nobody can be against accountability. The difficulty with the concept is that its fundamental premise is only partly right. The fact is that behavioral objectives are useful devices for dealing with the simplest, most primitive aspects of education, the things we already do quite well. Unfortunately, they do not serve us so well when they are applied to other kinds of objectives, such as intelligent behavior requiring a creative approach to a problem. Behavioral objectives do not deal with the problem of holistic goals. They do not help us in dealing with the things that make us truly human—the questions of human beliefs, attitudes, feelings, understandings, and concerns—the things we call "affective." Nor do they deal with the problems of self-actualization, citizenship, responsibility, caring, and many other such humanistic goals of educators.

Using this approach, we are evaluating schools and circumstances on the basis of what we know how to test. As a result, we are finding that our educational objectives are being established by default because the things we know how to test are the simplest, smallest units of cognitive procedures, which don't really matter much anyway.

We are spending millions and millions of dollars on this very small aspect of dealing with the educational problem, while the problems of self-concept, human attitudes, feelings, beliefs, meanings, and intelligence are going unexplored.

Although I do not oppose behavioral objectives, I do believe that those who are forcing accountability techniques on us need also to be held accountable for what they are doing to American education.

Performance based criteria is the method of big business, a technique of management, and we are now in the process of applying these industrial techniques to education everywhere. We ought to know better. When industry developed the assembly line and other systematic techniques to increase efficiency, what happened? The workers felt dehumanized by the system and formed unions to fight it. And that is precisely what is happening with our young people today. They feel increasingly dehumanized by the system, so they are fighting it at every possible level. Applying industrial techniques to human problems just won't work. A systems approach, it should be understood, is only a method of making sure you accomplish your objectives. Applied to the wrong objectives, systems approaches only guarantee that your errors will be colossal.

The trouble with education today is not its lack of efficiency, but its lack of humanity. Learning is not a mechanical process, but a *human* process. The whole approach to learning through behavioral objectives concentrates our attention on the simplest, most primitive aspects of the educational endeavor, while it almost entirely overlooks the human values. I believe we can get along better with a person who can't read than with a bigot. We are doing very little to prevent the production of bigots but a very great deal to prevent the production of poor readers.

Learning is a human problem always consisting of two parts. First, we have to provide people with some new information or some new experience, and we know how to do that very well. We are experts at it. With the aid of our new electronic gadgets, we can do it faster and more furiously than ever before in history. Second, the student must discover the meaning of the information provided him. The dropout is not a dropout because we didn't give him information. We told him, but he never discovered what that information meant.

I would like to give an alternate definition to the S-R theory most of us cut our teeth on: Information will affect a person's behavior only in the degree to which he has discovered its personal meaning for him. For example, I read in this morning's paper that there has been an increase in the number of cases of pulmonic stenosis in the state of Florida in the past two years. I don't know what pulmonic stenosis is, so this information has no meaning for me. Later in the day I hear a friend talking about pulmonic stenosis, so I look it up and find that it's a disorder that produces a closing up of the pulmonary artery. It's a dangerous disorder, and it produces blue babies. Now I know what it is, but it still doesn't affect my behavior very much. Later in the day I received a letter from a mother of one of my students who says, "Dear Teacher, we have taken Sally to the clinic, where we learned that she has got pulmonic stenosis, and she's going to have to be operated on when she reaches adolescence. In the meantime, we would appreciate it if you would keep an eye out for her."

This information has more meaning to me now because it's happening to one of my students, and my behavior reflects that meaning. I protect the girl, and I talk to other people on the faculty: "Did you hear about Sally? Isn't it a shame? She's got pulmonic stenosis. Poor child, she's going to have to be operated on."

Let's go one step further. Suppose I have just learned that my daughter has pulmonic stenosis. Now this information affects my behavior tremendously, in every aspect of my daily life.

This explains why so much of what we do in school has no effect on students. Sometimes we even discourage them from finding the personal meaning of a piece of information. We say, "Eddie, I'm not interested in what you think about that, what does the book say?" which is the same as telling him that school is a place where you learn about things that don't matter.

What do we need to do, then, if we're going to humanize the business of learning? We have to see the whole problem of learning differently. We have to give up our preoccupation with objectivity. In our research at the University of Florida, we find that objectivity correlates negatively with effectiveness in the helping professions we have so far explored.

Freud once said that no one ever does anything unless he would rather. In other words, no one ever does anything unless he thinks it is important. So the first thing we must do to humanize learning is to believe it is important.

Let me tell another story by way of illustration. In the suburbs of Atlanta there was a young woman teaching first grade who had beautiful long blonde hair which she wore in a pony tail down to the middle of her back. For the first three days of the school year she wore her hair that way. Then, on Thursday she decided to do it up in a bun on top of her head. One of the little boys in her class looked into the room and didn't recognize his teacher. He was lost. The bell rang, school started, and he didn't know where he belonged. He was out in the hall crying. The supervisor asked him, "What's the trouble?" and he said, "I can't find my teacher." She said, "Well, what's your teacher's name? What room are you in?" He didn't know. So she said, "Well, come on, let's see if we can find her." They started down the hall together, the supervisor and the little boy, hand-in-hand, opening one door after another without much luck until they came to the room where this young woman was teaching. As they stood there in the doorway, the teacher turned and saw them and she said, "Why, Joey, it's good to see you. We've been wondering where you were. Come on in. We've missed you." And the little boy pulled away from the supervisor and threw himself into the teacher's arms. She gave him a hug, patted him on the fanny, and he ran to his seat. She knew what was important. She thought little boys were important.

Suppose the teacher hadn't thought little boys were important. Suppose, for instance, she thought supervisors were important. Then she would have said, "Why good morning, Miss Smith. We're so glad you've come to see us, aren't we boys and girls?" And the little boy would have been ignored. Or the teacher might have thought the lesson was important, in which case she would have said, "Joey, for heaven's sake, where have you been? You're already two pages behind. Come in here and get to work." Or she might have thought that discipline was important, and said, "Joey, you know very well when you're late you must go to the office and get a permit. Now run and get it." But she didn't. She thought little boys were important. And so it is with each of us. We have to believe humanizing learning is important.

To humanize learning we must also recognize that people don't behave according to the facts of a situation, they behave in terms of their beliefs. In the last presidential election, those who thought that the Democrats would save us and the Republicans would ruin us voted for the Democrats. And those who thought the Republicans would save us and the Democrats would ruin us voted for the Republicans. Each of us behaved not in terms of "the facts," but in terms of our beliefs. A fact is only what we believe is so. Sensitivity to the beliefs of the people we work with is basic to effective behavior. In our research on the helping professions, we found the outstanding characteristic of effective helpers was that the good ones are always concerned with how things look from the point of view of the people they are working with.

Let me give another illustration of what I mean by being aware of the other person's point of view. A supervisor and a teacher were talking about a little boy: "I don't know what to do with him," the teacher said. "I know that he can do it; I tell him, 'It's easy, Frank, you can do it; but he won't even try." The supervisor said, "Don't ever tell a child something is easy. Look at it from the child's point of view. If you tell him it's easy and he can't do it, he can only conclude that he must be stupid, and if he can do it, you have robbed it of all its thrill! Tell him it's hard, that you know it's hard, but you're pretty sure he can do it. Then if he can't do it, he hasn't lost face, and if he can do it, what a glory that is for him."

So much of what we do in teaching is not concerned with people. It is concerned with rules, regulations, order, and neatness. I visited a school some years ago, and as I sat in the principal's office one of the bus drivers came in with a little boy in one hand and a broken arm from one of the seats of the bus in the other hand. How did this principal behave? He became very angry. It was as if the little boy had broken the principal's arm. And, in a sense, the boy had, I suppose.

In contrast to that, I am reminded of a visit I made to a school in Michigan. As I walked down the hall with the principal, a teacher and a group of children came out of one of the rooms of this very old building. We walked into the room and saw that it was in complete havoc. The principal said, "It's a mess isn't it? And it can stay that way. The teacher has raised the reading level of her classes by two grades every year she's had them. If that's the way she wants to teach, it's all right with me!"

We walked along to the gymnasium and looked in. He said as we looked at the floor, "That's the third finish we've had on that floor this year. We use it in the evenings for family roller skating!" There is a man whose values are clear. He is more concerned with people than things.

There are hundreds of ways we dehumanize people in our schools, and we need to make a systematic attempt to get rid of them.

In *Crisis in the Classroom,* Charles Silberman says that he believes one of the major problems in American education is "mindlessness." We do so many things without having the slightest idea of why we're doing them. One dehumanizing element is the grading system. Grades motivate very few people, nor are they good as an evaluative device. Everyone knows that no two teachers evaluate people in exactly the same terms. Yet we piously regard grades as though they all mean the same thing, under the same circumstances, to all people at all times.

I remember my son coming home from college and asking, "Dad, how can you, as an educator, put up with the grading system? Grading on the curve makes it to my advantage to destroy my friends. Dad, that's a hell of a way to teach young people to live." I'd never thought of it that way before.

Another thing we need to understand is the serious limitation of competition as a motivational system. Psychologists know three things about motivation:

1. The only people who are motivated by competition are those who think they can win. And that's not very many. Everyone else sits back and watches them beat their brains out.

2. People who do not feel they have a chance of winning and are forced to compete are not motivated. They are discouraged and disillusioned by the process, and we cannot afford a discouraged and disillusioned populace.

3. When competition becomes too important, morality breaks down, and any means becomes justified to achieve the ends—the basketball team begins to use its elbows and students begin to cheat on exams.

Grade level and grouping is another mindless obstacle to humanizing. All the research we have on grouping tells us that no one method of grouping is superior to any other. And yet we go right on, in the same old ways, insisting that we must have grade levels. As a result, we might have an eleven-year-old child in the sixth grade reading at the third-grade level. Every day of his life we feed him a diet of failure because we can't find a way to give a success experience to such a child.

If we want to humanize the processes of learning, we must make a systematic search for the things that destroy effective learning and remove them from the scene. If we're going to humanize the processes of learning, we must take the student in as a partner. Education wouldn't be irrelevant if students had a voice in decision making. One of my friends once said that the problem of American education today is that "all of us are busy providing students with answers to problems they don't have yet." And that's true. We decide what people need to know and then we teach it to them whether they need it or not. As a result some students discover that school is a place where you study things that don't matter and so they drop out. It's intelligent to drop out. If it isn't getting you anywhere, if it doesn't have any meaning, if it doesn't do something for you, then it's intelligent to drop out. But we seldom think of it that way. Most of us regard the dropout as though there is something wrong with him.

Part of making education relevant to the student is allowing him to develop responsibility for his own learning. But responsibility can only be learned from having responsibility, never from having it withheld. The teacher who says, "You be good kids while I'm out of the room" is an example of what I'm talking about. When she comes back the room is bedlam. "I'll never leave you alone again," she says. By this pronouncement she has robbed the children of any opportunity to learn how to behave responsibly on their own.

Not long ago, I arrived at a school just after the election for student body president, and the teachers were upset because the student who was elected president had run on a platform of no school on Friday, free lunches, free admissions to the football games, and a whole string of other impossible things. The teachers thought it was "a travesty on democracy" and suggested that the student body have another election. I said, "If you do that, how are these kids ever going to discover the terrible price you have to pay for electing a jackass to office?"

We know that what a person believes about himself is crucial to his growth and development. We also know that a person learns this self-concept from the way he is treated by significant people in his life. The student takes his self concept with him wherever he goes. He takes it to Latin class, to arithmetic class, to gym class, and he takes it home with him. Wherever he goes, his self-concept goes, too. Everything that happens to him has an effect on his self-concept.

Are we influencing that self-concept in positive or negative ways? We need to ask ourselves these kinds of questions. How can a person feel liked unless somebody likes him? How can a person feel wanted unless somebody wants him? How can a person feel acceptable unless somebody accepts him? How can a person feel he's a person with dignity and integrity unless somebody treats him so? And how can a person feel that he is capable unless he has some success? In the answers to those questions, we'll find the answers to the human side of learning.

3 / The Teacher as Psychologist

Every teacher is in his own way a psychologist. Everything he does, says, or teaches has or could have a psychological impact. What he offers helps children to discover their resources and their limitations. He is the central figure in countless situations which can help the learner to realize and accept himself or which may bring humiliation, shame, rejection, and self-disparagement.

What we are urging is that if all teachers could gain a clearer conception of what this psychological function is and what it might be, and if we could discover the kind of selection, training, and experience which might bring it to its fullest development, the result would be a happy one for all mankind.

—Arthur T. Jersild

The Teacher as Psychologist

Arthur T. Jersild

As was stated earlier, this publication is part of a project which proceeds from the hypothesis that schools can do more than they now are doing to help people gain in healthy self-understanding and in acceptance of themselves and others. This hypothesis poses many questions which the present limited effort does not begin to answer, but we would like in conclusion to comment briefly on certain questions, misgivings, and theoretical and practical considerations.

Let us look at some of the reasons advanced against the position that experiences at school in general and the influence of the teacher in particular can do anything to promote self-understanding and self-acceptance in a way that might have a significant impact on the learner's way of life.

One view is that if a child is already anxious there is little or nothing a teacher can do to reach him, and if he is not anxious he needs no help. The first part of this proposition may or may not be true. It poses an important problem, but as stated it represents an arbitrary prejudgment. No one knows enough about anxiety and its ramifications to make such a statement unless he has wisdom extending far beyond anything yet put into writing on the subject. One characteristic of the most illuminating literature about anxiety, in this writer's opinion, is that it is phrased tentatively, revealing that the person who is writing humbly recognizes that there is much yet to be learned.

Another misgiving is that teachers cannot enter into the kind of relationship which would enable pupils to grow in understanding of themselves. The teacher is a person in authority. He is a disciplinarian. He is the moral arm of society. He cannot allow the kind of permissive relationship which is necessary if there is to be anything approaching a free exchange or revelation of feeling.

If this claim is correct, it means that the teacher's role will be limited

Reprinted by permission of the publisher from Arthur T. Jersild, *In Search of Self.* New York: Teachers College Press, pp. 122–25. Copyright © 1952 by Teachers College, Columbia University.

133

mainly to rather superficial relationships. But to make this claim does not necessarily establish it. Some teachers will say that the situation is quite the opposite. When given half a chance, their pupils poignantly reveal themselves with a deluge of feeling. The writer believes that those claiming that the position of the teacher is such that pupils will inevitably hold themselves aloof and take on an attitude of self-defense are perhaps telling more about the teachers they happen to have known, or perhaps about their own difficulty as teachers in establishing relationships with pupils, than about teachers in general. This is a matter for study, not for prejudgment. In any event, common observation tells us that teachers differ considerably in their ability to establish a relationship of friendliness, trust, and emotional acceptance in their contacts with their pupils (and probably in a similar manner in their dealings with human beings in general). There may be some who support the claim above, while others are a living refutation of it.

According to another misgiving, even if the school tried to promote self-understanding it would make little or no real difference in a child's life. This draws upon the view that understanding and insight are at best only of incidental importance. One theory is that self-understanding (or insight) is something that happens to occur after a basic change in attitude toward self or others has already taken place. According to this view, understanding simply provides intellectual confirmation, so to speak, of something that has already occurred. This position has merit, presenting a matter we need to learn more about. As was mentioned earlier, it would be foolish to claim that learning something about oneself or about human beings in general will have any effect if it is perceived only on an intellectual level, as another academic fact. But that is not what we mean by self-understanding. So far as the position taken in this book is concerned, this misgiving is unrealistic and academic; for we maintain that a program to promote self-understanding must use all the resources the school can command—intellectual, social, and emotional.

Another misgiving is that teachers will do harm if they set out to be amateur psychologists. As was stated elsewhere by the writer (1), teachers might do psychological harm just as an amateur surgeon might harm the body. But this analogy oversimplifies the problem. For, whether they will it or not, whether they know it or not, teachers are already practicing psychology in their dealings with children. All the teacher's relationships with his pupils are charged with psychological meaning.

This does not mean that the teacher, by virtue of the work he is doing, should take on the role now occupied by the professionally trained psychologist or that the teacher should pretend to assume the functions of a psychiatrist. The psychiatrist is the person in our society who has the training and the responsibility to work with the most serious behavior disorders and the most acute forms of mental disease. He also works with milder disorders. The teacher, too, must deal with the severely disturbed children who happen to be in his class. He must work with them as best he can, but he cannot ethically or legally take it upon himself to "treat" such disorders as though he were a psychologically trained physician.

We are not proposing that teachers should try to take on or pretend that they might take on the role of a psychiatrist or highly trained psychological counselor. We do not want teachers to assume a role that is entirely new or different. We are simply saying that the teacher should try to function to the best advantage in the psychological role which he already occupies. As a teacher he already is in a position to have a profound psychological influence on his pupils, for better or for worse.

Every teacher is in his own way a psychologist. Everything he does, says, or teaches has or could have a psychological impact. What he offers helps children to discover their resources and their limitations. He is the central figure in countless situations which can help the learner to realize and accept himself or which may bring humiliation, shame, rejection, and self-disparagement.

What we are urging is that if all teachers could gain a clearer conception of what this psychological function is and what it might be, and if we could discover the kind of selection, training, and experience which might bring it to its fullest development, the result would be a happy one for all mankind.

The Boundary Line
Between Education
and Psychotherapy

Rudolf Ekstein

Before 1938, teachers and clinicians trained together in the Vienna Psychoanalytic Institute. Though not large, this group was distinguished by the fact that it represented a variety of different practitioners: elementary-school teachers, kindergarten teachers, child analysts and teachers specializing in working with severely emotionally or mentally handicapped children. We were all studying together to see whether psychoanalysis had something to offer the educator. During this training there was no clear boundary between psychoanalytic therapy and psychoanalytically oriented education.

I believe that the lack of clear differentiation had to do with the fact that psychoanalysis was then so new and so occupied with the causes of emotional illness and its prevention. The cause of emotional illness was seen primarily in the educational system, and I am referring now to the parent as educational agent as well as the formal school system. The educational system was considered over-strict, Victorian and traumatizing. The benefit derived from psychoanalysis was seen in an educational movement which stood for less restriction, for sexual enlightenment and for an effort to avoid traumatization of children. In those days we had achieved a sort of fusion (or, occasionally, confusion) between psychotherapy and analytically oriented education. Only slowly did we learn that this concept of education did not completely hold.

I could perhaps best illustrate this through an incident from one of the schools which we had organized at that time in Vienna. It was a progressive school with psychoanalytically trained teachers. One of the teachers told the following story about a little girl of eight who was highly disturbed. She had just been brought to this school in order to benefit

Rudolf Ekstein and Rocco L. Motto, *From Learning for Love to Love for Learning,* New York: Brunner/Mazel Publishers, 1969, pp. 157–63.

from its system after she had gone to one of the typical strict elementary schools. This little girl now found herself in a school where the children were asked: "What would you like to play?" "What would you like to learn?" The little girl answered, "I don't like it at all. As a matter of fact, I am very unhappy here. I like my old school much better." The teacher was puzzled. "Why?" And the little girl burst out, "Because in the old school the teacher helped me to be good."

I think that this anecdote tells us clearly that psychoanalytically oriented education has to do more than undo traumata, has to be more than a reaction to outmoded educational techniques. Since those days in Vienna, representatives of both disciplines have worked toward clearer boundaries between education and psychotherapy.

As I use the word "boundary," I suspect that it suggests the idea of limits beyond which one should not go. Such connotations are not very useful if they are colored by notions of hierarchy and status. My use of "boundary" is inspired, rather, by the concept of different functions, of different applications of the insights derived from psychoanalytic knowledge. I believe it is our task to note clearly that between teaching and healing, between education and psychotherapy, there is a boundary line not in terms of understanding the child, but rather in terms of differentiation of function, of purpose and purpose-geared technique. In the case of a child, who has acquired certain symptoms, the expressions of conscious and/or unconscious conflict, there is the need for psychotherapy. It is the task of the therapist, through psychotherapeutic intervention, to restore the lost function. It is the task of the teacher and the educator not to restore function, but to develop functions by helping the child to acquire skills, knowledge and correct attitudes.

From that point of view, one might say that the teacher's job, the educator's job, is a much broader and more important one. What the psychotherapists do is remove the inner obstacles which have been created in the child and which prevent him from making use of what life has to offer. The teacher comes to the child with a different purpose. The purpose of the teacher—and the parent—is to help the child to acquire various kinds of learning. One might say that the educator brings controls from outside, from without, to help the child to learn techniques to live. The psychotherapist helps the child—to use Fritz Redl's phrasing—to restore inner controls which have broken down.

Despite the attempt to differentiate between the function of the psychotherapist and the function of the teacher, frequent overlapping does occur. As a matter of fact, the younger the child or the more complex the illness, the more these functions do overlap. But I would like to emphasize that there are two different functions, as defined here, and both can or may make use of the generic knowledge which psychoanalysis offers.

Ordinarily, when we speak about psychoanalytic knowledge, we have only therapy in mind because psychoanalysis has become most widely known through its application as a therapeutic technique. When the first group of educators was training with the analysts in Vienna, they wanted to see whether psychoanalysis could be applied not only as a therapeutic technique but could also be used by the teacher as he helped the child acquire skills and knowledge and useful attitudes toward life. When this group left Europe after the first experiment in modern democratic government in central Europe had failed, a good many of us went to England. The first meetings that we had in England are relevant to the possibility of wider application of psychoanalysis. At them, Anna Freud addressed a large group of the recently arrived Viennese and many English friends who had joined us. The three addresses made by Anna Freud in London, in the fall of 1938, were for teachers. Many hundreds had come, and I think it is not incidental that she chose to address teachers first. I think she did so because psychoanalysts have always felt, even when they were primarily interested in therapy, that the therapeutic function makes social sense only when psychoanalysis can be applied to the educational process and is not utilized for therapeutic purposes alone.

In this social use of psychoanalysis, inquiry is needed. A task for psychoanalysts then is to help teachers distinguish between problems which are educational and those whose solutions are beyond the educator's sphere. Educational techniques might fail in certain situations because the appropriate technique may be a therapeutic one. Related to this task, therefore, is knowing how to refer parents and children to appropriate resources.

There is an area which teachers and analysts should investigate together. This is the area of collaboration in dealing with children who need treatment. Some of these children, even though sick, neurotic or psychotic, can and should continue their formal education with modified techniques. Most important, teachers and analysts must discover how to apply psychoanalytic knowledge in teaching itself. Concerns common to both disciplines include: the nature of learning; the differences between the kind of learning based on repetition and that which is based on insight; and the role of teacher-student relationships.

As some contributors to the field maintain, psychoanalysis has never offered a learning theory of its own. I will not challenge this contention seriously but—with tongue in cheek—I must insist if it does not offer a learning theory, psychoanalysis could well be considered an unlearning theory, since it brings about a kind of education in reverse. Freud spoke of it as *Nacherziehung,* a second education. He referred to its propositions concerning therapeutic change of symptoms, the pathological formations which had been "learned" and then, under the influence of therapeutic action, unlearned. If these propositions concerning unlearning could be turned inside out like a glove, they would pertain to the acquisition of functions through education, rather than the restoration of functions through therapy. They would then describe a learning theory.

I believe that pessimism concerning the applicability of psycho-analysis to formal education has much to do with the development of psychoanalytic theory. This pessimism derives from the history of both its application as therapy as well as the place that it held until recently in our school systems.

When I speak of its development as a theory I refer to earlier phases when instinct theory was dominant. At that time the topographic model of the psychic apparatus stood in the way of developing a theory which included the serious study of cognitive functions. Earlier therapeutic use stressed the emotional aspects of treatment: affect discharge, regaining mastery over instincts, making the unconscious conscious, reliving the infantile neurosis in the transference neurosis, etc. Consequently, school systems primarily saw the use of psychoanalysis in mental hygiene attempts, preventing emotional disorders and helping children who suffered from them. Desirable as these uses are, they have defined and limited the use of psychoanalysis by the educator, despite the changes in modern psycho-analysis.

Since Freud's inception of the structural model of the psychic apparatus, we have developed ego psychology, including a psychology of adaptation, as part of the total theoretical framework. This has influenced treatment techniques to the point that "to make the unconscious conscious" is no longer an adequate description of its goals. Freud's "Where Id was there shall Ego be" is a better summation; that is, higher psychic functions should be restored and brought to dominance. These higher functions include the concepts of insight, capacity for delay, capacity for problem-solving. The resolved unconscious conflict frees energy for ego function. Thus, instead of the compulsion to repeat an old conflict or an old and vain attempt to solve a problem, the capacity to solve new tasks is now available. These tasks include those of learning. The freeing process of therapy has given us an opportunity to observe the restoration and the use of cognitive functions. We now pay attention to problems in these functions as well as to emotional and interpersonal problems. It is no mere coincidence that psychoanalysts are now slowly catching up with the work of Piaget.

In previous considerations the emphasis was on conflict; equally stressed now is the task implied in a conflict. Conflict and task are but two sides of the same coin. The therapist is more concerned with conflict as he attempts to help the patient. The educator is more concerned with task, as he helps the student. The difference is one of focus, and each focus requires different skills since it implies different goals. Psychoanalysis practiced as a therapeutic technique is unlearning theory. Utilized in education, it is a learning theory, albeit presently available only in fragments, many of which are not very well tested or tried.

Erikson's "phases of growth" apply to this interrelationship between conflict and task, particularly the one that characterizes the latency period —the time when formal schooling starts. Erikson—who tried to describe in psychosocial terms what Freud had described earlier in terms of instinctual psychic development—has described the latency period as a time of conflict between inferiority and industry. Although "conflict" is a word that appears quite frequently in psychoanalytical literature, in my opinion it is not completely appropriate for facilitating the fullest understanding of the psychological issues involved. The word "conflict" is usually associated with ideas of psychopathology. It reminds one also of war, of something painful, of something that had better not take place. Thus, if we speak of the young child's conflicts, we may see him torn between the forces of industry and inferiority. In such a conflict, the parents or teachers certainly want industry to win over inferiority in order to permit the work required for the learning task. But such an outlook refers to the result of a process rather than to the process itself. I suggest now that this process can be better understood in an educational perspective if we refer to what takes place not only as a conflict but as a psychic task as well.

The child will meet this task well if he has resolved previous psychic tasks. He must have acquired basic trust, autonomy, the capacity to accept controls from outside—inner and outer discipline—and socialized initiative. Such a child was not crushed in the oedipal struggle; has learned to renounce early instinctual wishes; identifies with the role of the parent of the same sex. He is thus ready for the school task and for learning, so that he can someday fulfill the same functions as his providers of today who take care of him, on whom he is dependent and from whom he must finally grow away.

Latency rather than being a quiet period, is actually a very active one in which ego growth takes place. Defenses and adaptive psychic organizations develop. Then character formation takes place, and a readiness to learn becomes available.

But this learning readiness, which is discussed in chapter 6, is unsteady. Its acquisition, a slow process, is experienced at times as a serious struggle. The child who learns looks up to the parents and teachers, compares himself with competing peers, looks at the volume of work, and finds that he is wanting. Regardless of how well he will come out in the end, he must go through phases where he feels that he cannot do it, that he will never reach the educational goal. This anxiety-ridden feeling of inferiority can now become either the driving force towards learning, towards industry or the goal-inhibiting force. As the latter, it may force the child to become a dropout, a passive and inhibited learner, a school failure, an under-achiever, or whatever name we may choose to give him. But if he had no feeling of inferiority, if he thought of himself as somebody who already knows everything, he could not learn. He would then live in a megalomanic fantasy world, as our clinical work reveals many youngsters unfortunately do, and would achieve only in fantasy what he is unable to bring about in reality.

The complete lack of self-appraisal; the inability to know what one can do; the belief that one can do everything—in other words, the absence of any kind of sense of inferiority—would lead to an autistic world. This might be a universe of great success—within the skin; a kind of LSD Utopia; a new religion which would fall apart as soon as it had to be matched against realistic achievement. A certain sense, then, of "I do not know it as yet nor do I know if I can master it" is a necessary accompaniment to learning. The outcome of the oedipal struggle will dictate whether this new conflict can lead to the acquisition of the capacity to work and study, to learn and to master school problems. The conflict then is essential to the task, and, in many ways, is the task.

Educational methods have made use of this psychological fact. The system of grading, the competitive arrangement in the school situation, the use of that conflict, that particular attitude towards the task of learning within the socialization process, each is well known. Sometimes we see education only as external manipulation and forget about the intrapsychic meaning of the conflict. We then see education only in terms of a conditioning process, something that is being done to the child. In doing so, we miss the active tasks involved, the active conflict in which the child is engaged, and the intrapsychic events which take place in order to solve the problem.

In stressing the intrapsychic work necessary, the psychoanalytic contribution is to see the teacher not simply as a taskmaster. Rather the teacher is seen as someone who initiates in the child those processes by means of which learning and mastery can take place. The child then gravitates between the "I cannot" and the "I can do it very well." He has his ups and downs since he is constantly confronted with new tasks. As long as these tasks are only external tasks, he will meet them in the manner that one bears burdens. If these tasks become internal tasks, however, he will not only meet the tasks but also develop the capacities needed to solve them. The system of external rewards will be replaced by internal gratification. The work for love will turn into the love of work. It is at this point that repetition learning can begin to be replaced by insight learning and the pleasure that is gained from the development of cognitive processes.

Education, then, cannot avoid conflict, nor should it avoid conflict situations. The task grows out of conflict. The task is the child of conflict.

One might well say that the capacity for the solution of tasks grows out of the resolution of conflicts. An inner world without conflict could not lead to growth and mastery.

A systematically defined psychoanalytic learning theory would need to encompass propositions concerning individuation and separation, concerning the resolution of conflict, concerning internalization processes, concerning the parallelism between insight-learning in therapy, and problem-solving in education. This is to name but a few of the processes of development and maturation which are the professional concern of analysts and educators in their common quest.

While Freud said teaching, healing and governing are three impossible professions; he also said, "The voice of the intellect is soft, but it is persistent."

I think that the psychoanalysts and the teachers who are working together at present are united, both in the sense that they have chosen an "impossible" profession, as well as in the sense that they believe in the power of the searching intellect. In this union we are, then, soft but persistent in the pursuit of our "impossible" dedication: serving children through the fields of education and psychotherapy.

Education and Therapy

Walter M. Lifton

Symonds [1] makes the distinction between education and therapy in the following way:

> Education is concerned with helping an individual to adjust to his environment and to form the habits and skills which enable him to do so most effectively. Therapy, on the other hand, is concerned with helping an individual to work out for himself a personal reorganization, and to achieve new points of view, new attitudes, new courage and self-assurance, so that he may find it possible to become educated, that is, to adjust to the situation with which he is faced.

This definition of education seems to hinge on the role of information and skill development. To a degree it suggests dichotomy between mind and body. Perception and behavior are seen as discrete.

Although it is certainly true that the individual who is preoccupied with his own difficulties finds it very hard to consider new ideas, it is equally true that learning appears to take place when the individual is aware of how an idea or skill meets his needs and is relevant to his goals and aims in life.[2, 3, 4, 5] The conditions necessary for a good learning situation appear to be similar for both education and therapy. Both require that the student or client:

1. See a need to achieve something beyond his present status. (Unless a person has some discomfort with his present situation he has no motivation for change.)

2. Is secure enough in the situation to feel able to look at ideas or feelings which are threatening him. (The youngster who can't spell, like the man who feels inadequate, cannot explore his inadequacy in a setting where to admit weakness is to make himself vulnerable.)

3. The setting provides a basis for the person to check the reality of his perception of himself. (Do others see me as I really am, and

Walter M. Lifton, *Working with Groups,* New York: John Wiley & Sons, Inc., 1961.

if they do, what do they think of me? Also, if others see me differently, whose estimate of me is correct?)

4. Based upon a perceived need for new skills in relating or performing, he receives help in discovering (information) new ways of acting.

5. Have an opportunity to rehearse and practice these new skills or ideas until the person feels equally competent in their use to the ones he had before. This practice must be in a setting which is protected so that his mistakes will not hurt him. (The boy who is learning to dance starts with his sister who may tease him, but whom he basically knows is interested in helping him. He then moves on to his sister's girl friend. Only after he feels he has passed the grade here is he ready to consider asking *the* girl for a dance.)

Group Dynamics. Dissension about the definition of group process also has come from representatives of the group-dynamics movement who object to classifying every attempt to change attitudes in an educational setting as "group therapy." The point has been made in numerous studies [6, 7, 8, 9] that it is important to differentiate therapy groups from "problem solving" and "action" groups. The significance of this distinction is registered in the observations by researchers in those studies, focused toward therapy and using the group-dynamics devices of process-observer and the like, that the presence of a non-participating, judgmental person limits the security that individuals need in a therapeutic situation before they can afford to face the threat within them.

One solution to the semantic difficulties involved in distinctions between "group dynamics" and "group therapy" might be to reserve the former term for those processes employed to assist a group to achieve goals outside the group itself. In this setting, the needs of individuals become subservient to the goals of the group.[10] "Group therapy" would then cover those groups which are designed as a means through which people's needs and attitudes could be expressed. The therapy group would serve only as a vehicle for an individual's clarification of his own ideas and values as he tries them out on his peers.

For those who are disturbed by what would appear to be a dilution of differences between the needs of the disturbed individual and the normal person, or between the content needs of our society and its affective needs, it is important that there be a brief discussion of the role of limits. It has been stressed that true learning takes place only when a person feels secure in the setting. One of the first things that any group seeks to discover is the dividing line between what is acceptable and what is not. There are two kinds of limits. Those imposed by society and those internal ones we impose on ourselves. Society has the responsibility continually of determining which of its rules are unyielding and those that require change. The setting in which the group meets, the question of voluntary or forced membership, the societal expectations of the purpose of a group all will influence where the limit is set and how it is interpreted. People need security to see how the group can be useful to them and they to it. The group has the responsibility of setting limits to what it can offer. Some needs ought to be met elsewhere.

A GROUP VERSUS A MASS

For many people any grouping of people carries with it the concept of the loss of individual responsibility and identity. Freud [11] in describing the effect of group behavior on people was particularly concerned with the tendency for people to reinforce in each other the needs of an antisocial nature that could be expressed since a person's identity in a group was lost from view. This concept is not unlike that which we see in a lynch mob. The concept of a "group mind" as a unique entity that is the sum of the people involved but responsible to no one certainly has not become obsolete in popular thinking.

The definition of the characteristics of a group described by Loeser [12] is of interest in the light of our desire in some way to differentiate the labels we apply to numbers of people. Loeser states that groups have:

1. Dynamic interaction among members.

2. A common goal.

3. A relationship between size and function.

4. Volition and consent.

5. A capacity for self-direction.

Applying these concepts to a group of theatergoers one could possibly find every defined characteristic except the group's capacity for self-direction. As long as they were all reacting on an individual basis to the show they are watching, even if they are aware of other people, they more aptly could be called a crowd or a mass. They do not become a group until there is an awareness of their dependence on each other to accomplish a goal and an acceptance of their responsibility to each other in the process. An educative or therapeutic group demands that there is continual awareness of each person's behavior in the group and the acceptance of each person of responsibility for his own actions. Fundamental in a democracy to the use of any group technique is a concern over the rights and needs of the individual.

There can be little question that group processes such as those employed in the concentration camps can modify behavior and attitudes. When, however, the pressures for achievement need to arise from within each individual, it becomes very relevant that these motivating needs reflect the intrinsic values of each group member as he shares in developing group goals. Within this context, each term describing group techniques has to be considered as it relates to the way it facilitates or hinders individual growth. Within such a context, for example, group guidance is evaluated in terms of the conditions under which people develop the need for information and the environment which best facilitates the incorporation of the desired information.

THE GROUP DYNAMIC APPROACH

The articles and research in the area of group process reflect ideas about alternative roles available to members of a group. One body of publications seems to be focused primarily on how to help groups become more effective in achieving their goals.[13] This pragmatic orientation partially reflects the feeling that for democracy to prove its worth it must do so by demonstrating the results of group effort. For many, the yardstick becomes the speed with which a group achieves a goal external to the group. An illustration of this kind of concern can be seen in the writings of such people as Benne and Sheats.[14] The following table is an adaptation of the concept of group roles developed by them.

MEMBER ROLES IN GROUPS ATTEMPTING TO IDENTIFY,
SELECT, AND SOLVE COMMON PROBLEMS

A. Group Task Roles. Facilitation and coordination of group problem solving activities.

1. *Initiator contributor.* Offers new ideas or changed ways of regarding group problem or goal. Suggests solutions. How to handle group difficulty. New procedure for group. New organization for group.
2. *Information seeker.* Seeks clarification of suggestions in terms of factual adequacy and/or authoritative information and pertinent facts.
3. *Opinion seeker.* Seeks clarification of values pertinent to what group is undertaking or values involved in suggestions made.
4. *Information giver.* Offers facts or generalizations which are "authoritative" or relates own experience *pertinently* to group problem.
5. *Opinion giver.* States belief or opinion pertinently to suggestions. Emphasis on his proposal of what should become group's views of pertinent values.
6. *Elaborator.* Gives examples or develops meanings, offers rationale for suggestions made before, and tries to deduce how ideas might work out.

7. *Coordinator.* Clarifies relationships among ideas and suggestions, pulls ideas and suggestions together, or tries to coordinate activities of members of sub-groups.

8. *Orienter.* Defines position of group with respect to goals. Summarizes. Shows departures from agreed directions or goals. Questions direction of discussion.

9. *Evaluator.* Subjects accomplishment of group to "standards" of group functioning. May evaluate or question "practicability," "logic," "facts," or "procedure" of a suggestion or of some unit of group discussion.

10. *Energizer.* Prods group to action or decision. Tries to stimulate group to "greater" or "higher quality" activity.

11. *Procedural technician.* Performs routine tasks (distributes materials, etc.) or manipulates objects for group (rearranging chairs, etc.).

12. *Recorder.* Writes down suggestions, group decision, or products of discussion. "Group memory."

B. Group Growing and Vitalizing Roles. Building group-centered attitudes and orientation.

13. *Encourager.* Praises, agrees with, and accepts others' ideas. Indicates warmth and solidarity in his attitude toward members.

14. *Harmonizer.* Mediates intra-group scraps. Relieves tensions.

15. *Compromiser.* Operates from within a conflict in which his idea or position is involved. May yield status, admit error, discipline himself, "come half-way."

16. *Gatekeeper and expediter.* Encourages and facilitates participation of others. Let's hear. . . . Why not limit length of contributions so all can react to problem?

17. *Standard setter or ego ideal.* Expresses standards for group to attempt to achieve in its functioning or applies standards in evaluating the quality of group processes.

18. *Group observer and commentator.* Keeps records of group processes and contributes these data with proposed interpretations into group's evaluation of its own procedures.

19. *Follower.* Goes along somewhat passively. Is friendly audience.

C. Antigroup Roles. Tries to meet felt individual needs at expense of group health rather than through cooperation with group.

20. *Aggressor.* Deflates status of others. Expresses disapproval of values, acts, or feelings of others. Attacks group or problem. Jokes aggressively, shows envy by trying to take credit for other's idea.

21. *Blocker.* Negativistic. Stubbornly and unreasoningly resistant. Tries to bring back issue group intentionally rejected or by-passed.

22. *Recognition-seeker.* Tries to call attention to himself. May boast, report on personal achievements, and in unusual ways, struggle to prevent being placed in "inferior" position, etc.

23. *Self-confessor.* Uses group to express personal, non-group oriented, "feeling," "insight," "ideology," etc.

24. *Playboy*. Displays lack of involvement in group's work. Actions may take form of cynicism, nonchalance, horseplay, or other more or less studied out of "field behavior."
25. *Dominator*. Tries to assert authority in manipulating group or some individuals in group. May be flattery, assertion of superior status or right to attention, giving of directions authoritatively, interrupting contributions of others, etc.
26. *Help-seeker*. Tries to get "sympathy" response from others through expressions of insecurity, personal confusion or depreciation of himself beyond "reason."
27. *Special interest pleader*. Verbally for "small business man," "grass roots" community, "housewife," "labor," etc. Actually cloaking own prejudices or biases on stereotype which best fits his individual need.

A rapid survey of these labels quickly illustrates that the needs and personalities of the group members are judged by the way they facilitate the rapid movement of the group toward the predetermined goal. Let's see how this type of group might function.

The newspapers announce that there will be a meeting of all citizens interested in helping promote the local bond issue. Mrs. Smith decides that this is just the kind of volunteer work she would like to do. She is tired of being cooped up in the house and aches for someone to talk to. At the meeting that night Mrs. Smith pitches in with enthusiasm. She has found that to understand an idea she must put it in her own words. Since she isn't too clear about the issue, and since she likes to talk, she unwittingly monopolizes the meeting. At the end of the session, the group process observer points up the way in which her behavior slowed down the group. Since Mrs. Smith really wants friends, and since she is concerned over the group goal she sits quietly through the next couple of meetings.

How can we evaluate what happened? The group has exercised control over its members to insure maximum movement. Mrs. Smith has learned what not to do, but no longer knows how to participate since her normal method of functioning brings group disapproval. The group has achieved conformity at the expense of a member's individual growth.

Much of what has been presented so far reflects the philosophy of some members of the "group dynamics" movement. The term Group Dynamics actually covers all studies of group process and group roles.[15] There have been, however, a series of individuals who have developed techniques which they feel provide optimum group control for efficient problem solving. These techniques have been popularly labeled as the group dynamics approach. There is one other basic concept associated with this group. Stated simply it would be that man, through the use of logic and cognitive processes, can alter his behavior. Feelings and needs are subordinate.

THE COMMON DENOMINATORS

Common in most therapeutic groups is the feeling that basic to the development of any meaningful decisions or changes in behavior is the awareness and acceptance by group members of the needs or feelings which motivate their actions. Although groups may differ in the techniques they employ to facilitate self-understanding, all would accept the following concepts.

1. People need security in the group before they can afford to look at the underlying bases for their actions.

2. Topics form the basis for the group to pull together, but it is a vehicle rather than an end in itself. Therefore "digressions" are not seen as such, but rather an attempt is made to see what need the new topic is representing, and how it relates to the one it followed.

3. The group strives to put across the feeling which indicates a continued acceptance of the individual despite possible rejection of his behavior or idea. This concept reflects the epitome of the successful group. When group members can feel the continued interest and concern in them as people and not feel rejected when others disagree with their idea, the group has achieved the kind of security which maximizes spontaneity and puts the premium on individual difference. Jung [16] has stated the basic concept here in clear terms:

I fully approve of the integration of the individual into society. However, I want to defend the inalienable rights of the individual; for individuality alone is the bearer of life and is, in these times, gravely threatened by degradation. Even in the smallest group the individual is acceptable only if he appears acceptable to the majority. He has to be content with toleration. But mere toleration does not improve the individual; on the contrary, toleration causes a sense of insecurity, by which the lonely individual who has something to champion may be seriously hindered. Without intrinsic value social relations have no importance.

4. The group is a place to test the reality of an idea and it is the role of the leader or other members to react honestly.

5. Group members will present their feelings not only through the words they use but also by physical behavior.

6. The more a member participates in a group the more he gets out of it.

7. The group is strengthened by recognizing individual differences rather than merely focusing on the bases of similarity or consensus.

8. People react in terms of their present perception of a situation. This perception, however, is based on past experiences. To the degree that present perceptions can be related to the past, it is possible for the person to determine if he wishes to continue in the same direction for the future.

These are but a few of the common denominators to be found among groups that see the major reason for group life as being the means for most effectively recognizing and gratifying the needs of the individual. Like it or not, none of us lives in a vacuum. The ultimate lesson we have to learn is that we can find ourselves only as we relate to others.

RESTATEMENT OF THE PHILOSOPHY
EXPRESSED IN THE TEXT

It should be clear that my philosophy is biased toward describing personality as an ever-changing thing and holding that in dealing with an individual it is impossible to divide your relationship into levels. Accordingly, it is possible to use terms like teaching, counseling, or psychotherapy interchangeably without doing violence to the kinds of relationships that need to be developed in a group to achieve the goal of individual growth.[17] With this point of view it is possisble to draw from both the fields of education and psychology in our attempts to explore the problems and skills associated with group leadership skills.

The values I use as a counselor place me squarely in the camp of those who take a phenomenological and client-centered point of view. The following hypotheses about the nature of personality and way to achieve behavior change represent my theoretical position.

1. To help people we need to start with their perception of a situation.

2. Help is most useful if it is initially directed toward the problem causing an individual (or group) the most immediate concern.

3. Individuals (groups) have an innate capacity to heal themselves, if they are provided a setting where they can feel secure enough to examine their problems.

4. As an individual (group) is helped to feel more secure, his need to shut out unwanted bits of information decreases. As he broadens his perception of the problem he must by necessity include the

values and attitudes expressed by society. Particularly in a group setting, this means that the solution to a problem although it starts out as egocentric, must ultimately resolve the paradox that man can only get his needs met through others. The following sequence may explain this concept.

I want you to meet my needs.

For you to be willing to do so, I must give you
a reason for doing so.

It therefore follows that I can only meet my needs
after I have first considered yours.

I have learned then that I can start out being
as selfish as I like, but I cannot achieve
my goal without considering how others will respond.

5. A change in any part of an individual's life affects all other aspects of his being. A new perception today can cause all past experiences to have a new and different meaning.

Certainly these assumptions are not original. As indicated earlier they can be traced back to the words of such people as Rogers, Wertheimer, Rank, Taft, Bergson, and Rousseau.

Since any belief is manifest only by the way it employs tools and techniques, the following chapter will consider just how people can be helped in group situations.

DISCUSSION

This chapter provided many ethical and philosophical concepts worthy of further study. For the reader who is intrigued by the question of the appropriate role of the therapist or educator in our society, two books are especially recommended. Both Lindner's *Prescription For Rebellion* [18] and DeGrazia's *Common Errors in Psychotherapy* [19] will force you to examine your own beliefs.

If you find yourself somewhat confused by the brief survey of psychological theories, reading *Individual Behavior* by Snygg and Combs [20] will be helpful. Some may be disappointed by the absence of any specific discussion of learning theory. Its absence is not due to any question of the technical help learning theory has offered to practitioners. As a philosophy, however, except for the Pavlovian mechanistic approach to people, learning theory has made its greatest contribution when it has been used to explain phenomena within differing psychological systems. The symposium by Shoben,[21] Shaw,[22] and Combs [23] as well as the works of Dollard and Miller [24] provide examples of how these relationships are conceived from different frames of reference.

The question of where education ends and where therapy begins is highly controversial. An entire issue of *Progressive Education* (May 1955) has been devoted to this topic. Included are articles by philosophers, psychiatrists, group workers, educators, and psychologists. Also in this area, and presenting differing points of view, is the Volume VII, January 1957, No. I issue of the *International Journal of Group Psychotherapy* covering Group Dynamics and Group Psychotherapy.

Although not discussed in this chapter, the question of the need for adopting a theoretical position rather than developing a smorgasbord of techniques conveniently labeled an eclectic approach, deserves the careful attention of the serious student in the area. To help in an understanding of the difference between a philosophical stand which reflects personal consistency rather than rigidity, Carl Rogers' *Client-Centered Therapy* is highly recommended.[25] On the question of a philosophical eclecticism, the article the author wrote in *Occupations* (now the *Personnel and Guidance Journal*) entitled "A Reply to a Plague on Both Your Houses," [26] may amplify why eclecticism of philosophies is considered impossible.

Common to both of the last two references is the work by Lecky on the importance of self-consistency. Also helpful is the discussion by Corsini [27] on the relationship of a leader's personality and the methods he will employ.

For teachers, Arthur T. Jersild's *When Teachers Face Themselves* [28] carries out the same themes in the classroom setting.

A good historical summary of writings defining group work, group therapy, and group organization can be found in a book of readings edited by Dorothea F. Sullivan entitled *Readings in Group Work*.[29] It contains articles printed in a journal entitled *The Group* which is now out of print (New York Associated Press, 1952).

Particular violence was done in the extremely brief presentation of the activities of members of the group dynamics movement. It is suggested that the more mature reader will enjoy browsing through *Group Dynamics* by Dorwin Cartwright and Alvin Zander.[30] This book and *Dynamics of Groups at Work* by Herbert Thelen,[31] present excellent descriptions of the philosophy and techniques employed by people operating from that theoretical position.

BIBLIOGRAPHY

1. SYMONDS, PERCIVAL. "Supervision as Counseling." *Teachers College Record,* Vol. 43, 49–56, October 1941.

2. ALPERT, A. "Education as Therapy." *Psychoanal. Quart.*, **10**, 469–474, 1941.

3. BARUCH, DOROTHY W. "Therapeutic Procedures as Part of the Educative Process." *J. consult. Psychol.*, **4**, 165–172, 1940.

4. OJEMANN, RALPH. "Basic Approaches to Mental Health: The Human Relations Program at the State University of Iowa." *Pers. & Guid. J.*, Vol. XXXVII, No. 3, 199–206, November 1958.

5. ZLATCHIN, PHILIP. "Round Table: Education and Psychotherapy." *Amer. J. Orthopsychiat.*, Vol. XXIV, No. 1, 133–140, January 1954.

6. GORDON, IRA J. "The Class as a Group: The Teacher as Leader—Some Comments and Questions." *Educational Administration and Supervision*, **37**, 108–118, February 1951.

7. GORDON, IRA J. *The Creation of an Effective Faculty Adviser Training Program Through Group Procedures.* New York: Teachers College, Columbia University, November 1950, 224 p. (Doctor's thesis).

8. PEPINSKY, HAROLD B. "An Experimental Approach to Group Therapy in a Counseling Center." *Occupations*, **28**, 35–40, October 1949.

9. TROW, WILLIAM C., and others. "Psychology of Group Behavior: The Class as a Group." *J. educ. Psychol.*, **41**, 322–338, October 1950.

10. HERROLD, KENNETH F. "Evaluation and Research in Group Dynamics." *Educ. psychol. Measmt.*, **10**, 492–504, Autumn 1950 (Part II).

11. FREUD, S. *Group Psychology and the Analysis of the Ego.* London: International Psychoanalytic Press, 1922.

12. LOESER, LEWIS. *Intern. J. Group Psychother.*, Vol. VII, No. 1, 5–19, January 1957.

13. LIPPITT, RONALD, KENNETH BENNE, and LELAND BRADFORD. "The Promise of Group Dynamics for Education." *J. Nat. Educ. Assoc.*, **37**, 350–352, 1948.

14. BENNE, KENNETH, and P. SHEATS. "Functional Roles of Group Members." *J. soc. Issues*, Vol. 4, **2**, 42–47, Spring 1948.

15. JENKINS, DAVID H. "What Is Group Dynamics?" *Adult Educ. J.*, **9**, 2, 54–60, 1950.

16. ILLING, H. A. "C. G. Jung on the Present Trends in Group Psychotherapy." *Human Relations*, **10**, 77–84, 1957.

17. *Journal of the National Association of Deans of Women.* "Counseling and Group Work," Vol. X, No. 3, 99–124, March 1947.

18. LINDNER, ROBERT. *Prescription for Rebellion.* New York: Rinehart, 1952.

19. DEGRAZIA, SEBASTIAN. *Errors in Psychotherapy and Religion.* Garden City, New York: Doubleday, 1952.

20. SNYGG, DONALD, and ARTHUR COMBS. *Individual Behavior.* New York: Harper, Revised Edition, 1958.

21. SHOBEN, EDWARD J. "Counseling and the Learning of Integrative Behavior." *J. counsel Psychol.,* Vol. 1, No. 1, 42–48, Winter 1954.

22. SHAW, FRANKLIN J. "Counseling from the Standpoint of an 'Interactive Conceptualist.' " *J. counsel. Psychol.,* Vol. 1, No. 1, 36–42, Winter 1954.

23. COMBS, ARTHUR W. "Counseling as a Learning Process." *J. counsel. Psychol.,* Vol. 1, No. 1, 31–36, Winter 1954.

24. DOLLARD, JOHN, and NEAL E. MILLER. *Personality and Psychotherapy.* New York: McGraw-Hill, 1950.

25. ROGERS, CARL. *Client-Centered Therapy.* Boston: Houghton Mifflin, 1951, p. 9.

26. LIFTON, WALTER M. "A Reply to a Plague on Both Your Houses." *Occupations,* Vol. XXX, No. 6, 434–437, March 1952.

27. CORSINI, RAYMOND. *Methods of Group Psychotherapy.* New York: McGraw-Hill, 1957, pp. 125–127.

28. JERSILD, ARTHUR. *When Teachers Face Themselves.* New York: Bureau of Publications, Teachers College, Columbia University, 1955.

29. SULLIVAN, DOROTHEA F. *Readings in Group Work.* New York: Association Press, 1952.

30. CARTWRIGHT, DORWIN, and ALVIN ZANDER. *Group Dynamics.* Evanston, Illinois: Row Peterson, 1956.

31. THELEN, HERBERT. *Dynamics of Groups at Work.* Chicago: University of Chicago Press, 1954.

Teaching Emotional Education in the Classroom

Albert Ellis

For the last fifteen years or so I have been a teacher of sorts, for I am a very busy psychotherapist, and during this time I have given individualized remedial instruction—or what I call emotional education—to several thousand adults, perhaps a thousand adolescents, and a few hundred children. In addition, I have done group therapy—which is somewhat closer to classroom teaching than is individualized therapy—with another couple of thousand adults and adolescents. My group therapy clients, in fact, frequently refer to their "class" instead of to their "group," and they are not entirely wrong about this terminology.

I am, in other words, very frankly and consciously a philosophic or educational therapist. I have written and said on many occasions that the system I use and train others to use, rational-emotive psychotherapy, is uniquely didactic, cognition-oriented, and explicative. Perhaps more importantly than anything else, it teaches people to use the scientific method in their own lives just as they might tend to use it in one of the physical or social sciences. Like classroom instruction, it is designed to be a highly active-directive method and it makes notable use of specific homework assignments, and checkups during the therapeutic sessions on these assignments, for almost all the clients who are involved in it (Ellis, 1957, 1962, 1966).

One of the main aspects of rational-emotive therapy, moreover, is its frequent emphasis on teaching parents how to deal effectively with the emotional problems of their children and how to educate these children to live more comfortably with themselves. When I first started to use this form of treatment—which is called RET for short—with adults, I found that many of them, with or without my connivance, began to employ it with their own children, and often the results were quick and astounding. I also

Albert Ellis, "Teaching Emotional Education in the Classroom," *School Health Review,* November 1969, pp. 10–13.

found that many of my clients who were teachers and counselors began to use RET with children in grade schools, day camps, athletic teams, activity clubs, boy scout groups, Sunday schools, and various other kinds of young people's groups and classes. And again the results were frequently most gratifying.

At the same time, my associates and I at the Institute for Advanced Study in Rational Psychotherapy and at our branches in other parts of the country began to see children in individual therapy sessions and in group sessions, in our regular offices, in school systems, in homes for retarded and disturbed individuals, and in other settings. As a result of our collective experience in these respects, we thought that the time had arrived to give a regular workshop in "Teaching Children How to Think Clearly About Themselves and the World," and so we gave the first of these workshops in October 1966. Penelope Pollaczek, an experienced school psychologist and instructor in educational psychology, and I led the initial workshop series, and more than sixty individuals, the great majority of them teachers in the New York City public schools, attended various sessions of it and seemed to be most absorbed in its presentations.

Instead of lecturing on the principles of rational-emotive psychotherapy and how they could be used in classroom situations, Dr. Pollaczek and I asked the assembled teachers and counselors to bring up specific emotional problems of their pupils and counselees; by the use of role-playing, discussion, tape recording, and other methods, we showed them how these problems could be handled. Within a few weeks of the inception of the seminars, the teachers began to report back to the workshop group that they were actually using rational-emotive principles in regular classroom situations and that in most instances they were achieving surprisingly good results.

What we basically taught the teachers, during the workshop sessions, was that if a child is upset in the course of a classroom situation, he is invariably disturbed at point C not because of what happens to him at point A (such as his failing to recite well or another child's acting nastily toward him) but because of the philosophic assumptions he consciously or (usually) unconsciously makes at point B *about* what is happening at point A. At point B, he almost always, when he *feels* anxious or hostile or when he *acts* in a self-defeating manner, is signaling himself two meanings or attitudes: B-1, which is sane, and B-2, which is insane.

Thus, if eight-year-old Robert is so anxious that he cannot recite well in class, even though he obviously knows what the lesson is about, he is being forced, at point A, to recite and he is feeling, at point C, shame, blocking, numbness, or depression. At point B-1 he is usually telling himself the sane belief: "It would be unfortunate if I did not recite well, for then everyone would think I do not know my lesson and perhaps view me as a dunce. I certainly wouldn't like that!" This appropriate B-1 observation and conclusion normally induces him to have the equally appropriate C-1 feelings of concern about failing or of regret, displeasure, and frustration if he does fail.

At point B-2, however, Robert is usually *additionally* and irrationally convincing himself: "It would be absolutely awful if I failed. No one would like me at all, and I would therefore be a worthless slob!" This catastrophizing, overgeneralized conviction causes him to have, at point C-2, the inappropriate and self-sabotaging emotions of great anxiety, shame, and despair. Then, when he feels these inappropriate (and self-induced) reactions, he normally is so distracted and upset by them that he functions even more poorly at point A, and a vicious circle of poor behavior, catastrophizing conclusions, and increased poor behavior results.

Robert's teacher, Dr. Pollaczek, and I showed in the course of our workshop presentations, this self-negating and inefficiency producing process can be interrupted by asking Robert, immediately after he refuses to recite or recites badly, "What do you feel right now? What emotions are you experiencing? What are you telling yourself in order to create these emotions? Can you see the difference between telling yourself that it is unfortunate and that it is catastrophic to fail? How does giving a poor recitation make you, a total and very complex human being, a complete slob? Would your friend, Jimmy, be totally worthless if he failed to recite well? Where is the evidence that because you failed this time, you will *always* fail in similar situations? How do you know that everyone in the class will think you a dunce just because you don't recite too well at times?"

By asking these kinds of questions, and forcing Robert to think about his thinking and to understand exactly how and why he upsets himself when he may do, or actually does, poorly, the teacher can teach him a more scientific, more objective way of looking at himself. What is more, whether Robert learns this lesson or not, and thereby starts to become emotionally educated, other children in the class, who are listening to what is going on between him and the teacher, and who themselves are not likely to be too upset at this time, may well begin to learn it. As in other classroom situations, moreover, the teacher can involve the other children in solving Robert's problem. Thus, he can say: "Since Robert does not yet seem to see what he is telling himself in order to upset himself over reciting, who else thinks that he sees what Robert is saying to himself?" And: "Robert seems to think that all of you think he is a dunce for reciting poorly. Is that what all of you really think?" And: "If you, Marilyn, recited just as poorly as Robert did right now, what would you think of yourself? Would you think that you would always do just as badly in similar situation?"

Another common disturbance which arises in classrooms is a situation involving hostility, temper, or unmitigated rage. The workshop sessions showed how to deal with these problems, following a similar pattern. The teachers understood the principles that Dr. Pollaczek and I were trying to get over, and many of them made a serious effort to apply them in typical classroom situations (see the example below of emotional education in the classroom as reported by a workshop participant).

Now, two and a half years later, some of them are still in touch with me and have reported that they are continuing to apply rational-emotive principles in the classroom—in public, private, and parochial schools—and that they are often getting remarkably good results. Since that time, Dr. Pollaczek and I have taught these principles to other teachers, in her classes at the New School and New York University and in my workshops and seminars at the Institute for Advanced Study in Rational Psychotherapy in New York City, and we have had similar positive feedback in many instances.

> A teacher reported that one of her fifth-grade pupils, Jonathan, kept having fits of temper whenever he was thwarted and frequently threw objects around the classroom. We role-played this situation with her and showed her how, in all probability, Jonathan was falsely connecting A with C—was convincing himself that *because* he was thwarted at point A he "naturally" had a fit of temper at point C, and that he could not very well stop acting in that "natural" manner. Actually, B-1 and B-2 were the real "causes" of Jonathan's behavior. After the workshop session, the teacher attempted to apply the principle to Jonathan's behavior. She reported the results as follows: On one occasion Jonathan became very angry and punched another boy, Bill, because Bill blocked his way to the coatroom and prevented him from being the first one out of the class at lunchtime, as he usually managed to be. When the class returned from lunch, and the teacher asked Jonathan why he had punched Bill, he replied, "Bill made me very angry by blocking my way to the coatroom and making me late to lunch." "Oh, no," the teacher insisted, "this wasn't exactly what happened. Let's assume that Bill really did, for no good reason, block your way to the coatroom, and that you were therefore late to lunch. That's point A. And your getting angry and punching Bill is point C. But what did you tell yourself, at points B-1 and B-2, to cause yourself to get angry at Bill?"
>
> "I dunno," Jonathan insisted. "I didn't tell myself anything. I just got angry."
>
> "That's impossible," said the teacher. "We *just* don't do anything or feel anything. *First* we tell ourselves something—*then* we get angry. Now what do you think you told yourself, a split-second before you became—or, rather, made yourself—angry at Bill?"
>
> "Nothing," said Jonathan. "I just *did* get angry."
>
> "What do you think he told himself, Bill?" asked the teacher.

"Oh, I dunno. I guess he told himself that I was no good and deserved to be punched," Bill replied.

"Yes, something like that," said the teacher. "But something a little more specific, too. What do you think that was?"

Bill didn't know, or thought he didn't know. Sally, another member of the class, finally said: "I think that Jonathan told himself that Bill had no right to block his way to the coatroom; that Bill *shouldn't* have done an unfair thing like that."

"Yes," said the teacher. "That's probably what Jonathan told himself at point B-2. But what did he first tell himself at B-1?"

No one seemed to know. So the teacher said: "Well, didn't he probably tell himself, quite appropriately, at B-1: 'Bill blocked my way, for apparently no good reason; and that made me late to lunch. And *I don't like* being late to lunch; I *prefer* to be the first one downstairs. And therefore I think that Bill is unfair and wrong and I wish he weren't that way.' Isn't that what Jonathan probably told himself, or something like this, at point B-1?"

"Yes," said Jonathan. "That's *exactly* what I said to myself! For *I don't like* being even second or third down the stairs to lunch. I *do* want to be the first on line and the first to sit down at the lunch-table, so that I can get my favorite seat at the head of the table. And Bill has *no right* to block my way like he did, and make me late like that. Why, actually I was practically the last one to lunch, because of his unfairly blocking me!"

"Yes," said the teacher. But now you're going on to B-2 again. Let's first stick to B-1 and get that perfectly clear. At B-1 you very appropriately told yourself, as you have just said, 'I *don't like being* even second or third down the stairs to lunch. I *do* want to be the first on line and the first to sit down at the lunch-table, so that I can get my favorite seat at the head of the table. And now Bill is blocking my way, so that I won't be first on line. And that is————.' What is that?"

"That is terrible!" said Jonathan.

"No," said the teacher. "There you go running on to B-2 again. At B-1 you surely told yourself something milder than 'that is terrible!' What do you think you said at B-1?"

"I don't know," replied Jonathan. "I think I immediately said, 'That is terrible!'"

"No," Sally spoke up again. "I think you first said, at B-1, 'that is bad. I don't like what Bill is doing! I wish he weren't blocking me, like he is, so that I could be first on the lunch line.'"

"Well, isn't that the same thing?" asked Jonathan.

"No," said Sally. "It's not the same thing at all! 'I don't like what Billy is doing. I wish he weren't blocking me!' is a lot different from

'This is terrible! I *can't stand* what he is doing to me!' Can't you see the difference?"

"No," replied Jonathan. "Aren't the two the same, really? Aren't you quibbling? If I don't like what Billy is doing to me, then I *can't* stand it. It *is* terrible!"

"Why is it terrible?" asked Sally.

"Yes," said Bill. *"Why* can't you stand my blocking you? Even if I am wrong, and I'm unfairly keeping you from being first on the lunch line, why can't you stand being second or third or even last?"

"Obviously," said the teacher, "you *can* stand it. Since you actually were, you said before, practically last on the lunch line, and you're still here, aren't you? You didn't *die* from being last. You actually ate lunch, didn't you?"

"Yes," smiled Sally. "And as far as I can see, you ate more than usual, enjoyed eating it, and finally had a good time talking to the rest of us at lunch!"

"Yes," admitted Jonathan, finally smiling himself. "I guess I did. I guess I did stand it. I didn't *like* it; but I did *stand* it."

"Exactly!" the teacher pointed out. "Now do you clearly see the difference between B-1, 'I don't *like* Billy's blocking me. I *wish* he wouldn't!' And B-2: 'I can't *stand* his blocking me. That's terrible!'?"

"Yes," said Jonathan, a bit sheepishly. "I guess I can see the difference now. It didn't kill me to be almost the last on the lunch line. I still managed to enjoy eating and talking at lunch."

"Yes, you did," said the teacher. "And you normally can—if you don't insist that you can't stand it. "But I can see that you're now a little ashamed of your behavior, of thinking that you couldn't stand it, and of hitting Bill. Is that right?"

"I am definitely ashamed of being such a baby."

"Because you're telling yourself what, at B-1, about your hitting Bill?"

"I guess I'm telling myself that 'I was wrong to make myself so angry and to hit Bill, even though Bill was wrong to block my way, like he did, to the coatroom."

"Yes," said the teacher, "you're telling yourself, at B-1, 'I wish Bill hadn't blocked my way unfairly. But I didn't *have* to get angry at him and punch him.' And what are you telling yourself at B-2, to make yourself ashamed?"

"I dunno," said Jonathan.

"But you *do* know," Sally interposed. "I'm sure you do know. For the rest of us know, and you can know, too, if you look for your B-2 sentences.'

"Yes, I guess I do know," said Jonathan. "I guess I'm not looking at it closely enough. I guess I was telling myself, 'Isn't it *terrible* that I lost my temper at Bill, like I did. I *shouldn't* have been such a baby!' "

"Right," said the teacher. And you could change that B-2 thought, instead, to what?"

"I guess I could change it to, 'I was wrong to lose my temper at Bill. But I guess it wasn't so terrible. And next time I can try to see that Billy's blocking my way is unfair but that I can stand it, even if it does make me late to the lunch room, and that if I lose my temper toward him, I'm not so terrible a person for making this kind of mistake.'

This handling of Jonathan's anger and shame by the teacher, and her showing him and the rest of the class exactly what was going on in his head and how he could understand his own reactions and change them in the future, is a little too idealized. It is most probable that her task of emotionally educating her pupils didn't quite work out in this ideal manner (perhaps she reported the incident to the workshop too patly). But it did seem quite clear that the teacher understood the principle and was sincerely attempting to apply it in a classroom situation.

From this kind of experience, as well as with other experiences in showing parents, counselors, and other individuals who have close contacts with children how to handle the behavior problems of these youngsters, I have come to the conclusion that one of the best methods of evaluating a system of psychotherapy is to determine its effectiveness outside the usual kind of therapeutic relationship. For if a given system can only be applied to a small number of seriously disturbed people, and particularly to adults, who honestly admit that they have problems and are willing to come for steady treatment, it is indeed of limited scope and usefulness; while if it can be applied to great numbers of individuals, including children in the regular classroom situation, it will be much more valid and valuable.

The use of psychotherapeutic methods and application in educational situations is hardly new. Aichhorn (1955) and Freud and Burlingham (1943) used Freudian methods with children in the 1920's and 1930's; and the Adlerians (Adler, 1927, 1931; Adler and Deutsch, 1959; Dreikurs, 1950) have pioneered in emotional education since the inception of individual psychology in the first part of the twentieth century. More recently, Bessell (1969), Glasser (1969), and Leonard (1969) have been among the many innovators who have adapted various kinds of therapy techniques to classroom situations.

Which of these older or newer therapeutic applications will tend to become popular in educational circles is still in doubt. It does appear, however, that the use of rational-emotive principles of emotional education is quite practical in the classroom. J. Clayton Lafferty pioneered in using this approach, in the early 1960's, with fourth-grade students in the Dearborn, Michigan, schools, and, more recently, Lewis I. Raimist and his associates in the Diagnostic and Resource Teacher Program in three school systems in northern Virginia have been doing extensive experiments using a closely allied approach. As noted in this paper, a good number of individual teachers, many of them trained by Dr. Penelope Pollaczek, and by me, have been employing rational-emotive methods in various kinds of classroom situations for the past several years. Much more research and experimentation should be done, but the indications already are that emotional education is possible, both in a prophylactic and therapeutic manner, in regular school systems and that this kind of teaching is probably just as important as the conventional academic training.

REFERENCES

ADLER, A. *Understanding Human Nature*. New York: Garden City, 1927.

ADLER, A. *What Life Should Mean to You*. New York: Blue Ribbon, 1931.

ADLER, K. A. and DEUTSCH, D. *Essays in Individual Psychology*. New York: Grove Press, 1959.

AICHHORN, A. *Wayward Youth*. New York: Meridian Books, 1955.

BESSELL, H. Emotional Education for Children. Workshop at Esalen Institute, San Francisco, July 14–17, 1969.

DREIKURS, R. *Fundamentals of Adlerian Psychology*. New York: Greenberg, 1950.

ELLIS, A. *How to Live with a Neurotic*. New York: Crown Publishers, 1957.

ELLIS, A. *Reason and Emotion in Psychotherapy*. New York: Lyle Stuart, Inc., 1962.

ELLIS, A. *How to Prevent Your Child from Becoming a Neurotic Adult*. New York: Crown Publishers, 1966.

FREUD, A., and BURLINGHAM, D. T. *War and Children*. New York: Medical War Books, 1943.

GLASSER, W. *Schools Without Failure*. New York: Harper and Row, 1969.

LEONARD, G. *Education and Ecstasy*. New York: Macmillan, 1969.

4 / Sensitivity Education: Problems and Promise

In the midst of our current preoccupation with objective, mechanistic, cognitive, computerized education, it is good to know there are some who are deeply concerned with the human questions. The present curriculum scene is a depressing one for the humanist, and it is, therefore, reassuring to know that some persons are actively experimenting with humanizing innovations. Sensitivity education may not provide us final answers, but out of experiments with it will come new perspectives which cannot help but advance our understanding of the human aspects of curriculum development.

—*Arthur W. Combs*

Confrontation Techniques—
A Two-Sided Coin

Leonard Blank

COMMENTARY

Recently, there was a cartoon of two ladies sitting under hair driers. One remarked to the other, "I don't know what I'm getting out of my group but I certainly have got the goods on a lot of people." In other words, group techniques may have their disadvantages as well as advantages.

Basic encounters, marathons, and sensitivity or interactional training are confrontation techniques that are capable of mobilizing powerful inter- and intrapersonal forces in a most constructive manner. Moreover, these techniques are not restricted to patients or even clients but are available to any segment of the population—to people and people issues.

THE NEGATIVE SIDE OF THE COIN

There is, however, another side to the coin. That side reflects the misuse and abuse of interactional processes. We shall consider the equivocal training of many group leaders; the questionable objectives of participants, as well as those who guide them; the problems of cultism and the buckshot application of group techniques; and the misapplication of these techniques.

There is a vast and hungry demand for human interaction nowadays in education, government, industry, religion, and other organizations, not to mention legions of "unaffiliated" persons. Where there is marked demand, supply usually rises to meet it—even if the quality suffers. So we witness the phenomenon of large numbers of newly self-anointed group leaders, trainers, and encounter facilitators or guides. These "experts" often may have been baptized by participating in a one- or two-week training laboratory, having a week-end encounter experience, visiting Esalen, or reading *Joy* or the writings of Perls, Rogers, Maslow, *et al.* And they have decided that this work is more fulfilling and humanizing than accounting, personnel work, ministerial duties, or experimental psychology. They have seen the light and tasted the joys and poignancies of human interaction; so why shouldn't they lead and inspire others along these routes?

Perhaps more sophisticated is the diverse and amorphous group lumped together under the rubric of behavioral scientist and the helping professions. This includes, but does not exhaust, such occupations as sociologists, social psychologists, physicians, nurses, speech pathologists, rehabilitation workers, industrial relations managers, and management consultants. It is questionable whether the expertise of these specialists, which ranges from study of laboratory group process to enhancing increased business production, is suitable for the clinical and interpersonal and intrapersonal phenomena that are stimulated in encounter and interactional groups. More about this when we consider objectives.

There is question, as well, about the efficacy of the clinician who thinks in terms of a traditional medical model—the psychiatrist, clinical psychologist, social worker, psychiatric nurse, counselor, individual therapist, or even group therapist. One is reminded of the psychiatrist who accounted for an extremely large number of diagnoses of schizophrenia in the mental hospital at which he worked. The incidence of this diagnosis decreased sharply when he left for a position as a school psychiatrist. Schizophrenia, however, became a quite popular diagnosis at this school. The clinician is rather prone to stress psychopathology and therapy even though this may not be critically indicated or desired. And he will therapize or encourage group participants to therapize because this is what he knows and what gratifies him. The participants will also be gratified because "personal growth" is so desired. Then all will rationalize that great good has been achieved despite forgotten objectives (such as knowledge of group dynamics and interpersonal skills) and uncertain evidence of more-than-transient gains. One thinks of those psychology or sociology books we read to learn something; we soon get seduced by sexual material, intriguing gambits, and exotic case material. They are certainly worth reading for the fun of it, and we might learn a thing or two. But we have been cheated out of our objective of mastering specific knowledge.

In other words, unqualified or irrelevant training for group leaders may waste group effort or aggravate conflict. Now, this is not a brief for training versus perceptiveness, interpersonal skill, and humaneness, which are certainly not the restricted possession of the professional. But relevant training geared toward specific objectives is at least a minimal guarantee that the leader is not working out merely his own needs of filling his loneliness or satisfying his voyeurism, exhibitionism, or desire for power—that he at least recognizes these needs and is channeling them constructively in the service of the individuals who make up the group. Humanists tend to be antibureaucratic (or so it would logically seem), but some form of certification seems in order so as to provide protection for the public and the "science-art" of group leadership. I must hastily add that accreditation also has its drawbacks—certifying bodies or training centers may also become parochial, so that innovativeness is lost. I should think that a multidisciplined, varied-theory approach requires contribution from professional associations, universities, agencies, and impartial consultants.

What are the objectives of the myriad numbers of people who seek group or interactional experience? Some seek to learn about their style of interaction with others and the interpersonal techniques of others. Some want to learn about group process so they can function better in groups or utilize the productive learning and problem-solving powers that groups manifest. Others want to improve their communication or human side of themselves—they look for better human relations, race relations, or very generally personal growth. Many really want psychotherapy whether they appreciate this need or not. (Wise people seek personal growth—patients and sick people seek psychotherapy.) Some are looking for a spiritual, religious, or sensual if not orgiastic experience. A rather large number of people, I think, are searching to fill a void in their lives and many settle for going from one turning-on experience to another with nothing in between. The last group includes many persons who have tried or are still trying drugs, ESP, spiritualism, yoga, Eastern religion, mysticism, and what not.

I personally, believe that any of these objectives is legitimate and respectable. The only trouble is they are not clarified for the seeker or in the group facilitator's mind. Often, the rationale is that the group will work out its objectives once it forms, no matter what the group composition, the training skills, and the tactics of the trainer. It seems to me that the particular chemistry of a group and who and what the leader is and why he wishes to work with a particular group are extremely important. It also seems to me that different objectives require different techniques.

Therefore, screening procedures geared toward specific objectives can prove to be of crucial importance. They are insufficiently employed and what are substituted in some instances are pious rationales, silent prayers that psychotic episodes will be avoided, and the hope that more people will benefit than not. Incidentally, the danger of precipitating a psychotic manifestation tends to be overrated by critics of encounter groups. Nonclinicians, including many behavioral scientists, tend to view raw expression of emotion or vital expression of irrationality as uncontrolled madness. A cohesive group with a skilled leader provides control for these emotional storms to the vast benefit of the individual and the group. There are many ambulatory psychotics who, however, in their quest for human contact, find a group in order to "experience" with people. There is some doubt whether the group's objectives are most furthered by the discrepant needs of these individuals. There are many others who really are very threatened by human interaction or any type of personality uncovering but desperately seek help. Here again, more formal psychotherapy or a more homogeneous group seems indicated. Advertising for participants for training laboratories or encounters led by "Esalen-trained" or "NTL-experienced" leaders in newspapers and indiscriminately distributed brochures seems to be foolish as well as unethical for the very reason of disregard of screening.

The objectives of the newer, less experienced leaders in the encounter fields may also be confounded and contaminated. They know they have hold of a powerful vehicle and, therefore, looking for any substantial theory, believe they can apply interactional techniques to anyone, anywhere, for any reason. So the T group that worked so well for a group of educators or a marathon that clicked for students or patients is transferred lock, stock, and barrel to middle management in a medium company, black-white dialogues and confrontations, clergy, a P-TA meeting, or an American Legion convention. This is a buckshot approach—whoever is hit, fine; whoever doesn't bleed or emote has not responded because he remained out of the line of fire. Smacks of rationalization, doesn't it? (Campbell and Dunnette [1968] in their extensive review of sensitivity training conclude that there is little evidence to support the contention that T groups alter work behavior.)

More dangerously, faddism, cultism, and fanaticism seem to be creeping on the scene. "If you haven't experienced sensitivity training, you'll never know what we are talking about." "You need to enter a marathon to really be able to relate to people or know yourself." "If you don't take an annual trip to Mecca, that is, Bethel or Esalen, you are not really alive." "People will get along together only if they all participate in T groups." I have heard all these statements and even more extreme ones. We know that religion can be very helpful for pople but we also know that religiosity fans conflict, rivalry, and hatred. The same is true of cultism. And a beautiful and powerful experiment—the interactional approach—may be vitiated by breeding irrationalism, unquestioned faith, conflict, and suspicion—the very processes it seeks to counteract.

THE POSITIVE SIDE OF THE COIN

There is considerable interest matched with as much confusion about a variety of group phenomena—encounters, marathons, and sensitivity training, to name several.

Sensitivity training, or T groups, are the most commonly known and most unfortunately named. The term suggests to many an indoctrination or conditioning. In fact, the opposite is intended, for the objective of sensitivity training is the enhancement of self-awareness and awareness of one's relationships to others—the opening up of more options for communication. T groups originated with Kurt Lewin and his fellow social psychologists in New England who were concerned with the democratic process in small groups (Bradford, 1964). It was in New England, of course, that the town meeting became an essential ingredient of our budding democracy. This progenitor of the T group encouraged the frank and free interchange of opinion and attitudes among people concerned with and involved in the democratic process.

Nevertheless, there is a vocal segment of the populace who link sensitivity training and encounter techniques with brainwashing, communism, immoral experimentation, and such. To analyze why there is such polarized interest and criticism, let us consider the context or the psychosocial climate.

Fromm (1945) has discussed the increasing sense of alienation of people in highly industrialized societies. What seems to take place is a clash between two intense human needs—the need for individuality and freedom versus the quest for security. The latter apparently is prevailing for most people.

The mobility in our industrial society and the decline of the working family as a unit have attenuated that social unit and the security associated with it. Job specialization and fierce competition undermine security at work, and complexity of community and national affairs combined with international tensions generates insecurity with respect to one's place in society. When one adds, to the already steaming cauldron, differing and conflicting roles of youth and adult, male and female, white and black, white collar and blue collar, the entire issue of identity becomes shaky (Erikson, 1968).

Therefore, Fromm postulates, people attempt to escape from individuality and freedom because they need reference points and want to be protected and guided. One way to accomplish this is to search for strong leaders, whether benign father figures or stern authoritarians. Another, usually complementary choice is that of concrete symbols. These are oversimplified, distorted versions of flag, church, institutions, politics, cults, and fraternal organizations, but they do provide a sense of unification and belonging. Unfortunately, what is often sacrificed is the meaningful participation of, and respect for, the individual as well as team and group interaction. Yet another, and most pervasive, way of escaping from the threats and *responsibilities* of freedom is to assume rigid roles and insulate oneself from the needs (perceived as demands) of one's fellow man.

It feels dangerous to be too human. Roles must be chosen that minimize this danger by such techniques as:

Keep contacts minimal or at least shallow.
Don't really look at the other (or at least don't see him).
Never touch—unless for sex, to hurt, or to control.
Avoid listening, certainly do not hear (Rollo May, 1969).

Situations or interactions that do not permit such insulating tactics are threatening to people seeking to maintain security. Human relaions, group programs, confrontation experiences, and so on are perceived, therefore, by the threatened as ominous, unpatriotic, irreligious, and whatever other label can be scared up. The result is weak or superficial communication and stereotypic relationships.

A number of influences, however, have emerged to contribute to reaction against personal isolation or, more positively, as a stirring for interpersonal and group closeness.

EGO PSYCHOLOGY

The preponderance of personality theory, from such diverse sources as learning and behavior theory and traditional psychoanalysis, has explained personality as being fixed relatively early in life. The individual, these theories postulate, is conditioned and essentially reacts to his environment (Hilgard and Marquis, 1961). In the last decade or so, however, ego psychology has offered conceptualization and research data to indicate that man is more than reactive. He is adaptive, curious, interested in shaping his environment, and prone to experimentation (White, 1964; McClelland et al., 1953).

EXISTENTIAL THEORY

The popularity of another theory, the existential approach, with youth and intellectuals is also focussed on experimentation. As with ego psychologists, existentialists are concerned with the investigation and opening up of options for enhanced dimensions for living. The emphasis is on the present and the implications of future possibilities rather than on the limitations of the past on one's life (May, 1958).

GESTALT THEORY

Adding to the dimensions of adaptability, experimentation and existential reality, the Gestalt approach emphasizes the whole person, including the significance of the body and "gut" reactions (Perls, 1969). Gestalt concepts have been utilized in academic psychology for many years, but their application in psychotherapy and interpersonal interactions, particularly in combination with such therapeutic theories as Reich's (Reich, 1949), is much more recent. Stress on the body and its language and gestures, ipso facto, emphasizes the immediacy of the moment and validates the merit or distortion of verbal communication.

YOUTH EXPRESSION

Only a few of our youth are acquainted with the theoretic inputs just cited. Nevertheless, the psychosocial climate that seems to be nurturing the interest in these theories appears also to be stimulating the expression of youth in analogous claims: "I want to be me, to experiment in living, to be a person and a whole person—body and mind—and to live in the present." Apparently, there is a revulsion by youth against the impersonalization and dehumanization of huge populations, computerization, automation, and constant threats of bombs, radiation, pollution, and throttling in our own wastes. So a thrust for life and individuality and identity results (Fromm, 1945; May, 1969; Erikson, 1968).

MINORITY PROTEST

Although springing from different sources, the minority and civil-rights movement also is voicing its claim for identity and individuality. There is a commonality of goals and, even in the extreme forms of protest and militancy, shared objectives.

The concatenation of theoretic influences such as ego psychology, existential approach, and Gestalt theory and the struggle of youth and minorities to assert themselves is part of a social ferment. There is an increasing search for contact, communion, and engagement. This search for personal and interpersonal awareness is called *humanism* (Maslow, 1963; Bugental, 1967). The humanistic orientation has appealed to a spectrum of individuals as well as to educational, religious, and industrial organizations.

There has been a proliferation of groups and encounter phenomena to meet this appeal. Some of these situations are wild experimentation and others smack of cultism or fadism. Behavioral science, on the other hand, studies and applies knowledge of interpersonal dynamics and group processes to communication and personal growth. If we designate this area of interest as interactional processes (what the editors of this book have described as encounters in self and interpersonal awareness), the objectives are enhanced interaction and communication, especially sensitization to see, hear, and understand the other fellow in relationship to oneself.

BIBLIOGRAPHY

BRADFORD, L., GIBB, J., and BENNE, K. (eds.) *T-Group Theory and Laboratory Method: Innovation in Re-education.* New York: Wiley, 1964.

BUGENTAL, J. (ed.) *Challenges of Humanistic Psychology.* New York: McGraw-Hill, 1967.

CAMPBELL, J., and DUNNETTE, M. Effectiveness of T-Group Experiences in Managerial Training and Development. *Psychol. Bull.,* **70**:73–92, 1968.

ERIKSON, E. *Identity: Youth and Crisis.* New York: W. W. Norton, 1968.

FROMM, E. *Escape from Freedom.* New York: Farrar & Rinehart, 1945.

HILGARD, E. R., and MARQUIS, D. G. *Conditioning and Learning.* New York: Appleton-Century-Crofts, 1961.

HULL, C., and LINDSEY, G. *Theories of Personality.* New York: Wiley, 1970.

McCELLAND, D., et al. *The Achievement Motive.* New York: Appleton-Century-Crofts, 1953.

MASLOW, A. Fusion of Facts and Values. *Amer. J. Psychoanal.,* **23**:117–31, 1963.

MAY, R. *Existence.* New York: Basic Books, 1958.

MAY, R. *Love and Will.* New York: W. W. Norton, 1969.

PERLS, F. *Gestalt Therapy Verbatim.* Lafayette, Calif.: Real People Press, 1969.

REICH, W. *Character Analysis.* New York: Orgone Institute Press, 1949.

SCHUTZ, W. *Joy.* New York: Grove Press, 1967.

WHITS, R. *The Abnormal Personality,* 3rd ed. New York: Ronald Press, 1964.

Sensitivity Training and Education: A Critique

Clifford H. Edwards

The present popularization of sensitivity training (T-group experiences) and its widespread use by an ever-increasing number of semi-intellectuals and pseudo-professionals have created a need for a closer examination of the field along with its assumptions, practices, and outcomes. Sensitivity training has evolved from an early emphasis on the sociological aspects of group dynamics under the direction of its founders, Leland Bradford, Ronald Lippitt, and Kenneth Benne, to an orientation based more on the psychological.

Recognition of the power of the T-group has led to a high degree of experimentalism. Various applications of the technique have been developed to serve a variety of purposes. The earliest application formulated was designed for organizational development. Here the emphasis was on organizational change rather than personal development of participants. Sociological phenomena were studied while the psychological aspects of group behavior were ignored.

Subsequent to this a second category for sensitivity training became prominent. The major subcategories include encounter groups, marathon labs, and confrontation sessions. These types of training differ significantly from the organizational development application, in that greater stress is placed on the psychological aspects of group dynamics. In the encounter groups, for example, there is a direct exposure of values, beliefs, and feelings. The group is encouraged to operate almost exclusively on an affective basis. Uninhibited exposure of emotions is acceptable, while reserve and defensiveness are discouraged. Complete openness and honesty are the sought-after goals. Marathons differ from encounter groups primarily in terms of intensity of the experience. These sessions

Clifford H. Edwards, "Sensitivity Training and Education: A Critique," *Educational Leadership,* December 1970, pp. 258–61. Reprinted with permission of the Association for Supervision and Curriculum Development and Clifford H. Edwards. Copyright © 1970 by the Association for Supervision and Curriculum Development.

173

go "nonstop" and are designed to literally break through the normal defense patterns of participants as quickly as possible and thus move immediately to new levels of open behavior. Confrontation sessions consist of contrived racial encounters where white and blacks openly confront one another in an attempt to more vividly portray the nature of prejudice and the racial problems which exist. Such confrontations hopefully provide the participants with a more realistic perception of the racial issues and new perspectives in solving them.

More recently a third type of sensitivity training has invaded the field. This kind of training is by far the most experimental and consists primarily of a variety of nonverbal exercises. Techniques range from simple exercises with a minimum of body contact to more intimate associations. The objectives for this type of experience are unclear at best and the supporting theories are of questionable validity. Nevertheless, the technique is in wide use and is increasing in popularity.

Each of the approaches described above has been designed for a specific purpose. However, these purposes are presently being obscured by the experimental attitude of many participants. Currently the engagement of numerous quasi-professionals in the sensitivity training process is discrediting the whole field. These enthusiastic amateurs have discovered that only a minimum amount of experience and knowledge is necessary to stimulate initial responding by participants. They consider one or two T-group experiences or a small repertoire of easily learned exercises to be adequate preparation for the role of trainer. However, in every type of sensitivity training, considerable knowledge and sophistication are required to extract positive outcomes and protect individuals who may be adversely affected by such an experience. This fact serves as an indictment against these self-appointed experts and the gross misrepresentation of skills they perpetrate upon the public.

SENSITIVITY TECHNIQUES FOR SCHOOLS?

Support for sensitivity training was first won in industry primarily for the purpose of humanizing the job relationships between various personnel with the hope that greater productivity would result. Subsequently, social and behavioral scientists devoted various uses for T-groups. More recently education has indicated an interest in using these techniques for solving its multitude of problems. Each of the types of sensitivity training has received some trial in the schools. However, inappropriate identification of objectives and misapplication of techniques have plagued successful application in the school setting. For example, school coworkers who are involved together in the same sensitivity training group, and are thus unable to participate anonymously, often reveal information which deteriorates any future working relationship between them. The same polarization may also be produced when only part of a school staff is "trained" and the training they get alters their behavior sufficiently so that co-workers are aliented by them.

Increased alienation may also be produced between school officials and community members through sensitivity training. For example, insufficient knowledge and experience often render confrontations between school officials and minority groups highly charged and dangerous. Proper management of anxiety levels and degrees of resistance is imperative. The skillful relation of encounter experiences to specific educational problems and issues is also necessary. The trainer not only needs T-group skills but also considerable insight into the educational problems being considered. There is an obvious lack of individuals so prepared.

Nonverbal exercises have also been used to a limited extent in the schools. This usually consists of an unofficial attempt by a teacher to incorporate the "games" he has learned in his own T-group experience into the school curriculum. This is the least rational application of sensitivity training. The educational usefulness of "sensitivity" gained through various forms of quasi-intimate bodily contacts is subject to serious question.

In general, sensitivity training is said to offer several advantages. Foremost among assumed benefits is the sensitizing of an individual to the real feelings, values, and intents of others. Ordinarily, barriers to personal disclosure are developed to protect the tender psyche from attack by real or imagined exterior forces. Being sensitive to the communications of others and able to discern the real from the artificial is an obviously useful skill. However, widespread use of this skill by unsophisticated individuals may be more damaging than helpful. It may, for example, increase rather than decrease the defensiveness of associates. If may also encourage defensive individuals to expose themselves to the "sensitized" person, thinking that they can receive professional assistance from him when in reality they cannot.

A second benefit claimed for sensitivity training is its influence in eliminating defenses and setting the individuals free to be himself. Certainly most human beings may benefit from more openness. Supposedly, greater perceptual acuity and creative expression are made possible for the open individual. Yet we should be careful not to assume from this analysis that all defenses are damaging and should be stripped away. Defenses serve a useful purpose. We use them as a shield to protect ourselves from blunt and possibly harmful confrontations with the environment. Usually, environmental conditions are such that defense development is necessary to maintain a balanced personality.

T-groups ordinarily make no attempt to determine whether the nature of the individual's environmental conditions makes intervention by sensitivity training appropriate. Nor do they make any attempt to ascertain the nature of personal problems among group members that may be beyond the group's power to deal with properly. These groups generally assume that everyone will benefit from reduced defensiveness. The writer believes that a limited set of defenses is health-producing and is basically normal for the human organism. Also, many "defenses" identified by the T-group are in reality self-integrating preferences which contribute to individual identity. These components constitute the uniqueness of the individual and promote self-fulfillment and independent creative activity.

ROLE OF DEFENSES

One of the problems with sensitivity training lies in the way psychological defenses are dealt with by the group. Most frequently the individual with the "problem" is openly attacked. Once his weaknesses are exposed, the group converges on him in an attempt to lay the "problem" completely open. The tragedy is that the individual who has built extensive barricades against his tender psyche has done so out of necessity. The therapeutic tasks is not simply one of tearing away an exterior facade to reveal a healthy personality. It is more accurate to view the barriers as shorings developed to prop up a crumbling personality. Indiscriminate tearing of these defenses is obviously dangerous. If it seems advisable that a person's defenses be reduced, it is best done under the supervision of a trained professional, not in a T-group composed of inexperienced novices. If a highly competent individual is serving as trainer for the group, disaster may be averted; but, in fact, relatively few groups are so equipped.

In a group composed of emotionally mature adults with a competent trainer, certain benefits can be derived from sensitivity training. However, those presently advocating participation by youngsters in this kind of experience are openly courting trouble. Teenagers are usually in the process of developing their value systems. Admittedly they have rudimentary values which influence how they behave, but these values have not as yet been characterized. Nor do they have carefully defined rationales which support their beliefs and with which their behavior patterns can be defended. This leaves the young person defenseless in the face of the conflict developed in the T-group, especially if the attack is led by persons experienced in this kind of confrontation. These individuals frequently succeed in imposing their will upon the group.

The implication played upon is that values which one cannot defend must be worthless and in need of change. Judgments concerning change are ordinarily made in terms of emotional criteria only. Pressure from the group may thus supply adequate leverage to alter values which are rationally superior to those which the group advocates. In their quest to eliminate defenses, many groups do not adequately distinguish between self-disintegrating defenses and highly integrating values. They assault useful values which they assume to be inappropriate defenses. The major consequence is really one of evolving common values, with the more influential group members supplying the direction.

VALUE DEVELOPMENT

Values are developed to enhance personal adequacy and strengthen social identification. They also lend consistency to behavior which makes valid expectations possible in interpersonal associations. Ordinarily value formation occurs in a variety of contexts and prepares the individual for satisfying relationships in many social situations.

In the early stages of value development, criticism by the T-group members of home, family, friends, religion, attitudes, and beliefs produces disillusionment and value disintegration, and encourages acceptance of group values. This limits the extent of successful social relationships and in reality is confining and restricting rather than socially enlarging.

Sometimes the development of values through T-groups is championed because it is claimed that the individual is better able in this environment than in the home to develop his own beliefs in an atmosphere of freedom. It has been pointed out, however, that considerable pressure and coercion can be generated in the T-group as it moves toward acceptable common values. This pressure is particularly potent for youngsters because of their need for peer identification. Because of this need, they more readily succumb to the pressure developed by the group to accept common values. In addition, no topic is excluded from possible debate in the T-group setting. Beliefs long accepted as true by the individual are exposed to cursory examination by the group. Such items as old loyalties, family relationships, and religious convictions become subject to change. The person may then suffer disassociation from parents and others as a consequence of his altered beliefs.

Emotionalism is the mode of operation in almost all sensitivity training groups. Intellectualizing is strictly forbidden. The rational components of values are ignored. Even though this atmosphere provides unlimited exposure to emotion, it has questionable validity in terms of value formation. The stability of reason must always be present in this process because values have to be consistent with the reality against which they interact. The teen-ager who has been exposed to sensitivity training and perhaps persuaded to redefine his value structure still is a member of a family and still is required to interact with other family members. The quality of this association is more likely to deteriorate than be enhanced if values are changed as a consequence of his T-group participation.

In addition to possible interfamilial alienation through discussion of family problems and redefinition of values in sensitivity training, relations in other social contexts can also be jeopardized. It has been pointed out that some participants in T-groups exchange their own personal judgment, values, convictions, and morality for those of the group. Ironically these new values have limited transferability to society at large. Communication skills so gained also have limited usefulness. Intensive training out of a normal social context trains one primarily for association within that group. Outside the group, the individual's style of communication is likely to be ineffective and in some instances even alienative. This is especially true of those groups where the strongest personalities have values divergent from acceptable proprieties or where strong attachments and dependencies are developed.

In summary, sensitivity training may provide useful knowledge and experiences for some people in some situations. It should not, however, be considered as some sort of panacea for solving the various social and educational problems in our society. Too many critical questions are still unanswered regarding its general usefulness.

The present popularization of T-groups has produced far too many groups without proper supervision. This condition constitutes a crisis of considerable proportions. Any application of sensitivity training in education should be supported by a high degree of professionalism in T-group techniques as well as a comprehensive understanding of the educational problems under consideration. Emotionally disturbed individuals and young people with insufficient characterization of values should be screened out of such experiences.

Sensitivity Training:
Salvation or Conspiracy?

Thomas W. Wiggins

The past decade has produced a renaissance of interest in humanism in education. A growing interest in affective learning has gradually gained ground on the cognitive domain in schools. Many educators have been scurrying about searching for a safe way to get on the bandwagon while others have chosen to ignore the entire issue.

Throughout the nation, particularly in larger urban areas, educators have been attempting to apply various human relations training concepts and strategies to educational programs. The results are mixed and opinions vary. The present status of human relations programs is precarious, yet such programs frequently are characterized as a salvation or a conspiracy.

THE MOVEMENT

Sensitivity training is a nebulous term which is seldom used by professionals. This term loosely includes a variety of human relations training approaches, organizational development techniques, and group dynamics practices. The term has attracted a good deal of attention because of its illusory entertainment, exciting, and emotional reputation. At best, sensitivity training is a term with a questionable reputation and imprecise meaning, and it should be more appropriately called human relations training.

Generally, social psychologists and psychologists believe that human relations training could provide a significant contribution to the growing needs of school programs which prepare students for life in an increasingly complex and dehumanized world. However, efforts to establish programs

Thomas W. Wiggins, "Sensitivity Training: Salvation or Conspiracy?" *Educational Leadership,* December 1970, pp. 254–57. Reprinted with permission of the Association for Supervision and Curriculum Development and Thomas W. Wiggins. Copyright © 1970 by the Association for Supervision and Curriculum Development.

179

have met with myriad troubles: unclear or nonexistent objectives, ill-trained or noncertificated training personnel, the absence of evaluative procedures, and the lack of substantive research evidence which clearly establishes human relations training as beneficial to organizational effectiveness. Nevertheless, all levels of educational enterprises are investing time and money in programs and training strategies.

Human relations training programs are frequently directly or indirectly related to the National Training Laboratories (NTL) of the National Education Association (NEA). The NTL is the parent organization of most training enterprises. The NTL is concerned about expanding human potential across a wide spectrum of formal organizations, and generally, this group has earned the respect of social and behavioral scientists as a a professional organization. NTL provides training opportunities, certification programs, and program development for many schools throughout the nation. The Center for the Advanced Study of Educational Administration (CASEA), the Institute for the Development of Educational Activities (IDEA), the Western Behavioral Sciences Institute (WBSI), and innumerable other private and federally funded enterprises are engaged in rigorous longitudinal studies and applications of human relations practices, strategies for change, and affective learning techniques.

RESEARCH

Research involving various human relations enterprises in education is relatively sparse, methodologically questionable, and inconclusive. Imprecise objectives and ineffective evaluation have created a paucity of research data which indicate any justifiable stance on the question of the viability of training experiences in schools.

The research of Joyce and others [1] involved the use of a series of communications tasks which are designed to increase the sensitivity of teachers to the frame of reference of the learner. Sensitivity training intervention in teacher training programs produced little direct effect on the sensitivities measured. Although the program failed to achieve its principal objective, it did achieve an ancillary objective of increasing the ability of teachers to build rapport with each other and with students.

A symposium presented at the 1970 annual meeting of the American Educational Research Association dealt with the topic of "Curriculum Change Through Organizational Change: A Human Relations Training

---

[1] B. Joyce et al. "Sensitivity Training for Teachers: An Experiment." *The Journal of Teacher Education* 20 (1): 75–83; Spring 1969.

Program in a School System." [2] The presentations offered little explicit data to suggest the success or failure of programs in New Jersey public schools.

A comparative study of human relations training methods and the discussion-lecture approach in preparing undergraduate resident assistants was conducted at Ohio University during the 1967–68 academic year.[3] Groups exposed to human relations training methods were rated superior by students as compared to groups which were trained principally by the discussion-lecture method.

An experimental study was made in Tennessee to explore the effects of human relations training with classroom teachers and administrators at the elementary and secondary levels in public schools.[4] An experimental group was involved in a two-week human relations laboratory in the summer of 1968 and, subsequently, 14 weekly sessions during the following school year. Changes in the experimental and control groups were assessed by internal and external criteria. The data indicated that both teachers and administrators exposed to human relations training became less authoritarian, developed greater self-insight, improved interpersonal relationships, and improved leadership skills.

Various other research investigations are reported in the *Research Bulletin* of the Florida Educational Research and Development Council.[5] These studies suggest that no clear evidence has resulted from research which points to sensitivity training as a better means of achieving explicit training objectives in preservice and in-service teacher and administrator programs.

Research points an accusing finger at educators for applying training processes, the results of which are apparently unpredictable. Many educators neither look for nor perceive the same outcomes from human relations training programs. Nonspecific objectives inevitably produce nonspecific training programs and haphazard results. At the present time research suggests that what researchers call sensitivity training is a process, like a grabbag, which produces a few surprises, but only occasional and fortuitous functional products.

[2] See: *Abstracts/Two: 1970 Annual Meeting Symposia,* American Educational Research Association, 1970, p. 17.

[3] See: *Abstracts/One: 1970 Annual Meeting Symposia,* American Educational Research Association, 1970, p. 113.

[4] J. L. Khana. *An Evaluation of the Human Relations Program.* Project Upper Cumberland, Final Report, Title III ESEA, Contract #67-03525, Livingston, Tennessee, 1969.

[5] B. R. Ellis. "Sensitivity Training in Perspective." *Research Bulletin.* Gainesville, Florida: Florida Educational Research and Development Council, University of Florida, 1969.

SOME APPLICATIONS

Elementary schools through graduate colleges are using various human relations training methods with some explicit objectives in mind but mainly out of curiosity. Evanston, Illinois, recently held a five-week institute for elementary teachers and administrators, and enthusiastic responses have provided incentive to expand the program to all elementary schools. Bristol Township, north of Philadelphia, Pennsylvania, included the entire school staff of 700 teachers and administrators including the superintendent plus 100 community representatives, in one of two kinds of programs. They attended five-day workshops on leadership and minority group problems and two-day workshops for teaching personnel. Human relations training was conducted as a strategy for change.

Human relations training techniques and methods played a major role in Talent Awareness Training programs conducted in over six states involving over 20,000 elementary school teachers across the nation. The Institute of Psychoanalysis in Chicago is a pioneer group in providing human relations programs for teachers. Programs conducted at weekend retreats have been a major part of the Teacher Corps training program at the University of Oklahoma. The University of Rhode Island, UCLA, Harvard, the University of Michigan, Boston University, Case Western, SUNY at Buffalo, and MIT are reported by NTL as offering graduate programs which include sensitivity training.

Opinions surveyed and reported in the March 1970 issue of *Nation's Schools* indicated that educators are largely on the fence about sensitivity training. Relatively few schools (3 percent) provided intensive programs. Approximately 50 percent of the respondents in the survey have suspended judgment about using sensitivity training. Uncertainty about trainers and insufficient and conflicting information on the effects of extensive group experiences were the principal reasons given by school administrators for suspending judgment. The prevailing attitude seemed to be one of "wait and see."

DIRECTIONS

There appears to be general agreement that educational programs at all levels need to improve conditions under which affective learning can be knitted into cognitive and substantive subject matter. Teachers and administrators need to improve their skills in dealing with the emotional life of their students, themselves, and their colleagues. These educators need to foster school climates which permit and encourage personal development. At this time it is difficult to answer explicit questions regarding the role of human relations training in this process. Educators are still infatuated with the notion that training alleviates tensions and reduces resistance to change.

Although much of the personal liberation associated with sensitivity training may be conducive to the more effective accomplishment of specific tasks or goals of the institution, on the other hand it may not. The truth is that educators are making a calculated guess that it will help. Human relations training programs are potentially enormously useful as component parts of overall plans to increase educational effectiveness and efficiency.

In this sense human relations training can be a means to an end, but it is unlikely to be an end in itself. Organizational development laboratories, where applied problems are confronted and dealt with, are likely to provide a better model. Here the enhancement of human sensitivities such as improved perceptual acuity is stated as an objective, developed, and evaluated within the perspective of the organization.

There is an absence of any conclusive evidence which clearly demonstrates that human relations training improves the performance of educators' tasks. Perhaps educators should become involved with the behavioral-scientific fathers of sensitivity training in collaborative activities to build models applicable to preservice and in-service education and to curricular programs. In other words, let's go back to the drawing boards. Applications of specific human relations tasks can be tested and evaluated as means of facilitating behaviorally defined objectives.

In this way the present fear or infatuation can be replaced with a more rigorous examination and selection of explicit opportunities for experiences to achieve explicit tasks. The status of human relations training in educational programs would be greatly improved if:

1. The term sensitivity training were eliminated and replaced by the expanded concept of human relations training

2. Human relations training would be used only when clearly defined goals and behaviorally defined objectives are established

3. Research could be conducted to provide empirical evidence as guideposts to direct applications of human relations training

4. Standards for professional performance on the part of trainers could be developed and enforced to ensure quality control

5. Evaluation models to assess the results of training programs could be developed.

Maslow has called sensitivity training a new frontier in social psychology. To many it is a fad. To others it is a conspiracy, and to some a salvation. Whatever it may be or whatever it may be called, it appears as though it might be around for some time.

Critique of Sensitivity Training

Milton K. Reimer

The problems faced by educators and by the educational system have undergone profound changes over the past half-century. Perhaps none of these changes is making a greater impact on American education than the increasing tendency toward confrontation. Almost overnight, students at all levels seem bent on challenging all facets of the existing structure.

Educators, therefore, aware of their need to meet this challenge, but also painfully aware of the inadequacy of the traditional methods, have begun to search for new ways. Rogers made this point in a recent report to the governors of the Rocky Mountain States; it is impossible, he said, to speak to parents, teachers, and students "without realizing the tremendous challenges which education is facing today and the fact that it is not meeting them very well." [1]

One of the new ways which is receiving enthusiastic support from educators throughout the country—one that appears to be especially suited to the present problem of confrontation—is sensitivity training. As used at this time, the term can apply to a wide range of laboratory training approaches. However, these can be grouped generally into three broad areas: those intended to produce personal growth, understanding, and development—generally referred to as T-groups; those designed to develop better intergroup relations—often involving radical confrontation of hostile groups; and those designed to develop interpersonal understanding to improve work efficiency—focusing on actual institutional problems, rather than on therapeutic exchange. [2]

Depending, of course, on the nature of the problem to which sensitivity training is directed, the sessions will assume specific characteristics related to one of these groups. For example, industrial objectives have been geared largely to developing interpersonal understanding as a means toward improving work efficiency.

In education, the problems have been varied enough to call, at dif-

Milton K. Reimer, "Critique of Sensitivity Training," *School and Society,* October 1971, pp. 356–57.

ferent times, for the use of all three broad types of sensitivity training. But, regardless of the problems to be dealt with and the initial objectives of the sensitivity session, there is a strong tendency for any group focus to move toward therapeutic exchange. Thus, a session intended to focus on institutional problems often ends up probing deeply into personal matters that have little, if anything, to do with institutional function.

There is no consensus of opinion or firm agreement on the value of sensitivity training. Some eductors—like Norman M. Paris, professor of psychology, University of Cincinnati,[3] and Carl Rogers—are avid proponents of the experience. Others—such as Donald Thomas, superintendent of Community Consolidated Schools, Arlington Heights, Ill.—have their reservations, and question the validity of many of its common practices.[4]

This writer was involved in one laboratory situation extending over a period of about a week. Most of the points raised in this paper arise from this experience, and are compared with the experiences of others as expressed in their writings.

A sensitivity training group usually consists of 10–15 members and a trainer or group leader. An assumption is generally inherent that the members of the group will share their feelings in an honest and straightforward manner.

Theoretically, each person in the group is free to act and speak as he sees fit.[5] This should mean that he be allowed to share as little or as much with the group as he wishes. Indeed, there are many things which are inappropriate for a person to share with someone else,[6] and it certainly would seem unwise to share with the group what one would hesitate to share with any single member of that group.

The actual process of many groups, however, violates this freedom of action. Group leaders usually encourage the members of the group to ask each other questions, and these questions tend to become very personal in nature.[7] In reality, a group needs very little encouragement to ask personal questions. A collective psychology quickly unites the group against the person who fails to tell all. Once, this writer witnessed a group member actually being accused of trying to manipulate the group just because he had remained silent for a period of time. There was a pervading attitude that a person who did not enter into the discussion was an enemy of the group, and that the pack must pounce upon him.

Brown, who seems generally favorable toward sensitivity training, says that some people will ask for feedback so that they can give it in return. "I have observed," he says, "a number of situations where it seemed to me that feedback was being asked for because the asker wanted an opportunity to unburden himself to the person he had initially queried."[8]

In this writer's experience, the reverse situation was even more true. Members of the group would submit themselves to questioning so that they could have the opportunity of digging and prying into someone else's life. The implied consent principle works in both directions.

Most of the authorities on sensitivity training emphasize the importance of the group leader. Max Birnbaum, Boston University, warns against the "enthusiastic amateur" and the "enterprising entrepreneur." [9] Thomas is more pithy: "T-group experience with a good trainer may not help an organization, but T-group experiences with a poor trainer can create severe personal problems . . . and can be psychologically damaging to both individual and institution." [10]

Obviously, the group leader holds the key to the quality of experience in any sensitivity session. However, there are no accrediting associations for sensitivity trainers, so the effectiveness of any session will depend on the individual trainer and on the criteria used to determine success. Given the possible serious nature of the effect of in-depth probing, this casual selection of leadership seems somewhat suspect in an educational setting.

A major objection to the use of sensitivity training as an educational device is its tendency to be irrational. Critical, reflective thinking and an intelligent analysis of problems and values represent a time-honored approach to education. ("The distinguishing mark of an educated person is intellectual power." [11]) But sensitivity training either ignores critical thinking as a process or is virtually hostile to it. According to Birnbaum, sensitivity training emerged as an answer to those people who felt that the emotional factor was perhaps an even more important item in education than were content and skills. [12]

There are two specific operational fields in which sensitivity training concentrates and in which it is especially irrational. The first is that of emotions and feelings. In order for the group process to be successful, its members must be perfectly honest about their feelings.[13] Feelings about problems and about each other are shared honestly and openly, resulting in strong emotional responses.

While some claim is made to intellectual involvement,[14] there is very little evidence to support this. In this writer's group, any rational analysis of a problem was construed to be an evasion of the issue. The question was never, "What do you think about it?" but always, "How do you feel about it?" In fact, the group tended to become hostile toward anyone who injected thinking into the discussion.

The second focus, and one that is related to the extreme emphasis on feeling, is the concerted emphasis on the "here and now." [15] The objective is to prevent the evasion of uncomfortable issues. The end result is a further removal from rationalism. No intellectual analysis of an issue is possible outside of its context—past and future. But in this experience, feeling—apart from an intellectual context—becomes the criteria for evaluation and for the solution of a problem.

A related item, though perhaps incidental, nevertheless is further indicative of irrationalism in sensitivity training. The group leader frequently and officially is called a "trainer." The term provides a connotation of a conditioning session, rather than an educational experience.

Actual anti-rationalism and an increasing preoccupation with emotion, feeling, and affect are becoming evident in present-day education.[16] Indeed, it is a national trend in American thinking in all fields, and no doubt it comes as a reaction to the coldness and inertness of past intellectualism. Most people—including those who decry the abdication of intelligence to emotions—would agree to the need for greater understanding and better communication among all Americans of all ages. Sensitivity training, if properly conducted, doubtless could foster this in many situations. It seems, however, that regardless of how worthwhile the objectives may be, the means under consideration are suspect from an educational point of view. Educators should become more sensitive to the needs of others— both students and fellow teachers—but the sensitizing process need not be divorced from intelligence and the use of man's rational powers.[17]

NOTES

1. Carl Rogers, "Self-Directed Change for Educators: Experiments and Implications," in Edgar L. Morphet and David L. Jesser, eds., *Preparing Educators to Meet Emerging Needs* (New York: Citation Press, 1969), p. 57.

2. Thomas Cottle, "Strategy for Change," *Saturday Review*, 52:71, 79, Sept. 20, 1969.

3. Norman M. Paris, "T-Grouping: A Helping Movement," *Phi Delta Kappan*, 49:460–463, April, 1968.

4. Donald Thomas, "T-Grouping: The White Collar Hippie Movement," *National Association of Secondary School Principals Bulletin*, 52:1–9, February, 1968.

5. Donald Thomas, "Sensitivity Training and the Educator," *National Association of Secondary School Principals Bulletin*, 51:78, November, 1967.

6. David S. Brown, "Some Feedback on Feedback," *Adult Leadership*, 15:251, January, 1967.

7. Herbert A. Otto, "Depth Unfoldment Experience," *Adult Education*, 17:80, Winter, 1967.

8. Brown, *op. cit.*, p. 251.

9. Max Birnbaum, "Sense About Sensitivity Training," *Saturday Review*, 52:96, Nov. 15, 1969.

10. Thomas, "T-Grouping . . . ," *op. cit.*, p. 8.

11. Robert M. Hutchins, "Report of the President's Commission on Higher Education," 29:110, *Educational Record*, April, 1948.

12. Birnbaum, *op. cit.*, p. 82.

13. Thomas, "Sensitivity Training . . . ," *op. cit.*, p. 458.

14. Paris, *op. cit.*, p. 462.

15. Thomas, "Sensitivity Training . . . ," *op. cit.*, 458.

16. Mary Anne Raywid, "Irrationalism and the New Reformism," *Educational Leadership*, May, 1969, p. 744.

17. See Bruce Joyce, Peter Dirr, and David E. Hunt, "Sensitivity Training for Teachers: An Experiment," *Journal of Teacher Education*, 20:75–83, Spring, 1969.

Encounter Groups
". . . May Loom as a Potential Source
of Salvation."

John D. Black

The biggest movement to engulf the campus since LSD is the Encounter Group movement (which has, incidentally, supplanted drugs as a means of self-exploration for many students).

At Stanford University last year, well over 10 per cent of the student body of 11,000 are estimated to have participated in some formal encounter-group experiences. Some of these enrolled in credit-bearing classes offered by regular academic departments; others joined voluntary groups led by staff from the university's Counseling and Testing Center; some participated in groups conducted off-campus by the Mid-Peninsula Free University.

The largest number sought experiences on weekends at "Marathon" or "Minithon" groups arranged by an ad-hoc committee of students and faculty in cooperation with Esalen Institute. These sessions were usually held near the campus and required payment of a modest fee.

This year has seen no diminution in the demand, and the counseling center has staffed groups as diverse as a "sunrise group" (meeting at 5:30 A.M. outdoors and concluding with 7:30 breakfast), a group for "bogged-down Ph.D. candidates," and a "cowards' group" (for students fearful of a group experience).

If the movement were a local phenomenon, it would scarcely bear reporting, but it is not confined to Stanford. From the University of California at Davis, in northern California, to Johnson College at Redlands in the south (where student-faculty encounter groups are an integral part of the educational program), students are flocking to join encounter groups.

What are these groups anyway, and why are they so popular? Both questions are difficult to answer. Encounter groups consist usually of from eight to 20 people, including one or two leaders, who meet regularly over a period of time, or once or more for a protracted session—eight to 40 hours—during which the participants strive to achieve an atmosphere of honesty and openness for the purpose of learning more about themselves and experiencing more intimate communication with other human beings.

Beyond that definition lies an astonishing diversity. Some groups are purely verbal: others may emphasize a variety of nonverbal—physical and sensory—experiences designed to help people encounter each other and the immediate world around them in new and vital ways.

Some groups may utilize psychodrama or role-playing with group members helping one another achieve insight and understanding by acting out different roles. Others emphasize verbal "attacks" on participants, ostensibly to help them face themselves and experience feelings that may usually remain hidden.

Most groups tend to focus attention on the here-and-now to stimulate awareness of present emotions and interactions. Many groups achieve an atmosphere of warmth and mutual support which their participants have never before experienced, and which produces a degree of candor and openness as exhilarating as a drug "high" but with more potential for learning and growth.

What a group actually does is apt to depend both upon the convictions and the personality of its leader(s) and on the particular needs, desires, and characteristics of its members. A group of married couples will evolve a different agenda than a same-sex group of drug addicts. Many college groups focus on developing creativity through a new blending of the effective and cognitive aspects of personality.

A fraternity being torn apart by internal dissension decides to have a weekend encounter at a rural retreat. After much bickering, unsuspected feelings of envy and admiration of the "intellectuals" by the "jocks," and vice versa, begin to find expression and, before long, men who have never touched each other except in sports or jest are crying in each other's arms. In a faculty group, a strong department head, who has worked hard for his colleagues' welfare and felt very unappreciated by them, discovers how he has warded off their affection as they stroke his body and gently wipe his tear-stained—but joyous—face.

An intercultural group (led by a black counselor) attacks a Chicano who calls himself Spanish and claims he has never suffered prejudice; with their help, he sees facets of his personality that he had been forced to bury. A plain girl who has shown unusual sensitivity and a freedom to give support to other members of her group finally confesses how lonely and unlovely she feels. The outpouring of love from the group gives her such new feelings about herself that her face even becomes more beautiful.

Perhaps the most striking discovery in encountering is the untapped capacity for empathy which most people have; one can frequently become literally exhausted from sharing an intense emotional experience of someone sitting across the room. People also discover unsuspected reservoirs of emotion—hate, love, anger, joy, grief, tenderness—and, perhaps more significantly, that they can express such strong feelings without shame.

But there remains the question of why today's college students are so turned on to encounter groups. The answer is difficult to communicate to adults, but it seems very clear if one listens to students:

"I didn't come to college to learn how to make a living; I want to find out who I am."

"The courses I'm taking don't seem to have a damn thing to do with the real world."

"Rap sessions in the dorm are fun—except nobody ever syas he's scared or lonely, or screwed up—and I hate to think I'm the only one who is."

"I'm tired of always preparing for the future; I need to find some real meaning in the present, or I've had it."

One can hear several pleas here. Many students today are lonely and afraid. The campus is a frenetic, competitive, strident place. Everyone is too busy, too worried, too confused. Should I go to class now, or study, or go to the tutoring project, or join the Moratorium march, or write a letter home? Or should I go out to Pete's for a beer, or take a walk in the hills?

It is not simply that the range of choices is much wider on most campuses, for most students, than it was a decade ago: it is that students feel a much greater sense of responsibility to themselves, to others, and even to the world itself than any student generation before them.

They are, therefore, more troubled about what they *ought* to be doing with their own lives and, concomitantly, sometimes frustrated that they don't know what they really *want* to be doing.

Assaulted and appalled by the enormity of the world's problems, they see few and flimsy sources of security in the route their parents followed: developing a skill, finding a market for it, founding a home, and rearing a family (which may be faced with even more horrendous problems a generation hence).

In coping with these concerns, the student gets almost no help from the college curriculum. The pitifully few relevant courses are always oversubscribed. He receives little assistance from informal contacts with faculty members, who either avoid students or are themselves unwilling to confront the issues that concern students. And many of these questions are so gripping and threatening that they are not discussed in the normal social situations to which students have access.

In this context, the encounter group may loom as a potential source of salvation. There, with a group of his peers, in a relaxed setting where the basic rule is honesty, he may at least discover how others have answered the questions that bore in upon him; or, if they have not answered them, at least he may share others' uncertainties, and they his, and perhaps achieve a sense of community in doing so.

Then, too, perhaps by learning to share his own feelings openly and to experience the honest feelings of others, he may discover what it is to love, and to be loved—and perhaps life will acquire new meaning in the security of a deep and honest love relationship.

Finally, through the encounters in the group, he may learn for the first time how others really experience him and thereby develop a firmer sense of his own identity; after all, if external sources of security are dwindling in number and viability, perhaps one can only hope to find it within himself.

Are there dangers in encounter groups? Lurid tales are often circulated about groups degenerating into orgies or precipitating psychotic or suicidal behavior. Most such stories are fabrications or exaggerations. Virtually all experienced group leaders forbid the use of alcohol or drugs immediately prior to or during group meetings—even the marathon variety —because such substances tend to alter reality and obscure true emotional reactions.

On rare occasions, the "attack" method may precipitate a severe enough reaction to warrant brief psychiatric hospitalization in an already predisposed individual. An experienced leader can usually minimize such responses, and most universities provide access to psychologists or psychiatrists for students who may be "shook up" by the encounter experience. But the human ego is buttressed by all too many defenses and only very rarely do they disintegrate so completely, even in groups without trained leadership, that a psychotic reaction occurs.

People often ask whether the benefits of encounter groups are lasting. There is no definitive answer to this question. Many group members have intense insight-producing experiences; these may or may not result in lasting behavior changes. By whatever means achieved, insights hard to come by are wont to slip away.

But is the question a fair one in the first place? Do we apply the same stringent criterion to a course in history, a trip to Europe, reading a book, or seeing a movie? A successful encounter may give us a momentary glimpse of a deep and vital level of sharing, a refreshing insight into another's struggle with the problem of existence, a compassionate, if poignant, sense of what it means to be a human being. Perhaps this is as much as we should expect from such experiences: a memory and a vision of what man can occasionally know—and strive to find again.

Sensitivity Education:
Problems and Promise

Arthur W. Combs

The overwhelming problems of our time are human problems. Their solutions depend upon effective human understanding and interaction. If America's schools do not produce sensitive, compassionate, caring persons equipped to meet these problems, they will have failed all of us, students, parents, the nation itself. One promising movement aimed at achieving these ends is *sensitivity education.*

In the midst of our current preoccupation with objective, mechanistic, cognitive, computerized education, it is good to know there are some who are deeply concerned with the human questions. The present curriculum scene is a depressing one for the humanist, and it is, therefore, reassuring to know that some persons are actively experimenting with humanizing innovations. Sensitivity education may not provide us final answers, but out of experiments with it will come new perspectives which cannot help but advance our understanding of the human aspects of curriculum development.

Even if its potentialities for sensitizing students to themselves and to each other were not reason enough for experimenting with sensitivity education, the contributions it can make to the learning process itself would demand our serious attention. Sensitive awareness to self, to others, and to the outside world of ideas and events is the base line from which personal discovery of meaning begins. Billions of dollars and billions of man-hours are currently being expended in attempts to reform education. Unhappily, much of this effort is foredoomed to be wasted because it concentrates on the wrong problem.

Learning, psychologists tell us, always consists of two parts: exposure to new experience or information, on the one hand, and the discovery of

Arthur W. Combs, "Sensitivity Education: Problems and Promise," *Educational Leadership,* December 1970, pp. 235–37. Reprinted with permission of the Association for Supervision and Curriculum Development and Arthur W. Combs. Copyright © 1970 by the Association for Supervision and Curriculum Development.

its personal meaning for the learner, on the other. Teachers have long been expert in providing information. This is the thing we know how to do best. With modern technology we are now able to provide information faster and more furiously than ever before. Unfortunately, this is not the place where education is sick. Our major failures do not arise from lack of information. They come from the other half of the equation—our inability to help students discover the personal meaning of the information we so extravagantly provide them.

PERSONAL MEANING

The meaning half of the learning equation is the human half. It lies inside the learner and so is only indirectly open to external manipulation. We know a great deal about providing information. We know very little about the dynamics of helping learners discover personal meaning. We have, therefore, concentrated our efforts at educational reform on the things we already know how to do. As a consequence, the principle of overkill has come to education and we are in danger of drowning in a wave of information.

We are accustomed to overproduction in America, and such extravagant waste might be tolerated if it were not true that "what you make on the bananas you lose on the oranges!" We have seen how overproduction has fouled up our environment. It is doing the same for education. Our preoccupation with the information half of the learning equation has dehumanized our schools, alienated our youth, and produced a system irrelevant for most students.

The human side of learning cannot forever be swept under the rug with impunity. It will continue to plague us and frustrate our efforts whether we recognize its existence or not. The laws of learning cannot be suspended because they are inconvenient to consider. It is time we devoted ourselves and our treasure to the human side of the learning equation as an antidote to the terrible dehumanizing forces we have set loose in the past ten years. One small contribution in this direction is sensitivity education. It deserves our respect and encouragement.

Professional workers are great faddists, and educators are no exception. New movements in any of the professions begin with enthusiastic experimentation among their proponents. As a consequence they blossom out in dozens of variations, each staunchly defended by its adherents. So, the current scene in sensitivity training finds people operating at every conceivable variation under many different names. It appears, for example, under such names as discussion groups, T-groups, confrontations, sensitivity groups, and encounter groups. These also run for varying lengths of time from occasionally, to an hour or two a week, to 24-hour marathons, to weekends or retreats of varying lengths. They vary also in philosophy and practice, from nondirective to directive involving just talk or varying forms of controlled or permissive interaction, from sensitivity games to encounter in the nude.

INNOVATION INVOLVES RISK

With any new movement there is likely to be a need to examine the question as a pure case. Innovation always involves some risk. Inevitably, this experimentation includes some pretty far-out activities which seem reprehensible, dangerous, or immoral to more inhibited observers who may respond by rejecting the entire movement. This is unfortunate; it is also predictable.

Critical observers of beginning movements are very likely to deal with them in shades of black and white. Enthusiastic proponents are sure they have come into possession of all embracing solutions, while antagonists see the movement as irresponsible, dangerous, or evil. This, too, is probably inevitable. Thinking men need to see matters in clearer perspective and to avoid creating such yes/no dichotomies. Earl Kelley once said, "Whenever you find an idea that can be stated as a dichotomy, it is almost certain that both extremes are wrong!" Currently, there is much confusion in discussion sensitivity education. The term is a kind of umbrella. So many many different kinds of philosophies, practices, and arrangements are subsumed under this heading that one cannot be "for it" or "agin it." To form a rational judgment about a given group, it is necessary to know who is in it, who is running it, with what philosophy, with what experience and training, for what purpose, under what circumstances.

In time we shall know better how to judge these matters. In the heat of the present excitement it will often be necessary to proceed without all of the data we might otherwise like to have. Meanwhile, the pressing need incumbent upon all of us to deal with the human side of learning requires the widest possible responsible experimentation with the promising leads provided us by sensitivity education. There is not the slightest doubt that these approaches have immensely important contributions to make to educational theory and practice, and we need to exploit them to the full as quickly as possible.

The need for innovation in humanizing education is very great. But human beings are precious and cannot be wantonly expended. It is, therefore, necessary that those who experiment with sensitivity and encounter carry out such experiments responsibly. As a psychotherapist I have had the unhappy experience of having to "pick up the pieces" with clients who suffered bad trips from inept sensitivity encounters. Education is no haphazard process.

The things teachers do must be predicated upon a reasonable expectation of positive results. At the very least, this demands of those exploring sensitivity education: (a) an understanding of the goals and purposes of education, (b) a selection of methods of working clearly consistent with those purposes, (c) a reasonable expectation of positive results, (d) the provision of adequate safeguards against negative affects, and (e) a compassionate acceptance of responsibility for the welfare of all concerned in whatever processes are instituted.

At this point it is clear that sensitivity education has promise. It is also clear that it has problems. In time we shall know more clearly about its promise and will clear up its problems. One way to speed that happy day is through the kind of dialogue provided in this issue of *Educational Leadership*.

Encountering What?

John R. Silber

There is the crude police officer who mounts his movie camera on the top of a toilet booth in a department store—and then there is the highly sensitive person from the American Psychiatric Association or the American Psychological Association who administers encounter groups. The two appear to be radically different, but they have much in common: Both invade human privacy with reckless abandon. Though the encounter group psychologists detest the behavior of police officers, they may be more dangerous and corrupting in their subversion of the dignity of the person.

The encounter groups are blurring the distinction between authentic human relationships and the playacting that goes on in the typical encounter session. A relationship in which two people look at one another in an uncontrived atmosphere is quite different from a relationship in which two people look at one another in an encounter group, whether it be in a training session, a therapy session, or the usual Esalen kind of operation.

It is no great trick to look in a long and steady manner into the eyes of a young woman during an encounter session. That does not mean a thing. The same behavior in an uncontrived context might be quite different.

You cannot make public what is private without changing it. But the operators of the encounter group movement seem never to have been aware of the egocentric predicament nor to have realized that when it is bypassed it is not actually bypassed; it only appears to be.

We are now parasitic upon a cultural inheritance that few of us accept. In the process of rejecting the host plan, we are placing culture in a precarious situation. We have derived our sense of human dignity largely from the Judeo-Christian tradition and, to some extent, from the Hellenic tradition. In rejecting those traditions, we forfeit the basis for the respect of the individual person and his dignity. So, today, we pay lip service to human dignity without quite knowing why.

Reprinted, with permission, from the March/April 1971 issue of *The Center Magazine,* a publication of the Center for the Study of Democratic Institutions.

196

What bothers me most about the encounter group program is that the psychologists have not offered an anthropology worthy of the name. They have not offered a theory of man that explains the dignity of his being or justifies the concern society professes to have for his development and protection. Without such a theory, we are running a serious risk of destroying—in practices such as the encounter group—the very thing we are trying to protect.

I would not want to see a law passed prohibiting people from engaging in encounter group sessions, nor would I want to see one passed prohibiting people from going on Caribbean cruises. The Caribbean cruise does for some people what the Esalen weekend does for others. If either helps people to speak more freely with other human beings, and if they cannot do that in any other way, the excursions are relatively harmless.

What are harmful are the scientific pretensions that have become associated with the encounter sessions. What is dangerous is the claim that these sessions lead people to honesty, sincerity, and the expression of themselves. In fact, there can be as much masquerade in the effort to be honest, open, and direct in the contrived context of an encounter session as there is in a normal setting in which one deliberately tries to deceive.

The typical encounter experience is one-shot in character, lasting twenty-four hours, or forty-eight hours, a week, or even two weeks. Many of the people who engage in such experiences have been terribly disappointed. Some of the encounter group operators themselves say that within three to six months after an encounter session, people show only a five percent improvement, though I cannot imagine how they measure such things.

I question the claim that encounter sessions have therapeutic value. Carl Rogers argues that encounter is not worth a damn as therapy. He says that encounter may be all right for people without serious psychiatric problems but that it is very dangerous and should be used only with great restraint for people who are sick. I would not be satisfied or reassured to discover that there is about as much successful therapy in the encounter groups as there is in psychiatry or psychoanalysis as a whole. The rate of success in psychiatry and psychoanalysis is so pathetically low that to attribute improvement or cure to therapy instead of accident begs the question. Even if we had evidence of positive therapeutic results from encounter sessions, the lack of theoretical understanding of the procedure can jeopardize the fulfillment of man as a person.

There has been a great deal of criticism of university personnel who have been indiscriminate in their use of encounter sessions. Some group sessions have caused great harm, bringing people over the brink, exacerbating mental difficulties and problems that were relatively under control before the students participated in encounter sessions.

I would not deny that some people may benefit from an encounter group. Some people benefit from a drive in a high-speed automobile. People can benefit from a variety of things, and there may be no intellectual justification and no theoretical understanding of why the improvement took place.

There is a model for the encounter group—as the Esalen people recognized—in the prayer meeting. The prayer meeting had many of the essential features of the encounter group: singing together, engaging in group activities, a kind of public confessional, a testimonial for each participant about how hard things had been for him until his life was transformed. But the difference between the prayer meeting and an encounter session is that there was a theoretical position behind the prayer meeting. As you sang a hymn in the prayer meeting, there were no coverups. You were prepared to bare your soul before an Almighty God whose attributes as an all-knowing and understanding and loving Judge and Redeemer were accepted by everyone in the group. The Christian religion, as it grew more sophisticated, developed both a perfectionist ethic ("Be ye perfect as your Father in heaven is perfect") and a procedure for complete forgiveness and redemption ("Tho' your sins be as scarlet, they shall be as white as snow"). Christianity maintained a parity between God as Lawgiver and God as Redeemer: Redemption made a perfectionistic ethic viable in the lives of simple, sinful men.

Of course, if you lost confidence in the redemptive part of the Christian religion but still believed you should be perfect and meet the ethical standards set by Jesus, psychical disturbances were bound to arise. But the prayer meeting took place within a small, self-selective community that shared a religious and theological position. Disclosure could be made within that community under remarkably well-controlled circumstances. Occasionally, violence and emotional excesses occurred, and it was obvious that reason was by no means the guiding principle. But the fusion of mind and body, reason and emotion, was brought into it, and it could be beneficial to the person.

All that, however, is in striking contrast to an encounter session that lacks any kind of common theoretical context, bringing together people who do not share values or ideals and therefore cannot have much confidence in the kind of revelation that is taking place.

Of course, there are people who are not pathological but who are unhappy and unfulfilled and who might become happier and more fulfilled if they were less inhibited by the conventional norms of their society. But a great deal depends on how you decide to encourage relaxation in such people. The orientation session for incoming freshmen at the University of Texas, for example, sometimes takes the form of a mini-lab. Three hundred freshmen get up and begin the baroque movements of the encounter program culminating in the feely-feely, and so forth.

The results are terribly depressing in terms not only of the school but of the dignity of the person. By the time the orientation people get through with the freshmen, you wonder why we bother to educate these young men and women. There is sometimes a pretext of therapy in such sessions, but if all these freshmen are sick, then so are we. And who, then, are the healers?

I think there are ways in which one can break down some of the trivial inhibitions that society imposes on people while protecting the human spirit from attrition and abuse. A university orientation for freshmen could well take the form of an intellectual discussion of some problem that is really critically important to the students. A skillful teacher can open up the students and get them to talk freely about social norms, for example, and the relative importance of being limited by them. I see no reason why we should be intimidated by the notion that because such an orientation is more or less rational it is therefore contemptible.

It would be consistent in such an orientation to say something like this to the freshmen: "We don't want to know how many times you have lusted after your mother. That is something you have probably done because there is probably much truth in Freud's analysis at that point. But that is something you decide to keep to yourself and it is something that normally we do keep to ourselves. Indecent exposure can be verbal no less than physical, and we would prefer that you retain your dignity and avoid indecent exposure at this point. We know, too, that your vocabulary was powerful in all obscene aspects of life before you came to the university. We would suggest, therefore, that all of you write to your parents tonight and list all the obscene and profane words you know, just so your parents will realize you did not learn them at the university. And don't waste your time defining the words; your parents have heard them all and know what they mean."

I know that some can argue—although the encounter people do not seem to have had sufficient intellectual or theoretical interest to discover and develop this argument—that privacy is not an absolute and unquestioned value. The argument is that it is not healthy for people to be private about their deepest emotions and thoughts. The theoretical justification for this argument is rooted in the strong positivistic position that emerged in the twentieth century which holds that there are no values in nature and consequently there is no basis for judging people. In this view, people are not right or wrong; they can only be sick or well. Therefore, privacy is not something that is "invaded"; it is rather something to be overcome.

My reply is that there is value in nature and in man as part of nature and that the cost to the individual and to human dignity when privacy is overcome is exorbitant. Of course, we do judge. It may not be for the individual always to make the judgment, but judgments are to be made and we do have institutions for the purpose of making judgments. If we were to take an indiscriminate, nonjudgmental attitude toward the child molester, for example, or toward the child who is a parent molester, we would endanger the preservation of essential human relationships necessary for happiness.

My criticism of Freud is that by assuming that reality has no moral content and that nature is value-free and, hence, that the individual should achieve a strong sense of reality and move from a pleasure principle to a reality principle, he was left without any basis for distinguishing between fear and guilt. If there is no moral content in nature, then there is no such thing as the experience of guilt except as some form of pathological manifestation. Yet Freud was too great an empiricist ever to accept that implication. He provided a phenomenological distinction between guilt and fear that is as good as any I have ever seen, but Freud was never able to bring the phenomena and the theory into line. If he had, he would have had to talk about moral reality no less than natural reality.

The only bases for values or value concerns that Freud introduces are those imposed by society. In Freud's reality principle, you must take into account that if you kill somebody, for example, the community may discover it and kill you. You must take into account the social norms and the risks run by the psyche if those norms are ignored, but that involves the notion of fear, not guilt, and requires the recognition of a responsibility that is not socially enforced at all.

The Limits of Social Education

Joseph S. Junell

Ever since the discovery of the "affective domain" several decades ago, educators have been enamored with the possibility of a new role which they believe parents have largely abdicated in favor of the school, namely, the socialization of America's children. Their main interest to date has been focused on citizenship or the inculcation of values associated with a democratic way of life; however, they have not failed to include certain moral values as well. While recent Supreme Court rulings have introduced anomalies into this role, it continues as one of the dominant themes in American education.

The condition is a curious one, since it has led to all sorts of conclusions, some muddled, others extravagant, as to the objectives American schools should pursue, their manner of pursuing them, and the degree to which they believe these objectives may be achieved. Few educators, however, are fully aware of the vast and complex forces, many of them rigidly deterministic in nature, which have not only placed severe limitations upon the school's influence over children, but have ironically produced results that were opposite from those intended. I shall attempt to deal only with those few which seem to me most prominent in their impact on school children's lives and suggest some approaches which lie within what appears to be a narrow but extremely important margin of opportunity.

Representative of the kinds of influences which have created enormous difficulties for schools as they are now constituted, but which we now accept as eminently humane, are the early laws designed to protect children from industrial exploitation. The discovery, for example, that the aptitudes and aspirations of many youth do not flourish within the present academic system designed for school children is certainly not new. Yet, for years now we have wittingly or unwittingly inflicted on this learner a kind of refined cruelty upon which it would be exceedingly difficult to improve. Where it was once a relatively simple matter for him to put an end to an

Joseph S. Junell, "The Limits of Social Education," *Phi Delta Kappan,* September 1972, pp. 12–15.

intolerable situation by leaving school for the factory or farm, today's social pressures and stringent laws regarding compulsory attendance and child labor allow him no such avenue of escape. In large measure his response to grinding frustration cannot but take the form of compensatory life-styles which are on occasion unseemly, frequently disruptive, and sometimes seriously threatening to life and health. If much of this behavior has found sanctuary under threat of litigation, the bane of teacher and administrator alike, I cannot believe that it was brought about by any mere shift in school or parental authority. I am convinced it would have appeared in any case, as one of the many reflections of vast social change. Moreover, it will likely run its course for good or evil, in spite of all efforts to stop it.

An example of such change is what many critics view as a most sinister shift in allegiance among youth from the values of an adult society to those of the peer group. So significant is this change in social behavior, so foreboding of social disintegration and demise, that brief consideration must be given to the socializing process, for it is central to all problems regarding value and value change and largely determines the conditions under which values are internalized. Let us begin with the child. He enters the world, in the words of Shakespeare, "an infant, mewling and puking in the nurse's arms," with very little to recommend him at this stage of life or in the weeks which immediately follow. Only by the most deliberate exercise of our romantic sensibilities could we attribute to this behavior any of the virtues which set him apart as a human. And yet, if we may accept Erikson's assessment of this phase of his development, it is, in a social sense, the most crucial one he will ever pass through. For upon the quality of his oral and other physical experiences will be established his fundamental trust or mistrust of the world—a factor, Erikson goes on to say, which in no small part determines not only the success of his future interpersonal relationships but the kinds of values he will choose to live by.[1] If this sounds like a highly deterministic view of what happens to all of us, it is one which authorities such as Piaget and Sears, in addition to Erikson, tend by and large to corroborate.[2]

The primary mechanism by which socialization takes place, however, is known as identification, a learning principle to which educators must begin paying closer attention than they ever have in the past. There is yet a great deal to be learned about this principle and its effects on cognition; however, one of its key functions, under ideal conditions, appears to be that of enabling very young children to internalize smoothly and effortlessly the stabilizing behaviors of the preceding generation that are deemed imperative to the survival of the species.

The concept was first advanced by Freud and later amplified by Anna Freud, Erikson, Horney, Adler, and others. It is commonly described as a dependency relationship with some significant figure, generally a parent, whose functions are, among other things, nurturant and supportive; but crucial to the condition is that it be based on the child's "emotional tie with the object." [3]   Moreover, it is unique, according to Sears, in that it is entirely self-motivated, operating without need of reinforcement or special training.[4]

As we read some of the recent and fascinating literature on imprinting among animals, we find a strange parallel in which a specific kind of experience must match a particular phase in the animal's maturation, if normal development is to occur.   Bettelheim, for one, views this phenomenon, or something similar to it, as one of the key factors in the relationship between emotional and cognitive development and in his own studies has found that when children have been deprived of this crucial experience, both socialization and cognitive ability are often seriously impaired.[5]   The timing, to be sure, is far less critical in humans; but the most sensitive period appears to begin at about the age of two and a half or three and continues at a decelerating rate until puberty, when it is largely, though not entirely, extinguished.[6]

Two factors seem most predictive of the success or failure of this learning principle: the quality of human contact and the length of time in which the principle is allowed to operate.   Any extraneous forces altering these two factors are very likely to bring about parallel changes in social behavior.

One of the better accounts of how this socializing principle has been profoundly affected by the impact of technology and the consequent altered styles in family life may be found in Bronfenbrenner's comparative studies of American and Russian patterns of child rearing and education (*Two Worlds of Childhood*).   In his analysis of the two cultures, he carefully pinpoints the various influences within each society—mass media, modified family habits, enforced peer relations—as they impinge upon the child. From these he extrapolates the probable effects on the child's behavior.   All lead up to a startling, carefully documented conclusion: Russian children make significantly more choices favoring adult values than do American children.   This in itself would not merit critical attention were it not for his further well-established observation that such choices are far more consistent with acceptable behavior than are those of peer-value oriented children who are more prone to engage in misdemeanors, violence, and other acts of an antisocial nature.[7]

At first Bronfenbrenner had reason to interpret his findings in terms of a growing tendency in American families toward greater permissiveness in the rearing of children.   Later, in the light of new data, he was forced to reassess his position.   Although still "consistent with the trend toward permissiveness," it now probed more deeply into the heart of the matter.

Of greater significance was the discovery of a "progressive decrease, especially in recent decades, in the amount of contact between American parents and their children." Along with this, moreover, he noted a relative lack of emotional tone and intensity in the relationship. To summarize, "whether in comparison to other contemporary cultures, or to itself over time, American society emerges as one that gives decreasing prominence to the family as a socializing agent. . . ." [8] From this, one may logically infer that, apart from the quality of the child's contact with adults, the degree of the child's allegiance to adult values is directly related to the amount of time in which the identification principle is allowed to operate.

In what exact way this affects student behavior is hard to determine; however, one logical assumption is that enforced and prolonged peer relations must ultimately lead to a serious questioning of much that is commonplace and ritualized in adult behavior to which time has given an aura of veneration and acceptance. Such questioning can be both good and bad. Where it exposes moral phoniness and appearance, it is to be lauded. Where its energies are directed toward forms of withdrawal, irrational violence, and destruction, it is most dangerous, particularly when its manifestations show increasing brutality and can no longer be accepted as youthful larks.

Also seriously affecting the identification principle is the limitation inherent in the philosophy to which schoolmen by and large adhere. In America, no less than in other nations, schools are regarded, among other things, as instruments for perpetuating the prevailing form of government. In the United States, one might say, the objective is to discover means of relating the ideals of democracy to the amount of social cohesion that is necessary to realize their fulfillment.

With this objective I am in full agreement. It is when we examine what social cohesion means in terms of these ideals that I am in doubt. I question, in particular, the heavy emphasis placed on the teaching of "rational processes" as a means of achieving these ideals. The format, as we know, is usually one in which students, through the application of inquiry techniques, are encouraged to "make up their own minds" on matters involving social and moral issues. As a technique for teaching values, I find it difficult to accept on two counts. First, I question its effectiveness from a logical point of view. Second, I view with considerable trepidation its implied dictum: *To follow wherever scientific intelligence may lead us.* I shall take up these matters point by point.

My first point involves the relationship of truth to behavior, or, more precisely, the demonstrated proof of a belief as a basis for behavior. Obviously, some beliefs are easy to prove; others are not. Let us take the democratic ideal, *the right of equality,* as an example of the latter. Now, it must be admitted that whatever value we attach to this ideal, it will stem primarily from our feelings regarding it rather than from any demonstrated proof that all men do in fact have this right. In point of fact, in any kind of moral reasoning, as in the making of moral judgments or decisions, the one question which must take precedence over all others is the ultimate question of our feelings about good or evil—whether a thing is right or wrong, good or bad. But many statements such as *the right of equality,* as one distinguished philosopher of logical analysis points out, are linguistic utterances having only an expressive function, not a representative one. They have no theoretical sense; they contain no knowledge; they can be proven neither true nor false.[9] This is what Joseph Wood Krutch meant when he said that science cannot prove that compassion is better than cruelty.[10] It is also what Bertrand Russell meant when he talked about "things which are legitimately matters of feeling" whose investigations lie outside the province of science method.[11] As feeling states (intellectualized to be sure) they cannot be rationally tested, except in relationship to other feeling states, which suffer from the same limitations.

Our feelings, in short, are central to the issue. Thus when hearing statements which attempt to equate moral reasoning ability with moral character, one doesn't know whether to laugh or cry. It is like saying that benevolent simpletons make wiser observations about moral principles than intelligent scoundrels.[12] I recommend that anyone suffering this delusion observe the psychopathic ward of any mental hospital.

The condition is a slippery one for the proponent of scientific methods, for there is nothing in his repertoire of techniques which enables him to cope with the central issue of value, which is feeling. Since he can only deal with data that can be proved or disproved, he must of necessity put all beliefs, either moral or intellectual, to the same test, without regard for the distinction that may greatly separate them. Finally, he must assume that children will automatically select what is demonstrably true over what is demonstrably false as a valid basis for behavior. Surely the most naive of all assumptions, it is tantamount to saying that when youth at last learns the truth about drugs, the problem will cease to exist.

Let us not delude ourselves. It is feeling, not reasoning, that keeps alive many of our most widely held moral beliefs and provides us with the motivation for following their precepts. An investigation may well reveal one of them as being deleterious in relationship to some other more fundamentally held value or social norm, but once this determination has been made, any attempt to induce new models of behavior that does not utilize the emotional component as the primary anchor point in the learner's experience is by and large doomed to failure.

My second point concerns the grave danger I believe to be couched in a method of teaching that holds scientific intelligence as the chief arbiter of the decision-making process. Paradoxically, the sentiment expressed in the statement, *"to follow wherever scientific intelligence may lead us,"* is typically identified with many men who combine great powers of thought with deep moral insight. When we examine carefully the lives of such men, however, we often find a strange contradiction. Almost invariably their intellectual powers have been employed in the interests of promoting some profound moral outlook that suspiciously resembles an absolute. This assertion could be made of John Dewey no less than of Bertrand Russell. While such men would argue that action based on intelligence is better than action derived from simple moral conviction, they readily admit that unscrupulous men are often very intelligent. As leading advocates of scientific intelligence, they are in fact guilty of practicing what their formal systems of thought strongly disapprove: advancing arguments in terms of abiding moral reference points.

In the classroom, however, such practices by the teacher are viewed with reservation. Moral reference points are, after all, what they are—fixed beliefs strongly tinged with emotion—and therefore highly suspect. Thus, one day, after watching a fourth-grade teacher listen proudly while her youngsters ticked off documented reasons for our Vietnam involvement, I inquired.

"What do you think of the decimation of whole villages, the mutilation of bodies, and mass killings?"

She was surprised. "I think it's horrible."

"Then why don't you tell them so, with all the passion you can muster? If they think well enough of you, they just might start believing as you do."

She still hesitated. "Yes, but you see, that's not the way inquiry is taught. . . ."

No, that was not the way inquiry is taught. The ideal teacher is one who never persuades but rather guides his students to sources of information that will substantiate or refute their own beliefs. The term currently used, I believe, is value clarification, a process by which students, using all sorts of knowledge for testing their values, are supposed to arrive at a new moral synthesis.

Whatever reservations I may hold regarding the possibility of such an occurrence, this is not intended as a condemnation of value clarification, which has its own purpose and need. On the contrary, I consider it a matter of utmost importance for a person to discover if his values are those of a scoundrel, a saint, or a homicide.

The question of who is or who isn't a homicide, for example, deserves a moment's comment, since it bears distinctly on the average teacher's ability to use the "process of reasoning" in his own private judgments on important moral issues. Within the meaning of the term I would include a majority of the public at large. My feelings that this might be true were first formed in the early years of the Vietnam war when any number of people I talked to assumed a strongly belligerent stance on policy questions about which they had only the foggiest information. I was dismayed, but not without hope. There were still the teachers, in whose hands the prospects of a more humane world were safely ensconced. Armed with the new techniques for discovering truth, they were the largest and best educated teacher group in the world.

Alas, I had reckoned without checking my facts. As I entered into conversations with these persons, I found many of them amazingly truculent and warlike. It was a great disappointment to learn that, in spite of their sophisticated arguments, they were no different from the others. In vain did I try to point out how incompatible was our moral position with the facts of our own historical development—arguments that were being brilliantly and movingly advanced by Norman Cousins in the editorial pages of the *Saturday Review*. I had discovered a bitter truth: Teachers, like the rest of the people, are far more interested in exterminating their enemies than they are in the possibility of planetary extinction or of finding means of peaceful coexistence.

Even so, I should have been reluctant to take a public stand on this were it not for an incident that occurred several years later in which a large local branch of the National Education Association was asked to respond to the following resolution:

> Whereas the United States has been involved in Indochina for more than 20 years and whereas professional educators have a duty to voice their consciences concerning a terrible and unjust war, we . . . call for an immediate withdrawal of all United States personnel from Indochina. . . .

The resolution was turned down by a vote of five to two.[13]

Nowadays, of course, it has become fashionable to condemn the war on the ground that it was a gross blunder on the part of someone else. But whether or not this new outlook reflects any fundamental change of heart is a matter upon which I look with the greatest suspicion.*

I suppose my morality and the way I think morality ought to be taught in school is terribly old-fashioned, but it is difficult to have lived nearly 60 years without gaining some awareness of the cunning and rapacity of which men are capable in their determination to promote the good of mankind. Hence I tend to view civilization as a fragile veneer constantly in danger of being ripped away by the most carefully reasoned acts of violence. It is for these reasons that I find myself returning again and again to a consideration of the need for an inner discipline based on a

---

* Actually, I believe people become bored with an enemy whose lack of capability for retaliation ceases to arouse their desire to eliminate him.

few moral beliefs held in common by a great many men. Thus, in the interests of perpetuating democracy and its ideas, I see the school's major objective as one of combining children's need for a life of freedom with the amount of emotional conditioning that seems to me imperative to the maintenance of social stability.

I recognize that the word conditioning strikes terror in some hearts, for it smacks ominously of indoctrination. And there is indeed a sense in which conditioned allegiance to value is predominately absolute and irreversible. If the ego is involved, thus giving to allegiance a strong emotional component, it is especially imperious and demanding, a jealous mistress who brooks no trifling with the claims of rival beliefs. Even more unfortunate, the condition often poses at one and the same time the alternate paths of survival or annihilation. Few have pointed out more dramatically than Malinowski the survival value of taboo in primitive cultures where the social and economic life of the populace is reasonably stabilized. When stability is threatened, however, powerfully induced modes of behavior become virtual deathtraps which have rung the curtain down on more than one society, including many among our own Indian tribes.

I suppose that considerations like these have to some degree caused educators to look askance at all educational systems leading to rigid belief. Any system, however, that attempts to strike a compromise between the philosophies of unbridled freedom and totalitarianism must take a calculated risk, and I, for one, would rather see that risk taken on the side of what appears to me to be man's predominant genetic tendencies to behavior, namely, that he is primarily a creature of emotion, that his adherence to reason in the role of decision making is more figment than fact, and that his philosophies are far more the product of his ego needs than his ego needs are the image of his philosophies. What powers of reason he does possess, however, are among his most unique attributes and are not to be underestimated. But unless he is taught early in life to use these powers in support of a few strongly conditioned attitudes and beliefs to which all men can accede, his presence on earth will continue to grow steadily more uncertain.

Educationally speaking, the one—and perhaps only—avenue left open to him is narrow but fairly well defined. It must incorporate the primary socializing principle by which all humans are made more humane. In previous articles * I have tried to show how this may be in part achieved when teachers adopt the role of social critic and become adept in the art

---

* See Joseph Junell, "Can Our Schools Teach Moral Commitment?," *Phi Delta Kappan,* April, 1969, pp. 446–51; "Is Rational Man Our First Priority?," *Phi Delta Kappan,* November, 1970; and others.

of dramatizing materials in terms of social and moral conflict. Now I should like to consider briefly what Rosenthal (*Pygmalion in the Classroom*) has called the "untrained educational style" and its possible effect on the lives of very young children.

The notion deserves a moment's comment. Surely one of the grim aspects in American society, which we have already noted and to which we may no longer close our eyes, is the frightening list of deviant adolescent behaviors reflected by a growing alienation between adult and child. While rebellion against adult standards has always characterized youth, it is also true that there must be maintained between generations a baseline of mutual respect, communication, and agreement on some very fundamental ways of thinking and acting if social stability is not to be seriously impaired.

Are some teachers in fact instrumental in maintaining and perpetuating this baseline? The pre-school environment is unquestionably the single most influential factor in developing it. Nevertheless, there is good reason to believe that certain teachers also may be affecting it constructively, at least in part. Evidence of this is logically implied in Bronfenbrenner's analysis of the Soviet child's unbringing [14] and in Bandura's extensive explorations into modeling.[15] An experimental search for this teacher seems to me one among several of the highest priorities to which educators may address themselves.

The concept of single and multiple modeling itself demands equal attention, for it utilizes identification as its key operating principle. Bronfenbrenner, in particular, is convinced that modeling carries provocative implications for educational and social programs. In the relationship between teacher and child, he rates *teacher status* as the most essential quality. Indeed, in order for the "teacher . . . to function as an effective model and reinforcer, she must possess the characteristics which we have identified as enhancing inductive power; that is, she must be perceived by pupils as a person of status who has control over resources. . . ." [16]

Whether or not Bronfenbrenner's choice of catalyst (teacher status) is the correct one remains to be seen. However, in the current frantic search for expertise in behavioral objectives, performance criteria, and other related materials, the concept of modeling strikes me as the most fruitful and significant approach to make its appearance within the past decade. Apart from experimentation with drugs, sleep therapy, hypnosis, or forms of medical and biological intervention, I can envision little else that would make a real difference.

The fact remains that in the realm of attitudes and values we find ourselves in a quicksand world where good or evil so often hinges on mere impulse, right or wrong on simple conviction, and truth or falsehood on the heart's desire. As inadequate for making judgments as these criteria may be, we cannot entirely escape them. Because so much of our "rational thought" is dominated by our past emotional conditioning, our only hope, as I see it, is that we learn to reverse this blind process by deliberately inculcating our very young children with a few attitudes calculated to ensure a more humane utilization of reason in the pursuit of ideals consistent with happiness and survival. The greatest of all ironies might well turn out to be simply this: The *modus operandi* which at one time or another enslaved so much of the world is the only one that can free it.

FOOTNOTES

1. Erik H. Erikson, *Childhood and Society*. New York: W. W. Norton, 1963, pp. 247–51.
2. Henry W. Maier, *Three Theories of Child Development*. New York: Harper & Row, 1969, pp. 212–24.
3. Urie Bronfenbrenner, "Freudian Theories of Identification and Their Derivatives," *Child Development*, 1960, pp. 15–40.
4. Robert R. Sears, "Identification as a Form of Behavior Development," in *The Concept of Development*, D. B. Harris, editor. Minneapolis: University of Minnesota Press, 1957, pp. 149–61.
5. Bruno Bettelheim, *The Empty Fortress*. New York: The Free Press, 1967, p. 231.
6. Maier, *op. cit.*, pp. 188–226.
7. Uri Bronfenbrenner, *Two Worlds of Childhood*. New York: Russell Sage Foundation, 1970, pp. 95–119.
8. *Ibid.*, pp. 95–99.
9. Rudolph Carnap in *The Age of Analysis*, Morton White, editor. New York: Mentor Books, 1961, pp. 203–25.
10. Joseph Wood Krutch, "A Humanist's Approach," *Phi Delta Kappan*, March, 1970, p. 378.
11. Bertrand Russell, *A History of Western Philosophy*. New York: Simon and Schuster, 1945, p. 834.
12. This is in large part the major argument of the Committee on Religious Education in the Public Schools of the Province of Ontario, Canada. See pp. 41–70 in their publication titled *Religious Information and Moral Development*, 1969.
13. *Bellevue American*, Bellevue, Wash., p. 1.
14. Bronfenbrenner, *op. cit.*, pp. 70–91.
15. Albert Bandura, in *The Young Child: Reviews of Research*, Willard W. Hartup and Nancy L. Smothergill, editors. Washington, D.C.: National Association for the Education of Young Children, 1970, pp. 42–59.
16. Bronfenbrenner, *op. cit.*, p. 154.

Irrationalism
and the New Reformism

Mary Anne Raywid

Among the ideas which may soon come to influence education most significantly, two stand out—both by way of gathering momentum, and by
virtue of the changes they would bring to any and all institutions affected.
The first of these ideas—or, more accurately, these sets of ideas—is what
might be called irrationalism or, in its extreme form, anti-rationalism. The
second constitutes a very special type of reformism, taking its character
and flavor from the anti-rationalism which in part inspires it.

To assess the sort of impact these two interrelated ideas may have
on schools, we must first examine their nature and form. Although an
exhaustive attempt might fill a book, perhaps we can here look at two
outstanding features of each of these sets of ideas: the circumscribing of
reason's role and the expansion of the role of emotion, as represented
in contemporary irrationalism; and the irrationalism and rejection of
democratic process which mark the new reformism.

ANTI-RATIONALISM

First, just what sort of anti-rationalism is present? Actually, it
seems to constitute a broad trend, displaying a range of conviction with
respect to the role of rationality in life. It includes those disappointed heirs
of the Enlightenment who have come to question whether reason and
knowledge will ever yield the solutions we had hoped. And in more extreme form, the movement also encompasses those who no longer question
but are convinced that for contemporary man, reason has become more
bane than boon. A direct, frontal attack on reason has played a prominent

Mary Anne Raywid, "Irrationalism and the New Reformism," *Educational Leadership,* May 1969, pp. 743–48. Reprinted with permission of the Association for
Supervision and Curriculum Development and Mary Anne Raywid. Copyright ©
1969 by the Association for Supervision and Curriculum Development.

part in many of the activities of the New Left, Black Militants, and student demonstrators across the nation. It is not merely that critics seem justified in charging these groups with anti-rationalism. The significant point is rather that so many have openly claimed anti-rationalism for themselves. For an overt rejection of logic, reason, and knowledge is one of the most frequent themes of these groups—even if its expression is often parenthetic and almost offhanded. Indeed, it is almost as if a rejection of the processes and products of reason has already become an unquestioned operating assumption for these groups. Thus, such rejection needs stating only in handling outsiders and their challenges.

On such occasions, one hears the message over and over again: " 'On the New Left, we're not so logical,' " proudly proclaims one young interviewee. And furthermore, " 'It is not possible to be logical when you're with us.' " [1] At the recent Princeton seminar held by the International Association for Cultural Freedom, observer Walter Goodman was struck by the frequency with which these groups expressed their suspicion toward reason.

This attitude went well beyond impatience with the tedium of such traditional practices as discussion, analysis, and weighing of alternatives. It was not that these were merely dull or unnecessary: They were downright undesirable. Moreover, the several representatives of the newer politics condemned repeatedly the "lack of passion" of the others gathered at Princeton. One put it hands down: " 'Cool reasonableness is . . . not preferable to a political hysteria.' " [2]

This introduces a second facet of anti-rationalism, which is really but the other side of the coin. For if reason, knowledge, and analysis are found wanting when it comes to choosing a program or deciding an issue, it is feeling and passion on which one should depend instead. Indeed, among this group, passionate conviction and involvement provide the very procedural ground for decision and choice—just as detachment, objectivity, and calm appraisal were once urged as the qualitative ground important to valid choosing and deciding. These latter, traditional qualities, suggest the present group, are in fact better calculated to becloud and invalidate choosing; for the yield of detached choice will surely lack the sort of "gut commitment" that provides the only legitimate warrant for acceptance and action.

A man may become intellectually convinced by objective experiment and demonstration that "Water boils at 212°F."—or cognitively

[1] Quoted by Lionel Abel in: "Seven Heroes of the New Left." *New York Times Magazine,* May 5, 1968, pp. 30 and 129.

[2] Quoted by Walter Goodman in: "The Liberal Establishment Faces the Blacks, the Young, the New Left." *New York Times Magazine,* December 29, 1968, p. 30.

informed by factual reports that numerous deaths from malnutrition are occurring daily in Biafra—but neither item is likely to rouse him to passionate relevant partisanship. And unless something evokes feeling *in* him, then it lack "authenticity" *for* him, and he is just as well off not believing it at all. Without the crucial, sanctioning emotional quality, sheer knowledge or belief is meaningless and useless or worse: productive of inauthenticity or hypocrisy.

Intense emotion, caring, and passion stand then as contemporary irrationalism's cure for the ills of today. Yet not all the individuals and ideas comprising the growing irrationalist trend are as openly hostile to reason as are the youth groups and militants so far identified. There are proposals in many fields which do not involve *direct* assaults on reason and its efficacy or desirability—but which nevertheless lead to quite similar consequences. For the irrationalist, as well as the anti-rationalist, urges the substitution of feeling and emotion in approaching tasks we have been assigning to reason and knowledge. Explicit and implicit, the evidences and manifestations of this milder irrationalist tendency abound in various spheres, and from diverse sources.

The impressive popularity of Marshall McLuhan provides one kind of case in point, for McLuhan almost contemptuously dismisses the "linear," one-dimensional logic which has provided the model for the rationalist tradition. For him, such logic is simply obsolete and passé. And although as scientist and scholar McLuhan must keep one foot in the old-fashioned rationalist camp, both the method and style of his works reveal an increasingly familiar impatience with traditional ways of working out and supporting conclusions. The imagery in which he deals, and the often obscure connections and associations by which he proceeds from one idea to another, suggest a style of inquiry which has aptly been dubbed more psychedelic than scientific or rationalistic.

Indeed, in education itself—and not just among the youth protesting the Establishment—one finds a growing preoccupation with emotion, feeling, and affect among the most widely read newer books. As one interpreter observed, the education books of the 'Sixties differ markedly from those most prominent a decade ago. The latter called for an "intellectual upgrading" within education; today's cry is instead for "humanizing" the schools, and the concern is with affective development, not cognitive.[3]

A remarkable recent addition to this literature bears the telling title *Education and Ecstasy.* Criticizing almost all education past and present for its omission of "the Dionysian factor," the author asks and answers the critical educational question this way:

[3] Harold W. Sobel. "The New Wave of Educational Literature." *Phi Delta Kappan* 50(2): 109–11; October 1968.

What, then, is the purpose, the goal of education? A large part of the answer may well be what men of this civilization have longest feared and most desired: *the achievement of moments of ecstasy.* Not fun, not simply pleasure, as in the equation of Bentham and Mill, not the libido pleasure of Freud, but ecstasy, *ananda,* the ultimate delight.[4]

It is unfair to the author, *Look* editor George Leonard, to over-simplify his plan for achieving this goal. But encounter groups constitute a major and continuing method to be diffused and pursued in some form in most teaching and learning. And he also suggests that schools can learn much from such personalistically-oriented endeavors as the unusual Esalen Institute, with its program of "meditation, intensified inner imagery, basic encounter, sensory awareness, expressive physical movement and creative symbolic behavior." Criticizing the distorting bias of education as we have known it, the author suggests that today's schools typically produce "emotional imbeciles," "sensory ignoramuses," and "somatic dumbbells."

Mr. Leonard does not indulge in open anti-rationalism. There is no overt denigration of the cognitive nor denial to it of an important role, either in education or in living. But what we have seen does seem to place him squarely among the larger group who have concluded that we simply cannot ask of reason and knowledge all that we of the 20th century have expected from them. And this adds up to a plea for an enlarged sphere and role for the irrational in man. Leonard obviously joins the ranks of those who want to pursue answers to life's major questions by consulting emotion in preference to reason. And his rationale is presumably quite similar to that previously mentioned: the demand for passionate involvement in the replies to those questions, and a continuously intense emotional engagement with life itself. "The future," he warns, "will very likely judge nothing less appropriate than detached, fragmented, unfeeling men."[5]

THE NEW REFORMISM

Since he is also a bearer of the new reformism earlier mentioned, Mr. Leonard provides a good introduction to this second set of ideas which may also exert profound educational influence. Last year he

---

[4] All quotations are taken from *Education and Ecstasy,* by George B. Leonard, as it originally appeared in three installments of *Look:* "How School Stunts Your Child," 32(19): 31–34+, September 17, 1968; "Visiting Day 2001 A.D.," 32(20): 37–40+, October 1, 1968; and "The Future Now," 32(21): 57–60+, October 15, 1968.

[5] *Ibid.*

promulgated "A New Liberal Manifesto" in which he explained why traditional liberalism "failed" and has become "irrelevant":

> Many liberals suffered a disabling flaw. Their liberalism did not extend below their eyebrows. . . . they were liberals of doctrine, ideology and the intellect. . . .[6]

As this suggests, the heart of the new reformism is just that: heart. Its affinity with anti-rationalism is clear because it seeks to extend the general style and specific procedures of irrationalism to apply to sociopolitical issues and decisions. The new reformism stands as a recommendation to the effect that irrationalism provides the answers, not just for the individual's life style and choices; it also recommends the appropriate posture for nations, and the general means of working out our collective problems.

Within the new reformism, as among the anti-rationalists, there is a wide spectrum of opinion—all advocates displaying, however, a common tendency. We see it in its mildest and perhaps incipient form in such a program as the Mothers March for Peace—which, in contrast to its contemporary organizations, seemed to represent nothing so much as the reflection of, and demand for, genuinely *emotional* response to the horrors of war. But the Mothers March was perhaps mere prologue, with its plea for attending the affective dimensions of problems inevitably intellectualized and abstracted when pursued as affairs of state. Subsequent reformists have demanded a far more prominent role for the affective. Witness again, for example, testimony at Princeton for political hysteria in preference to "cool reasonableness." It came, incidentally, not from a youngster, but a professor at Harvard.

This preoccupation with feeling, and the demand for continuous passionate engagement, seems to represent one feature of the new reformism's two-pronged ideological base. The second part consists in an almost wholesale rejection of our sociopolitical system—government, of course, but also other major institutions as well. Most important, what is rejected—rendering the new reformism actually far more revolutionary than reformist in character—are the procedural provisions regulating the way all particular decisions are made.

American theorists have gloried in the claim that our political system permits of and virtually even *institutionalizes* change—allowing for extensive alterations, while taking as its only constant or unalterable arrangements, the procedural: the broad outline, that is, of *how* we shall decide. Thus, it is doubly significant that this decision process itself is perhaps a major target of the new reformism.

[6] George B. Leonard. "A New Liberal Manifesto." *Look* 32(11): 27; May 28, 1968.

This, it appears, is precisely what is at stake in "confrontation" politics, the program increasingly pursued by the new reformism. The strategy seems to be to force particular decisions directly, thus circumventing or reversing the legal processes by which the issues would otherwise be resolved.

There is nothing radically new, of course, in a minority's resort to direct action in attempting to wrest or assure its own rights as against those of a majority. What does seem relatively new, however, is the extension of such measures to apply also in other situations, resulting in attempts to compel majority performance when minority rights are not primarily or prominently at issue. To cite several examples: the demand that Afro-American history courses be offered in schools can easily be read as an insistence on minority rights; the demand that such courses be made compulsory for all students is something else. While even opponents might be willing to understand the first demand as an assertion of minority rights, the second seems to represent a new construction of minority entitlement— and a construction it is hard to reconcile with a commitment to the majority's right to govern itself.

Similarly, the assertion of one's right to refuse to be drafted is one thing; a demonstration denying anyone admission to an induction center is another. Or again, the boycotting and picketing of a meeting is a time-honored privilege; its disruption to the point where it cannot occur at all has not been. (It is not that our history has been devoid of such attempts. What does seem new and qualitatively different, however, is, on the one hand, the morally righteous posture assumed by the perpetrators, and on the other, the tolerance which has met such efforts. It was, after all, not so many years ago that we associated such measures only with those "kooks" and sneaker-shod old ladies populating what was then described as a "lunatic fringe.")

Thus, the new reformism seems to advance a view that is antithetically opposed to traditional decision-making arrangements. It should be noted that the denunciations and rejections of what may loosely be called "democratic procedure" are not limited to the extravagances of a few, or the excesses of frenzied moments. The opposition to democratic processes is both frequent and predictable, because it is built right into the ideology which directs many of the new reformists. Both Herbert Marcuse, the philosopher-prophet of the New Left, and Frantz Fanon, the intellectual sire of Black Militancy, argue in effect that reform—pursued within the system and according to its rules—is simply impossible.[7] Significant re-

---

[7] Marcuse's case is generally to the effect that the all-powerful system has absorbed effective opposition, turning the very instruments and processes of dissent to its own advantage and support. Fanon's argument is that the condition existing between colonizer and native is total opposition or war. In consequence, it is a

form requires systemic change tantamount to revolution. For in order to succeed at all, dissidents must reject the entire system, and with it, the ground rules which sustain and make it possible.

ROLE OF EDUCATION

And what is education to make of all this? If anti-rationalism and the new reformism are the emerging ideologies they seem to be, what should be the posture of the schools with regard to the new *Weltanschauung?* In one sense, of course, the question comes after the fact—for schools in many metropolitan areas have already felt the effects of the new reformism. But whether or not we can control all of these effects, we can certainly question their desirability and the acceptability of the ideologies inspiring the events.

I am afraid I find little potentially positive contribution in that part of the new reformism seeking to scrap democratic processes. History has seen too many instances of ends which at some subsequent point in time are supposed to justify and exonerate whatever means have been used in their attainment. Irrespective of the forcefulness of the arguments of Marcuse and Fanon—and they are, indeed, forceful—I fear the abandonment of procedural democracy, because that may well reintroduce all the old-fashioned tyrannies democracy evolved to prevent.

If we scrap democracy's procedures for decision making, the only thing that remains to be seen is whether the ensuing despotism will prove benevolent or otherwise.—Unless, of course, the new reformists have devised an improved alternative, with new protections and safeguards. And sadly, the chances are that they have not. For not only are their mentors silent on this point, but the followers seem not yet to have come to the question. It is precisely at this point that the two features of the new reformism considered here come together in ominous combination. For on the one hand we have the opponent of democracy's processes—the revolutionary who is willing to use whatever force is necessary to overthrow present institutions and procedural guarantees; and on the other hand, he also represents irrationalism—telling us, in effect, "I don't know what to substitute. We will destroy first—and only *then* decide what to build in its place."

Yet the irrationalism by itself may have real virtues. For insofar as the movement represents a recommendation to the effect that in our per-

---

situation which cannot be discussed, compromised, adjudicated, or otherwise politically and peaceably resolved. Force is the only recourse. (Militants have rendered Fanon's work on colonial nations relevant, by likening the situation of Blacks in this country to that of the natives of a colonized state.)

sonal lives we pay greater heed to emotion, perhaps it is a message many of us need. And insofar as the new reformism represents the extension of the anti-rationalism to regulate our impersonal negotiations and inter-actions—among groups, institutions, and states—possibly this, too, is a message we should hear very attentively. For there may be few better hopes for ending war, poverty, and injustice than to bring to them the kind of feeling and resolve we would surely experience if those we loved were the victims. Surely in this sense, the anti-rationalism of contemporary reformism has much to offer.

More directly, a considerable part of the irrationalist message may have something important to say—and perhaps it is just the antidote for those of us who are least able to recognize it! For it is surely the case that the traditional liberal has been reared on the counsel that he should distrust his emotions. Indeed, much of what he was taught with respect to finding out, concluding, and deciding was designed precisely to the pur-pose of counteracting and compensating for his preferences and biases, and thus assuring they did not lead him away from truth and down false by-ways.

This, after all, is exactly what we in education have been up to as we have dedicated ourselves to teaching children "how to think," or to "think critically," or to be "intelligent problem-solvers." We have adopted, and tried to adapt to all life's circumstances and demands, the methods of science—particularly as enunciated by John Dewey, who was, after all, a consummate rationalist with unlimited faith in the power of reason and knowledge to guide man and enhance his state.

Perhaps it is the case, then, as antirationalism contends, that we have vastly oversold ourselves on reason's promise, as well as on its pervasive relevance to all life's circumstances.

If this be so, what ought education to be and do? Hopefully, we can arrive at some proper "mix" of reason and emotion for man—in his life, and consequently in that part of equipping him for it that we call education. It is not, of course, a new problem—for philosophy or for education. Yet it is surely one that acquires new urgency from the ideological currents examined here. And just as surely, to propose that we evolve some appro-priate *mixture* of the intellectual and affective for man and his instruction is a rather weak solution. For not only is it no solution at all: it even fails to direct us in seeking one (or, indeed, recognizing one should we stumble upon it). How does one appropriately conduct the search: looking pri-marily to reason or to emotion as guide? With only a handful of excep-tions, the Western philosophical tradition all the way from Plato to Dewey would have agreed on reason as the proper instrument. It is precisely because of the revolutionary character and impact of the ideas examined here that we no longer enjoy such agreement.

Differentiating Affective Concerns

Morton Alpren

I teach a large graduate class in curriculum. Teachers and administrators who take the course, as well as invited speakers, often call for more affective learnings in school. Both this call for personal-social input into educational programs and the more humane concerns reflected in the literature of the past five years have become quite absorbing. Many writers are addressing themselves to it.[1]

It seems to me that there is much confusion in these advocations about problems that are not directly of a curriculum and instructional nature and those that are. The advocates of dealing with humane and affective concerns frequently attack on all fronts and most often without resolutions that might lead to specific changes. When some apparent changes in practices are revealed, they are quite temporal. Some analysis of this dilemma would appear to be in order so that our roles and functions might become clarified. This can offer hope for some long-range solutions.

The confusion seems to focus on a disparity between directions of the concerns. Some are directed toward the conditions for learnings. Youngsters are hungry or sleepy or drugged and are poor subjects for any school-associated learnings, as a result. Some concerns are directed to an overemphasis upon adult expectations in learnings associated with a disciplinary curriculum. The call here appears to be to lessen such expectations in favor of more personal-social inputs into the curriculum. Last, we see concerns about inhumane instruction. Teachers fail to see youth as people and either do not teach for or fail to create environments that allow for adequate respect or motivation to learn.

---

[1] To cite but a few: Norman Newberg and Mark R. Shedd in the latest yearbook of the National Society for the Study of Education, *The Curriculum: Retrospect and Prospect,* Part I. Chicago: University of Chicago Press, 1971; the writings of Paul Goodman, John Holt, Edgar Friedenberg, Mario Fantini, and Gerald Weinstein.

Morton Alpren, "Differentiating Affective Concerns," *Educational Leadership,* April 1972, pp. 627–30. Reprinted with permission of the Association for Supervision and Curriculum Development and Morton Alpren. Copyright © 1972 by the Association for Supervision and Curriculum Development.

These concerns have commonality in their aspects of humaneness and personal foci. However, they also depart in terms of who must address themselves to them.

Many of the concerns are not directly related to school programs. Some who advocate more humane concerns for children and youth reveal the necessity to cope with students who suffer from conditions that retard their attention-giving to life in a classroom. The conditions refer to fear of or absorption with gangs on the street (that may or may not be in evidence within a school building), addiction to drugs, lack of sleep or nourishment, and emotional problems that may emanate from home and family situations.

Now one can argue that education, even formal education, is a necessary requirement as a long-range step to cope with gang warfare and drugs. However, it is most ostrich-like for one to think that he can alleviate such conditions in the immediate future so as greatly to diminish such problems in the minds of learners where these problems exist. As educational programs go, in terms of likely attainability for the here and now, one is hard pressed to think that schooling can be addressed to their solutions where they result in lessened conditions for learning.

It is also difficult to see how curriculum and/or instruction offer solutions for students deprived of sleep, food, or the emotional strength to function in daily activity. This does not necessarily imply that they should not be concerns for school personnel. However, to be affectively oriented toward a student in such cases may have much more meaning in terms of securing federal money for free lunches or consulting with a parent about home conditions than in terms of looking for solutions through curriculum and instruction. The major point here is that the schools have been poorly equipped to deal with affective concerns in terms of any prompt solutions to serious problems.

The curriculum can help in terms of dealing with gangs—but it will not necessarily halt the gang problem and its deleterious effect on children and youth. The same applies to drugs. It may be quite sadistic on the part of a teacher to be harsh to a student who is unable to be attentive due to a home-related problem. Yet to be humane, in such cases, does little to alleviate the problem and, hence, improve the conditions for learning.

Those who seek more personal-social input into the curriculum are really vying with two highly influential forces. One is the traditional concern for the disciplines as a major input, a movement that has seen renewed vigor through the reforms of the 1950's and 1960's. It has a time-honored base in that it represents the cultural heritage of a given society, in particular, and advances in civilization, in general.

The other is the behavior modification movement, which is represented by the more recent advances in technology, the behavioral objectives boom, and the accountability deluge evidenced in the desire for performance contracts.[2] The fact that the humane people are vying with two potent camps is initially forwarded not as a new fact but as a consideration to which they have failed to address themselves. They must not only begin to recognize the differentiations that form the theme of this writing, but should also face more squarely the consequences of deciding what they will specifically do without, and why, in competing for time in educational programs. It is not enough to say, "We can cut out some of the traditional subjects and skills."

One argument going for them is evidenced in a recent historical piece by Kliebard.[3] He attacks the behavior modification movement in terms of its use of the corporate, efficiency model of the business world. Furthermore, schooling, he says, suffers from using a model that is not adaptable to goals for educating children and youth as much as for training them.

What are some feasible curriculum inputs that the personal-social camp can opt for? One form would be small group enterprises that focus upon personal and social concerns of students. Another is a course that specifically deals with race relations and prejudice. A third is drugs and narcotics. A fourth is sex education. And so forth. The list is potentially a long one and is summarized by three features that differentiate it from the other two competing forces. They focus on:

1. Attitudes and values

2. More student input (less adult expectation)

3. Interdisciplinary or guidance efforts.

These conclusions do not necessarily reflect the romantic aspirations of many of those with humane concerns. (As a matter of fact, one is correct in noting that I accuse many of those with good intentions of failing to think out just what it is that they are about.)

Another way of summing up the curriculum input desired by those with affective concerns is that they believe it imperative to help youngsters today see themselves, other people, and institutions as schools have never before attempted to do.

Affectively concerned persons are probably most concerned about

[2] These movements, viewed as inputs into educational programs, were neatly classified as personal, social, systems approaches, and information processing in a taped dialogue with Bruce Joyce, Professor of Education, Teachers College, Columbia University, February 1971. This author took prerogatives in simplifying them as three inputs, namely, personal-social, behavior modification, and disciplinary curriculum reforms.

[3] Herbert Kliebard. "Bureaucracy and Curriculum Theory." In: *Freedom, Bureaucracy, & Schooling.* 1971 Yearbook. Washington, D.C.: Association for Supervision and Curriculum Development, 1971. Also result of taped dialogue, University of Wisconsin, March 1971.

the ways in which teachers have received and acted out their roles. The goals for teachers might run as follows:

1. Like and respect children and youth

2. Not be coercive or punitive with youngsters

3. Concentrate on aiding learners in being better motivated to learn —even learn more in terms of what the learners wish to learn

4. Develop and implement more local (even individual teacher-class) curriculum that will utilize value and attitude learnings.

In this arena there is little new that has not been advocated (really exhorted) over a half-century of teacher education. There are few who dispute such statements and their related slogans. However, in all fairness to the existing situation, the failure to have realized on such statements would seem to require less fault-finding and guilt-placing than to inquire about the reasons for not attaining more humane teachers. I do not think it is enough merely to blame an impersonal "system."

In any event, such is the distinction that appears to separate the affective concerns here from those that deal with the conditions for learning and the curriculum. Are these concerns in some ways related? Of course. Yet they are also separable and, in this regard, it becomes plausible to seek some conclusions and implications.

IMPETUS FOR CHANGE

Most of the problems associated with the conditions for learning are not school controlled and cannot be resolved without societal action. Law enforcement must control drug traffic and gang violence. At best, the school can cooperate in these efforts. If educators continue to sell the old game of schools' solving such problems, these problems will go unsolved unless the society recognizes this ego centered view of educators and refuses to heed those of our romantic notions that do disservice to children and youth. The affective, humanistic camp has not aided us toward solutions in the area of conditions for learning much beyond the pressure exerted for school lunch programs.

In terms of curriculum concerns, the humanistic group should receive support for thought-out reexamination. The onus is on the personal-social people to be clearer in their goals and to recognize that they cannot and should not expect a turnover without clear notions of what can be altered in what may well be a monolithic set of school offerings. The affective people are justified in desires to provide settings for process-oriented, personal-social programs that serve guidance functions, and they have some reason on their side for both their and student input into determining and developing this phase of the school's curriculum. Where such efforts require interdisciplinary developmental tasks, they need to be joined by those who are more concerned about substance, or the curriculum developed is likely to be weaker, temporal, and lose impetus for change.

For both curriculum and instructional components, changes are less likely without recognizing the need to rethink and revise teacher preparation and in-service education programs. On the other hand, caution is needed in such reexamination. If we are to teach teachers to deal more with values and attitudes, the question of which values raises its ugly head again. The risk of indoctrination comes into play here and, while the risk may be well worth taking, it is fraught with danger. When the goal becomes one of turning over an established system, we need to take care that we are not moving toward one that may be more dictatorial than the one we wish to replace. Who has the corner on good values and attitudes, and when do such judgments, when idiosyncratic, prove better than those represented by societal norms?

Those affective concerns that relate to emotional well-being often are based on the implicit assumption that teachers are therapists. At this point in time, they are not (nor are most of those who make the assumption). At this point in time, without a new teacher preparation (which may or may not be an attainable one) we might best argue for more school psychiatrists or cooperation from other agencies. Much as this latter point may infuriate the personal-social camp, what is the alternative?

This examination has led to raising the question, once again, about what schools can and cannot do. I tried to examine this in a 1969 writing.[4] Many of the questions and issues are still relevant, though I admit to oversimplification for the present era. However, until school and broader educational priorities are reexamined, many of the present dilemmas, including the affective arguments, will be difficult to resolve. Glatthorn and I will propose such a solution in a work to be released in 1972,[5] in the form of alternative educational programs for youth. This will not likely prove magical but will be representative of a wish we might make of a genie. It is that all substantive, scholarly oriented people could focus on being more humane and that all affective, romantic, personal-social oriented people could focus on being more substantive and scholarly.

---

[4] Morton Alpren, editor. "A Priority of School Functions." In: *The Subject Curriculum: Grades K–12.* Columbus, Ohio: Charles E. Merrill Publishing Company, 1967.

[5] Morton Alpren and Allan A. Glatthorn. *Planning Educational Programs for Adolescents.* Worthington, Ohio: Charles A. Jones Publishing Company, to be available in 1972.

Encounter Groups and
Brainwashing

William R. Coulson

I have the embarrassment of being one of the substitutes for Dr. Carl Rogers at the Center for Studies of the Person. By no means is this unequivocally a bad deal for me. Doors open which otherwise wouldn't. Last year, for example, I had the singular honor of being the keynote speaker at the annual convention of the National Catholic Guidance Conference—because Carl Rogers couldn't come. I have been to Cleveland, Salt Lake City, Winston-Salem, Dallas, and Pacoima, California, all because Carl Rogers wasn't able to make it.

It is bad only when I walk in and the audience still is expecting the great man. Something diminishing happens to one's spirit if too often faces fall when one enters a room.

Another bad time is when people approach me because what they

William R. Coulson, "Encounter Groups and Brainwashing," *Notre Dame Journal of Education,* Summer 1971, pp. 140–52.

Acknowledgment: I owe the distinction between group learning and individual learning to Weldon P. Shofstall. Currently Superintendent of Public Instruction for the State of Arizona, Dr. Shofstall is a former college professor and dean of students, and patriot many times honored. I was his student for several years, and he in turn "became mine" when my own experience in encounter groups accumulated more rapidly than his. He has since been an innovator in applying the encounter group to the classroom, where, as he has pointed out, the typical pattern has been that students have not talked to one another as persons but to the group as a whole, a situation better made for speechifying than real learning. When encounter is adapted for classroom learning, Dr. Shofstall points out, "How, when and by whom the subject matter is introduced into the group becomes a major problem. . . . If the goal is a group goal rather than the individual goals of the members, then the introduction of content into the group makes the group almost certain to be a brainwashing group."

I am afraid that Dr. Shofstall will think me unfair to many of his friends in the way I lump conservatives in this chapter. I want him to know that I can lump him with no one and take him very seriously indeed. But the indiscriminateness of many conservative voices makes them hard to take seriously; their sound is suspiciously collective itself, in its slogans as unindividuated as any left-wing party line.

But I owe Dr. Shofstall not so much this defense of any intemperateness in my writing as gratitude for what I consider his happy influence.

really want is to get to Carl; as if their message might travel better if I carried it for them.

Another bad time (bear with me, I'll feel better when this is over) is when I don't know whether or not they've already asked Carl for something and he's turned them down but suggested they come to me. It's bad, because I would like to believe that now and then I am somebody's first choice; but if I would believe that and it turned out not to be true, I would feel foolish.

It might be that your editor will clear up the present case in a footnote, because I don't know how it is with me and the *Notre Dame Journal of Education* and Carl Rogers. It's a little confusing, because the letter inviting my participation in this issue also said that if I preferred "to present an article coauthored with Dr. Rogers, this would certainly be most acceptable."

I am not taking the co-author route, as you can see, but I will recommend to you Dr. Rogers' new book, *Carl Rogers on Encounter Groups.*[1] If you will read that soon, the sense of what I am going to say will be added to, for Rogers presents what I would call a healthy version of encounter groups.

Then there are some other approaches, and this article is about them.

THE ENCOUNTER AND THE INDIVIDUAL

The encounter process and effect are not a group matter but within the individual participant himself, making him stronger, more able to do what he wants where he wants, even to the point of resisting the group if it imposes. When done well, encounter groups have nothing to do with groupness. That is precisely the reason they were originally exciting to people and valuable. In the past, encounter groups gave people a chance to try themselves out without performance expectations, a chance to see what they were like when they didn't arrange other people's reactions.

But there are approaches to encounter other than this free-form one. You have seen the extreme in the news magazines lately: Hot-bath Esalen Institute nudes earnestly engaged. Communal flower sniffing. Group lifts. The Gunther sandwich. Like . . . an X-rated summer camp.

Many in the "group movement" think they know now what everybody needs in our culture: they need freeing up. Which is not defined as being free (for who then could name what it would mean?) but is a set of prescribable behaviors: recapturing our sense of smell, say; or learning to express hostility; or becoming more graceful in body movement—that is,

[1] New York: Harper and Row, 1970.

learning to move your body more as I have learned to move mine. Many group leaders today approach their work as if the encounter were something predictable, a nameable bit of business which should occur among the participants, some preferred way time ought to be spent in encounter groups, and some desired outcome to group interaction. When this happens, the conservatives who shout that "encounter groups are a Communist plot" are right (if not to shout, at least to worry), for the process becomes like brainwashing.

(When I have thought of the possibility my own younger children might be in school-based encounter groups, I have realized that I would be very hesitant to let them participate when I did not know the group leader. I do not want my children in an encounter group led by someone I am not reasonably assured is a good person. I cannot say what would define a good person, but I know what he would *not* be: he would not be someone who has *his* goals for *my* children, who would set out to reform them. It is enough that the formative influences of our lives should be between my children and me, for only we are likely to be around for one another in the future to take responsibility for our reciprocal effect. It is not the group leader who will be there, not he who can be morally accountable.)

When encounter groups were invented, we didn't know how to act in them, and thus they were a good opportunity to try ourselves out free-form. Now, I am afraid, most of the invention surrounding such groups is the invention of new things for people to do in them, as if the opportunity to try oneself out isn't enough. Can you guess what has been happening to bring this about? A profession has been emerging, the group-leader profession, with standards, qualifications, ways of objectifying success and earning reputation. Perhaps the quickest, cheapest way to become known in this new profession is to be the inventor of techniques, for the list of possible clever group activities is endless. ("Maybe we could get people to clean one another's ears and talk about their reactions," one wag suggested. "Or pick one another's noses . . . .")

Do you think I am only kidding? A colleague in the publishing business sent me a manuscript to review, a manual offering ways in which encounter groups might reform education. It is one of a number now in preparation or already published. The author presents a list of "encounter games" and develops a rationale for them. For example, to get at the "vibrations" by which people "get to know each other," he suggests "Hand Contacts Hand," in which participants are in one stroke to be carried beyond our cultural inhibitions about touching strangers, to a new and freeing set of non-verbal acquaintanceship maneuvers. Members are told to "explore" one another and afterward to talk about what they felt as they did so. A good explorer, we are told, will bypass the issue of whether or not his partner wants to be explored, for feelings of reluctance can also provide grist for the mill when later we talk about our reactions:

> Frequently, you will find that girls do not like to be touched and might hold back, at least in the beginning. A boy in our experimental group noted that when he confronted one girl, she was almost trembling.
>
> When asked to make eye contact also, a second girl sat with her head buried in her lap and afterward questioned why she could not do the exercise. Others admitted they did it because they felt they must, and they tried to get it over as quickly as possible. Still others enjoyed it and pursued contact with force. We found these differences provided excellent discussion material. . . .
>
> Now when you switch to the left hand and then both hands together, you find the whole realm of encounter dramatically expanded. There seems to be something more meaningful in such meetings. They are new and refreshing experiences which complement the more familiar and stereotyped right-hand encounters. . . .

Aside from its naivete, its completely unfounded meaning claim ("If you think you met me in my right hand, wait till you try my left!"), this gamey, microcalisthenical approach to encounter shouts, "I KNOW WHAT IS GOOD FOR YOU!" One doesn't even have to know at whom he shouts: we all need this medicine, and if not, no matter, for then we can talk about *that* after the game. The escalation of technique has gone so far toward the impersonal that a large communications firm has now issued a set of tape-recorded group-game instructions (at $300 a copy). We are so advanced as a technological culture, that a tape recorder can tell us how we should act in order to be free. "This is your tape recorder speaking. Take your partner's left hand. Careful now . . . ."

A journalist was fascinated by what he'd heard about encounter groups. He wanted to try one. He joined a "marathon," a kind of non-stop, round-the-clock encounter group in which participants' psychological defenses are supposed to yield more thoroughly than in the more leisurely paced encounter, because of fatigue.

As the group started, one of the participants was asked by another what he did for a living. He answered, "I don't think that matters here. Call me Rumpelstiltskin—if you have to give me a name." It turned out later he was a psychiatrist, co-leader of the group.

By the group's fifth hour, the journalist had begun to doze:

> It was some time after 1 A.M. that I was jarred awake by hearing Rumpelstiltskin ask Felicia, a woman with the voluptuous but strangely asexual body of a *Playboy* foldout, whether she would go to bed with him. His question used the coarsest word possible.
>
> Felicia, her face blank, answered, "I don't know what that word means."

"Come on, you know what it means," Rumpelstiltskin said, goading her.

"I've seen it on walls but I *don't* know what it means," insisted Felicia. "I was brought up very religiously."

"Take a guess, then."

Felicia suggested a very unconventional form of coupling that took me aback even more.

"No," Rumpelstiltskin corrected her, "it means sexual intercourse."

"Well, I've never slept with a man," protested Felicia in a small voice.

"Anyway, let's hear you say the word. Go ahead, say it," insisted Rumpelstiltskin.

Felicia said it in an emotionless voice and added several other four-letter expletives. "What's so great about that?"

"You've got a real mothering hang-up, Felicia," continued Rumpelstiltskin. "You use it to hide your fear of offending people. You wear it like I wear this sweater which identifies me as Bob, the Great White Therapist." (Although this was the first admission we'd had from Rumpelstiltskin that he was . . . the psychiatrist, none of us was surprised.) "Now," he went on, "I want you to go around the room and say the nastiest thing you can think of to every person here. . . . And every time you hesitate or fail to say something nasty enough, you've got to get down on your knees and crawl across the room, and kiss my hand." . . .

Felicia turned to Rod, the Irish type, and said, "I think you're a pompous ass."

"Fine," said Bob, "but you looked back to me for support. Come on. Crawl.'

We all watched, spellbound. Slowly, Felicia sank down beside Bob's chair. . . .

"You're no better than your husband," she said to Louisa.

"My God, your life is a mess," she said to the painter's wife, Bonnie.

"I'll bet you really use women," she said to me.

Though ashen, Felicia managed to say something rude to all 18 people in the group, but three times she looked back at Bob, and three times he made her crawl across the room and kiss his hand.[2]

If it sounds cruel, it is supposed to be for the person's own good. Of himself, Rumpelstiltskin might say, "You think it's easy for me to be a mean bastard? I'll tell you, it costs me." Of Felicia, he might say her sweetness was a coverup for the hostility lurking beneath, unexpressed and

---

[2] From "Get Down and Crawl," by James Halpin, *Seattle Magazine, Dec., 1967.*

therefore unexamined, a barrier to her emergence as a genuine person. Although Felicia resisted at first the crudeness of the suggestion that she change her behavior—"Do it! Now!"—she might have agreed later that the psychiatrist was right about her and meant well. When the journalist checked with Felicia a week afterward, in fact, she said it had been a growthful experience, one she would like to repeat. "Me, I'm not so sure," the journalist said.

(Yes, Virginia, there actually are such "encounter groups," though I hope no one I love ever finds himself in one. What if he didn't resent that kind of treatment? What if, like Felicia, he actually was grateful? What would he have learned? "Thank God for the Doctor. How could I ever be myself if not for him?")

My newspaper headlines, "She Sues Over Judo in Sensitivity Course":

> The sensitivity session recommended to Constance Grant by her employers . . . advertised that it would "increase . . . self-understanding . . . interpersonal effectiveness . . . confidence and ability to work in group situations"

> So Miss Grant went. . . .

> Toward the end of the course, Miss Grant and one of her classmates, Sandra Pine, were encouraged "to physically demonstrate aggression and hostility."

> According to . . . Miss Grant's lawyer, what resulted was a judo hold that sent Miss Grant to the hardwood floor of the sensitivity training room flat on her back.

> Miss Grant has filed a lawsuit for $500,000. . . .

She didn't have to do it if she didn't want, did she? That's right. Unlike the bad example with which I began this chaper, the Manual for Educational Reform, most group exercises have an "option out" clause. The $300 tape recording, for example, cautions the group to respect the wishes of any member not to participate. "No one should be forced to do any exercise of which he is shy." (Maybe that's why it costs $300: a tape recording with a conscience.)

But it's hard to pull that off, you know: not participate when everyone else seems to be doing so easily. A person who had enough strength to say No when everyone else was saying Yes, wouldn't need an encounter group. He could start his own program.

Even when the leader doesn't operate as if his job were to force on group members gimmicky guides-to-live-by, sometimes there can be subtle, compelling pressures in the group nonetheless. Loring Woodman reports:

> We got into the subject of sex in our group, and I was explaining some of my frustration at being caught between what I actually felt and the

cultural norms, between a kind of honest approach and the strange feeling that somehow I ought to be living up to a different cultural model, a model I had partly incorporated into myself but which yet was still somehow alien to the way I usually react.

In trying to bring this discussion down to the "here-and-now," as it were, I think I got talked into saying something about my feelings toward one of the girls in the group which was not really me. What started out as a general, personal attraction to this girl came out instead, under the "guidance" of the group, as a straight "I want to screw you" type approach. On looking back at this now, I feel as though I'd been conned into saying this when it was not an adequate representation of how I felt toward her. . . . Somehow, at the time, I didn't think this episode had made much difference to me—but the amount of time I spent thinking about it afterwards belies that thought. It seemed like the group had "gotten what it wanted" and was now ready to move on to someone else.

Encounter groups distort what they are good at, which is a chance for a person to try himself out and make his own value discoveries, when they attempt to teach values, as in Loring's group: "You should say what you feel. Say it with directness. No need to hide here what would embarrass you elsewhere." Under that kind of pressure, a person might say, and sometimes do, considerably more than he means. Apparently Loring did, realizing it only later.

A number of years ago the research staff at our Center got involved for a while in the "encounter movement." We went to a "growth center" for a workshop and shared group leadership with the staff there. We felt some uneasiness afterward and surveyed our reactions to see if we could tell what was discomfiting about the experience. One of the leader reaction sheets reported:

More than in the previous workshops I've attended, there was in the air at ———— a demand to "let go." While I know that letting go, simply experiencing, has its beneficial effect, the pressure at ———— carried with it, as I saw it, the demand to suspend judgment, to suspend critical awareness, simply, indeed, to be irrational. The demand (and the atmosphere itself, rather than any one person generating it), the demand to "let go," became a demand to "go along," to go along with the group mind, to go along and not to think but to feel.

Sometimes one succumbs to that pressure, feels a vague uneasiness while doing so, but only afterward realizes what happened. This is the way in which encounter groups become dangerous, when subtly they cause individuals to yield their own judgment.

I wrote the report above myself. It was after only my third encounter experience. But I have since continued to attend encounter groups and still recommend them to people. Why? What answer can there be to brainwashing charges [3] and to my own suggestions that the charges are not entirely without merit?

1) People are resilient. People are not so easily bent as the conservatives imply. When something bad happens to people they know it. Loring did. I have. You probably would too. Could it be that we worry about *other* people?

Yes. For example, I said I worry about my children. If one of them were looking over my shoulder, he might say, "Dad. I worry about you."

But in nature, what better sensing-judging equipment is there to take care of people than their own? Sure, some people go crazy. And all of us hurt ourselves in stupid ways from time to time, not knowing our own good. But if in the long run each of us didn't know his own good, couldn't

---

[3] Here is a sample of the charges:

1) Rev. W. S. McBirnie's booklet, *Sensitivity Training: The Plan to Brainwash America,* quotes former chief W. Cleon Skousen in "The Police Chief's Manual": ". . . the promotors of [encounter] programs are trying to *homogenize* the members of the group. *Individualism* must be sacrificed. Group dependency must be established. When one member holds out for a conviction or moral value which is above the norm of the group ,the tendency is for the group to gang up on that member in an attempt to justify their own lower values. Ridicule, sarcasm and other 'honest' feelings are expressed against the hold-out." (Emphasis in original.)

2) McBirnie also quotes Congressman John G. Schmitz on sensitivity training: "It appears to be aimed at destroying the independence, self-confidence and self-reliance of the individual—the foundations of both liberty and good government."

3) The conservative documents usually quote one another so repeatedly that often one can't find where a particular charge emanates. But here is what the San Diego County Federation of Republican Women's Clubs reports, though I don't know where the descriptive portion comes from (I gather that most of the conservative critics have not participated in encounter groups themselves):

" 'We were told to hold hands and not speak for two hours . . . we bunched close together pressing against the person in the center—a sort of group bundling. . . . I tell you there is a look on those kids that I can't describe to you. . . . They are all embracing and kissing one another in the most weirdest fashion . . . it produces the emotional binge. One of the veterans even broke down and bawled.'

"This whole process is designed to make the members feel completely dependent upon the group and instill a reluctance to think or do anything different from the rest of the group. After criticism of family, friends, home and moral, political, and religious belief, his old values are weakened and he is ready for a new set. Does this sound strangely familiar? This same method of group criticism was used to brainwash American prisoners of war in Korea. . . ."

4) On the "method of group criticism" itself, Rev. McBirnie quotes Army psychiatrist, Major William E. Mayer, who studied repatriated American prisoners of war from Korea: "Very rapidly the soldier who was talking gets the feeling . . . that he had gone too far; he had exposed himself too much. . . . So when ten men would walk out of a self-criticism group, they would walk out in ten separate directions, divided like sticks in the Old Testament that you can break so easily when they are apart but are so strong if they're together."

speak best for himself, wasn't to be trusted with himself, then nature would have made human beings upside down—and *that* would be crazy, for the rest of nature seems to be well suited to its life.

There is less magic in the world than the superstitious would lead us to believe. And that includes brainwashing. It's not a magic process which happens to you and you don't know it. If it happens, you know it. Eventually. And then you can correct it.

That is what the conservatives themselves have done. They have lived under what they would call a "liberal government" for a long time, and they're not brainwashed. They are resilient. Aren't we all?

2) People are not evil. The conservatives claim there is a conspiracy which aims to do us dirt. There may be. I'm sure I couldn't prove there wasn't. If I looked into it and said there was no evidence of a conspiracy, they could say, "See how insidious it is! The conspirators fooled you (you dupe)."

A life conspiracy theory is an example of an "other people" claim, in which we assert that what is not true of ourselves (that we are Communist conspirators) is true of others, who seldom are present to account for themselves. This sort of claiming, not only about conspiracy but about life, tends to get overcome in encounter groups. If you and I were in an encounter group together and you said, "People are evil," I might be impressed for a while, then I might think twice, and then I might say, "Well, really, I don't think I am. At least I don't mean to be. I don't mean harm to people." Or an aggressive group member might say to you, "Why don't you speak for yourself? Are *you* evil?" And if you said, "Yes," he'd say, "Why don't you talk about that instead of wasting our time with people who aren't here." And if you said, "No, I'm not evil," he'd say, "Then how come you make claims about other people which aren't true of you?"

"Why don't you speak for yourself?" is one of the demands which tend to be made in encounter groups, and I don't think it's a bad one, for how will we locate truth unless people say what they mean? A characteristic of ordinary social discourse is that we make sloppy claims about the world and about those who people it, and we never, ever make contact with one another in social discourse because the others don't pause to consider that deep down they don't believe these things we say but instead rush ahead to pile their own crap on top of the conversational pile. Nobody stops to see whom he is with. No one speaks for himself. In encounter groups, because there is a lot of time and nothing to do, people do stop to consider. And if *you* don't, if you rush ahead, making sloppy, ill-considered claims about "everybody," then someone finally will challenge you. He'll ask you to consider that fact that in his own deepest heart he doesn't feel that he is an example of what you're saying, and he'll ask you to consider whether or not you think *you* are an example of it—"And if not, then why don't you just shut up for a while?"

But, again, are people evil? Apparently not, when you consider them in their singularity. But when enmeshed in institutional purposes, they often work counter to the immediately experienced good, even their own. A recent president escalated our involvement in a war nobody wanted, and another asserted, "I am not going to be the first American president to be said to have lost a war." One was trying to do a good job; the other was concerned about his reputation. It's the same thing. In both cases, for what they saw as common, institutional good, they ordered young men to maim and kill other young men—and old ladies, and little children. . . . Yet each loves his daughters, is undoubtedly good to his friends, and would never by personal choice pour fire on an old lady.

What encounter groups are about is speaking, acting for yourself, no longer institutionally. And there—it seems so clear when you're in a good encounter group—is where you can trust people and where they're lovable. Personally.

It is the possibility of excess in the loving which probably frightens many of the conservatives about encounter groups [4] ("embracing and kissing one another in the most weirdest fashion"), but, really, you can't have it both ways. Either participants in encounter groups will get too close and, for love of one another, abandon their traditional commitments—*or* the encounter process will prove divisive and weaken solidarity among participants because each feels he has "exposed himself too much" and has to watch his step now with the others. But it doesn't make sense to charge that the groups are both ways at once.

What would people have to be like for the conservative assumption about encounter to be correct, that you have to watch out because the groups brainwash their participants? Human nature would have to be at the same time very weak and very depraved; participants would have to be weak and malleable and leaders wicked. I don't find either to be true, and if the conservatives do, they will have to show more cases and offer less hearsay. In the meantime, I think we have to assume that people in encounter groups are like people we know elsewhere, and that includes ourselves: basically decent. Again, I am. And if I shouldn't assume it of you, you will have to tell me.

Don't call me a Pollyanna, for I know there are times when any of us might seem depraved indeed, even demented. But there are other times, better times, when we are not.

---

[4] I don't want to put this just on "the conservatives," for I fear it too at times. And in my own best, non-institutional self, I have no wish to put good people in a bag marked "conservative."

I know I can be trusted, for example, when I am paying attention and not harassed; but if you catch me when I am busy, when my mind has not been brought to attend on what you wish to trust me with, then I might deal with your concern very sloppily.

I know I can be trusted when I see that I am needed. I think this is true of all of us and probably accounts for how good most people are, even to strangers, when all are under natural disaster.

I know I can be trusted when I am secure in the moment, when I am not afraid. I know I can be trusted if you will let me see you and if, with that assist, I can come to recall who I am too. In that moment I know that if we had enough time, we might find one another as brothers.

There are conditions under which people appear wicked and when one would be ill-advised to trust them. There are other conditions when they are magnificent. And if you agree with my partial list of trust conditions, then I will add that they are some of the very conditions which were captured in the early encounter groups.

But lately, increasingly as the movement gains momentum, encounter groups lose their early promise. Often they are gamey now. Sometimes they are coercive. Nudity, blind walks, trust formation games, arm wrestling, judo. These are some of the tricks by which the public now knows encounter groups. But all of the gimmicks could be eliminated without eliminating the core of the group itself, and that is the sensing of community. To characterize the encounter group by its coercive, vulgar elements is to define the whole by its worst abuses. To attack it on its begimmicked grounds is to be concerned with non-essentials. But to offer it on these grounds is likewise to distort what the experience might provide. As a free-form experience in community the encounter group is a valid, even necessary social invention in these days of weakened family ties, days when we have forgotten how strong the bonds can be between people and how unalienated from their fellows they can feel, days when we need somewhere to be reminded of this so that we can have it again at home.

When done in this way, that is, freely, encounter groups are conservative institutions. Their effect is on the individual, strengthening him; and in their process aspects, they are best to be seen as occasions for personal responsibility. Because sessions typically are lengthy and thus have time for the minutiae of each participant's existence, the individual eventually finds vanishing the excuses by which habitually he gets off the hook of self-responsibility. Because encounter groups are exhaustive in this way, the individual no longer can say he didn't have time to express his meaning. There is time now. And if he cannot communicate at this his leisure, cannot find himself under his freest of communal opportunities, then finally he can see clearly who is responsible. No longer can he lay to lack of opportunity the failure to be what he wants. No longer, then, need he wait.

Accordingly, he emerges from the encounter with an enhanced sense of personal potency. There is something to be done after all. He waits no longer for an unknown other to save him.

Toward freedom and community and self-responsibility is not, however, the way the encounter *movement* is going. It is going toward performance and thus becomes undistinctive and unnecessary, for existing social institutions sufficiently expect the individual to perform. Founded to serve the individual and protect him, our traditional institutions have turned rule-ladenly upside-down, the individual now expected to serve purposes lined out for him institutionally. So to the begamed encounter group, though a bit more insidiously. It assigns people—O marvelous contradiction!—to behave freely. It teachers them to strike poses of openness. It gives the participant new ways out of responsibility: "I did it because the doctor said I should."

A symposium on encounter groups appeared recently in a journal of the American Psychological Association.[5] The majority of the symposium contributors, professions and academicians expert in group work, demanded assurances from group practitioners that participants "would be helped to learn" in encounter groups. As against a human being model of group participation and leadership, the experts wanted expertise: they wanted structure, they wanted performance expectations and the security of replicable technique, they wanted leaders who could point out to participants what they were learning. They wanted group members to know where the group was going before it began, and at the end, most assuredly, they wanted understanding nailed down of where the group had been.

Such a guided-tour model of the encounter group necessitates a leader who has already been where the group might go, lest he fail as a guide. But who wants to travel only the ground staked out by the human relations professionals? Who says the best places to go already are known?

I told the symposium participants about the group filmed by W. H. McGaw, Jr., of the Center for Studies of the Person, the film which won the Academy Award for documentaries, *Journey Into Self.* I told them about Jerry, one of the men in the group, who had been very guarded until about the fifth hour, when he spoke movingly of having no friends, in spite of his hail-fellow style. In the eighth hour Jerry cried. Several of the other group members cried, too, as they saw him. I guess he was feeling then more deeply what he had said before about having no friends. But people respected his privacy. They didn't quiz him about his tears. It was as though, in that moment, Jerry was able to express meaning, as one human being no longer afarid of others. There was nothing to do then but love him for it.

[5] *The Counseling Psychologist,* II, 2, 1970. Pp. 1–76.

But one of the participants in that APA symposium suggested an alternative approach than the one in the film, where the facilitators had just let the group happen:

> . . . in the eighth hour, rather than what did transpire, the trainer might ask the group to explore how the norms about the expression of friendship or concern had developed within the group, what sub-groups or cliques had formed within the group, which persons felt most part of the group and which members felt that they were not part of the group, and so on. Presumably, the trainer's interventions generally are directed at the purpose for which the group was organized, in this case a better understanding of how groups develop and function.

"We all know why we're here, let's get on with it."

Well, it seems to me that some of the most productive learning experiences follow when we *don't* know why we're here, none of us, or when our original purpose for being here is upset. For then, no longer knowing what's going on, we finally find it difficult to manipulate events into old ruts. Only then, it seems to me, do we face the possibility of moral growth, when we step beyond what we already "knew," no longer able to treat our fellow tactically because we find we don't know where to steer them anymore. It seems to me that any "trainer" should long to find himself in such a place, where he no longer knows what's happening.

"We know how groups develop and function," the trainer approach says. "Better than telling it to people, however, is letting them see it in the example of their own group interaction." This is why some encounter groups are called "laboratories." It is a form of indirect teaching, where the professor draws out of the class itself the points he wants to make. It is supposed to be more effective than straight lecture. Many students resent it as manipulative and dishonest. Unless he is perfectly content to sacrifice himself for the community, living a lonely-knowing life, it seems to me the professor should resent it too.

THE ENCOUNTER MOVEMENT

There are two poles to the encounter movement (and in the middle, the body of good guys, me and my friends). On one pole is the tricky approach, as exemplified by the Esalen nude: "If you take your clothes off, there will be lots to talk about." This, and other group gimmicks, are called "generating data," as if the fact that each of us has been trying to live his life wouldn't give us enough to talk about.

At the other end is the analytic approach, exemplified by people at the National Training Laboratories, those who call themselves "trainers" (as in "animal"). They have data generating devices, too, but are reputed to keep their clothes on, being from the East Coast. Their forte is helping the group come to a shared understanding of its own process (and thereby of group process generally), as if people weren't able to see their own experience without the help of Ph.D.'s.

The analytic approach strikes me as totalitarian. If there is something for the conservatives rightly to fear in the encounter group this is it; where we are all expected to learn the same thing together, and where, as a group analyzing our shared experience, we can come to acknowledge what that something is. Though the trainer could have told us before we began what we were to learn, it is better that he didn't, this approach says, for when we come to it ourselves (with the help of his "interventions") the learning is more likely to stick.

It would not do just to have a moral revulsion to this kind of manipulation, for it is not so much a magic process of brainwashing, as it is an utter waste of time and a missed opportunity for the kind of accelerated personal learning which can go on in community. It seems to me that the only assuredly honest and lasting learnings are individual learnings—if you will, secret learnings, learnings stimulated within the community but which the individual speaks to no one save himself. The possibilities of dishonesty and of self-coercion and of eventual value compromise (fabricating learnings to please the group—"Yes, I learned what you learned") are very great when group learning is emphasized and when learnings are to be announced. For me, the encounter group has always been a chance to get away from such learnings, from organization and performance, and fiinally to be with people, just to be.

"There is a view of life," Soren Kierkegaard said, "which conceives that where the crowd is, there also is the truth . . .":

> There is another view of life which conceives that wherever there is a crowd there is untruth, so that . . . even if every individual, each for himself in private, were to be in possession of the truth, yet in case they were all to get together in a crowd—a crowd to which any sort of decisive significance is attributed, a voting, noisy, audible crowd—untruth would at once be in evidence.
>
> . . . if there were an assemblage even of only ten—and if they should put the truth to the ballot, that is to say, if the assemblage should be regarded as the authority, if it is the crowd which turns the scale—then there is untruth.[6]

We need all the power of occasion we can muster, it seems to me, in which individuals can seek their truth for themselves, for the collective's

[6] S. Kierkegaard, "The Individual," in *The Point of View for My Work as an Author.* New York: Harper and Row, 1962, p. 110.

lack of success in finding it has been notable. Too bad it is that the conservatives have made "the collective" their own catchword of warning, for shouting the word in assemblage empties it of meaning. But the word is useful in this consideration of encounter groups. In his own day Kierkegaard spoke of the distinction between the individual person and man-as-specimen, and he rued the "modern notion"

> . . . that to be a man is to belong to a race endowed with reason, so that the race or species is higher than the individual, which is to say that there are no more individuals but only specimens.[7]

I think it is concern about being turned into specimens which motivates the conservative alarm—and I am with them, if not so much in alarm at least in regret that the better opportunity to attain true manhood in community is being missed as the encounter movement gathers momentum, as people exhibit themselves now as types of repeatable group learnings.

The particular potency of the encounter group lies in its being an occasion for the individual to know himself better, to be able to decide for himself about himself, no expert able to direct him as well as he can himself upon entering community with his fellows. At its best, the encounter group is thus a benign anarchy, where if participants accrue similar learnings it is only because it turns out that way, never because it can be arranged in advance. All the learnings of encounter are private, individual ones, to which the group has no claim whatsoever.

But encounter groups can offend as dreadfully as any political collective, yet more immediately, when they roll along on the energy of a crowd, when they become a court which decides about the individual, which calls on him to perform, which claims right of access into his secret heart.

When that happens, I want no part of them.

[7] *Ibid.*, p. 111.

5 / "I Learn by Going Where I Have to Go."

I wake to sleep, and take my waking slow.
I feel my fate in what I cannot fear.
I learn by going where I have to go.

We think by feeling. What is there to know?
I hear my being dance from ear to ear.
I wake to sleep, and take my waking slow.

Of those so close beside me, which are you?
God bless the Ground! I shall walk softly there,
And learn by going where I have to go.

Light takes the Tree; but who can tell us how?
The lowly worm climbs up a winding stair;
I wake to sleep, and take my waking slow.

Great Nature has another thing to do
To you and me; so take the lively air,
And, lovely, learn by going where to go.

This shaking keeps me steady. I should know.
What falls away is always. And is near.
I wake to sleep, and take my waking slow.
I learn by going where I have to go.

–"The Waking," *by Theodore Roethke*

Human Relations Training
for Elementary School Principals

Terry A. Thomas

Educators agree that awareness of group processes and interpersonal skills is of primary importance for effective school administration. Griffiths maintains that not only are an individual's skills essential for effective human relations but certain personal qualities are also vital:

> First of all, he knows himself—his strengths and weaknesses. He is aware of his own attitudes and assumptions. He has an inner security which enables him to consider new ideas and can work to bring about orderly changes in both the system and the people in the system. He is skillful in understanding others' words and behavior because he accepts viewpoints, perceptions, and beliefs which differ from his own. He works to create an atmosphere of approval and security for all his organization. He knows that all he does or fails to do has an effect on his associates. Human skills have become an integral part of his whole being.[1]

Ineffective, although otherwise wholly qualified, elementary school principals may fit Bennis' description of being ". . . badly cast to play the intricate human roles required of them . . . [their] ineptitude and anxieties lead to systems of discord and defense which interfere with the problem-solving capacities of organizations." [2]

To establish and maintain a fully functioning school, a principal must be aware of his influence on his staff. Feedback on others' perceptions of his behavior must be readily available to him—a situation possible only in a climate of mutual trust, one that is open, honest, and satisfying to the staff. A relationship of trust between a teacher and a school principal depends primarily on the skills and knowledge employed by the principal.

Terry A. Thomas, "Human Relations Training for Elementary School Principals," *The National Elementary Principal,* May 1971, pp. 59–62.

A NEW EMPHASIS IN TRAINING ADMINISTRATORS

In the last few years, human relations training for school administrators has received increased recognition. Traditional college courses for school administrators emphasized school buildings, personnel administration, finance, and school management. Now, more emphasis is placed on the application of the behavioral sciences to educational problems. The focus of administration is on people.

Many school administrators who were trained several years ago find this new emphasis helpful, and its popularity as a method of continuing education is evident in the number and variety of opportunities we have to participate in such experiences. *Sensitivity training, T-grouping, encounter groups, human relations seminars, and laboratory training* are among the terms used to identify these formal opportunities to improve our interpersonal relations skills and to learn about ourselves, to become more "aware."

The form of these training sessions may vary from a two-week conference, a weekend marathon meeting, or a few hours regularly scheduled each week. The participants may be strangers from different walks of life, people with the same job responsibilities, or an entire school faculty.

Participation in laboratory experiences requires a large investment in time and money. What do the participants and the sponsoring organizations receive in return for this investment? Can laboratory training really help a person become a better school administrator?

THE LABORATORY EXPERIENCE

An opportunity to study the effects of laboratory training on the relations of principals with their teaching staffs was provided by the Oregon Elementary School Principals Association, which sponsored a five-day residential laboratory on interpersonal relations for educators from all over the state in cooperation with the Oregon Secondary School Principals Association, the Northwest Regional Educational Laboratory, and the Oregon State Department of Education. This laboratory was held at the University of the Pacific, Forest Grove, Oregon, in June 1968.

The author conducted a follow-up study of 14 elementary school principals who were participants in the program in order to discover: 1) what observable behavioral changes resulted from laboratory training, and 2) what effect these changes had on the social-emotional climate of their schools.

The laboratory training staff, secured by the Northwest Regional Educational Laboratory, was headed by John Wallen, Regional Coordinator for the NTL Institute for Applied Behavioral Science. Each staff member was highly qualified in the areas of laboratory training and the behavioral sciences and had a wide background of professional experience in conducting training sessions.

OBJECTIVES

The following laboratory objectives were stated in the material handed to participants:

1. To increase each person's understanding of:
   a. Ways he sends messages—how others see his actions differently from the way he sees them.
   b. His tendency to misread other people's behavior.
   c. How feelings influence behavior—his own as well as the behavior of others.
   d. His silent assumptions (those he has been unaware of) that give rise to his feelings about other people's actions.
2. To increase each person's skill in:
   a. Understanding the feelings and ideas of others; using skillful checking responses to decrease damaging misunderstandings.
   b. Communicating his own feelings and ideas in ways that are maximally informative and minimally hurtful to others.
   c. Dealing with conflict and misunderstanding.

Numerous sources outline activities typically pursued at a human relations laboratory, and the Oregon laboratory did not deviate markedly from these.[3] Among the learning outcomes emphasized were: openness about feelings, emphasis on the "here-and-now," encouragement toward using others as "auxiliary nervous systems" or "social mirrors," and reception of "feedback" in relation to one's own behavior.

EXPECTED OUTCOMES

What kinds of behavioral changes could one expect in elementary school principals as a result of laboratory training? It was hypothesized that an administrator would become more tactful in dealing with his teaching staff. He would become more sensitive to the needs of others and would not abuse other people's feelings. Because he would feel less threatened, he would find it easier and more desirable to develop closer relationships with his staff. Instead of being coolly formal and relying on his status in order to influence his staff, he would tend to become aware of their individual differences and willing to relate to them as persons rather than just staff.

He would also communicate more effectively, employing skillful speaking as well as effective listening. His staff members would feel freer to bring professional or personal problems to him. The principal would also become more effective in his efforts to improve staff performances, and he would involve teachers in making policy decisions for the school.

These changes could also be expected to have certain effects on the whole school organization. Teachers would tend to accept the organization's goals more completely and to work more effectively toward their fulfillment. The staff would become a more cohesive group and would gain more satisfaction in the accomplishment of their tasks. They would have a higher level of morale and would become more open to innovation and change. Such a school would provide a better education for young people.

To determine if these changes actually occurred, a follow-up study was designed to measure changes for the following variables:

1. Changes in the elementary school principals:
   a. status emphasis
   b. communication effectiveness
   c. directiveness and dominance
   d. tact
   e. use of collaborative decision making
   f. leadership directed toward improving the quality of staff performances

2. Changes in the elementary school organization:
   a. group cohesion
   b. morale
   c. staff perception of administrative tasks
   d. social-emotional climate

Measurement of these changes was accomplished through a questionnaire completed by 204 teachers working in 28 Oregon elementary schools. The questionnaire was based on the Organizational Climate Descriptive Questionnaire (OCDQ) developed by Halpin and Croft,[4] the Executive Professional Leadership scale (EPL) developed by Gross and Herriott, a tact (or Social Support) scale, also from the National Principalship Study of Gross and Herriott, and included questions devised to determine the extent to which the principal shares with teachers certain decision-making responsibilities.[5]

The items contained in the questionnaire were selected because they most clearly represented the interpersonal behavior hypothesized to change as a result of laboratory training and because these dimensions of behavior were considered vital to the effective operation of an elementary school. The reliability and validity of these measures were considered satisfactory for the purpose of this study.

PARTICIPANTS

In order to determine the effects of laboratory training on the interpersonal behavior of elementary school principals with their teaching staff, each experimental group principal was matched with a control group principal. Prior to the laboratory session, its preregistrants were invited by letter to participate in the follow-up study. Each of the 14 principals who agreed to participate in the study supplied names and addresses of all teachers who were planning to remain in his school for the following year.

Each principal also completed a personal data sheet containing information about: 1) the number of teachers in his school, 2) his years of experience in his present principalship, 3) his total years of experience in educational administration, and 4) his age.

On the basis of the size of their schools, principals who had not preregistered for the laboratory were also invited to participate in the study. Those who agreed to participate in the study also completed the personal data sheet. From these principals, a matched control group was selected.

COLLECTION OF DATA

Questionnaires were sent to teacher-observers of the participating principals, both experimental and control groups. The first set of data was collected in late spring, just before the laboratory sessions were scheduled to begin. Nine months after the sessions, a follow-up questionnaire was sent to the same teachers. After-measures were accepted from only those teachers who completed the before-measures. In this way, the data contained pairs of before- and after-measures from the same sources, thus reducing the possibility of variance attributable to the teacher-observers and emphasizing the variance of the principals' behavior due to change. Both groups could, of course, be expected to change during the nine-month interval of the before-measures and the after-measures, but it was assumed that any systematic differences would be attributable to the five-day training laboratory.

FINDINGS

The results of the analysis provided support for the following hypotheses:

The experimental group principals became more considerate of the individual needs of the staff.

The experimental group principals used more tact

The experimental group principals moved toward a collaborative approach in the area of deciding how the teachers should be supervised.

The experimental group principals increased leadership in improving staff performance.

The staff of the experimental group principals gained higher group morale.

The experimental group principals' schools became more open.

INTERPRETATIONS

The elementary school principals who participated in the five-day laboratory training did alter certain aspects of their behavior in working with their staff. They became more aware of the conditions that facilitate effective group functioning and altered their interpersonal behavior with the school staff. They felt less threatened by their teachers and thus were more willing to engage in democratic decision-making processes.

Being more tactful, considerate, and democratic with his staff can help a principal overcome the interpersonal barriers associated with helping a teacher improve his performance. Evidence indicates that a principal's EPL is closely associated with both teacher and pupil performance,[6] and the experimental group did exhibit more change toward higher EPL than did the control group.

Does an elementary school principal change his behavior as a result of a five-day training laboratory? The findings of this study indicate that not only did the principals' interpersonal behavior change but the changes were desirable both administratively and educationally. The staffs of the experimental group displayed more change toward higher group morale and apparently derived more satisfaction from their work. They were also more open to educational innovations.

These findings support the use of laboratory training as one means of effecting change in the interpersonal relations of elementary school principals with their teaching staffs. The changes appear to have important, positive consequences for the quality of the educational program of an elementary school.

RECOMMENDATIONS

In view of the above, school districts and professional associations should consider the training laboratory when seeking innovative inservice programs for school administrators. However, one should keep a number of factors in mind.

The study reported in this article found positive results from a five-day laboratory conducted by highly qualified professional training staff. An individual or organization contemplating participation in a laboratory training experience should determine carefully the qualifications of the training staff. The duration of training is also important. The marathon or "quickie" weekend training laboratory has not shown the effectiveness of other forms of training. Durable and significant behavioral changes require time to become fixed or internalized by the participant. Moreover, those who are considering participation in a training laboratory should enter the laboratory with open minds. They must be prepared to change themselves and their interpersonal behavior rather than merely to help other people change.

The training laboratory evaluated in this study was conducted in the spring after the school year was over. Its participants had a normally busy summer season prior to the opening of school in the fall. Although the changes they made during the laboratory session were still evident the following spring, it seems probable that a laboratory conducted just prior to the opening of school in the wall would have even greater effect.

The present study indicates that an elementary school principal's laboratory training in interpersonal relations affects both his behavior with his staff and the social-emotional climate of his school. However, more research is needed to confirm that principals who are involved in such laboratory training undergo helpful behavioral changes that improve the learning climate of a school.

FOOTNOTES

1. Griffiths, Daniel E. *Human Relations in School Administration.* New York: Appleton-Century-Crofts, 1956. P. 10.

2. Bennis, Warren G. *Changing Organizations.* New York: McGraw-Hill Book Co., 1966. p. 116.

3. Especially useful references are:

Bennis, Warren G. *Changing Organizations.* (See footnote 2.)

Bradford, Leland P.; Gibb, Jack R.; and Benne, Kenneth D. *T-Group Theory and Laboratory Method.* New York: John Wiley & Sons, 1964.

Marrow, Alfred I. *Behind the Executive Mask: Greater Managerial Competence Through Deeper Self-Understanding.* New York: American Management Association, 1964.

Schein, Edgar H., and Bennis, Warren G., editors. *Personal and Organizational Change Through Group Methods: The Laboratory Approach.* New York: John Wiley & Sons, 1965.

Weschler, Irving R., and Reisel, Jerome. *Inside a Sensitivity Training Group.* Berkeley, Calif.: Institute of Industrial Relations, University of California, 1960.

4. Halpin, Andrew W., and Croft, Don B. *The Organizational Climate of Schools.* Chicago: Midwest Administration Center, University of Chicago, 1963.

5. Gross, Neal, and Herriott, Robert E. *Staff Leadership in Public Schools: A Sociological Inquiry.* New York: John Wiley and Sons, 1965.

6. See footnote 5, p. 22.

The Personal Approach
to Good Teaching

Arthur W. Combs

To plan effective programs for teacher education we need the very best definition of good teaching we can acquire. That seems clear enough. How to arrive at such a definition, however, has proved to be a most difficult task. Despite millions of dollars and millions of man-hours poured into research on the problem over the past 50 years, the results have continued to be frustrating and disappointing—until recently. It now appears that our failure to find useful definitions may be due to the inadequacies of the frame of reference from which we have attacked the problem.

THE TEACHER AS KNOWER

The earliest conception of the good teacher was that of the scholar. It was assumed that a person who knew could teach others. Of course it is true that a teacher has to know something but, even without research, it is apparent to anyone who looks that "knowing" is simply not enough. Most of us recall out of our own experience the teacher who "knew his subject but could not put it across." In some places there can even be found good teachers whose depth of information in a particular field is woefully lacking! This is often a shocking discovery to some critics of education who still equate teaching with scholarship. One of my own studies on good teaching demonstrated that *both,* good teachers and bad ones, knew equally well what a good teaching situation *ought* to be like (Combs, 1961). Knowing is certainly important to teaching, but, it is clear, good teaching involves much more.

Arthur W. Combs, "The Personal Approach to Good Teaching." *Educational Leadership,* 21(6):369–377, 399; March, 1964. Reprinted with permisison of the Association for Supervision and Curriculum Development and Arthur W. Combs. Copyright © 1964 by the Association for Supervision and Curriculum Development.

THE "COMPETENCIES" APPROACH TO TEACHING

A second approach to defining good teaching has been in terms of teacher "competencies." The thinking goes something like this: If we know what the expert teachers do, or are like, then we can teach the beginners to be like that. This is a straightforward, uncomplicated approach to the problem and seems logically sound.

This idea has produced great quantities of research into the traits of good teachers and their methods. This has provided us with long lists of competencies supposedly characteristic of good teachers. In the beginning these lists were quite simple. Since, however, what people do is always related to the situations they are in, every situation calls for a different behavior and the more situations the researchers examine, the longer the lists of competencies have become.

The following, for example, is a list made by a conference of "Superior Teachers" in 1962:

Good teachers should:
Know their subject
Know much about related subjects
Be adaptable to new knowledge
Understand the process of becoming
Recognize individual differences
Be a good communicator
Develop an inquiring mind
Be available
Be committed
Be enthusiastic
Have a sense of humor
Have humility
Cherish his own individuality
Have convictions
Be sincere and honest
Act with integrity
Show tolerance and understanding
Be caring
Have compassion
Have courage
Have personal security
Be creative
Be versatile

Be willing to try

Be adaptable

Believe in God.

This is but a short list. There are much longer ones!

At first, attempts to discover the competencies of good teachers were highly specific. Hundreds of attempts were made to demonstrate that good teachers had this or that trait, used this or that method—all to no avail! Good teaching simply could not be defined in terms of any particular trait or method. In 1959, the American Association of School Administrators commissioned a team to review the research on the problem. Out of this the school administrators hoped to find some guidelines which might help them make the practical decisions about a high quality of teaching necessary in carrying on their jobs. Sadly, the team was forced to report that there is no specific trait or method sufficiently associated with good teaching to provide clear distinctions (Ellena, 1961).

Some investigators have thought better discriminations might be found in generic, rather than specific studies of the "teaching act." Accordingly, they have turned their attention to the *general* traits or methods used by the teacher. Approaching the problem in this way they have been able to find fairly stable distinctions in such general terms as, "good teachers are considerate," or "child centered," or "concerned about structure." The most significant of these is a study by Marie Hughes (1959) under a grant from the U.S. Office of Education, Cooperative Research Program. Dr. Hughes developed an exhaustive system for analyzing teacher behavior and applied this system to time sample observations of teachers in the classroom. She was able to demonstrate a number of general classes of behavior seemingly characteristic of good teachers. Among these were such categories as controlling, imposition, facilitating, content development, response, and positive or negative affectivity.

Similar attempts to analyze teacher behavior have been carried out by Flanders (1960), Smith (1961), Bowers (1961), Filson (1957), and Medley (1959). These attempts to examine the more global aspects of effective teaching have been somewhat more successful in discriminating between good and poor teaching than research directed at specific or detailed descriptions of behavior, or methods. But they still do not provide us with the definitive distinctions needed by the profession. Good teaching, it now seems clear, is not a direct function of general traits or methods.

Some Practical Difficulties
of the Competencies Approach

The attempt to develop a teacher education program based upon the competencies approach runs into some very knotty problems. In the first place, it is a fallacy to assume the methods of the experts either can, or should be, taught directly to the beginners. It is seldom we can determine what should be for the beginner by examining what the expert does well. I learned this some years ago when I was responsible for teaching failing university students more effective methods of study. At first glance it would seem logical to determine what should be taught to the failing students by determining the study habits of successful ones. Such an approach to curriculum construction, however, is disastrous!

Successful students study most whimsically. They operate without plan, go to the movies often, indulge in all sorts of extracurricular activities and generally behave in ways that would be suicidal for students teetering on the brink of failure. It simply does not follow that what is good for the expert is good for the novice too! Nor is it true, that the way to become expert is to do what the expert does.

Some of the methods used by the expert can only be used *because* he is expert. Many experienced teachers have learned to deal with most classroom disturbances by ignoring them. Yet beginners cannot ignore them! The expert is able to ignore matters precisely because he *is* expert. Some methods cannot even be comprehended without adequate prior experience. One must grow to achieve them. Asking the young teacher to use methods which do not fit him may only turn him loose in the blackboard jungle to fight for his life with inappropriate weapons.

The creation of long lists of competencies is likely to be deeply discouraging and disillusioning to the young teacher for another reason. Evaluations of "goodness" or "badness" become attached to methods, and students thereafter are expected to judge their own adequacies in these terms. The net effect is to set such impossible goals of excellence that no one can ever hope to reach them. This is a terribly depressing and discouraging prospect.

Discouraging and disillusioning as the competencies approach is for the young teacher, it has equally unhappy effects on the more experienced teachers. A vast complex of competencies, all of which are demanded as criteria for good teaching leaves the individual defenseless before criticism. No matter what he does well, it is never enough! There is always so much more that he might have done, or should have done, that he can rarely find pleasure or satisfaction in what he actually has done. Add to this the fact that many of the competencies demanded do not fit his particular personality, and so could probably never be achieved anyhow, and the defeat of the individual becomes almost inevitable. In time, feeling of inadequacy produced by continual failure to meet impossible goals undermines professional pride and is likely to produce a guilt-ridden teacher suffering from a secret feeling of being "too little and too late." It should not be surprising if, after years of this kind of experience, the will to try shrivels and dies on the vine.

To use particular competencies as a measure of good teaching, irrespective of personalities, situations or purposes, leads us to the ridiculous conclusion that some of the very people who taught us most, were poor teachers. When I hear young teachers-in-training remark, "Oh, he is a lousy teacher but you sure learn a lot!" I am forced to conclude that the determination of the goodness of teaching on the basis of competencies is highly questionable.

The methods people use are highly personal. These methods cannot be judged apart from the personality they express. No one, after all, looks well, feels well, or behaves well, in another person's clothing. Methods, like the clothes we wear, must fit the people we are. Good teaching is a highly personal matter.

THE PERSONAL CHARACTER
OF GOOD TEACHING

Is there a better approach? I think there is. As we have seen, the research on good teaching is unable to isolate any common trait or practice of good teachers. Yet these unanimous results, themselves, represent a most important commonality. They demonstrate the uniqueness and individuality of good teachers! The very failure of research to define common factors is, itself, a demonstration that a good teacher is primarily a personality. If good teachers are unique individuals we could predict from the start that the attempt to find *common uniqueness* would be unfruitful!

A good teacher is first and foremost a person. He has competence, to be sure, but not a *common* set of competencies like anyone else. Like the students he teaches, he is infinitely unique and becoming more so all the time. The fact of his personness is the most important and determining thing about him. The personal character of good teaching can be documented by almost any of us from our own experience. If one thinks back to his own school days he will probably discover that the good teachers he had in his own lifetime did not all behave alike or, even, with great similarity. Rather, each stands out as a person, an individual, some for one reason, some for another.

Apparently, there can be no such thing as a "good" or "bad" method of teaching. The terms "good" and "bad" can be applied to results, outcomes, purposes or ends. The methods we use to achieve these ends, however, only derive their value from the goals and purposes for which they are used. The good teacher is not one who behaves in a "given" way. He is an artist, skillful in producing a desirable result. The result may be considered "good" or "bad," but not the method.

THE "SELF AS INSTRUMENT" CONCEPT

This shift in our thinking from a mechanistic to a personal view of teaching is by no means confined to our profession alone. In fact, most other professions dealing with human problems have preceded us in this direction. The effective professional worker, in medicine, social work, clinical psychology, guidance or nursing is no longer seen as a technician applying methods in more or less mechanical fashion the way he has been taught. We now understand him as an intelligent human being using himself, his knowledge and the resources at hand to solve the problems for which he is responsible. He is a person who has learned to use himself as an effective instrument (Combs, 1961).

If we adapt this "self as instrument" concept of the professional worker to teaching, it means that teachers colleges must concern themselves with *persons* rather than competencies. It means the individualization of instruction we have sought for the public school must be applied to the teachers colleges as well. It calls for the production of creative individuals, capable of shifting and changing to meet the demands and opportunities afforded in daily tasks. Such a teacher will not behave in a set way. His behavior will change from moment to moment, from day to day, rapidly adjusting to the needs of his students, the situations he is in, the purposes he seeks to fulfill and the methods and materials he has at hand.

The good teacher is no carbon copy but stands out as a unique and effective personality, sometimes for one reason, sometimes for another, but always for something intensely and personally his own. He has found ways of using himself, his talents and his environment in a fashion that aids both his students and himself to achieve satisfaction—their own and society's too. Artists sometimes refer to "the discovery of one's personal idiom" and the expression seems very apt applied to teaching as well. We may define the effective teacher *as a unique human being who has learned to use his self effectively and efficiently for carrying out his own and society's purposes.*

The production of this kind of person is not a question of teaching him what to do. Modern perceptual psychology tells us that a person's behavior is the direct result of his perceptions, how things seem to him at the moment of his behaving. To change an individual's behavior, it is necessary to help him see himself and his world differently. It is here that teacher education must direct its effort. The modern giant computer is able to provide "best answers" to vast quantities of data depending upon the formulas built into the machine. In a similar fashion, the effectiveness of the teacher is dependent upon the internal "formulas" which select and control his behavior as he is confronted with changing situations. These human formulas are the perceptions he holds of himself, his purposes and the world in which he must live and operate.

Whether an individual can behave effectively and efficiently in a given situation, according to the perceptual psychologists, will depend upon how he is perceiving at the time. To change his behavior, furthermore, it will be necessary to produce a change in his perception of himself and his world. This means for teacher education, we need first to know how good teachers perceive. Knowing that, we may then be able to help teachers perceive themselves and their tasks in those ways.

A PERCEPTUAL VIEW OF GOOD TEACHING

What kinds of beliefs, understandings, values and concepts make up the perceptual organization of good teachers?

This way of looking at teacher education is so new that we do not yet have the precise research we need to guide us. This need not deter us, however, for there is evidence enough at least to start us thinking on new tracks, designing new techniques and planning for the research we need. To this point we have the following sources of information to draw upon for defining the probable dimensions of good teaching in perceptual terms:

1. Perceptual psychological theory, especially that having to do with the nature of the self and fully functioning behavior
2. Research on the perceptions of good practitioners in other helping professions (Combs and Soper, 1963)
3. The research already existing in our profession
4. The experiences accumulated by thousands of teachers engaged in day to day "action research" in the classroom.

Drawing upon these four sources it would appear that a good teacher is characterized by typical perceptual organizations in six general areas:

A. His knowledge of his subject
B. His frame of reference for approaching his problems
C. His perceptions of others
D. His perceptions of self
E. His perceptions of the purpose and process of learning
F. His perceptions of appropriate methods.

Under each of these major headings a series of hypotheses can be drawn concerning the teacher's characteristic perceptual organization in that area. The following is a list developed at the University of Florida by the author and his colleagues over the past five years. These were originally drawn up to serve as suggestions for future research. The list is presented here both as an amplification of the "self as instrument" concept and as possible propositions for further research by others who may be interested in the problem. The list is by no means a complete one but it serves as a point of departure for consideration of the self as instrument approach. It is presented as a promising series of leads which may excite other researchers, as it has my colleagues and me, to explore these matters further. Some of the following hypotheses (marked by *) we have already corroborated in research on good and poor counselors (Combs, 1963). Others (marked by †) are currently being explored in several researches on the perceptual organization of good teachers. Each hypothesis is stated as the two ends of a continuum with the perceptions presumed characteristic of the good teacher at the left and those of the poor teacher at the right. Those hypotheses already studied or currently under investigation include more extensive definitions. Several items, not yet subjected to research test, do not have definitions included.

Hypotheses Regarding the Perceptual Organization of Effective Teachers

A. *A Good Teacher Has Rich Perceptions About His Subject:* The good teacher will need to be well informed about the subject matter he is responsible for teaching. That is to say, he must have a rich and extensive field of perceptions about his subject upon which he can call as required. The good teacher is not stupid. This aspect of good teaching provides us with nothing new. It is the aspect of the teaching function we have known best and developed most fully in the past.

B. *The Good Teacher's Frame of Reference:* The good teacher is always keenly aware of how things seem from the point of view of those with whom he works. His frame of reference for approaching problems and people is humanistic rather than mechanistic. He is deeply sensitive to the private worlds of his students and colleagues and accepts their feelings, attitudes, beliefs and understandings as legitimate and important data in human interaction.

Hypothesis 1*†—Internal-External frame of reference: The teacher's general frame of reference can be described as internal rather than external; that is to say, he seems sensitive to and concerned with how things look to others with whom he interacts and uses this as a basis for his own behavior.

Hypothesis 2*†—People-Things orientation: Central to the thinking of the teacher is a concern with people and their reactions rather than with things and events.

Hypothesis 3*†—Meanings-Facts orientation: The teacher is more concerned with the perceptual experience of people than with the objective events. He is sensitive to how things seem to people rather than being exclusively concerned with concrete events.

Hypothesis 4*†—Immediate-Historical causation: The teacher seeks the causes of people's behavior in their current thinking, feeling, beliefs and understandings rather than in objective descriptions of the forces exerted upon them now or in the past.

Hypothesis 5—Hopeful-Despairing.

C. *Perceptions About What People Are Like and How They Behave:* Teaching is a human relationship. To behave effectively good teachers must possess the most accurate understandings about people and their behavior available in our generation. Each of us can only behave in terms of what we believe is so. What a teacher believes, therefore, about the nature of his students will have a most important effect on how he behaves toward them. Let us take a simple example to illustrate this point.

If a teacher believes his students have the capacity to learn, he will behave quite differently from the teacher who has serious doubts about the capacities of his charges. The teacher who believes his students *can,* begins his task with hope and assurance that both he and his students may be successful. He can place confidence and trust in his students and be certain that, if he is successful in facilitating and encouraging the learning process, they can, they will learn.

The teacher, on the other hand, who does not believe his students are capable approaches his task with two strikes against him. He is licked before he starts. If you do not believe that children *can,* then it is certainly not safe to trust them. False beliefs about the nature of people can only result in the selection of inappropriate ways of dealing with them. A prime function of the teachers college must be to assist its students to clear and accurate understandings of the nature of people and their behavior.

Hypothesis 6*†—Able-Unable. The teacher perceives others as having the capacities to deal with their problems. He believes that they can find adequate solutions to events as opposed to doubting the capacity of people to handle themselves and their lives.

Hypothesis 7*†—Friendly-Unfriendly: The teacher sees others as being friendly and enhancing. He does not regard them as threatening to himself but rather sees them as essentially well intentioned rather than evil intentioned.

Hypothesis 8*†—Worthy-Unworthy: The teacher tends to see other people as being of worth rather than unworthy. He sees them as possessing a dignity and integrity which must be respected and maintained rather than seeing people as unimportant, whose integrity may be violated or treated as of little account.

Hypothesis 9†—Internally-Externally motivated: The teacher sees people and their behavior as essentially developing from within rather than as a product of external events to be molded, directed; sees people as creative, dynamic rather than passive or inert.

Hypothesis 10*†—Dependable-Undependable: The teacher sees people as essentially trustworthy and dependable in the sense of behaving in a lawful way. He regards their behavior as understandable rather than capricious, unpredictable or negative.

Hypothesis 11†—Helpful-Hindering. The teacher sees people as being potentially fulfilling and enhancing to self rather than impeding or threatening. He regards people as important sources of satisfaction rather than sources of frustration and suspicion.

Hypothesis 12—Unthreatening-Threatening.

Hypothesis 13—Respectable-Of no account.

D. *The Teacher's Perception of Self:* Perceptual psychology indicates that the behavior of the individual at any moment is a function of how he sees his situation and himself. In recent years we have come to understand the crucial importance of the self concept in affecting every aspect of a person's life. It makes a vast difference what people believe about themselves.

The behavior of a teacher, like that of everyone else, is a function of his concepts of self. Teachers who believe they are able will try. Teachers who do not think they are able will avoid responsibilities. Teachers who feel they are liked by their students will behave quite differently from those who feel they are unliked. Teachers who feel they are acceptable to the administration can behave quite differently from those who have serious doubts about their acceptability. Teachers who feel their profession has dignity and integrity can themselves behave with dignity and integrity. Teachers who have grave doubts about the importance and value of their profession may behave apologetically or overly aggressively with their students and with their colleagues. It is apparent that, if the self concept is a fundamental in producing the behavior of an individual as has been suggested by modern psychology, then teacher education programs must give it a vital place in the production of new teachers.

Hypothesis 14*†—Identified with-Apart from: The teacher tends to see himself as a part of all mankind; he sees himself as identified with people rather than as withdrawn, removed, apart or alienated from others.

Hypothesis 15*†—Adequate-Inadequate: The teacher generally sees himself as enough; as having what is needed to deal with his problems. He does not see himself as lacking and as unable to cope with problems.

Hypothesis 16*†—Trustworthy-Untrustworthy: The teacher has trust in his own organism. He sees himself as essentially dependable, reliable, as having the potentiality for coping with events as opposed to seeing self in a tentative fashion with doubts about the potentiality and reliability of the organism.

Hypothesis 17*†—Worthy-Unworthy: The teacher sees himself as a person of consequence, dignity, integrity and worthy of respect; as opposed to being a person of little consequence who can be overlooked, discounted, whose dignity and integrity do not matter.

Hypothesis 18*†—Wanted-Unwanted: The teacher sees himself as essentially likeable, attractive (in personal, not physical appearance sense), wanted, and in general capable of bringing forth a warm response from those people important to him; as opposed to feeling ignored, unwanted, or rejected by others.

Hypothesis 19—Accepted-Not accepted.

Hypothesis 20—Certain, sure-Doubting.

Hypothesis 21—Feels aware-Unaware.

E. *The Purpose and Process of Learning:* Behavior always has direction. Whatever we do is always determined by the purposes we have in mind at the time of our behaving or misbehaving. What teachers perceive to be their own and society's purposes makes a great deal of difference in their behavior. The teacher who believes schools exist only for the able and that "it is a waste of time to fool with the poorer students," behaves quite differently from the teacher who perceives society's purpose as that of helping *all* children become the best they can. Similarly, what the teacher believes about how students learn will markedly affect his behavior. One teacher, believing children must be molded, teaches loyalty to country by carefully censoring what students read and hear about democracy and communism. Another teacher, believing children learn best when confronted with all kinds of evidence, takes a different tack in teaching his class. The clarity and accuracy of perceptions about the purposes and processes of learning will have profound effects on the behavior of teachers.

How the teacher sees the task of teaching, in the immediate sense, as it applies to moment to moment operations in the classroom, or in the broadest sense, of society's needs and purposes, will determine the way he behaves on the job. The teachers college must help him find these understandings and make them a part of his very being. Only the best and most accurate perceptions will suffice.

Hypothesis 22*†—Freeing-Controlling: The teacher perceives the purpose of the helping task as one of freeing, assisting, releasing, facilitating rather than a matter of controlling, manipulating, coercing, blocking, inhibiting.

Hypothesis 23*†—Large-Smaller perceptions: The teacher tends to view events in a broad rather than narrow perspective. He is concerned with larger connotations of events, with large, more extensive implications than the immediate and specific. He is not exclusively concerned with details but can perceive beyond the immediate to future and larger meanings.

Hypothesis 24*†—Self revealing-Self concealing: The teacher sees his appropriate role as self revealing rather than self concealing; that is, he appears to be willing to disclose himself. He can treat his feelings and shortcomings as important and significant rather than hiding them or covering them up. He seems willing to be himself.

Hypothesis 25†—Self involved-Self withheld: The teacher sees his appropriate role as one of commitment to the helping interaction, as opposed to being inert or remaining aloof or remote from interaction.

Hypothesis 26†—Furthering process-Achieving goals: The teacher sees his appropriate role as one of encouraging and facilitating the process of search and discovery, as opposed to promoting, or working for a personal goal or preconceived solution.

Hypothesis 27—Helping-Dominating.

Hypothesis 28—Understanding-Condemning.

Hypothesis 29—Accepting-Rejecting.

Hypothesis 30—Valuing integrity-Violating integrity.

Hypothesis 31—Positive-Negative.

Hypothesis 32—Open-Closed to experience.

Hypothesis 33—Tolerant of ambiguity-Intolerant.

F. *Perception of Appropriate Methods:* The methods teachers use must fit the kinds of people they are. An effective teacher must have an armamentarium of methods upon which he may call as these are needed to carry out his teaching duties. These may vary widely from teacher to teacher and even from moment to moment. Whatever their nature they must fit the situations and purposes of the teacher and be appropriate for the students with whom they are used.

The teacher education program must help each student find the methods best suited to him, to his purposes, his task and the peculiar populations and problems with which he must deal on the job. This is not so much a matter of *teaching* methods as one of helping students *discover* methods.

While methods must always be highly personal, certain perceptions about appropriate methods may be characteristic of good teaching. Among the hypotheses we hope to explore in this area are the following:

Hypothesis 34—Helping methods seen as superior to manipulating methods.

Hypothesis 35—Cooperation superior to competition.

REFERENCES

N. D. BOWERS and R. S. SOAR. *Studies in Human Relations in the Teaching Learning Process* V. Final Report, Cooperative Research Project No. 469, 1961.

A. W. COMBS. "A Perceptual View of the Nature of 'Helpers,' in Personality Theory and Counseling Practice." Papers of First Annual Conference on Personality Theory and Counseling Practice. Gainesville, Florida: University of Florida, 1961, p. 53–58.

A. W. COMBS and D. W. SOPER. "The Perceptual Organization of Effective Counselors." *Journal of Counseling Psychology* 10:222–26; 1963.

W. J. ELLENA, M. STEVENSON and H. V. WEBB. *Who's a Good Teacher?* Washington, D. C.: American Association of School Administrators, NEA, 1961.

T. N. FILSON. "Factors Influencing the Level of Dependence in the Classroom." Unpublished Ph.D. Thesis. Minneapolis: University of Minnesota, 1957.

N. A. FLANDERS. *Teacher Influence, Pupil Attitudes and Achievement: Studies in Interaction Analysis.* Final Report, Cooperative Research Project No. 397, U.S. Office of Education, 1960.

MARIE M. HUGHES. *Development of the Means for Assessing the Quality of Teaching in Elementary Schools.* Report of Research, Cooperative Research Program, U.S. Office of Education Project No. 353, 1959.

DONALD M. MEDLEY and HAROLD E. MITZEL. "A Technique for Measuring Classroom Behavior." *Journal of Educational Psychology* 49: 86–92; 1958.

B. OTHANEL SMITH. "A Concept of Teaching." *Language and Concepts in Education.* Chicago: Rand McNally & Company, 1961.

Helping Teachers Improve
Classroom Group Processes

Richard A. Schmuck

The studies reported here assumed that informal classroom group processes affect students' attitudes as well as their academic performances and that teachers can modify these group processes constructively. Three action research interventions are described in this paper which, in various degrees and in different ways, helped teachers improve the informal group processes in their classrooms.

The major intervention of Project 1 was a teacher development laboratory with seven core training activities: (1) sensitivity training and related human relations experiences, (2) didactic discussions on basic research about classroom group processes, (3) problem-solving techniques for improving group processes, (4) analyses of diagnostic data from the teachers' own classrooms, (5) discussions about useful classroom practices developed by other teachers, (6) role-play tryouts of new classroom practices, and (7) follow-up discussions during the school year. This laboratory was compared with a seminar in which the participants experienced all phases of

Reproduced by special permission from *The Journal of Applied Behavioral Science*, Richard A. Schmuck, "Helping Teachers Improve Classroom Group Processes," November 4, 1968, pp. 401–35. Copyright © 1968, National Institute for Applied Behavioral Science.

This paper summarizes over three years of action research on improving classroom group processes in schools in the metropolitan areas of Detroit, Michigan, Philadelphia, Pennsylvania, and Portland, Oregon. Acknowledgments of organizational assistance are extended to the Cooperative Research Branch of the United States Office of Education and the Center for Research on the Utilization of Scientific Knowledge of The University of Michigan for Project 1; to The Mental Health Association of Southeastern Pennsylvania and the Group Dynamics Center of Temple University for Project 2; and to the Oregon Compact and the Center for the Advanced Study of Educational Administration of the University of Oregon for Project 3. Many persons from these organizations contributed to the studies reported here. Special thanks are given to Denis Carville and Mark Chesler who worked on Project 1; to Anne Edelmann and Steven Saturen, co-workers in Project 2; and to Philip Runkel who collaborated in Project 3.

262

the laboratory except for sensitivity traininng, related human relations experiences, and role-play tryouts of new classroom practices. Both the laboratory and seminar were compared with a control group in which no interventions were attempted. An overview of the results indicated that the laboratory teachers and students made more positive changes in their group processes than those in the seminar group; both of these groups were more improved at the end of the school year than the control group.

In Project 2, psychological consultants attempted to enhance teachers' capabilities for coping with group processes in the classroom. The consultants spent four hours each week for 15 weeks in small-group discussions, classroom visitations, and individual conferences. The contacts between consultants and teachers were problem-oriented, centering on the teachers' reactions to classroom processes and how the teachers might try to improve group interaction in their classrooms. The consultants attempted to explore how teachers might relate to students with interpersonal problems, low self-esteem, and disinterest in learning. Results indicated that cognitive and attitudinal changes did occur in the teachers, but that these were not also accompanied by behavioral changes that made a difference in their classroom groups. Constructive changes in classroom group processes and students' attitudes did not occur as a result of the consultations.

Project 3 involved an organizational development laboratory for a school faculty which was aimed at improving such organizational processes as interpersonal relations and feelings, communication patterns, and group norms of the staff. The laboratory included structured group exercises, small-group discussions relating the exercises to school processes, total staff discussions on their own group processes, and problem-solving techniques applied to total staff problems. A majority of the teachers, quite unexpectedly, tried new group procedures in their classrooms patterned after their laboratory experiences, even though classroom applications were never formally mentioned during the laboratory.

It was concluded that an organizational development laboratory encourages a faculty to try out new group processes in the school organization or in the classroom. Problem-oriented and self-reflective discussions with consultants help teachers perceive that they can improve classroom group processes by modifying their own behaviors. But the regular presence of a psychological consultant does not appear, by itself, to change teachers' actual behaviors in the classroom. A teacher development laboratory which includes problem-solving techniques, sensitivity training, and role-play tryouts increases the likelihood that changes in teachers' cognitions and attitudes will be accompanied by behavioral changes in the classroom. These three interventions can fit well into integrated action programs that might be used by school systems for improving classroom group processes.

Classroom groups, like other groups, have both formal and informal aspects. The formal aspects have to do with ways in which various members work toward carrying out the official or specified goals of the group. In the classroom, for instance, one formal feature is the way in which any child performs the role of academic student, as it is defined by the teacher, school system, and adult community at large.

The informal aspects of a group involve the manner in which each member relates to other members as persons. In the classroom, an informal aspect is the way affection, or students' friendship for one another, is distributed. These informal features often have an important bearing on the formal aspects. Many of them, such as the amount of liking members have for one another or their willingness to help and support one another, may be thought of as positive and enhancing classroom group processes.

Informal classroom group processes, in the form of peer relations and norms as well as students' perceived group statuses, can have consequences for the students' self-esteem, attitudes toward schoolwork, and academic achievement. In previous studies (Schmuck, 1962, 1963, 1966), we showed that classroom groups with diffuse patterns of friendship and influence, compared with those with more hierarchical patterns, had greater cohesiveness and more supportive norms for learning. Most students in these diffuse groups perceived themselves as having high group status, while in the hierarchical groups only students who actually had high status perceived themselves as having it. Students who perceived themselves as having high peer status tended to have higher self-esteem, more positive attitudes toward schoolwork, and were applying their intellectual abilities better than other students. Students' academic performances were shown to be conditioned by affective contents associated with their self-concepts as peers and students; and these self-concepts were influenced, in part, by the students' friendship and influence relations with their classsmates.

Other studies have shown that teachers can influence classroom group processes. Flanders and Havumaki (1960) showed that teachers' support and constructive praise were likely to increase students' sociometric position among their classmates. In contrived classroom settings teachers interacted with and praised only students seated in odd-numbered seats, while in comparison groups all students were encouraged to speak and the teachers' praise was directed to the whole class. Students in the odd-numbered seats, in the former situation, later received more sociometric choices than students in the even-numbered seats. In the comparison classrooms, the difference between sociometric choices of students in the odd- and even-numbered seats was insignificant: The peer choices were spread around more evenly, indicating greater general acceptance.

In another study (Schmuck & Van Egmond, 1965), the results of a multistage analysis indicated that when the variables—familial social class, perceived parental attitudes toward school, perceived peer status, and satisfaction with the teacher—were compared for their relative relationship to academic performance, pupils' satisfactions with the teacher and performance were associated when the effects of the other three variables were held constant. The results indicated that the teacher, especially as a social-emotional leader, had an effect on the academic performances of both boys and girls which was independent, to a significant degree, of the effects of parents and peers.

Further research indicated that teachers of more cohesive classroom groups, compared with other teachers, attended to and talked with a larger variety of students per hour (Schmuck, 1966). Many teachers with less positive classroom group processes tended to call on fewer students for participation and seemed especially to neglect the slower, less involved students. Teachers with more supportive peer groups tended to reward students for helpful behaviors with specific statements and to control behavioral disturbances with general, group-oriented statements. Teachers with less positive climates tended to reward individuals less often and to publicly reprimand them more often for breaking classroom rules. All of these results indicated that teachers can and do influence classroom group processes. The three action research interventions described below illuminate how teachers might be helped to create more psychologically supportive classroom group processes.

Project 1:
TEACHER DEVELOPMENT LABORATORY

In Project 1 we assumed that for classroom changes to be effective and viable, teachers need to learn more than theories, research facts, and specific innovative practices or techniques. Teachers must integrate theories, facts, and techniques into their value systems, emotional styles, and role conceptions. Sensitivity training and role-playing experiences accompanied by a scientific problem-solving orientation were hypothesized to facilitate such a reeducation process. These experiences aim to encourage a teacher to search for alternative ways of teaching, stimulate him to try out new ideas, and press him to collect feedback from colleagues and students on the new practices.

Seven core training activities were carried out: (1) sensitivity training and related human relations laboratory experiences, (2) didactic discussions on basic research about classroom group processes, (3) problem-solving techniques for improving group processes, (4) analyses of diagnostic data from the teachers' own classrooms, (5) discussions about useful classroom practices developed by other teachers, (6) role-play tryouts of new classroom practices, and (7) follow-up discussions during the school year.

Twenty teachers participated in all of these activities and formed Laboratory Group A. Twenty other teachers participated in all the activities except sensitivity training, related human relations laboratory experiences, and role-play tryouts, and formed Seminar Group B. Ten teachers rounded out the design, received no special treatment, and formed Control Group C.

This project began in the spring of 1965 when a brochure announcing a four-week summer laboratory for upper elementary teachers went to 12 school systems in Metropolitan Detroit. The selection of school systems was accomplished by sampling broadly across social classes and racial and ethnic groups. Chief school officers in all systems agreed to inform their upper elementary teachers of the program. Over 75 teachers applied, and 20 teachers were placed in Laboratory Group A and were matched with 20 others who constituted Seminar Group B. The 10 teachers in Control Group C were selected later from other schools in the same school systems. The final selection of the entire sample was based on principles of demographic heterogeneity of students within the experimental categories and demographic similarity among the categories. All three categories of teachers, then, had students with a full range of social characteristics, but were quite similar to one another in their constellations.

The training period lasted six months for Laboratory Group A, starting in July and ending in December 1965. Seminar Group B met from September to December. There was no training for Control Group C. The program for Group A began with a six-hour daily intensive laboratory during the four weeks of July, and was followed up with feedback discussions with individual teachers and bimonthly discussion sessions from September to December. The program for Group B constituted weekly seminar meetings and individual conferences.

Laboratory for Group A

The first week of the four-week laboratory consisted almost entirely of general human relations training; the T Group, focusing on personal sensitivity, was the core of this program (Bradford, Benne, & Gibb, 1964). Twenty teachers were divided randomly into two T Groups that met separately for two-hour periods twice daily. While a skilled trainer was present in each group to maximize learning, the teachers created a group with their own concepts and in their own ways. Through this semi-structured process, some of the teachers became more aware of how groups are formed, some, of the significant events in group development and of the kinds of functions they personally perform in groups. Many participants gained the insight that their manner of speaking and relating to others could be just as important as the content of their communication.

Theory presentations, discussions, and skill exercises supplemented these T Groups. Theoretical lecturettes and discussions dealt with topics such as "Roles persons play in groups," "Communication and feedback," and "Personal styles in groups." Often skill exercises were based on these theory sessions. For instance, the discussion on communication and feedback was followed by a skill exercise in which the teachers gave feedback to one another in small groups and, at the same time, were required to indicate that they were "hearing" by paraphrasing what another had just said. In another combination session of theory and skill training, the teachers privately completed the *Edwards Personal Preference Inventory,* received their own scores on ten psychological needs, were informed of what the scores meant conceptually, and then role-played how such need patterns would be expressed behaviorally in the classroom.

During the second week T Groups continued to meet but only once each day, as the laboratory's discussions centered on the classroom as a human relations setting. Three categories of information were presented during the second week:

1. Some basic research on classroom group processes were presented to the teachers.

2. A problem-solving scheme was presented and included these stages:

   a. identifying classsroom group problems

   b. diagnosing the classroom problems

   c. developing a plan of action

   d. trying out the plan, and

   e. getting feedback and making an evaluation (Schmuck, Chester, & Lippitt, 1966).

3. Classroom diagnosis, the second stage of the problem-solving scheme, was explored in depth and included the following topics:

   a. assessing the classroom learning climate

   b. social relations in the classroom

   c. peer group norms

   d. student-teacher interaction

   e. outside influences on students' learning

   f. parental influences on school adjustment

   g. the student's self-concept, and

      h. students' attitudes toward school and teachers (Fox, Luski, & Schmuck, 1966).

Pairs or trios of teachers took one of these diagnostic topics and were responsible for teaching the entire workshop group how to use questionnaires and other measurement procedures on that topic. The trio working on teacher-student interaction received special instructions in Flanders' Interaction Analysis and used this procedure for collecting data on the teachers' instructional styles as the others taught about the various diagnostic techniques. After all of the other teachers had completed their instruction, this group reported on interaction analysis by giving feedback to all of the instructional teams on how they behaved according to the observation categories. Discussions on diagnosis were completed by the end of the second week.

Next, the teachers were assigned to skim through a booklet containing other teachers' practices and to decide tentatively on some practices they would like to try to improve classroom group processes or, more specifically, to solve classroom peer relations problems (Kaufman, Schmuck, & Lippitt, 1963). The teachers' techniques, devices, and special procedures included in this booklet were examined for their soundness by skilled teachers, educational administrators, and social psychologists. A few examples drawn from the booklet are:

Development of a classsroom group government to assist in social relations management. Early in the year the class votes for a Rules Committee which sets up a Bill of Rights for all students and presents it to the rest of the group for discussion and approval. A Judiciary Committee is constituted to enforce the rules and serves for four weeks. Every day a member of the Judiciary Committee puts a schedule of the day's activities on the board, including the name of the committee member who will be responsible for supervision of behavior during each period. The Judiciary Committee and the class officers meet to arrange the class seating plans and rearrange them as necessary. Every month four students who have not been on the Judiciary Committee are elected to serve, and this method is followed until all students have taken part.

Formation and clarification of peer group behavior standards. The teacher divides the class into small subgroups for discussion of behavioral standards. The groups initially are led by sociometrically high students who are given some leadership training before commencing with the groups. Each subgroup reports its findingns orally to the class, the whole class identifies the standards they like best, and these become classroom rules. These subgroups meet once every week, and each student receives some leadership training and a chance to lead a group.

Role playing for helping to teach a better understanding of group behavior. The teacher asks the class to create a play and the class discusses what the content of the play should be. The class is advised to choose a plot that would be familiar to all and that includes at least one group relations problem. The play is written, actors are chosen, and the play is enacted. Discussion takes place on applications of the play to life together in this classroom. Human relations in the classroom peer group in general are discussed.

Teaching human relations skills. Short class meetings are held three times each week concerning human relations topics. Some of these discussions are taped so that they can be played back later and evaluated by the students. The students also are encouraged to express their opinions by answering questions such as "What did you like about today?" and "What do you like (or not like) about our school?" When problems are identified, role-playing situations are set up and enacted. The students suggest alternative ways of behaving during the role-plays and discuss the meaning of role-plays for their classroom group relations.

On Monday and Tuesday of the third week the T Groups discussed the teachers' perceptions of the classroom practices presented in the booklet. Each teacher was asked to develop at least one practice that he wished to try out as a way of improving classroom group processes. On those same days, several two-hour sessions were held on the rationale for, and some ways of using, role playing (Chesler & Fox, 1966). Also one session was given on collecting feedback from students. From Wednesday of the third week to Wednesday of the fourth and final week, each teacher spent one hour simulating part of his chosen practice in a role-play enactment using the other teachers in roles as students or as outside observers.

During the last two days of the laboratory the teachers made specific plans for how they would implement these new classroom procedures during the school year. Lewin's field of force analysis was presented so that each teacher could estimate the restraining forces that would deter him from following through with the plan (Coch & French, 1948). After considerable thought was given to implementing the plan, each teacher conferred with a staff member about his plan. This conference took the place of a final examination and was tape recorded. A schedule was formed for playing the tape early in the fall at a similar conference as a reminder and motivational device for supporting tryouts of the plan.

From September until December of 1965, the teachers continued to be involved in the program. Early in September, data were collected on the quality of group processes in all classrooms. Some data were immediately presented to the teachers. Next, the teachers listened to their tape recordings with a person from our staff and made more realistic plans based on the new data and their summer plans. Group discussions were held bimonthly during which the teachers discussed the strong and weak points of their teaching experiences. Attempts were made to support the teachers' efforts to follow through on their plans and to help the teachers to engage continuously in the problem-solving process. The program of training for Laboratory Group A was ended with an informal gathering one week before winter vacation.

Seminar for Group B

Group B met weekly from September to December, 1965. They were initially presented the same problem-solving sequence used by Group A. They learned about the uses of diagnostic tools and received group processes data from their classrooms for analysis. Basic research findings about classroom group processes also were presented to them, and they read about the classroom practices of other teachers and discussed ones they would like to try. The principal activities omitted from the Seminar for Group B were sensitivity training and role playing.

Results of Project 1

Early in the fall, during the school year, and again late in the spring, students completed self-report questionnaires on classroom group processes and their attitudes toward peers, school, self, and teacher. Teachers in Groups A and B kept diaries concerned with their planned attempts at improving group processes. Every teacher was also observed for an hour's duration three or four times during the school year. Data were collected on teachers in Group C only during the spring. The assumption made was that Group C classes, in which no interventions were tried, would more nearly reflect the fall than the spring patterns of classes in Groups A and B.

An overview of the results indicates that the Laboratory Group A teachers and students made more positive changes in their group processes than those in Seminar Group B and that both Groups A and B were more improved at the end of the school year than Control Group C.

Perhaps the most obvious difference between teachers in Groups A and B was their group cohesiveness. The *esprit de corps* in Group A was extremely positive, while almost none existed in Group B. Group A teachers telephoned one another 25 times about professional matters, while only two such calls were reported by Group B teachers. Fifteen of the 20 teachers in Group A visited socially during the school year; only three from Group B met informally. Numerous instances of sharing classroom teaching ideas occurred in Group A, while the teachers in Group B talked about their practices only during seminar time. Group A teachers talked more about their classrooms before and after class and during coffee breaks. Group A initiated a party at the end of the laboratory, and many members indicated strong desires to continue or at least to keep in touch. Group B teachers showed more interest in receiving college credit than in one another.

These differences would not be very significant in themselves if they were not accompanied by changes in classroom practices. Evidence from diaries and observations indicated that the Group A teachers were much more innovative than the Group B teachers. Teachers in Group A produced more elaborate plans of action and attempted more practices for improving group processes than the Group B teachers. Group B teachers typically tried one or two practices during the year to improve group processes, while teachers in Group A tried from five to 17 different procedures with their students. Indeed, the enthusiasm of two teachers was discussed by several students critically when they wrote on their questionnaires that they wished their teacher would keep one grouping procedure for at least two weeks instead of the usual one week. Even though some similar criticisms were aimed at other Group A teachers by their students, these represented a minor percentage of the students.

The most emphasized goal of the practices tried by Group A teachers was increasing openness in classroom communication among peers and between students and teacher. Communication was encouraged by using activities such as summarizing data from student questionnaires and discussing their meanings, role playing difficult classroom situations, discussing critical statements placed in a suggestion box, discussing thoughts about what makes for a "good" or "bad" day in classs, and reviewing how the class had been proceeding by holding a once-weekly evaluation and review-discussion. Group B teachers used a few of these practices but tried fewer per teacher and continued using them for shorter durations.

The most widespread interest, manifested by 15 out of the 20 Group A teachers, was in raising students' participation levels in deciding upon classroom regulations and procedures. In seven Group A classrooms, student governments were formed and functioned successfully throughout most of the year. Teachers with such governments attempted to increase the diffusion of influence in the peer group by encouraging all students to take part at some point in the classroom government.

We also collected before and after self-report questionnaires from the students in Group A and B classrooms in the fall and spring of the school year. Students in Group C completed questionnaires only in the spring. Averages from the fall measure taken on students in Groups A and B were used as estimates of the before data in Group C.

In general, the questions centered on the students' perceptions of their influence and friendship statuses in the classroom group and the extent to which they supported one another and felt a part of the group. Students were asked to estimate whether they saw themselves in the highest part (quarter) of the class, the second highest part, in the third part, or in the lowest part on these two questions: (1) *Influence*—"Compared with others in the class, how often can you get others to do what you want them to do?" and (2) *Friendship*—"Where would you place yourself on the basis of how much the others in the class like you?" Improved group relations would be indicated by the students' feeling that they were more influential and had more friends in the spring as compared with the fall.

Furthermore, we asked students to describe, through a symbolic drawing, the friendship structure of the classroom group as they saw it. Students were presented the five rectangles as shown in Figure 1. Each rectangle represents a different group pattern. Students selected the rectangle that best represented their view of the peer group, or drew their own version in the blank rectangle. About 40 per cent of the students drew their own picture of the group. Each student also was asked to place an "X" within one circle that would stand for his own position in the group.

We defined a friendship group as more than two circles in a cluster and compared the average number of these perceived to exist in the class early and late in the school year. We also categorized the place a student perceived his own position to be in the group during fall and spring by using these four categories: (1) at the center of a larger group, defined as more than four circles; (2) at the periphery of a large group; (3) in a smaller group, defined as four or fewer circles; and (4) alone or isolated. Finally, as a means of getting some idea of the supportive nature of the group, especially with regard to academic matters, we asked a series of questions about the frequency of supportive behaviors in the classroom. The one presented here differentiated thus: The students in this class help one another with their schoolwork (a) almost always, (b) usually, (c) seldom, or (d) almost never.

The data on perceived influence clearly supported the hypothesis that the Laboratory for Group A would result in greater benefits than the Seminar for Group B, and that both would show gains over the Control Group C. The data on friendship were not so clear but did suggest the same pattern. Results shown in Table 1, on the perceived influence status of each student early and late in the school year, indicated the positive significance of the laboratory experience for the Group A classrooms. The students with Group A teachers, who perceived themselves as high (above the median) in peer group influence, increased significantly from 53 per cent to 61 per cent during the school year. Students in Group B, on the other hand, showed no significant change from fall to spring on perceived influence. In the Control Group C classes, the results were that the stu-

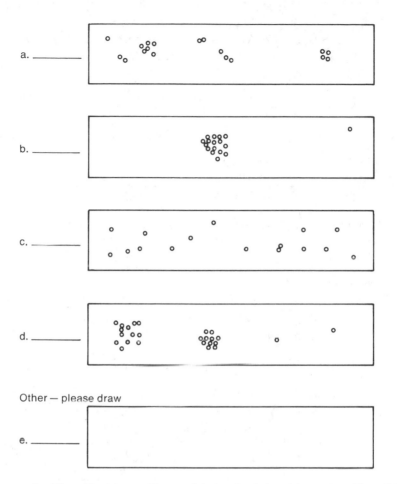

FIGURE 1. *The Classroom Group (A Method for Measuring Friendship Structure)*

If you were to think about this class as a group, which one of these drawings would most nearly resemble your class?

Pretend that each circle stands for a person in this class. Circles that are close together stand for people who are frends. (Check the one most like your class.) Place an "X" within the circle that stands for your position in the group.

dents became significantly more negative in their perceptions of influence. While 49 per cent viewed themselves as high in influence during the fall, only 44 per cent perceived that they were high in the spring.

Results in Table 2 indicated that positive gains in perceived friendship status were made in all three categories of classrooms during the school year. Comparisons of the chi-square totals as well as the per-

TABLE 1. *Student Perceptions of Influence Status in Their Classroom Groups, Early and Late*

		Laboratory Group A				Seminar Group B				Control Group C			
										Estimated			
	Perceived Influence Statuses	Fall		Spring		Fall		Spring		Fall		Spring	
		No.	Per Cent	No.	Per Cent	No.	Per Cent	No.	Per Cent	No.	Per Cent	No.	Per Cent
High	Highest part	55	10	28	5	45	9	44	9	31	10	29	9
	Second part	236	43	309	56	168	35	154	32	126	39	113	35
Low	Third part	206	37	155	28	187	39	202	42	124	38	120	37
	Lowest part	55	10	60	11	80	17	80	17	42	13	61	19

chi-square $= 48.90$ chi-square $= 2.39$ chi-square $= 10.16$
$df = 3$ $df = 3$ $df = 3$
$p < .005$ $p =$ NS $p < .025$

TABLE 2. *Student Perceptions of Friendship Status in Their Classroom Groups, Early and Late*

		Laboratory Group A				Seminar Group B				Control Group C			
										Estimated			
	Perceived Friendship Statuses	Fall		Spring		Fall		Spring		Fall		Spring	
		No.	Per Cent	No.	Per Cent	No.	Per Cent	No.	Per Cent	No.	Per Cent	No.	Per Cent
High	Highest part	79	14	99	18	101	21	91	19	56	17	58	18
	Second part	237	43	326	59	221	46	278	58	143	44	171	53
Low	Third part	171	31	105	19	106	22	72	15	87	27	55	17
	Lowest part	65	12	22	4	52	11	39	8	37	12	39	12

chi-square $= 92.39$ chi-square $= 29.84$ chi-square $= 17.37$
$df = 3$ $df = 3$ $df = 3$
$p < .005$ $p < .005$ $p < .005$

centages indicated that the positive gains made in Laboratory Group A were greater than those made in either Seminar Group B or Control Group C. Fifty-seven per cent of the students in Group A classrooms viewed themselves as highly liked early in the year. This number increased to 77 per cent in the spring, an increase of 20 per cent. Percentage increases in Groups B and C were significantly positive also, but were only half as great as the increase in Group A. We conclude that in most classrooms students tended to perceive that they were liked by more people in the spring than in the fall, but the laboratory teachers appear to have increased this positive trend even more than the others.

Additional data indicating changes in classroom friendship patterns are summarized in Tables 3 and 4. In general, these data also supported

TABLE 3. *Student Perceptions of Number of Classroom Friendship Groups, Early and Late*

	Laboratory Group A		Seminar Group B		Control Group C	
	Fall	Spring	Fall	Spring	Estimated Fall	Spring
Number of Friendship Groups	Per No. Cent	Per No. Cent	Per No. Cent	Per No. Cent	Per No. Cent	Per No. Cent
0 or 1	157 30	89 17	143 31	83 18	97 31	70 22
2	100 19	68 13	78 17	83 18	57 18	73 23
3	22 4	37 7	41 9	37 8	20 6	16 5
4 or more	245 47	330 63	199 43	258 56	143 45	158 50
	chi-square $= 69.17$ $df = 3$ $p < .005$		chi-square $= 43.37$ $df = 3$ $p < .005$		chi-square $= 14.38$ $df = 3$ $p < .005$	

our expectation that the laboratory would have positive benefit for Group A classroom groups. Results in Table 3 showed that positive gains in the number of friendship groups perceived by the students to exist in the class were made in all three categories. As in Table 2, comparisons of the chi-square totals as well as the percentages in Table 3 indicated that the positive gains were greatest for teachers in Laboratory Group A. Whereas 51 per cent of the students in Group A classes saw three, four, or more friendship groups during the fall, 70 per cent perceived that same number during the spring. Comparable increases in Group B, 52 per cent to 64 per cent, and in Group C, 51 per cent to 55 per cent, though statistically significant, were not so great.

Results in Table 4 emphasized the success of the laboratory even

TABLE 4. *Student Perceptions of Own Position in a Classroom Friendship Group, Early and Late*

| | Laboratory Group A | | | | Seminar Group B | | | | Control Group C | | | |
| | Fall | | Spring | | Fall | | Spring | | Estimated Fall | | Spring | |
Own Position in Friendship Group	No.	Per Cent	No.	Per Cent	No.	Per Cent	No.	Per Cent	No.	Per Cent	No.	Per Cent
At center of large group	96	20	120	25	48	16	51	17	55	18	81	27
At periphery of large group	120	25	97	20	72	24	66	22	74	25	66	22
In a small group	158	33	245	51	151	50	155	51	119	40	117	39
Alone	106	22	18	4	31	10	30	10	52	17	36	12

chi-square $= 131.35$	chi-square $= 0.81$	chi-square $= 18.10$
$df = 3$	$df = 3$	$df = 3$
$p < .005$	$p =$ NS	$p < .005$

more than those in Table 3. Here significant changes occurred in the extent to which students viewed themselves as being an integral part of either large (four or more persons) or small (three or fewer persons) friendship groups in the class. Fifty-three per cent of the Group A students saw themselves at the center of a large or small group during the fall. This increased to 76 per cent by the spring. The comparable increase in Control Group C classes was from 58 per cent to 66 per cent, representing a minor increment compared with the laboratory classes. No significant change was made during the year in the Seminar Group B classroom groups on perception of friendship group position.

Finally, the data in Table 5 indicated that the students in both the Group A and Group B classrooms increased during the school year in the degree to which they were helpful to one another with their schoolwork. A comparison between Groups A and B indicated that Group A classes made greater gains in helpfulness. For instance, in the fall 45 per cent of Group A students reported "almost always" or "usually" helping one another, while in the spring, 58 per cent reported similarly, representing a gain of 13 per cent. Group B, on the other hand, increased from 49 per cent to 57 per cent, an increase of only 8 per cent. Students in the Group C classroom groups showed no difference from fall to spring in helpfulness.

TABLE 5. *Student Perceptions of How Often They Help One Another with Schoolwork, Early and Late*

| | Laboratory Group A | | Seminar Group B | | Control Group C | |
| | Fall | Spring | Fall | Spring | Estimated Fall | Spring |
How Often They Help One Another	No. Per Cent	No. Per Cent	No. Per Cent	No. Per Cent	No. Per Cent	No. Per Cent
Almost always	56 11	86 17	71 15	71 15	42 13	48 15
Usually	172 34	206 41	162 34	200 42	110 34	107 33
Seldom	187 37	171 34	157 33	162 34	113 35	120 37
Almost never	92 18	44 8	85 18	42 9	58 18	48 15

chi-square = 49.19	chi-square = 30.81	chi-square = 3.09
$df = 3$	$df = 3$	$df = 3$
$p < .005$	$p < .005$	$p = NS$

PROJECT 2:
CLASSROOM MENTAL HEALTH CONSULTATION

In Project 2 skilled psychological consultants attempted to enhance teachers' capabilities for coping with group processes in the classroom. Our hypothesis was that through problem-oriented discussions with mental health specialists teachers would develop a better understanding of and be more skilled in working with the social-emotional aspects of classroom groups (Edelmann & Schmuck, 1967). Consultation sessions centered on the relationships of consultant to teachers, teachers to teachers, and of teachers to the children they taught. Since the project was carried out in Metropolitan Philadelphia, some attention was given to increasing teachers' facilities for working with groups of students from disadvantaged families.

Six highly trained consultants, two psychiatrists, two clinical psychologists, and two social workers were employed for the project. The bias of the consultants was psychodynamic and interdisciplinary. Only the social workers, however, had had professional experience in public schools. The consultants were assigned one to a school for half a day each week for 15 weeks. Three consultants worked in schools with mostly middle class children, while the others worked in schools with culturally disadvantaged youngsters. Forty upper elementary teachers received consultation. Three consultants worked with groups of six teachers each; the other consultants worked with five, eight, and nine teachers, respectively.

Two additional schools, one middle class and one lower class, were included for comparison purposes. The 20 upper elementary teachers in these two schools received no consultation.

The consultants received special training prior to and concurrent with their work with the teachers in the schools. Drs. Eli Bower (Hollister & Bower, 1967) and Ruth Newman (Newman, 1967) were responsible for much of this training. They discussed their respective approaches to school consultation and guided the six specialists through problematic situations that would arise during the consultations.

This project began during the fall of 1966 when pre-data were collected; consultation took place during the fall and winter months, and final data were collected in May 1967, three months after the consultations were completed. The consultants spent two hours each week in group discussions with the teachers. They also visited classrooms to make observations which would often culminate in individual conferences. The project plans called for both the group discussions and the individual conferences to center on teachers' own reactions to the classroom groups, especially to problem incidents involving several students. The consultants were to emphasize the development of trust in the group and to open up new pathways of behavior and new understandings of desired changes only after some trust had developed. Finally, they were to explore in depth how teachers might interact with students with interpersonal relations problems, low self-esteem, marked disinterest in learning, or recurrent daydreams and inattention.

Consulation Sessions

The consultants wrote historical accounts of every meeting with teachers, whether in group discussions or individual conferences. Along with these detailed descriptions of each encounter with teachers, the consultants were asked to jot down at the close of each session any problems they were having in establishing themselves as helpful and to specify any changes they saw in the schools, especially changes in the teachers with whom they were consulting.

Analyses of the consultants' reports indicated that certain recurrent themes appeared during the 15 weeks. During the first several sessions, classroom group problems were viewed as resulting from forces outside the control of the teachers. The teachers primarily ventilated their antagonistic feelings toward the "impersonal and unhelpful central office," the "authoritarian principal," the "incompetent counselor," the "uninterested parents," or the "intransigent students." These parties were seen as limiting the level of effectiveness that could be expected of the teachers. Some teachers felt that membership in the consultation group was involuntary, feeling that a school counselor, parental group, or the principal had really organized the group. Others needed reassurance that the principal or central office personnel would not be involved directly in the consultation groups.

After the teachers had a chance to voice these feelings in a supportive atmosphere, without being sanctioned by the consultants, they were more likely to discuss problems present in their classrooms and to see themselves and their students as jointly involved in them. As classroom group or individual problems were brought up for discussion, the teachers looked to the consultants for the solutions. They expected the consultants to recommend concrete actions that could be taken to solve the problem. At times, they expected the consultant to direct the principal or central office administrators that certain students perceived as mentally unhealthy should be removed formally from the regular classroom and placed in special education classes. The consultants generally assumed the point of view that they could only help teachers find their own answers, that these answers would most likely involve the teachers' changing their own classroom behavior, and that they did not have the authority to remove youngsters from classes.

Toward the end of the 15-week period, the teachers talked more about their own insecurities, doubts, and lack of knowledge and skills. During this phase the teachers turned more to one another for sharing ideas on handling classroom group problems. They offered to meet with one another at other times during the week to share teaching practices. The consultants' role became less prominent as the teachers conversed more freely and openly about their own classroom problems.

Results of Project 2

The consultants generally agreed that significant and positive changes occurred in many teachers as a consequence of the consultations. Perhaps the most striking change was in teachers' asking one another for help. Early in the year, many teachers reported that they were ashamed to ask for one another's assistance. The teachers were generally discouraged or indifferent about staff relations. But after the consultations many teachers had formed a strong group feeling, had a new sense of challenge and interest, and were using one another outside the sessions to talk over problems, trade materials, and respond to new ideas. Some teachers who had decided during the fall to give up teaching changed their minds as they noted how much support they felt from their colleagues.

Another general direction of change in the teachers was toward a more differentiated examination of their standards and attitudes, with somewhat greater leeway for accepting a variety of student behaviors.

One consultant noted that his teachers showed more interest and ability to deal with individual differences. Another commented that a number of students had been perceived by their teachers as being disturbed, but that during the course of consultations this was changed to perceiving the students as more energetic, restless, and child-like than disturbed. According to one consultant, because the teachers' behaviors toward these children changed, some classroom problems seemed to disappear.

Some teachers were seen as reaching a stage in which they could examine their own behavior as a factor in creating undesirable behavior in their students. Other teachers spoke less judgmentally of students and parents at the end of the consultation and instead were more likely to explore their own relationships to their students. Some began to sort out their own needs from those of the students, while others noted publicly that "problem students" often ceased being problems when a teacher extended special help, affection, and arranged for some success.

Early during the fall and again late in the spring, four self-report questionnaires were collected from the total group of 60 teachers. Three teachers' questionnaires focused on perceptual variables, measuring conceptions about self as teacher, ways of categorizing students, and conceptions of positive mental health in the classroom. Two skilled raters who had no contact with consultants scored the results of these three questionnaires without knowing whether the teachers being rated were in the consultation or comparison groups. Their initial ratings were in high agreement, generally above 90 per cent, but they continued to score items about which they disagreed until they achieved 100 per cent agreement.

The fourth questionnaire queried teachers on how they might handle a variety of problematic situations in the classroom. Each consultant scored all of these protocols. The consultants did not know what teacher or school they were scoring, nor did they know whether they were scoring the fall or the spring data. Scores of plus, zero, minus, or question mark were given. A plus meant that the situation was handled effectively. A score of minus meant that the consultant viewed the teacher's response as ineffective. A zero meant that the consultant was unable to make a judgment because the verbal content required a certain kind of nonverbal response or context. A question mark meant that the response was unclear and therefore could not be coded. In the analysis of these data, we required that four or more of the consultants agree before giving the response a plus, minus, or zero score. When only three or fewer consultants agreed, we scored the item with a question mark. The consultants did not see any results of the four questionnaires until after the consultations were completed.

In measuring the teachers' self-concepts, they were asked to write down ten phrases which described themselves as teachers. Then they were asked to go back to each phrase and to place a double plus sign if they considered that characteristic very positive, a single plus sign if they considered it somewhat positive, and a negative sign if they thought of it as somewhat negative, or a double negative sign if they considered it to be very negative.

We anticipated that the consultations would lead to a more balanced view of oneself as a teacher. We thought that those teachers who viewed themselves in the fall as quite negative and insecure would gain a greater sense of competence and self-esteem from the consultation. On the other hand, we considered that those who saw themselves as solely positive and effective in the fall would begin to uncover some areas within themselves that required some improvement. Thus the raters judged as more positive those self-concept patterns which became more balanced, containing both positive and negative attributes, or which changed from more negative to more positive, and judged as more negative those patterns which remained predominantly negative or defensively positive.

In the questionnaire on categorizing the students, teachers were given a set of cards with the names of all students, one to a card, and the following instructions:

> In your mind, there are probably many ways in which the students can be seen as similar to and different from one another. Place these cards in piles in as many different ways as might occur in your thinking. Each time you place the cards into piles, you should have some main idea in mind and a descriptive title for each pile.
>
> For instance, in your mind, you might divide the class into boys and girls. Then you would sort the cards into two piles, the main idea is "sex difference" and the descriptive titles of the piles are "boys" and "girls." Another division which might occur could be color of hair. Then "color of hair" would be the main idea, and "blondes," "brunettes," and "redheads" could be the descriptive titles.

We expected the teachers to develop in several ways as a consequence of the consultation. For one thing, we considered that teachers with consultation would use more main ideas having to do with emotional factors, attitudes, motivations, and interpersonal relations at the end of the school year. We expected more categories on topics such as anxiety, security, self-esteem, attitudes toward school, and peer relations. Further, we expected that the teachers who received consultation would increase the number of differentiations that they made under the main categories. We felt that the consultation would facilitate a more sophisticated and differentiated view of the students. We expected that the teachers might see their students more in terms of feelings but also as being increasingly different from one another.

The third questionnaire was aimed at measuring teachers' cognitive structures concerning "mental health" in the classroom. Each teacher wrote about his ideas of good mental health practices and conditions in the classroom by placing one idea each on a maximum of 25 small index cards. The teachers received the following directions:

> Let us suppose that the following situation occurs. A visiting teacher from a foreign country engages you in conversation about school practices in this country. Assume that your visitor knows very little about American teaching practices. He wants to know what you consider to be good mental health practices and conditions in the classroom. What sorts of things would you include in a list which he could refer to as he tries to learn about classroom mental health?
>
> Using these cards which have been provided, write one word, phrase, or sentence on each card which describes good classroom mental health practices or conditions. Use as few or as many cards as you need. A total of 25 cards is supplied.
>
> In order to ensure that the foreign visitor understood you, try to organize the items you listed on the cards. Do this in the following way: Lay out in front of you all the cards you used in listing mental health practices and conditions. Look them over to see whether they fall into some broad, natural groupings. If they do, arrange them into such groups. Now look at your groups to see whether these can be broken into subgroups. If they can, separate the cards accordingly. It is also possible that these subgroups can be broken down still further.

The range of groupings generally included physical properties of the room and school, physical properties of teachers or students, intellectual skills, personality characteristics including attitudes and motives, interpersonal relations, and group social relations, climate, and cohesiveness. We expected that after the consultation the teachers would emphasize students' attitudes, feelings, and motives, as well as classroom interpersonal relations and group climate. Although physical characteristics might be included, we viewed these as less central to effective classroom group processes. We further considered that the mental health categories would have more detailed subgroupings and that the teachers would relate these more directly to the students in their class.

The fourth questionnaire, titled "Classroom Situations," was made up of 44 situations which were taken from actual classrooms and presented in the form of dialogues. The teachers received these directions:

> Pretend you are the teacher in each situation (even if you have not met such a situation or would not have allowed it to develop). When the dialogue closes, write the exact words or nonverbal responses you would use at that point.

Data collected from the teachers generally indicated positive and significant changes during the school year in their perceptions of self as teacher, their cognitions of mental health categories, and their views on how to work with problematic classroom situations. The data on categorizing students did not change greatly during the year. These data are summarized in Table 6. Fisher's Exact Test, applied because of the very small sample, requires a two-by-two contingency table, and thus for purposes of this statistical analysis the data labeled "more negative" were dropped. In each case, except for the data on categorizing students, results of Fisher's Exact Test showed probabilities less than .01 (Hays, 1963). We can assume that these data indicate significant changes and therefore that the consultations altered many teachers' cognitions related to successful teaching.

The students also were asked to complete four questionnaires in the fall and spring. One questionnaire measured students' perceptions concerning the informal group processes in the class. Each student answered 12 questions on how he saw others in the class behaving, with one of four answers: almost always, usually, seldom, or almost never. Some of the items were: "Help one another with their schoolwork," "Laugh when someone misbehaves," and "Work well with one another." The second questionnaire measured attitudes toward school and self-esteem with incomplete sentence stems. Examples of items used to measure the former were: "Studying is ," "Homework is ———," "Learning out of books is ———." Self-esteem was measured with stems such as "When I look at other boys and girls and then look at myself, I feel ———," "When I look in the mirror, I ———," and "My teacher thinks I am ———." The third questionnaire presented sociometric questions on friendship and helping relations, asking students to choose the four other students in the class whom they liked the most and the four who were most helpful to other students. They also estimated their own status in the group on being liked and helpful. The fourth questionnaire dealt with students' attitudes about academic work and school in general. The students were asked about such things as how hard they saw themselves working, whether the teacher really understood them, and whether the students helped one another.

An overview of the results indicated that positive and significant changes did *not* occur in the consultation classes. The students' attitudes toward school and self did not improve in either the consultation or the comparison groups. The informal group processes appear to have remained about the same throughout the year, except for some evidence that helpfulness increased in the consultation groups.

The overall results do, however, obscure some positive changes that occurred in a few classrooms. Out of the 40 consultation classes, six

TABLE 6. *Summary of Teachers' Perceptions of Self, Students, and Classroom Processes by Group, Fall and Spring*

Evaluation in Spring Compared with Fall	Self-Concept				Categorizing Students				Mental Health Categories				Classroom Situations			
	Consultation Group		Comparison Group		Consultation Group		Comparison Group		Consultation Group		Comparison Group		Consultation Group		Comparison Group	
	No.	Per Cent	No.	Per Cent	No.	Per Cent	No.	Per Cent	No.	Per Cent	No.	Per Cent	No.	Per Cent	No.	Per Cent
More positive	14	35	2	10	5	12	0	0	15	38	0	0	19	48	3	15
No change	24	60	16	80	35	88	20	100	24	60	20	100	14	35	13	65
More negative	2	5	2	10	0	0	0	0	1	2	0	0	7	17	4	20
Probabilities From Fisher's Exact Test	$p < .01$				$p = $ NS				$p < .01$				$p < .01$			

showed distinct improvement and these, interestingly, were all within two schools. In these six classes, the friendship and helpfulness patterns became more diffuse over the course of the year. Moreover, significant changes occurred in the positive self-esteem of many of these students. In contrast with this, no changes whatsoever occurred in the students' attitudes toward school.

It appears that the cognitive and attitudinal changes which occurred in the teachers were *not* also accompanied by behavioral changes that made a difference in their classrooms. The teachers grew in their intellectual awarenesses about interpersonal relations in the classroom and in their willingness to explore new ways of handling them, but they did not in fact make major shifts in their classroom behavior. Any behavior changes that did occur, as reported by the consultants, were probably short-term and motivated out of desires to please the consultants. The group processes in the classrooms, by and large, remained unaffected by the consultations.

PROJECT 3:
ORGANIZATIONAL DEVELOPMENT LABORATORY

In Project 3, we did not attempt to influence directly teachers' capabilities for working more effectively with classroom group processes. Rather we assumed that the social relations of a school set the stage for classroom innovation and that more effective organizational processes support teacher innovativeness and performance in the classroom (Lippitt, Barakat, Chesler, Dennerell, Flanders, Worden, & Schmuck, 1966). Some aspects of effective school processes that we assumed to be related to classroom innovativeness and productivity were the interpersonal relations and feelings, communication patterns, and group norms of the staff.

This project was aimed at improving school organizational processes in the short run so that classroom innovations might be made more easily in the long run. It employed an organizational training program to help a junior high school faculty to become more aware, open, analytic, and skillful about its interpersonal relationships, communication patterns, behavior norms, decision-making processes, and group problem-solving skills.

A six-day laboratory was held before the beginning of school, 1967, and involved the entire faculty—except for two with illnesses in their families—including the head custodian, head cook, and administrative secretary, making a total group of 54 participants. The laboratory staff was composed of five trainers. The laboratory was designed to help the staff discuss its interpersonal relations, identify and explore its communicative problems, and move toward tentative, working solutions through group problem solving. Several follow-up training sessions were also scheduled during the 1967–68 school year. Some early developments warrant inclusion here because of the light they shed on helping teachers improve classroom group processes. A report is currently being written (Schmuck & Runkel, in press).

Laboratory for the Faculty

During the first two days of the laboratory the design called for a series of structured group exercises which were to lead the faculty into discussions about its own organization processes. For instance, a "NASA Trip to the Moon" exercise was employed in which five groups of 10 or 11 persons formed to decide on those items that would be most important to carry on a fictitious 200-mile trip across the moon's surface. The underlying theme of this exercise concerned the efficient uses of individual resources in making group decisions. After the exercise was completed, discussions were initiated by the trainers with such questions as: "What were your reactions to the exercise?" "How did you feel?" "What were you thinking?" "How similar or different were your behaviors here from the way they usually are in school?" and "What implications does this exercise have for your staff?" These discussions were followed by a general assembly of the entire faculty in which staff members gave their reactions to what they learned during the exercise. Each group chose its own way to report back on what it had experienced. Some elected a spokesman, while others held a group discussion in front of the general assembly. These group processes also were discussed as they took place. The trainers attempted to support openness and the giving and receiving of helpful feedback during these sessions.

Subsequent sessions during the first two days were similar in form. They began with a structured activity, were followed by discussion in small groups about the activity, and ended with some sharing of various insights on organizational processes within the entire faculty. Some of the structured activities involved nonverbal cooperation, preparation of murals depicting psychological views of the school, planning and executing a complex puzzle requiring coordination, and a communication and feedback exercise in which staff members gave feedback to one another in variously sized groups and were required to indicate that they were "hearing" by paraphrasing what the other had just said. In all of these activities the faculty members regrouped each time using the criterion of seeking out persons with whom they had communicated very little.

The remainder of the laboratory was spent in working through a six-stage problem-solving process. The staff was asked to choose "real" issues that were bothersome to the organizational functioning of the school. Three problems were identified as being the most significant: (1) a lack of role clarification, (2) low degrees of staff involvement in meetings, and (3) the nonuse of staff resources. While proceeding through the initial problem identification stage, several group formations and processes were employed that would be useful forms for the staff's operations during the school year.

After the three problems were identified, staff members volunteered to work jointly on one of them and proceeded through the problem-solving processes that involved five more steps: (1) further problem refinement and operationalization, (2) force field diagnostic exercises, (3) brainstorming action alternatives to reduce restraining forces, (4) designing concrete plans of action, and (5) trying out the plan with a training activity involving the rest of the staff.

The three training activities designed by the problem-solving groups represented high points of the laboratory. The group who worked on role clarification felt that a lack of trust among the staff was one important restraining force keeping staff members from clarifying their roles. They carried out a variety of nonverbal exercises to explore feelings of trust in the total staff. Each of these was followed by discussion on its meanings for the organizational functioning of the faculty. The second group, on staff involvement, organized several small discussion groups and acted as outside observers. During these discussions, persons who had been talking a great deal during the last five-minute interval were asked by the observers to move back from the group and to stop talking. Others still in the group were told that those who had moved back were not to answer any questions asked of them. When only two persons were left, discussions were held in each group on "feelings toward involvement during staff meetings." The third group, involved with using staff resources, set up several small groups, each of which was a simulated mini-staff of a junior high school. A crisis was pictured in which no texts or materials were available, but youngsters were coming to school the next day. Each staff person was told to specialize in an area other than his own subject matter and to seek help from others in his group. The fictitious staffs were to construct a curriculum by using one another's resources. The whole faculty assembled at the end to discuss implications for their organizational functioning.

The laboratory ended with a "strength exercise" that was designed to raise members' self-esteem and contribute to group cohesiveness. The staff divided into small groups of seven or eight. Each staff member spent a few minutes reflecting alone on his own strengths as a staff member and the unique strengths of others in his group. The time spent alone was followed by a sharing of these "strength perceptions." No admissions or observations of weaknesses were allowed. Every group included each of its members in its discussion and then the entire faculty discussed meanings of the exercise.

Results of Project 3

Faculty members were asked to complete several self-report questionnaires just prior to or during the laboratory. These were designed to measure the school's organizational climate, reactions to staff meetings, staff communication patterns, and perceptions of the principal. The research evaluation also called for some interviews and observations to be collected during the school year, as well as these same self-report questionnaires again in the spring. All the measures, whether they were questionnaires, interviews, or observations, were designed originally to center only on organizational processes. They did not include questions about classroom innovations.

We learned only inadvertently about the teachers' making use of experiences from the laboratory in their classrooms. The first signs came immediately after the laboratory when a one-page questionnaire was filled out by all faculty members on their reactions to the laboratory. Even though no question about classroom applications of the workshop was asked, seven teachers mentioned plans to make use of some laboratory experiences in their classrooms.

A second indication came in some of the essays about the laboratory written by 21 teachers. All workshop participants had the opportunity of receiving two hours of university credit for active participation. Twenty-one teachers desired three credit hours and were required to prepare an essay on their laboratory experiences. Their assignment was to write about any changes, positive or negative, in the school's operation which they considered attributable to the laboratory. They were asked to complete the essay no later than six weeks after the end of the laboratory. Most papers came in about one month after it closed. We expected to receive analyses of the school's organizational functioning primarily. Many of the faculty members, however, wrote extended reviews of how the laboratory had positively influenced their classroom performances. Some were quite specific about having used, with their students, some of the group formations, techniques, or processes employed during the laboratory.

Finally, a third sign of classroom application came about six weeks after the laboratory closed when we visited the school to interview staff members about the faculty's organizational processes. Again, even though no question was asked formally in the interview about classroom innovations, 15 teachers mentioned using new group processes in their classrooms. With these unanticipated data, we added one question to the interview schedule for the next round of interviews. The question was, "Has the laboratory experience influenced your classroom teaching in any ways? If yes, in what ways?" Of the 20 teachers who were interviewed on the second round, 19 answered yes to the question.

The teachers' comments on "in what ways" the laboratory influenced their teaching divided into three categories. Some teachers mentioned only very general outcomes such as "a change in my general approach to students," "a better atmosphere in my classroom," or "more attention to the feelings of the students." Another small group of teachers commented on specific attitude changes such as "I am more comfortable this year," "I am sensitive to students' feedback," or "I am more relaxed in letting the students discuss things." Eleven of the 19 teachers fitted into the third category. They mentioned specific group procedures that they actually were using in their classrooms such as "using small groups for projects," "using nonverbal exercises to depict feelings about the subject matter being studied," "using 'theatre in the round' or 'fishbowl' formations for having students observe one another," "using a paraphrasing exercise to point out how poor classroom communications are," "using the problem-solving sequence and techniques in social studies classes to learn more about social problems," and "using small groups for giving and receiving feedback about how the class is going." As far as we know, none of these practices was used by these teachers before the organizational development laboratory.

DISCUSSION AND CONCLUSIONS

The three interventions discussed above helped teachers, directly or indirectly, to work toward improving classroom group processes.

The organizational development laboratory for a school staff, described in Project 3, set the stage unexpectedly for staff members' attention to classroom group processes by encouraging them to experiment with innovative group procedures in the school organization. Training activities carried out during the laboratory presented group forms, techniques, and procedures that could be used just as appropriately in the classroom as at staff meetings. The laboratory was a living example of McLuhan's dictum that "the medium is the message" (McLuhan, 1964). A majority of the teachers tried new group processes in their classrooms that were directly patterned after their organizational laboratory experiences.

In Project 2, regular discussions about classroom group processes with psychological consultants helped improve teachers' perceptions of self as teachers, their cognitions of mental health categories, and their views on how to work with problematic classroom situations. However, these cognitive and attitudinal changes were not accompanied by behavioral changes in the classroom. This is not surprising since verbal learning is quite different from skill learning. Persons do not learn to play baseball, to dance, or to give speeches by reading books or through discussions. Nor should a teacher be expected to improve the complex skills of classroom instruction through mere discussions. Discussions on classroom group problems, students' psychodynamics, and different approaches to teaching can be expected to assist a teacher to think, talk, or write more intelligently about the issues, but actual behavioral tryouts and experiences are necessary before new skills are used easily in the classroom.

A teacher development laboratory which included problem-solving techniques, sensitivity training, and role-play tryouts did lead to behavioral changes in the classroom. The sensitivity training and related human relations activities seemed to challenge teachers' cognitions of interpersonal relations, to lead teachers to introspect on their effects on others, to encourage teachers to explore their values about teaching, and to develop colleague norms of support and helpfulness. The problem-solving procedures helped teachers think more systematically about new patterns of classroom behavior, and the role-play tryouts helped build psychological connections among new cognitions, attitudes, and behaviors.

Taken together, these interventions can fit well into integrated action programs that might be employed by school systems for improving classroom group processes. Two integrated programs of different durations can be mentioned here.

One would take place over an 18-month period. It would commence with an organizational development laboratory during the latter part of August, just prior to the beginning of the school year. Following this, teachers would be asked to volunteer for a program of consultation and training in classroom group processes. A psychological consultant, skilled in interpersonal relations theory and classroom processes, would work with them two hours each week for the entire academic year. Then, during the following summer, a teacher development laboratory would take place. Follow-up discussions could occur during the fall semester to help the teachers follow through on trying out new procedures and to reinforce continuously any insights or new skills developed during the previous year.

Another, shorter program, lasting for only about six months, would be launched with an organizational development laboratory just two weeks before school begins. Since many school systems now grant some days prior to the schools' opening for inservice training, it would be possible to extend those days into a week and to spend that week in a teacher development laboratory. This two-week, back-to-back laboratory program would facilitate the translation of group processes found to be useful during the organizational laboratory into classroom innovations during the teacher development laboratory. Then, during the fall semester, follow-up discussions could be led by psychological consultants who would emphasize the problem-solving process and give support to teachers trying to implement their plans.

Many other action designs might be developed using these three basic interventions as the elements. We hope that behavioral scientists and educators will collaborate in trying some of them.

REFERENCES

BRADFORD, L., GIBB, J., & BENNE, K. *T-group theory and laboratory method.* New York: Wiley, 1964.

CHESLER, M., & FOX, R. *Role-playing methods in the classroom.* Chicago: Science Research Associates, 1966.

COCH, L., & FRENCH, J. R. P., JR. Overcoming resistance to change. *Human Relations,* 1948, *1,* 512–532.

EDELMANN, A., & SCHMUCK, R. Pilot study in exploring the use of mental health consultants to teachers of socially maladjusted pupils in regular classes. Unpublished final report. Philadelphia, Pa.: Mental Health Association of Southeastern Pennsylvania, 1967.

FLANDERS, N., & HAVUMAKI, S. The effect of teacher-pupil contacts involving praise on the sociometric choices of students. *J. educ. Psychol.,* 1960, *51,* 65–68.

FOX, R., LUSZKI, MARGARET, & SCHMUCK, R. *Diagnosing classroom learning environments.* Chicago: Science Research Associates, 1966.

HAYS, W. *Statistics for psychologists.* New York: Holt, Rinehart & Winston, 1963. Pp. 598–601.

HOLLISTER, W., & BOWERS, E. (Eds.) *Behavioral science frontiers in education.* New York: Wiley, 1967.

KAUFMAN, M., SCHMUCK, R., & LIPPITT, R. *Creative practices developed by teachers for improving classroom atmospheres.* Document No. 14, Inter-Center Program on Children, Youth, and Family Life. Ann Arbor, Mich.: Institute for Social Research, 1963.

LIPPITT, R., BARAKAT, H., CHESLER, M., DENNERELL, D., FLANDERS, MARY, WORDEN, O., & SCHMUCK, R. The teacher as innovator, seeker and sharer of new practices. In R. Miller (Ed.), *Perspectives on educational change.* New York: Appleton-Century-Crofts, 1967. Pp. 307–324.

McLUHAN, M. *Understanding media.* New York: McGraw-Hill, 1964.

NEWMAN, RUTH. *Psychological consultation in the schools.* New York: Basic Books, 1967.

292 / Schmuck

SCHMUCK, R.   Sociometric status and utilization of academic abilities. *Merrill-Palmer Quart.*, 1962, *8*, 165–172.

SCHMUCK, R.   Some relationships of peer liking patterns in the classroom to pupil attitudes and achievement. *School Rev.*, 1963, *71*, 337–358.

SCHMUCK, R.   Some aspects of classroom social climate. *Psychol. in the Schools*, 1966, *3*(1), 59–65.

SCHMUCK, R., CHESLER, M., & LIPPITT, R.   *Problem solving to improve classroom learning.* Chicago: Science Research Associates, 1966.

SCHMUCK, R., & RUNKEL, P.   Organizational training for a school faculty. Eugene, Ore.: Center for the Advanced Study of Educational Administration, in press.

SCHMUCK, R., & VAN EGMOND, E.   Sex differences in the relationships of interpersonal perceptions to academic performance. *Psychol. in the Schools*, 1965, *2*(1), 32–40.

Sensitivity Training:
The Affective Dimension
of Inservice Training

Raymond L. Jerrems

Fred was a middle-grade teacher at the school; I was the principal. We were participating in an inservice workshop with about a third of the school staff. The workshop—a one-week residential session just before the opening of the school—included some intensive T-group experiences. Fred and I were not in the same group, but after the regular activities had ended late one evening, several of us were discussing some issues raised in the workshop. I am not sure what led up to the incident, but I suddenly found myself in direct confrontation with Fred. He described his grim perception of me: I was merely an office bureaucrat who passed on orders from "downtown" and shuffled papers. I was efficient and ran the school well but not in the best interests of the students or the teachers.

I found myself responding with my perception of Fred. I saw him as uninvolved. He put in his time at the school and did an acceptable job in the classroom, but there was no fire in him. I thought of him as being more interested in fine clothes and an active social life than in his career. Several others on the staff were listening, but at the time we were too immersed in the issue to be aware that anyone else was there. It struck me that if Fred was as unfair in his perception of me as I thought he was, perhaps my opinion of him was equally unfair.

We discussed this idea for a while, and then I suggested an activity I had used in similar workshop situations. Fred and I would stand facing each other. There was to be no spoken communication, but we were to take turns being the mirror image of the other. We were standing very close to each other, and I was intensely aware of the look in Fred's eyes and the expression on his face. We slowly moved our arms up and down

Raymond L. Jerrems, "Sensitivity Training: The Affective Dimension of Inservice Training," *The National Elementary Principal*, May 1971, pp. 63–69.

293

and twisted our necks for several minutes, each of us leading in turn, until I found myself getting into a highly uncomfortable position. I was following Fred's lead, bending to the left and reaching down with my left arm almost to the floor, until the tension in my back and legs became more and more painful and we both ended the activity.

We then sat down to talk. Fred began by saying that when I had put us into the painful, twisted position, he was determined not to be shown up and had continued to follow my lead in order not to be outdone. I responded that I had thought he was leading at that point. We had just proved to ourselves that we didn't always understand what the other was doing. We had also spent several minutes trying to become aware of the other's every movement and very thought. Now the way was open for us to learn to know each other, to build a different relationship, which we did during the rest of the workshop. Our relationship in school after the workshop was quite different. Because Fred trusted me more, he felt free to take a more active role in school activities. Because I trusted him, I encouraged him and was more responsive to his suggestions. Our experience in the workshop increased our effectiveness on the job. Four years later, we are still good friends, even though we now work in different schools.

Sensitivity training has become an omnibus term for group activities that range from staid discussions of individual problems to far-out orgies. For some, the word conjures up images of people crawling on a floor, covered with sheets, groping around in open fields while blindfolded, or congregating nude in heated pools. Others envision groups sitting silently in a circle for hours or prying and probing into each other's innermost secrets. Sensitivity training is a key topic in education today and an emotonally loaded one. As its use has spread throughout the behavioral sciences, reactions have been strong and they usually polarize. Most people are either for it or against it; few are neutral.

Wide exposure to the use of sensitivity training with special groups like drug addicts and mental patients overshadows the fact that most participants are groups of ordinary businessmen, factory workers, college students, church members—in short, groups of people. This is an account of sensitivity training in one elementary school. Some activities may seem strange or inappropriate to a serious educational endeavor, and this will probably always seem so to those who have not directly encountered them. Sensitivity training is something that can be described but not really understood or appreciated by anyone who has not experienced it. It is not a classroom kind of learning. It is a laboratory experience, sometimes called *experiential learning* in order to distinguish it from classroom learning. The improvement of interpersonal relations is an important objective of sensitivity training. Interpersonal relations are what schools are all about —not just the relations between teacher and student but those between teacher and teacher, student and student, teacher and principal, teacher and parent. To generalize, we can say that most school activity consists of a multitude of interchanges between person and person. Sensitivity training develops understanding and skill in person-to-person relationships. One example of such a skill is communication, an essential element in any person-to-person relationship.

School is a verbal place, and teachers are verbal people. We consider the best teachers to be those who are highly literate and articulate. Our language arts curricula usually include "communication skills," generally defined as the aural ones of speaking and listening and the visual ones of reading and writing. Schools might, therefore, be considered centers of effective communication, but this is not necessarily true, for the implication is that all communication is cognitive and verbal. Communication of emotions and nonverbal modes of communication, such as facial expression, physical contact, or body movements, are ignored. Guidance classes sometimes deal with emotions but usually in the context of learning how to control and suppress rather than how to communicate them. If a student tells a teacher, "I hate Mary because she always gets the highest marks," the teacher will probably respond, "You shouldn't say that" or even, "You shouldn't *feel* that way." The general pattern is that all communication is verbal and must be "nice." Strong or "negative" feelings must be suppressed. Of course, we know that strong feelings *cannot* be long suppressed; if they are, they emerge in dysfunctional ways, as in fighting, arguing, lying, stealing, or withdrawal. When this occurs, teachers frequently insist that they be dealt with abstractly and indirectly, in terms of "right" and "wrong," "good" and "bad," permitted and forbidden behavior.

A major goal of sensitivity training is to help us become sensitive to such feelings and acquire more effective ways of sharing and understanding them. Here is an example of these issues in a classroom activity:

A teacher has just finished explaining the day's lesson in a mathematics class and asks, "Are there any questions?" Peter raises his hand and says, "I don't understand why you put the decimal point after the two."

The teacher responds in a gentle and patient voice, "You are not paying attention, Peter. I explained that you count over three places, didn't I, class?" The other students nod, some smugly. "Are there any other questions? Yes, Marcia?" Marcia asks, "What do you do with the remainder?" "That's a good question, Marcia," replies the teacher, "I haven't explained that yet, have I? Now, this is what we do. . . ."

This is an example of ineffective communication. Peter's question should have been received as feedback about him, a message to the teacher that Peter—and perhaps others—did not understand the lesson. Instead, the teacher heard feedback about himself—that his presentation was unsuccessful—and he protected his bruised ego by hurting Peter and seeking reassurance from the rest of the class that he *did* do a good job in explaining. He rewarded Marcia for asking a question, one uncritical of his performance, that put him back in control of the lesson.

There is no doubt that a teacher feels threatened when confronted with evidence that children are not learning all he expects. It comes as no surprise, of course. Nevertheless, it is difficult to deal with this fact publicly. One way out is to discourage questions and feedback from the class. If, however, a teacher encourages feedback, he needs some way to deal with the anxiety it engenders. An experienced teacher has learned to deal with this so he will not feel threatened, but he often continues to use the punitive responses that he adopted when he was less experienced and felt more threatened.

Sensitivity training helps us cope with a situation like the above. Participants in a T-group learn to interpret feedback correctly and develop skills in responding to it. They learn to deal with the feelings generated in two-way communication; they come to understand that such feelings are legitimate and that they are more effectively met if they are recognized rather than repressed.

Let us look at a more effective response to Peter's question. The teacher might say, "That's an important point, and I want to be sure everyone understands. Are there others who are not sure why the decimal point belongs after the two? Now, I said we find the place by counting over three places. Let me try to explain it another way. . . ."

Here, the teacher rewards Peter for asking a question and uses his question to clarify the rest of the lesson. The relationship between the teacher and the children has changed. Students have some control over the direction of the lesson. We no longer have "good" questions, which go in the direction the teacher wants, and "bad" questions, which do not fit the teacher's expectations.

This is the meaning of "sensitivity." The teacher was insensitive to both Peter's feelings and his own. It takes practice to develop this kind of awareness, and it requires help from someone who understands interpersonal communication. This was an aim of our workshops.

The following events occurred during a three-year period in the Raymond School, a large public school in Chicago's inner city.[1]

In the 1966-67 academic year, the school began an inservice project, financed with $18,000 from the Weiboldt Foundation. A major criterion used in the development of the project was that its goals and directions be set by the school staff, including teachers, paraprofessionals, maintenance, and other auxiliary personnel. There were three major workshops the first year: a one-week residential program the week before school opened and two weekend workshops during the school year. The major theme of the year's work was organizational development. Our goal was to develop better programs and systems in the school by providing its staff with skills in communication, problem solving, and decision making. Inservice activities focused on the problems and the people in the school. Sensitivity training, in a broad sense, was the technique used to keep the program functional and in focus.

By the end of the first year, the staff had written a proposal for further activities, and a staff committee obtained $20,000 in grants from the Weiboldt Foundation and the Chicago Community Trust. The direction of the project was then firmly in the hands of the staff, who planned additional workshops and chose consultants to conduct them, made funds for special projects available to individual staff members and supervised and evaluated them; and planned inservice activities and coordinated them through the staff steering committee, a policy-making body representing the entire staff.

Sensitivity training teaches specific concepts and skills. The success of the Raymond School project depended on an individual's concept of his relations with others. Each participant asked himself these questions:

How do I appear to others?

How do I wish to appear to others?

How do I feel about others? How do I express these feelings?

We learned to communicate feelings as well as ideas and to accept the feelings of others as legitimate and important even if they were sometimes negative.

In addition, we learned group skills: We learned how to distinguish between the *task* of a group and the *process* it uses to deal with the task; how to negotiate and to collaborate. And we learned problem-solving procedures, the mechanics of group formation and maintenance.

We used structured experiences as well as group activities. Sometimes called *skill exercises,* these are specific activities for practicing specific behavioral skills.

Like physical skills, effective communication is facilitated by practice. For example, a golf pro will help a beginner perfect his golf swing by breaking the action down into many parts and helping him improve each one in turn. The novice will practice his grip on the club, his stance, addressing the ball, the backswing, head movements, and so on—and then integrate these small pieces of behavior into a coordinated action.

The same procedure is used in laboratory learning of interpersonal skills. A person identifies a specific kind of interpersonal exchange with which he has difficulty, and others help him practice it by role playing. He may alternate roles to learn how it appears from the "other side." He may watch others play the role to see how they handle the interchange. He also gets feedback on his own behavior from the other participants. In addition to providing practice for a specific behavioral objective, this activity teaches him a great deal about others' styles of behavior. We learn who excels in reasoned persuasion, mediation, confrontation, and so on.

As an example, in one workshop activity, we were grouped into threes and each person was asked to describe an interpersonal situation with which he had difficulty. I was working with Lucy and Bill. Lucy explained that she always had difficulty saying "no" to a request for help, especially if the request were made by a superior. She mentioned an instance when I had asked her if she would be willing to make a sign for a forthcoming parade. It was on very short notice, and, since the school year was coming to a close, she was busy. Lucy explained that she had agreed to make the sign but had been quite upset since she did not really want to do it.

We set up a game, with Bill playing the role of principal and Lucy being herself. Bill asked her to take on a special supervisory duty. Lucy demurred very gently, but when Bill pressed her she agreed to do it. This gave me a deeper insight: Even in a make-believe situation, where Lucy was expected to refuse a request, she couldn't do it. The activity helped Lucy focus on a specific problem and understand herself better. She continued to work on the skill of saying "no" throughout the workshop. It also helped me. I had asked Lucy to do the sign because she has some artistic talent, and I had thought that she would not mind. Now I could at least try to avoid putting her in such a conflicting position the next time I wanted help.

This interchange between Lucy and me was followed by another. At a session later in the week, several group members were telling me how I appeared to them. They remarked that my voice got louder, my face got red, and my behavior became threatening whenever I became deeply involved in a discussion that appeared to be going against me. My response was that I realized this was true but that it was an unintended and unconscious reaction on my part. Lucy spoke up and said that she couldn't press her views in a discussion when I acted like this, but she thought she could do something to change this.

In one of our discussions the next day, I was suddenly aware of Lucy's hand on my arm. I realized immediately that I was tense and speaking loudly to emphasize a point. I stopped talking, relaxed, thanked Lucy, and began to listen to what the others were saying. Lucy continued to sit next to me and help me realize when my actions became dysfunctional. Even now, four years later, I sometimes discover myself "coming on too strong" in a meeting and remember the feeling of Lucy's hand on my arm.

As we learned these new behavioral skills, we applied them. One of the problems we had initially indentified related to the steering committee, which was composed of a number of faculty members and had the task of setting policy and dealing with school problems. The committee had had variable success. Its policies were often not supported by the school staff, and it usually took an inordinate amount of time in coping with problems. As one member put it, "We spend all our time discussing the problem and no time solving it."

With the help of consultants, the steering committee worked to improve its own organization and skills in problem solving during the workshops. One of the first issues the committee faced was finding a chairman. When the question was raised, each member looked around, and there was silence. Then there was a round of nominations, followed by a round of refusals. The consultant pointed out that it looked as if this activity were designed to hinder rather than help us find the best chairman. He suggested that instead of trying to push someone into the chairmanship, we spend the time discussing why everyone was reluctant to be chairman. The discussion was illuminating, for everyone agreed that the chairman usually ended up doing most of the work. The committee often made decisions that required some action, but no one would volunteer to help. At this point, the consultant suggested that we were unlikely to get anyone to serve as chairman unless we gave him prior assurance that he would get whatever help he needed.

We then discussed what qualities were important in a chairman and who on the committee exemplified them. At this point, Joanne's name was mentioned. A quiet, reserved, and highly respected fifth-grade teacher who had not been an active leader in the school, she agreed to be the chairman temporarily, with the understanding that the committee would provide her the necessary assistance. She did the job effectively, the temporary appointment was later made permanent for the school year, and the steering committee began solving problems.

The overriding aim of our workshop activities was to improve the school program. It seemed clear that the instructional program would improve if the staff members became more sensitive to the needs and feelings of children and more skillful in working with people. Although it would be foolish to credit all improvements in the school to our inservice program, many were an obvious consequence of it. The following is an example:

Kathy, a fourth-grade teacher, came to tell me that her class was upset because they had missed their gym period. The gym teacher had been asked to supervise a special film showing for the school, necessitating the cancelling of some gym classes. Kathy explained that when she discussed it with her class, she found that the students were upset because they felt completely helpless to do anything about it. It soon became obvious to her that they felt that whatever happened at school occurred at the whim of the teachers and principal. Their opinion was never sought; if it was offered, no one listened. Kathy promised to ask me to discuss their complaint with them. She and her students had also discussed what they should say, and they had agreed that the problem would be more likely to be solved to their satisfaction if they could suggest alternative ways to run the movies.

When I conferred with the students, they told me how many times they had missed gym that year and how bad they felt about it. They suggested that I schedule the films on a rotating basis or find someone else to run them. I hadn't realized that the schedule had been unfair, and I agreed with the students that I should make some changes. Kathy's awareness of, and concern for, her students' feelings resulted in a better program and encouraged them to participate actively in it.

During the second year of the project, the sixth-grade teachers examined procedures for grouping students. There were three sixth-grade classes, grouped homogeneously according to reading levels. I suggested that it might be worthwhile to consider permitting students to form their own groups and showed them some studies of alternative grouping methods.[2]

The teachers displayed some anxiety when we discussed the idea. What would we do if one of the teachers had no requests to be in her group? Or if most of the students asked for one particular teacher? Was this giving the children too much freedom? Could the children make wise decisions about their own placement?

We talked about the teachers' individual differences. Lorraine had been in the school for over 30 years and was loved and respected by the whole community. Henrietta had been there for several years and was popular with the students and talented in music and art. Anne was quite a bit younger, had been there only a year, and was also liked by the students. Everyone agreed that it was likely that Lorraine would get the most choices and Anne the fewest and that no one should feel hurt about this since there were good reasons for it.

The sixth-grade teachers decided that they would ask each fifth-grade student to write his first, second, and third choices for his sixth-grade teacher and his reasons for his choices. The results were reassuringly predictable, but we were able to give each student either his first or his second choice. The students' reasons for their choices were revealing and encouraging to the staff. Typical reasons were:

"I want to go to Mrs. Smith because she makes you work hard." "I want to go to Miss Roland's room because my sister had her last year." "I want to be in Mrs. Adams' room because I like to sing."

The results of the new method of grouping were also encouraging.

Teachers reported that their relations with their students were better because they felt secure in their knowledge that their students had asked to be in their classes. They found that the heterogeneity of achievement levels led them to change their teaching procedures, but they also found that the quicker students could help the slower ones.

During the first year of the project, the staff worked to plan and finance its continuation. They wrote a proposal for continued activities that would cost about $100,000. They again wrote to the Weiboldt Foundation, which granted them an additional $10,000; and to the Chicago Community Trust, which also granted $10,000. This money was used in the second year of the program to continue the workshops away from school and to finance individual projects. Teachers were encouraged to request up to $500 for projects to improve their own part of the school program. If two or more teachers wanted to conduct an activity together, they could ask for up to $1,000. There were many proposals, and 11 were funded in amounts ranging from $400 to $1,000 for projects that included special field trip activities, a paperback bookstore, the development of a nature project on the school grounds, special reading experiments, a project in photography, and a free milk program for the kindergartens. These projects were planned by staff members and approved by a staff committee with a minimum of red tape and a strong feeling that they belonged to the staff—unlike most experimental programs that originate outside the school. Eight of the 11 projects were successfully carried out, and four were continued the following year, without special financing. One, the nature center, was so successful that the Board of Education took over its financial support and provided a special teacher for it. It eventually became the first operational part of an environmental studies program that is now being expanded throughout the city.

The benefits of the special grant program were many. In addition to affecting the children who were directly involved, it contributed to staff and student morale as the school became a place where many innovative and exciting things were happening. The staff felt encouraged when they were trusted to make their own plans and spend money with a minimum of supervision and red tape. On several of the projects, the staff worked with students from the entire school. This paved the way for a new norm of looking at the school as a whole, replacing the previous one that assumed that each teacher was responsible only for her own class. As teachers worked together on the projects, a new openness reinforced the cooperative activities that had begun in the workshops. Teachers felt that the ideas generated at the workshops could now be implemented since funds were now available to buy materials and to pay for staff assistance.

Most of the school staff are now more effective, more closely knit, and happier. However, some of the staff refused to come to any of the workshops. One teacher participated in the first workshop but became quite upset and refused to attend any more.

As new behavioral norms for the staff were tried, many found them uncomfortable. Calling each other by first names, expressing disagreement or disapproval directly and openly, talking about feelings rather than just ideas, getting everyone's views before taking action were sometimes cause for discomfort or confusion. Picture a janitor sitting in at a staff conference about a disturbed child while the teachers listen raptly to his analysis of the problem; a lunchroom cook telling the principal about his shortcomings; a teacher aide sitting on the funds committee; the engineer custodian conducting parlor meetings in the local housing project to encourage more parents to participate in school affairs.

The norm is now to deal with people as *people*. Of course, we still recognize them in their roles as students or teachers or secretaries or cooks. But they are people first, and the resources they have as individuals should not be limited to role expectations.

As principal, I, too, found much of this threatening. If I gave the steering committee the freedom to set policies, what would I do if it made some I did not approve of or which were in violation of Board of Education policy? How should I respond when my "expert" ideas about science textbooks were unanimously repudiated by the staff? How should I deal with my superiors when they questioned the propriety of nonprofessional staff operating outide their traditional roles?

I still have some of these uncomfortable feelings, but they are overshadowed by a much stronger sense of security and satisfaction. If I trust the staff and they trust me, we will help each other solve problems, not create them.

FOOTNOTES

1. A part of this project was described in a previous article: Pedersen, K. George. "Inservice Education: A New Model?" *Selected Articles for Elementary School Principals.* Washington, D.C.: Department of Elementary School Principals, National Education Association, Washington, D.C., 1968. Pp. 91–97.

2. Thelen, Herbert A. *Classroom Grouping for Teachability.* New York: John Wiley & Sons, 1967.

Sensitivity:
A Superintendent's View

James A. Kimple

Our rapid transition from an agricultural to a technological society, from a marginal existence to affluence, has intensified old human problems and created new ones. Since we were unprepared to cope with the mass migration to urban centers, changing employment patterns, disruption of family and community mores, the demands of minority groups, along with a host of other problems, such rapid change has produced massive cultural shock.

Our young people, well aware of the inconsistencies in our society, in search of meaning in their lives and lacking clearly defined roles, tend to add to our confusion by challenging our beliefs, our assumptions, and our institutions.

However, as we search for direction and focus, we could do worse than listen to the responses of two high school juniors who, when asked, "What do you think you need to learn to do?" replied:

1. To communicate with all sorts of people

2. To learn how to learn

3. To cope with ourselves

4. To make a (wise) decision

5. To help other people

6. To adapt to change

7. To solve problems

8. To learn how to put all of these things together in order to take constructive action.

James A. Kimple, "Sensitivity: A Superintendent's View," *Educational Leadership,* December 1970, pp. 266–69. Reprinted with permission of the Association for Supervision and Curriculum Development and James A. Kimple. Copyright © 1970 by the Association for Supervision and Curriculum Development.

To say that schools need to change in these directions is one thing; to help school personnel to develop the necessary attitudes, behavior, knowledge, and skills necessary to do so is quite another. Change does not come easily to adults or to institutions.

The problem then is to find the training methodology and to develop the vehicles which will enable personnel to acquire the new attitudes, knowledge, behavior, and skill necessary for schools to become dynamic self-generating institutions. Such schools will be capable of responding to and planning for changing needs and conditions in a systematic way.

Our first attempts to create change in schools through the use of group dynamics occurred nearly 20 years ago. During the intervening years we used the methodology in a variety of ways, at first with poor results. We were able to send a few people to the National Training Laboratories at Bethel, Maine, for a two-week session; but these people often expressed frustration at their inability to find others in their school who were willing to take a look at the process of group work.

However, these early attempts and the development of an inquiry-based summer laboratory school in 1953 for youngsters in grades 4–12 led to the development of the design of the model used for training during the three-year period from 1967 to 1970.

Our first really successful use of group dynamics occurred about 1955 when this process was combined with individual counseling, group counseling, self-analysis of academic achievement, and intensive training in effective writing, thinking, and methods of study. High school juniors and seniors (my oldest son among them) were completely turned on and, although they officially met from 7 to 11 P.M., unofficially they convened at 6 and continued until 2 A.M. in the local diner. This was voluntary participation with no extrinsic rewards and the results were phenomenal. Conducted over a three-year period, most of the young men and women were transformed from mediocre to high achievers.

A CONTINUING EFFORT

Our second successful application of group dynamics and organizational development work started in 1963 in the South Brunswick Public Schools when all administrators attended a training session of the National Training Laboratories in Bethel, Maine. This effort has continued through 1970. From 1967 to 1970, training has been provided through an ESEA Title III grant Number 68-3566-1.

In our proposal we noted that during recent years the South Brunswick Public Schools had been making significant strides toward developing a meaningful educational program for every child in the district. However, we had found that supplementary programs and cultural enrichment activities would be of relatively little value until all administrators and teachers were able to examine, and where necessary modify, their attitudes and behavior, especially toward children and their parents.

In our guiding principles, we indicated that: (a) one of the most important needs facing public schools is to bring classroom practice more nearly into line with current knowledge in the areas of child growth and development, human relations, and learning theory; (b) curriculum is more than cognitive learning and it embraces everything which occurs in a school; (c) teacher personality and behavior have a profound effect upon the lives of children; (d) if schools are to become more positive forces in the lives of children, schools must change; (e) the only way to change schools is to change the perceptions and behavior of administrators and teachers.

Detailed objectives we described as: (a) to develop and demonstrate an in-service training program for administrators and teachers which will result in significant changes in teacher perceptions and classroom practices; (b) to accomplish this purpose we shall attempt to: (1) develop trust among staff members; (2) increase sensitivity to the effects of one's own behavior upon others; (3) increase sensitivity to the needs of children; (4) free teachers of rigid restrictions imposed by fixed courses of study, inflexible time schedules, inflexible grouping practices, etc.; (5) help teachers develop skill in goal setting, planning, systematic recording of information, and evaluation of learning activities; and finally (6) help teachers become more productive as team members.

The basic design of the training model included a six-week summer session and the equivalent of two weeks for follow-up during the school year. The summer session included:

2 weeks	*4 weeks*	
Group	A.M.	Teaching in a summer laboratory school
Dynamics	P.M.	Continuous evaluation and planning of morning program by teaching teams; training groups continue work in group dynamics

This training program involved all but two or three members of the staff of a new middle school, elementary and secondary school teachers. In addition, we developed a unique and highly successful undergraduate teacher intern program. Seniors from Newark State College participated in the summer training and then spent a semester with a teacher or teachers of their own choice.

REACTIONS OF PARTICIPANTS

Although the evaluation is not fully completed, the reactions of the participants and our own observations indicate that the program has been even more successful than we had originally thought it might be. No person has been harmed in the process and no participant thought it a waste of time.

Experienced teachers expressed themselves as follows:

"The most significant experience to me this summer was having a group of educators embark upon trying to understand each other. Too often schools are merely a place to work with no significant interest in the other people who work alongside of you."

"For the first time in many years of teaching I was able to become involved with people. These were not teachers to me, they were people whom I grew to know. I also regained a feeling of importance that I had not felt in recent years."

"I see the administration not as a threat but rather as a resource to me. I can work without a sense of 'big brother' watching over me and I feel the freedom to try new things."

"The feeling of freedom that I experienced in dealing with students has enabled me to feel a total commitment to this school. Knowing that the administration is truly sincere in its desire for innovation has made me able to make innovations."

Interns and cooperating teachers said:

"In the beginning, the group was composed of uncertain individuals, each regarding the others as either a threat or just indifferent. As we proceeded to discuss personal feelings we became aware of each other's fears and expectations. The turning point (I feel) came after we split into subgroups and probed personal experiences and feelings. After reassembling into a large group, we (as a group) were able to share and better understand each group member's feelings. From there we have continued to grow and strengthen our relationships to each other and with the group as a whole. Each day we have continued making progress and evaluating our failures and successes (as a T-group) in a more realistic manner."

I am now even more enthusiastic about the potential of group dynamics, sensitivity training, and especially organizational development work than I was when first introduced to this process 20 years ago. Not once in these years have I observed any harmful effects upon any participant, student, teacher, administrator, or parent; quite the contrary, I have watched people blossom and become far more capable individuals, and have seen faculties become self-directing.

I have been especially impressed with the intern program—with some minor modifications this model could be profitably used by every teacher education institution.

PRECAUTIONS AND SUGGESTIONS

We do not pretend that we know how to take full advantage of the potential of organizational development work. We have, however, learned a few things that may be helpful to another school district or institution contemplating use of organizational development work for the first time.

We believe that organizational development work should begin with or include the administrator. Unless he is involved in and committed to the complete process, he may be threatened by the expertise developed by staff members and may find ways to prevent effective work.

All participants should be volunteers. Some staff members resist any activity which they feel may expose their inadequacies. If forced to participate, they may cause irreparable harm.

Do not expect miracles. This is hard, exhausting work which may have no effect upon some. It takes time, so allocate six weeks during the summer for your initial effort.

Provide time for follow-up during the course of the school year. There seems to be a very substantial wash-out effect within six months, especially in group dynamics training.

Be careful whom you select as trainers or consultants. If a trainer offers you a package promising extraordinary achievement, I suggest that you proceed cautiously. It's your organization, not his. He can walk away from the consequences. You can't. If the trainer is not interested in your organizational concerns and is unwilling to plan cooperatively, find someone else.

We prefer to conduct organizational development work on site. Individual growth opportunities for those who desire them are available at well-known training centers. Send some personnel who wish to attend.

Be careful that training exercises are used judiciously by teachers in their own classrooms. Some are most appropriate—others take more expertise than teachers can develop in a short time.

Anticipate some conflict. No matter how carefully you plan you will receive some criticism. The results are worth the risk.

Avoid giving the impression that there is something mysterious about training. There isn't, but the impression is easy to create.

Provide extended training for key personnel. Training for new staff members and follow-up sessions for "old ones" will continue to be needed.

Sensitivity training, group dynamics, or organizational development will not cure a sick institution. If a staff feels that it is doing the best possible job and if it blames others for its own shortcomings, this training probably won't help.

Conversely, organizational development work will aid an institution which is healthy and wants to improve its performance.

Sensitivity training can help staff members develop mutual trust and confidence, become aware of the effects of their own behavior upon the group. However, this personal growth does not teach the individual to solve problems. Other processes must be used in conjunction with it. It will not, for example, teach teachers how to teach reading.

Involve as many members of a total staff as possible. "Outsiders" tend to create dissension.

Be prepared for different rates of change among staff members. Some acquire news skills rapidly, others may need three years, and still others may never change.

Permit staff members—a group of teachers or a teacher—to try different teaching techniques and to proceed at their own rate. Nothing makes a school as stagnant as expecting all to move at the same time.

Keep the board of education and the community informed of your progress. If possible, involve them in training.

Allow ample time for staffing and planning—at least six months.

Limit your objectives realistically.

6 / Teaching with Feeling

Whether it is a newly acquired reassurance or an aroused anxiety, these feelings affect her performance in the classroom. They affect the teacher's patience in dealing with children, the teacher's ability to discipline children successfully, and especially the teacher's ability to sustain exciting, interesting learning for children. Here again is lost opportunity. Often these feelings are considered irrelevant; usually they are ignored. At best the teacher is expected to "control" them, which usually means to mask, cover up, and deny what the teacher deeply feels. Shouldn't such feelings be recognized rather than ignored, dealt with directly rather than masked, considered natural rather than shameful or a sign of weakness?

—Herbert M. Greenberg

Positive Focus

Robert C. Hawley

If you ask a teenager to list his personal strengths on one side of a page and then turn the paper over and list his personal weaknesses on the other, chances are that he will come up with about six items on the strengths side, but that he'll write on and on and even ask for more paper on the weakness side—listing about seven times as many weaknesses as strengths.[1] Our culture is so heavily over-balanced toward focusing on the negative, on weaknesses, on what we can't do, that there is little time left to build on the positive, on our strengths, on what we *can* do. And the average classroom is no exception, reflecting the focus of the larger culture not only in the attitude of the students and of the teacher, but in the way that students relate to one another and in the way that the students relate to the teacher and to the school. One of the questions that I am most often asked by teachers is, "How can I make my classroom a positive, growth-enhancing place when my students and I habitually focus on weaknesses, where the climate of the larger community is so hostile?"

Furthermore, we learn very early that it is bad manners to show too much praise or admiration for others, and it is absolutely in the worst of taste to take pride in or even to acknowledge our own accomplishments and strengths. The person who goes out of his way to praise or affirm the strengths of others is considered "unrealistic," a "Pollyanna," or a "brown-noser." The person who takes pride in his accomplishments or affirms his strengths is known as conceited, boastful, stuck-on-himself. We prefer understatement to praise, modesty to self-affirmation. And yet in maintaining this culturally acceptable facade we drain our own personal energy and reduce the energy of others so that there is a diminished amount of energy available for constructive social action.

In an experiment designed to show the effect of positive and negative

---

[1] Unpublished study conducted by Dr. Herbert Otto.

Robert C. Hawley, *Human Values in the Classroom*. Amherst, Mass.: Education Research Associates, 1973, pp. 83–89.

311

personal feedback,[2] a class at a major eastern university was rigged so that the students, about twenty in a graduate history section, had special instructions. The professor was unaware of the experiment or of the fact that he was being video-taped by a concealed camera. At the beginning of the tape the professor is lecturing, head down, hands grasping the lectern, reading from his notes in a monotone. The students are sprawled in various postures of inattention and boredom. At a given moment the students start to act more interested in the lecture—they sit up, nod their heads, smile, lean forward, and give other non-verbal signs of interest and support. Like a flower unfolding, the professor moves away from the podium, begins to use his hands in expressive gestures, speaks more energetically, develops eye contact with members of the class, and has become a more lively and interesting speaker. He grows and blossoms under conditions of positive relationship with his class. The experiment continues, however, as, on a clandestine signal, the students return to their original postures of boredom and inattention. In less than three minutes the professor is back behind the safety of his desk, hands clenching the lectern, droning on from his lecture notes, a withered shadow of the person that had been. This is what we can do for each other: We can enhance each other's lives, build on each other's strengths, or we can tear each other down, enervate and cripple.

Teachers are seemingly forced into the role of providing negative focus. Grading compositions, correcting tests, marking off for spelling, diagnosing reading problems all have a distinctly negative focus, and I am convinced that these practices are at least as damaging as they may be beneficial. Not only do these negative-focus teacher behaviors diminish the students' feelings of self-esteem, but also where a teacher identifies a learning deficiency such as a "spelling problem" or a "calculating problem" or a "reading problem," then this labeling in effect gives the student permission to allow that "problem" to continue until the teacher does something about it. The "problem" becomes the teacher's and there is a subtle shift of responsibility for learning from the student to the teacher. (I suspect that this is one reason that remedial reading programs have in general been so abysmally ineffective: When he is classed as a "remedial reader," the student realizes that he has a special problem about which he really can do nothing without the help of an expert. The problem of dyslexia will not be resolved until it is seen as one aspect of a larger problem which also includes a lack of self-respect, feelings of powerlessness, etc.).

Grades foster a negative focus. Even an *A minus* is a sign of nega-

2 Described to me by Dr. David D. Britton, to whom I am indebted for introducing me to the notion of positive focus and to much of the material in this chapter.

tivity. Points are always taken *off*. I know an English teacher who would have given Shakespeare only 98 for *Hamlet* because, after all, no one is perfect. Standardized testing is another school institution that often focuses on the negative: Did you realize that half of the school population is only average or below on any given standardized achievement test? A third generally negative focus in the school situation is the use of comments instead of or in addition to grades. Teachers almost always feel that they must make a balanced comment, stressing both the strengths and the weaknesses of the student. (In fact, many parents would question the teacher's ability if the comment sheet showed only positive comments). But given a page divided equally between positive and negative comments, many people will see only the negative ones. Any attempt to maintain a "realistic" focus on both negative and positive ultimately winds up focusing strongly on the negative.

But to return to the problem: How can we build a classroom climate that is positive and growth-enhancing? How can we and our students learn to identify and build on our own strengths and the strengths of others? I see two stages—first to foster an awareness of the general negative focus to the degree that it exists; and second to develop skills in positive focus.

One useful technique for the awareness stage is brainstorming. The class can be asked to brainstorm for five minutes all the things that students can do to each other and that teachers can do to students that get students down or create feelings of defensiveness in them. Then another five minutes are spent brainstorming all the things that students can do that raise feelings of self-esteem and supportiveness. A general discussion can follow, focusing on how to change so that the class becomes more supportive of each other. Another possibility is to ask the students to brainstorm all the self-put-downs that they can think of—that is, all the things that they can say and think about themselves that make them feel less worthy. And then they should brainstorm all the things that students can think about themselves to make themselves feel more powerful, more worthy. This can be followed by a discussion of why we put ourselves down so much and how we can change.

For the second stage, developing skills in positive focus, perhaps the first thing is to stress that positive focus can be considered a skill, and just as in learning a new game, like tennis for instance, no one is expected to be perfect at first. We can accept our sometimes clumsy attempts to give each other positive feedback because we are, after all, learning a new skill. A second step is to ask the students to monitor their own self-put-downs and to try to change to statements of self-affirmation. Students can try to catch each other at self-put-downs: "I'm hearing you putting yourself down. That's against the rules in this class." And as a forfeit, when a student is caught putting himself down, he must frame a statement of self-affirmation. The other students can help: "I caught you putting yourself down; now you have to make a self-affirming statement. I like the way you smile; I like the way you listen; I like the way you stand up for what you think is right—How about one of those?"

A third way to practice skills in positive focus is for the teacher to call for a validating round.[3] Validating rounds generally come at the end of small group discussions of personal topics such as "My happiest moment from early childhood," or "The one day I would like to live over again because it was just about perfect," or "If I could do anything I wanted to for two whole days, I'd . . ." Or the validating round can occur after the students have read their compositions to each other in small groups or tried to reach consensus on a forced-choice problem, etc. To begin the validating round, each person writes the name of each of the other persons in the small group, skipping four lines between names. (Generally this activity works best when the class is divided into groups of four or five). Then the teacher asks the students to write two positive statements about each of the other students in the group, being as specific as possible, and using, if they wish, some of the following sentence starters: *I like the way you* . . . or *You're a lot like me when you* . . . or *It made me feel good when you said . .* or *You are . . . .*

The teacher should remind the students that this is a skill-building exercise: It's probably going to feel uncomfortable reading each of your validating statements, and it most likely will seem embarrassing to hear them read to you; but this is practice in both giving and receiving positive feedback, so do the best you can, and remember that we can all make allowance for not being perfect at a new skill.

Then the teacher asks that in each group the students focus on one person at a time and everybody read his validating statements about that one person. Then the focus moves to the next person, and so on around the group. *Caution:* It is important to allow enough time to complete this activity within the class period. Generally twenty minutes is enough for a group of four, especially if the teacher warns the class of the time five minutes before the bell. If there is not enough time for the validating round, it is better to postpone it until the start of the next day's class.

Positive focus requires practice and faith. It is not easy to go counter to the general norms of our culture and the beliefs and attitudes of so many of our fellow humans. But over time, a continuing and steadfast focus on the positive in life, on our strengths, and on the strengths of others can help to restore in our students their personal energy, their feelings of power, their sense of worth so that they can see themselves as positive forces who can contribute to the task of building a better world.

[3] This activity owes its inspiration to Sidney B. Simon's elaboration on the validating principles in Harvey Jackman's re-evaluation counseling technique.

Sensitivity Modules

Howard Kirschenbaum

> *"You never really know a man until you stand
> in his shoes and walk around in them."*

In every school building there is a wall which keeps the rain and cold out
and the children in. It is a wall made of concrete, steel, wood or asbestos,
and glass. We have all seen this wall, would readily acknowledge its existence and usefulness, and therefore need not dwell upon it.

However, there is *another* wall which separates the school from the
outside world—one which deserves our more serious attention. This is a
wall which many people say they cannot see and many others do not want to
see; although research shows that it is seen more easily by students than
by their parents or teachers. It is called the *wall of unreality,* and it pre-
vents students from making any vital connection between what they learn
in the classroom and what they know is happening in the seething world
outside the school.

One recent study showed that from September, 1968 to March, 1969,
there were over 2000 student disruptions in secondary schools across the
country. It seems that if we, as teachers, do not do something quickly to
tear down the *unreal* walls of our school buildings, then the students are
very likely to tear down the real ones.

In one mostly white, suburban classroom, an eleventh grade, social
studies class was discussing poverty, race, guaranteed annual income, police
brutality, welfare and other related issues. This, in itself, was a positive
first step toward relevance and away from unreality. But the teacher sensed
his students had no real *feeling* for or *experience* with the issues they were
discussing. Their comments seemed to reflect a cross between their parents'
opinions and the 6 O'clock News—nothing personal. The teacher felt the
need for a greater reality-orientation in his classroom, so he gave the
following assignment:

Howard Kirschenbaum, "Sensitivity Modules," *Media & Methods,* February 1970,
pp. 34, 36–38.

Do *two* of the following within two weeks. At that time we will discuss your experiences in class and relate them to the subject at hand.

Wear old clothes and sit in the waiting room of the State Employment Office. Listen, observe, talk to some of the people sitting next to you. Read the announcements on the bulletin board, etc.

Attend church services some Sunday in a store-front church.

Go to an inner-city elementary school and read a story to a child in kindergarten or first grade. The child must be held on your lap.

Go to magistrate's court and keep a list of the kinds of cases brought before the magistrate. Who are the "customers"? How are they handled?

Spend a few hours in a prowl car traveling with a team of policemen. Listen to the squad car radio. Ask questions. If the policemen park and walk a beat, walk with them.

Sit in the waiting room of the maternity ward of a city hospital whose patients are mostly charity cases. Strike up a conversation with any other persons in the waiting room.

Live for three days on the amount of money a typical welfare mother receives to feed a son or daughter closest to your own age.

Spend a morning making the rounds with a visiting nurse.

Read at least two issues, cover to cover, of the *Tribune, Afro-American, Monitor* or other Negro newspaper.

Go to the community health center and take a seat in line. Watch the attitude of the personnel who work in the health center. Talk to some of the other patients coming for help.

Compare the prices of the same brands and models of record players, TV sets, and transistor radios at your local stores with those on display in a credit store in the downtown area.

Turn the heat off in your own house some night in January or February and spend the night in a cold house.

Read *Autobiography of Malcolm X* or *Manchild in the Promised Land* or some other book which tells what it is like to grow up black in America.

Attend a meeting of a civic group such as the Human Relations Committee, the Welfare Rights Organization, or the Neighborhood Association.

Try to call City Hall with a complaint that your landlord did not give you heat, or has not repaired a roof leak, or that the toilet is not working.   Better yet, find a neighbor with a real complaint and offer to help him get it fixed.

Walk four or five blocks between 13th and 18th on Broadway at lunch hour and buy a sandwich and a cup of coffee in a luncheonette in which you will be the only white person.

Spend a weekend with the American Friends Service Committee on one of their weekend workcamps, which are a combination of seminar and clean-up, paint-up projects.[1]

Two weeks later, after doing many of these sensitivity modules, the students had developed a *personal* concern for the subject, a wealth of experiences to draw upon and dozens of pertinent questions needing answers. Had it been an all-black school, the sensitivity modules would have been constructed accordingly, so as to enable the black students to become more sensitive to the realities of the white world.   Needless to say, such experiences generate many powerful feelings and often considerable confusion in students—especially when their preconceptions about the world are challenged.   But then, what is learning all about?

Yet, sensitivity modules do not all have to be on such controversial subjects.

One teacher, when the class was reading Helen Keller's *Story of My Life,* had her class walk around the school and their homes blindfolded for a day, so they might be more sensitive toward Helen Keller's way of experiencing the world.

An elementary school teacher who was doing a unit on inventions and inventors "who have changed our way of life" asked each class member to invent some useful object for his home.

A math teacher tried to bridge the gap between the reality of the classroom and that of the outside world by asking his students to help their parents calculate the family's yearly income tax—using the *long* form.

A history teacher had the members of his class work for political candidates of their choice, during an election year, as one way of studying how politics work—a realistic addition to the textbook version.

[1] Note: Whites will not be overly welcome these days if they come a-slumming in black ghettos. This issue needs to be examined and all the realities explored clearly before any team goes out on the first module. For a list of additional sensitivity modules on this subject, send a long, self-addressed, stamped envelope to: Howard Kirschenbaum, College of Education, Temple University, Philadelphia, Pa. 19122.

In fact, for just about any subject we teach, and at just about any level, sensitivity modules can be created.

Some students wonder why they have to learn to write formal letters in junior high school. So some teachers ask that those letters take the form of letters-to-the-editor or to Congressmen, and they actually get sent. Of course, the students are encouraged to learn more about the subject they are writing on, and the letters contain the students' own views, not the teachers'.

In teaching elementary children the period of world exploration and the discovery of America, one teacher had her children go out and actually "discover" new parts of the city. One instruction was to "find a new and faster route to the ball field." She stayed a half block behind them, but they had to do the discovering themselves. And the gap between the world of Columbus and their own risk-taking world in the city was narrowed.

One high school class studying the second world war took a trip to a Veterans' Hospital where the students interviewed many of the patients.

Children studying the great "melting pot" that is America have visited with each other's grandparents and people in old-age homes to inter-view people who *were* the real-live immigrants at the beginning of this century and to find out about their experiences.

A good book or movie, a trip to a museum, a guest speaker—any number of traditional teaching devices can serve as a sensitive module—*if the student is truly involved in the experience* and if it is a *new experience* for him. All new experiences are risk-taking experiences, because we never know how they might turn out. Generally, the more the student has to *do,* the *newer* the experience is for him, the greater the *risk* he has to take, the deeper will be the sensitivity which results from it. The more passive the student's role is in a sensitivity module, the less he gets out of it. Naturally, students' ages will be an important factor in creating sensitivity modules, as will be an intelligent concern for their safety. *But risk cannot, and should not, be eliminated, because it is central to the experience.* Teachers who take fewer risks in their classroom and in their own lives will probably be less disposed toward the newer, more unpredictable modules than teachers who frequently experiment, try out new behaviors and ideas and otherwise take risks in their own lives.

One word of caution for the teacher: Experience does not necessarily lead to wisdom or sensitivity. We humans are notoriously capable of translating new experiences and information so as to fit neatly into our old, fixed and often prejudicial way of thinking. That is why it is essential that students have the opportunity to validate their experiences and learnings with those of their peers and to check out these learnings with the accumulated body of knowledge which we can make available to them. The sensitivity module, then, is only one aspect of a more encompassing learning experience.

Many parents and teachers will probably object to the sensitivity module—if not in its conception, then in its application. They might argue that there are enough unpleasant realities which their children cannot avoid in this world, without having to seek out new ones. They might also say that the schools really have *no right* to ask students to take risks, that is, to put themselves in situations where the outcomes are uncertain and may be unsettling.

We believe that, although these arguments are probably offered for the "children's own good," they do a great disservice to those same children and to our society. In a world that seems ready to explode because of lack of understanding and communication among groups and nations, it is frightening to think what sheltered lives most of our students lead.

Roger is white, wealthy, suburban, and until his twelfth year in school, had never shaken hands with a black person. Denise is twelve and has never had more than 25 cents of her own. Ellen has never been hungry a day in her life. Mike, when he dropped out of his inner-city school, had never ridden on the city's subways, for fear he might get lost underground. Geraldine believed that every family who lives in the suburbs has a sleep-in maid.

Are these children exceptions? We wonder. Over the years, as we have gotten to know our students, we have continued to be amazed at what little experience they have in worlds outside their own neighborhoods or communities. But, really, this should not be so surprising.

As small children, their friendships follow the socio-economic patterns of their neighborhoods and their families' social circle. Thus, their friends are of the same race and social class and frequently of the same religion. When there are exceptions to this rule, it is not unusual for the parents to intervene and subtly or explicitly explain that "*we* don't play with *them*." In many areas, the neighborhood school perpetuates this pattern of homogeneous socio-economic grouping, as does ability grouping in schools. By the time the student reaches high school, he still probably has little feeling for how most people in the country or world, aside from his own closed circles, live. That is why the first year in a college dormitory is usually such an eye-opening experience for freshmen.

But the problem goes even deeper than these structural realities of school and society—social class, friendship patterns, neighborhood schools, ability grouping. As we view the schools' curricula and teaching methods, it seems as though the schools had *a stake in keeping their students ignorant* of many of the realities of the world around them.

Why else would the reading matter be so carefully screened, lest *real* ideas or *real* language influence the students? Why is controversy, certainly the norm in the *real* world, still frowned upon in more schools than it is welcomed? Why are students still allowed such little choice in school subjects, while in the *real* world they have to make all sorts of important choices about how they will spend their lives? Why are students often burdened with so much homework, especially the brighter ones, that they have little time to discover the *real* world on their own, in their own fashion? What are we trying to protect?

It's as though schools were afraid that students might develop the "wrong" ideas, the "wrong" attitudes and beliefs. Wasn't it Jefferson who asked, "Who ever knew truth to be the loser on a free and open market of ideas?" Yet, apparently this is the fear that runs our schools—the fear that constructs a wall around the school to keep the realities of the outside world from intruding and interrupting "business as usual."

But the students in the 1970's, even more so than in the '60's, will not allow that artificial wall to stand. They want desperately to get an education that will help them make sense out of and live in the world around them, and they will try to get it with or without the school's help.

The sensitivity module is only *one* of many methods teachers have for helping students in a search for real understandings, based not only on academic knowledge, but on life's experiences as well.[2] Harper Lee wrote, "You never really know a man until you stand in his shoes and walk around in them." By helping students to walk around in many men's shoes, the sensitivity module helps to tear down the wall of unreality that too often separates schools from life.

---

[2] For many more methods which help the student connect his classroom experiences to the world around him, see Raths, Harmin and Simon, *Values and Teaching*. (Columbus, Ohio, Charles E. Merrill Books, 1966).

Guidelines for Sensitivity Training in Your School

Larry J. Krafft and Leland W. Howe

Sensitivity training can be boon or doom to an educational program. It is important that the educational practitioner understand clearly when sensitivity training methods are likely to be helpful and when they are useless or even damaging.

Numerous articles have extolled the virtues of sensitivity training and T-group methods; a few have cautioned against use of these approaches. Sensitivity training as an important innovation for school change is not in question. The concern is that educators may turn to a methodology which, if not used correctly, can easily create as many problems as it solves.

Sensitivity training methods are used to: 1) reduce personal alienation; 2) relieve interpersonal and intergroup tension; 3) learn interpersonal process diagnostic and facilitation skills; 4) "personalize" learning ("sensitivity education" and "affective curriculum" are now common terms in educational jargon); 5) develop individual and group problem-solving skills; and 6) provide the basis of decision making, leadership training, conflict management, community involvement, and various types of organizational development objectives.

Any of these may be legitimate outcomes of sensitivity-training methods. But cogent planning is necessary if the achievement of specific goals is to be reasonably assured. The difference between success and failure may lie in the user's ability to heed the following guidelines:

1. Carefully diagnose the current situation. What are the problems? What is prompting resolution? What are the real causes? What are the priorities of need? What are the short- and long-range goals? What are the methods available for meeting objectives? What are the possible losses as well as gains which may be outcomes of each method? Change in one part of a

Larry J. Krafft and Leland W. Howe, "Guidelines for Sensitivity Training in Your School," *Phi Delta Kappan*, November 1971, pp. 179–80.

school organization will produce adaptive changes in other parts. This means that a gain in one area may be offset by a loss in another.

   Much more is known today than was known only five or 10 years ago about change and the outcomes of various change strategies. Use this newly acquired knowledge, or find those who have it, to decrease the risk of embarking on a new strategy.

2. Limit the objectives. It is tempting to use sensitivity training to try to change a whole system, both in breadth and in depth simultaneously. This seldom, if ever, works constructively. When one has unrealistic expectations he will be disappointed; this disappointment may lead to disillusionment with the experience and make it less likely that, despite the method's merits, an attempt will be made to use it again. Sensitivity training *can* help to bring about meaningful changes in the system, but it will not bring utopia. Changing an educational system is a long and difficult struggle which requires much more than mass participation in a T-group or two.

3. Specify the objective(s) as well as the depth of the intervention and stick with it. For example, T-groups might be designed to improve participants' understanding of the effects of cooperative and competitive behavior and to develop skills in managing these strategies constructively. If, instead, the T-groups are allowed or led to focus on personal problems and personal growth, it is probable that specified objectives will not be attained. The unanticipated consequences will, in the long run, produce more harm than good.

4. Specify the point of intervention and a rationale to support it. If the change is to be the adoption of a new model for teaching foreign languages, the point of intervention may easily be defined as the contact between all foreign language teachers and their students. However, it may be more difficult to determine the initial and subsequent intervention points where, for example, the aim is to achieve lower-level involvement in school decision making. Questions arise. Shall students, teachers, administrators, or parents be the first to be "trained"? Or a cross-section of these? The strategy, if it is to result in the desired change, should include a rationale, based on goals and resources, for these decisions. Don't leave these decisions to intuition, chance, or political pressures.

5. Give each person an opportunity to choose whether or not to participate in sensitivity training. We find that it is usually un-

wise to coerce people to participate in processes with which they are, by their own self-knowledge, too uncomfortable. Choice ought to be based on adequate knowledge. Fear and resistance to sensitivity training are often results of too many unknowns.

6. Do not allow sensitivity training to polarize the school. If sensitivity training is rejected by part of the school population it may be wise to abandon the idea and try alternative methods to reach the same objectives, or go ahead with a pilot training group of those willing to participate. It is crucial that part of the pilot group's learning be aimed at relating productively with the resisters. We have found that too often people who get involved in sensitivity training do not gain these skills and thereby tend to increase any existing polarization.

7. Transfer of learning should be the primary concern in every training intervention. An individual's attitudes and behaviors may improve in the protected T-group environment, but this is no guarantee that his behavior will improve in the day-to-day situation. Time schedules must be met. Products must be delivered. Reports must be completed. And there are outside forces, such as peer group pressures and family demands.

   Therefore, participants must be educated concerning the differences between the contexts of the sensitivity training laboratory and of daily life. This education might take two forms: lectures, simulations, and role plays of specific situations in the home-school environment, and follow-up sessions in school in which participants can share their successes and failures. The follow-up sessions are most helpful in facilitating transfer of learning because participants have an opportunity to reexamine their goals and design alternative strategies based on their tests of personal and organizational realities. Follow-up sessions also support isolated individuals and groups who endeavor to promote their newly learned behaviors.

8. Sensitivity training will not solve human problems in one part of the school system unless parallel and complementary changes are made in other parts. For example, if the goal is to have students assume greater responsibility for their learning goals and methods, it cannot be met very effectively if teachers continue to impose the learning criteria and reward and punish accordingly. Teachers must develop new skills and receive support for their new and more appropriate behavior. This means that the school's criteria for reward and punishment (social recognition, pay, and promotion) must be consistent with criteria related to

increased student responsibility. However, should the school be unwilling to alter its tangible reward system, the stated goal of increased student responsibility becomes unrealistic.

9. Seldom is it desirable to apply sensitivity-training methods directly to the school situation. The school system is much larger and more complex than a T-group; it usually has different goals and a different set of factors to deal with. Learning to become more sensitive to processes and persons' values and feelings is an important educational goal, but teachers must continue to help students gain cognitive understandings and skills.

   Thus it may be inappropriate for teachers to conduct their classes in T-group fashion or for the principal to act as a "trainer" to his staff. It is more appropriate and productive to incorporate sensitivity training into the processes of learning/teaching/administering than to institute it as a special incident in the life of a school.

10. Find and use competent human resources. Since most school systems do not have sensitivity-training experts on their full-time payroll, an external consultant or staff member with some familiarity with sensitivity methods usually designs and carries out a program in the school system. The question is, How do you tell if he is qualified? The following criteria may be helpful:

Choose someone who openly states his own values, perspectives, and criteria for decisions and who can be trusted to do whatever he can to accomplish what he states he will accomplish. His goals should be consistent with the school's defined goals.

Seek someone who has a broad range of intervention experiences, rather than experience only as a T-group trainer or with some other limited set of methods. The latter tend to be biased in the diagnostic process.

Select a person committed to an organized but flexible problem-solving approach. Avoid someone who seems to have all the answers prior to, or even after, thorough diagnosis.

Be wary of someone who has a packaged set of techniques applicable to a broad spectrum of objectives. A package can be appropriate only if it meets a specific need which has been carefully diagnosed.

Be encouraged by the consultant who insists on careful diagnostic data. If he is to help plan adequately he must be able to assess facilitating and hindering factors and predict outcomes based on alternative approaches.

A consultant who states outcomes in vague, universal, or poorly defined terms is also unlikely to deliver a "product" consistent with organizational objectives. He should be able to define specific objectives and describe why certain methods are more appropriate than others.

Health—The Affective Approach

Orvis A. Harrelson

Imagine yourself to be in an elementary school classroom. (I know that's not difficult for most of you.) Now imagine that thirty children, all nine years old, are sitting still, raptly intent on the task at hand. (Still no problem?) All right, now think of Jimmy, who is usually picking, gouging, poking, pestering, or talking (or any combination of any or all of these) and realize he is watching with great interest. And even Debbie, who usually is gazing out the window or daydreaming, is with the class one hundred percent. (That's really straining the old imagination.) It is a situation most teachers experience infrequently but imagine often.

This is not, however, an imaginary class I'm describing. This is a real, live class with a real teacher in a "typical" classroom in a big midwestern industrial city. The class participation is the kind most elementary educators dream about. They are watching a television program and are really involved. No, they are not watching "Mission Impossible," the Saturday cartoons, or even "All in the Family." They are viewing a field tryout of a new educational television film, "Living with Love," from a health education series of thirty, fifteen-minute programs for eight- to ten-year-old youngsters. The series is called "Inside/Out." It is produced by the National Instructional Television Center.

The program is designed to help children identify expressions of love and to explore how one feels when one is loved or not loved. It is anticipated the teacher will follow the film by helping the class consider the idea that love is necessary for human well-being and that we all vary in our abilities to receive and to express love. The follow-up may also include classroom discussion as to how one might cope with a lack of love in one's life.

"Living with Love" provides the viewing children with a day-to-day documentary story of Mrs. Dorothy Smith and all of her children. Mrs. Smith works for the Cuyahoga County Welfare Department in Cleveland,

Ohio. She works at home, for her job is to care for children who are waiting to be adopted. Although it is a foster home for them and, because of that, a temporary one, the home Mrs. Smith makes is full of love. Throughout a typical day in their lives, there are countless ways that show how well love brings them all together and lets them live as a family. Love is expressed in many ways—through gentle words, touch, and the warmth of human feelings. Love is shown as affection, respect, discipline, sharing, concern, and caring.

The children who have viewed the film identify closely with the children and Mrs. Smith and watch intently as the program is shown. They also want to talk when the film is over. The teacher hears of pets and loving moms and dads, of den leaders and Little League coaches, and of grandparents. She also hears of people who hate, and of children who have been neglected, and from those who feel unloved. "Living with Love" seems to call forth feelings and emotional ideas rarely dealt with in the classroom. And teachers and pupils seem pleased with the process.

The series and the individual films are part of a growing body of books, pamphlets, films, tapes, filmstrips, and records designed for use at the elementary level by teachers who believe children need to know about human emotions, and to know themselves. The materials are part of affective education and take their place alongside materials aimed primarily at the cognitive or factual areas of education. The greater part of the materials is designed to produce introspective responses in the children and teachers and to stimulate classroom interaction and communication as the prime educative processes. Such teaching makes different demands on teachers and pupils. The affective education process requires different teaching techniques from those areas which deal in facts or physical skills.

In the classrooms where pupils and teachers have had the most successful discussions following the films and have enjoyed the affective process the most, the teacher has viewed her function as a guide trying to arrange conditions so that each student will feel free to express himself openly and will feel part of the discussion. She has been flexible and relaxed enough to use silence well and to be willing to accept differing points of view. Though the teacher holds her own options she views the enterprise as a quest for creative, affective thinking rather than as a debate or instruction. She views the process as an attempt to analyze and clarify issues and to develop alternative means of dealing with childhood problems and developmental tasks. She is fair to positions represented by a minority or not represented at all. Rather than seeking or proposing a right answer she attempts to find means by which values of children may be pursued without clash, and she helps them respect the values of others.

In most instances the spontaneous response to the film plus the teacher's leading of the discussion have resulted in thirty minutes of give-

and-take. The teacher has been able to close off discussion while enthusiasm was still high, but not before children had a chance to express their feelings. A promise to return to the topic the next day has been greeted most of the time with enthusiasm.

Teachers have used many activities as follow-through on the first discussion. One activity which is succesful is having each child develop a "Peanuts" cartoon of love. Another which leads into other areas of physiology and anatomy (part of the traditional health education course) is having children collect pictures showing the physical effects of love on the human being. Role playing or making up skits showing what they think love is has also proven to be popular. Most gratifying but perhaps most likely to cause teachers anxiety are those contacts with pupils who, spurred on by discussions of feelings, come to the teacher for help with problems of lack of love in their lives. There is also the pleasure of hearing children express their joy because of the love in their families and because of love for their teacher.

Love is an unusual topic for school and school television. It is, however, an integral part of mental health education as part of a total school program of health instruction. For the person who believes health education to be blood and bones, vitamins and brush your teeth, germs and pollution, the consideration of love as a health topic is confusing. However, the teachers who have participated in planning and previewing the films of the total series have found that taking an affective approach to health education increases the enthusiasm and participation of pupils and teachers and still provides an avenue to state- or school-district-mandated health education topics.

"Living with Love" is only one example of the feelings approach to health education which is in the series "Inside/Out." The series—available in videotape or 16mm films—is designed to help each child by focusing on certain elements in his life—using growing, loving, hurting, enjoying, fearing, and hating. Through an understanding of the emotions involved, the child will come to accept and respect himself, then his family and the persons around him, and eventually the people in the larger world beyond his current range of experience and knowledge. In the process he will discover how to care for his own life in relation to the lives of others. Topics included in individual films in addition to love include moving, divorce, prejudice, death, joy, and coping with a bully, among others.

The series is supported by a consortium of thirty-four state departments of education, state educational television networks, and large city school systems.

National Instructional Television Center of Bloomington, Indiana, organized the consortium, provides financial support, and serves in the executive producer capacity. The films are being produced by WVIZ-TV,

Cleveland, Ohio; KETC-TV, St. Louis, Missouri; WNVT-TV, Annandale, Virginia; and the Ontario Educational Communications Authority, Toronto, Canada.

Fifteen films will be ready for distribution in January 1973, along with a partial teacher's guide. The complete series and guide will be available to school districts for broadcast in September 1973. For further information regarding this series contact the National Instructional Television Center.

This article began with a request for you to imagine a class, a room, and a teacher working together on an affective, feelings approach to health. Now imagine that teacher to be you, with your class in your teaching area. Do you have trouble with that one? I don't, for the elementary teachers I know can do almost anything you can imagine.

Letting Go:
Emotion in the Classroom

Kent Owen

Nine-year-old Eddie squirms at his desk, unable to keep his mind on what his teacher is saying. His spells of restlessness are more and more frequent, his schoolwork sketchier.

When he gets home from school, he knows his mother will screech at him and his father will torment him. He's wondering about his chances of running away from all the squabbling and bickering he has to live with day in and day out.

Linda is an alert, sensitive fourth grader, whose grandmother has just died of pneumonia. She can't understand why her grandmother will never come back, why her parents are so subdued and upset.

Linda's feelings churn inside her as she puzzles her way through a maze of bewildering events—the arrival of relatives, the strangely changed atmosphere of her home, the preparations for the funeral.

Each week Eddie and Linda study health as a regular part of their schoolwork, but it's awfully hard to memorize the bones of the inner ear or which foods are rich in protein when you're thinking about how mean your mother and dad are to each other or how much it hurts when someone you love dies. Somehow there should be a time to talk about how you feel inside.

It's not just Eddie and Linda who feel that emotions need to be discussed in the classroom. Health educators, too, have increasingly urged that an "affective" approach to the health curriculum be tried out.

Ever since the publication of the School Health Education Study in 1965, educators in this field have been caught up in wide-ranging examinations of content and teaching practices. They have now reached the conclusion that important as factual information is to the establishment of good health habits, cognitive knowledge alone is not enough to help stu-

Kent Owen, "Letting Go: Emotion in the Classroom," *The PTA Magazine*, 700 North Rush St., Chicago, Illinois 60611, March 1974, pp. 33–35.

dents achieve well-being. Affective knowledge—or a knowledge of the emotions—is important also.

Given the strong support that the affective approach has gained from health educators in recent years, the next question was, how could this new method be introduced into the schools quickly and tellingly? It usually takes almost fifteen years to disseminate new ideas through such established institutions as universities and professional organizations.

In the fall of 1970 the National Instructional Television Center (NIT) initiated a series of discussions with leading health educators throughout North America to determine whether classroom television could be of any use in improving instruction in health education.

A nonprofit agency with headquarters in Bloomington, Indiana, NIT is dedicated to strengthening education by developing, acquiring, or adapting television and related materials for wide use as major learning resources. In the planning and production of these materials, NIT works closely with content specialists, teachers and students, educational administrators, broadcasters, and national professional organizations.

Over the years, NIT has sought to establish television as a progressive force in education, harnessing the technology of broadcasting with important advances in teaching and learning.

When NIT was founded in 1962, only one of every sixteen American students was regularly using television as part of his formal education. By 1970 one of every four students (more than thirteen million) was using television in classes on a regular basis.

As it stands now, school television has reduced the time it takes to introduce new ideas to less than five years. That's quite an improvement, as educators are quick to admit.

Even more important, television as a medium possesses that much-discussed singular ability to create an immediate, intimate rapport with its viewers. Almost uncannily, as Marshall McLuhan has explained at length, television conveys a sense of authenticity that lends special authority to whatever it presents.

In 1970 the connection was clear enough to health educators: The affective approach to health was made for classroom television. The next step was to assemble a working group who could design a health curriculum for a television series.

Shortly thereafter, NIT brought together several health educators whose thinking reflected both diverse fields within the discipline and the viewpoints of different regions. Their meetings led to a basic statement of purpose—that as a result of watching the proposed series a student should:

"Experience thinking, feeling, and concern related to health problems facing him in such a way that he is better able to deal with them.

"Understand and appreciate the wonder of his body, and as a result, do or not do certain things that affect its function.

"Be motivated to seek experiences and information that will aid him in making decisions about personal goals.

"Better sort out the reasons for accepting others as they are, find comfort in accepting anger or rejection, and, as a result, handle these experiences in a more satisfying manner.

"Better experience and channel idealism so that constructive activities may follow."

On this basis NIT laid out specifications for a series of thirty fifteen-minute programs designed for eight- to ten-year-olds, generally the third, fourth, and fifth grades, plus a thirty-minute program for teachers.

With the endorsement of prominent spokesmen in education, including then U.S. Commissioner of Education Sidney P. Marland, Jr., the project gained the support of twenty-seven state educational or broadcasting agencies. Overall, the $600,000 plus budget was the largest ever in this country for a series created specifically for the classroom.

More important still was the scope of participation that a consortium of this size ensured. Most of the third, fourth, and fifth graders in the United States would be able to view the programs.

In addition, Exxon Corporation (formerly Standard Oil of New Jersey) awarded a grant of almost $200,000 to NIT to make possible the publication and free distribution of teacher's guides to all teachers whose classes would view the series. The Exxon grant also provided for the production of a short film about the series, to be shown on public television stations, and the development of materials to be used in workshops for teachers.

The thirty programs focus on various elements in the life of every child—using, growing, loving, hurting, enjoying, fearing, and hating.

Through an understanding of the emotions involved, the child is helped to accept and respect himself, then his family and the persons around him, and eventually the people in the larger world beyond the range of his knowledge and experience. In the process he discovers how to care for his own life in relation to the lives of others. This interplay between the inner self and the outer world inspired the series' name, *Inside/Out*.

Without *moralizing* or indoctrinating, *Inside/Out* considers a variety of situations common to youngsters. In no sense is the series sensitivity training or psychotherapy; it does not attempt to change behavior in relation to prescribed values or standards.

Instead *Inside/Out* presents in documentary and dramatic form incidents through which children can learn about the vital connections between their feelings and their actions. Accordingly, the programs illuminate problems familiar to children; they do not offer simple answers or solutions.

The programs, individually and collectively, express an interdisciplinary as well as an affective approach to the traditional concerns of health education.

One program, "Because It's Fun," deals with the good feelings a child can have by skillfully engaging in physical activities of all kinds or by playing for the sheer joy of it. It focuses on an intensely competitive boy who believes that winning is the only thing that matters. He balks at accepting the fact that his classmates can have fun by jumping rope, roller skating or just playing around.

Another program, ". . . . But Names Will Never Hurt," looks at how prejudice separates one person from another and affects the feelings of everyone involved. It concerns two boys, one French-Canadian and the other English-Canadian, whose rivalry in hockey flares into an ugly name-calling incident.

"You Belong" studies the intricate balance between human beings and their surroundings. The program shows that because everything in creation has its own function, man must learn carefully what to preserve and what to destroy.

Other programs in the series deal with how persons express what they are really thinking and feeling; the tensions between freedom and responsibility; the choices involved in taking dares; ways of dealing with feelings brought about by the death of a person or pet; the consequences of ridiculing others; the effects of strong emotions on the body; and the meaning of love as it is expressed in many ways.

Inside/Out is a pioneering project in the affective approach to health education. It cannot and should not tell students what to think and feel. Rather, it encourages children to talk out their feelings in the classroom. Within the freedom and openness of conversation, feelings of misunderstanding, confusion, and dread can be turned into an awareness of the range of choices that lead to good health and well-being.

Educational Applications
of Humanistic Psychology

Dennis Romig and Charles C. Cleland

Summary: *Maslow's theory of human motivation contains the nuclear ideas for a model of a transcendent human survival. While critics have decried the absence of empirical support for the theory beyond the level of physiological or safety needs, Maslow's ideas are none the less generating a number of studies, some of which clearly reflect on the higher-order needs of man. This paper presents a hypothetical school, along with suggestions concerning the teacher-curricular composition that would help operationalize Maslow's theory in the schools The aim and objectives of the hypothetical school seek to reduce the animal in man and to produce truly human beings. Attention is also given to certain relevant aspects of the theory that are often ignored in the zeal of educational innovators to totally equate learning with happiness. Many ideas presented in this paper have been applied by different educators in a variety of settings. However, this paper discusses the systematic implimentation of the research and theory current in humanistic psychology circles.*

Currently numerous attempts are addressed to revising and reforming education, and many educational dissidents behind these movements invoke the theory of Abraham Maslow for the support of their innovations (Lyon, 1971; Rogers, 1969). This paper will present certain characteristics of a school, suggesting specific and systematic examples that may assist educators and school psychologists in accurately translating Maslow into the classroom.

Dennis Romig and Charles C. Cleland, "Educational Applications of Humanistic Psychology," *Journal of School Psychology,* 1972, Vol. 10, no. 3, pp. 289–98. Copyright © 1972 by Behavioral Publications, 72 Fifth Ave., New York, N.Y.

PHILOSOPHY AND GOALS

For Maslow the crucial component of *every* educational system is its goals. Frequently school systems do little more than write up some flowery sounding general goals, easily acceptable to most, and lock them in a closet safe for the annual visit of an accreditation team. The real goals are observed in what the system values and emphasizes and the kind of student it attempts to produce. The school psychologist can be catalyst in any school system to facilitate the articulation of the schools' goals and their implementation in terms of behavioral objectives for the staff and students. Much of Maslow's philosophy of education is related to his concept of the self-actualizing person. "To the extent that it (education) fosters growth toward self-actualization, it is 'good' education" (Maslow, 1962, p. 197). However, he indicates that man has a hierarchy of needs which must be met before the individual can reach the highest needs, the self-actualizing needs (Maslow, 1954). The first task of the school, then, is to facilitate the child's attempts to have his basic needs met while teaching the child how to meet his own needs, growing away from an immature dependence on parents and other adults. The instructional supervisor and the school psychologist should ascertain that each teacher is aware not only of the general developmental needs of all the children in his classroom but also that children differ in need level; he should know how these needs can be met. A cardinal principle of a humanistic school is that while it is meeting society's need by training children to become productively integrated into the society, the school demonstrates to the child the benevolence of the society by simultaneously meeting the needs of each individual child.

The various hierarchical needs, even the so-called "lower-order" needs, are, in a true Maslowian interpretation, difficult to translate, just as food relates to more than just satisfaction of the immediate hunger drive. Food can be directed both at physiological need satisfaction and the self-actualization of a given child. This can be demonstrated by the teacher's bringing in foods of different cultures and nationalities as those countries are studied in geography or social studies. Most communities have access to foreign exchange students, ex-Peace Corps volunteers, and individuals visiting from other countries. These persons can, as consultants, broaden the food horizon in children of all ages. Variety and styles of preparation of food and drink can introduce novelty, variety of taste sensations, and, prior to the onset of cultural ossification of tastes, indicate to students that trying new things can be rewarding.

On a more concrete level the authors recall a teacher of elementary children whose students produced a Greek play. The central figure ate seven seeds of a pomegranate and was destined to seven years in Hades. To invoke realism, this teacher brought pomegranates for the class and the students ate the seeds to learn more of Grecian life and foods. To this day several of her students relish pomegranates and also have a keen appreciation of Greek plays. This teacher translated Maslow's physiological need and led several students toward a fuller appreciation of a higher-order need.

The child can learn to meet his physiological needs by having classrooms designed to include a water fountain, restroom, and food, all easily accessible to the child throughout the day. On school entry the child can be instructed that these facilities are free for his use and he does not have to raise his hand or get a restroom pass. Through a variety of foods, as well as architectural modifications, students can gain appreciation of many different cultures and a sense of security for lower-order needs that simultaneously promote security and invoke a wonderous curiosity of life.

Education teaches the child about meeting his safety needs through instruction in perception and by neutralizing apparent dangers through knowledge about them. To teach young children how to utilize traffic signals to cross streets safely, the teacher might take the class on a field trip to the center of town where the appropriate behavior could be learned. Many teachers presently teach "Stop, Look, and Listen" to the children as they approach a street corner. The teacher could heighten auditory perception by blindfolding the children and taking them in small groups around the school and neighborhood environment. By exercises in olfactory perception the child would have a heightened awareness of smells that might lead to recognizing a fire out of hand or a gas leak.

Maslow (1954) also indicated a child's need for safety is reflected in his preference for some degree of order and routine. Much of the child's world is being modified daily, and he learns that he needs some routine in order to provide a degree of stability around which change can freely occur. Many advocates of "free schools" or "creative schools" thought they were doing a service to their children by abolishing all schedules and routines. However, it was observed that abolishing schedules caused a marked rise in frustration and acting out, negative behavior. While departures from the routine such as field trips or visiting lectures are desired, it is important to explain these variations to the child in advance. The teacher can provide variation and surprises within the framework of the schedule and have an exciting productive classroom.

The safety need is sometimes ignored when a child is expelled from the classroom, which creates insecurity in the entire class because each child secretly wonders, "Will I be next?" Redl and Wineman (1952) suggested many alternatives that can be attempted with deviant children— expelling the child from class is the last of their alternatives. They show

how strongly group morale can be destroyed when even one child is asked to leave. Some of their suggested alternatives include the teacher's preventing deviant behavior by intervening with "hurdle help"—restructing a group, changing the activity, moving close to an explosive situation, or using humor to help a child handle his frustration.

In the classroom children continually interact with each other, forming and reforming friendships in an attempt to have their love need fulfilled. Children gravitate to other children they like throughout the day as the need expresses itself: on the way to a reading group, before lunch, to show off their art work, and whenever they have a feeling that must be shared. Unfortunately the teacher may inadvertently discourage and even punish such attempts with threats or by sending these children to the principal for "fooling around and talking." The teacher could structure into the routine certain visiting/talking periods which not only would encourage friendship, but would also allow children to practice speech skills in an appropriate and fun way. Most teachers, by allowing such an activity, would quickly see who the socially isolated children are and could report this to the school psychologist for his assistance. To the objection that the teacher is protecting those children who do not want to be bothered, would it not be more helpful and effective to allow the child to handle the situation himself with the teacher assisting? A teacher who has children of his own, close friends, etc., could bring his loved ones into the child's world by discussing them and occasionally having them visit. Modeling and imitation will occur and it would be desirable for children to model positive emotional feelings of adults.

The last basic need the child should learn how to fulfill before reaching self-actualization is the esteem need. This need is met by the child's achieving mastery or competence in various tasks and skills and through deserved praise by others. In school the child can learn how to achieve successfully by being given structured learning tasks that are neither too easy nor too hard. At this point the school psychologist would prove helpful in providing the teacher concrete information regarding each student's abilities. Such information would include not only intellectual ability but special aptitudes (musical, artistic, conversational, and even humor). In other words, the school psychologist's concern would be to broaden the development of assessment measures that would discover normally ignored interests and aptitudes. Later, as the child is taught how to evaluate his ability and aptitude in various situations, he will be allowed to structure the level of difficulty himself utilizing programmed instruction. The teacher can protect a child's esteem subtly by not inviting others to criticize him since children tend to follow example. The fulfilling of these four areas of basic needs is crucial in the further growth of the child.

In the humanistic school, the school psychologist would explain to the parents how they can work with the school in meeting the needs of their children. Besides helping the teacher evaluate each individual student, the school psychologist helps coordinate the use of this knowledge in the development of a program that will include the parents. Initially and throughout the school year the psychologist would provide workshops and talks to the parents that would underscore the relevance of self-actualization and its many facets to the mutual hopes of teachers, parents, and society that each child will become a productive, happy, emphathetic member of society. Organizations like the PTA could become involved in cooperating with the school in meeting the needs of the children. In fact, the parents might get the indirect payoff of seeing how they can meet their own needs and become more self-actualizing.

The second area of goals center more specifically around promoting self-actualization. "The role of the environment is ultimately to permit him or help him to actualize his own potentialities," not its potentialities (Maslow, 1962, p. 151); this statement has implications for curriculum development. The usual approach carries the implicit assumption that all children should be expected to do equally as well in all areas. The report card and grading system is based upon this assumption. In our society's desire for equal educational opportunity for all children, it has assumed equal levels of interest and ability for all children for all curriculum areas. The school teacher supports this concept by reinforcing those students who most conform to this standard.

According to Maslow, all people are composed of a unique inner core which is fundamentally based upon heredity and the experiences of the first few years of life. Even newly weaned infants in a dietary selection study (Davis, 1928) demonstrated satisfactory choice and reflected normal health and growth; by the first grade children clearly exhibit more ability and interest in some activities than others. One can observe that elementary school children given a choice of free-time activities usually are quite active and seem to accomplish a lot. Such observations challenge the conventional "wisdom" that very young children are incapable of intelligent decision. As children are successfully creative in their own area of potential, the teacher can reward the child but not necessarily publicly praise him in a way that is done in the regular classroom, where along with verbal praise is the connotation, "Why can't the rest of you do something like this."

It has been hypothesized by Maslow that one explanation for the rareness of self-actualizing individuals is that this inner core of potential is basically weak and easily suppressed. With the use of television videotapes, movies, and live performances, children can be given the opportunity to observe other children of comparable age who have developed exceptional ability in some activity. By exposing children to age-peers having a variety of well-developed talents, in contrast to the usual practice of employing a talented adult model, children can be impressed early with the idea that they too have almost unlimited potentials. Too often young learners are led to expect that they must achieve mastery. Teachers can prevent this unintentional suppression by encouraging divergence and by avoiding the harsh, personal criticism that adults often levy when children make mistakes or misbehave. In our hypothetical school a child will not be criticized for making mistakes. Instead, he will be encouraged to evaluate his own performance with the teacher providing informational feedback.

A goal which would receive considerable attention would be the development of individuals who would be able to help the larger society while meeting their own needs. Maslow (1954) has discussed Benedict's description of a synergic society where a person who contributes the most to the welfare of the community is held in the highest esteem. Cleland and Swartz (1969) have suggested a "peace obstacle course" to promote cooperative behavior with mentally retarded children—the polar opposite of war obstacle courses designed to generate hostility. The "obstacles" would be various goals to be achieved which required the utilization of the intellectual or physical resources of the whole class, teacher included, e.g., a rope-pulling obstacle would activate an electric relay connected to a bell only when all the children of a particular class were pulling together. Such activities followed by group rewards would help balance out the present overly competitive orientation of the public schools.

Other examples from experimental social psychology on conflict resolution could be usefully employed, e.g., Sherif's Robber's Cave experiment (Sherif, Harvey, White, Hood, & Sherif, 1954) in which the hostile competitiveness of two groups of children was dissolved when both groups were required to work together in an "emergency" situation. The classroom teacher can encourage cooperative behavior in getting the classroom ready for an activity, cleaning up, or in planning and carrying out a field trip by involving all children in some task. He can then make the point, "Look what we can do when we work together." The teacher can also divide the children in various ways (pairs, triads, or small groups) with a specific task to accomplish, but with the oblique goal of teaching cooperative behavior.

The child's capacities clamor to be used and to grow, which most of the time will be reinforcing to the child. However, Maslow (1952) has stated, "Growth has not only rewards and pleasure, but also many intrinsic pains and always will have" [p. 120]. Attention needs to be focused on this painful side of growth, as too often educators become discouraged with their efforts when the students complain and appear to be experiencing difficulties that are painful. If educational reformers are aiming for a utopian school situation where the child will always be happy, according to Maslow, they are predestined for failure. The teacher in the self-actualizing school will be sensitive to the child's growth and to the fact that he may need extra encouragement and protection in these instances. The teacher needs continually to recall his own education and how painful some learning and growth was.

With the public school's emphasis on daily evaluation and grades and the implicit threat and pain they provide for children, we can understand how this negative threat, combined with natural growth pains, could conceivably turn children off to school. Part of the natural pain of growth occurs when a child becomes impatient with his rate of learning compared to his expectations or the model provided by the teacher. To neutralize this type of negative experience, the teacher can provide the child with a sense of time perspective. For example, a child impatient with his progress in some skill such as handwriting could be told by the teacher that by Thanksgiving he will likely have the skill mastered. The child can be shown on the calendar how far away Thanksgiving is and can even be instructed to ask his parents when and how far in the future Thanksgiving is, so the child will learn that different, but significant adults, teacher, and parents are reliable and consistent.

Viewing internal and external control of the behavior of the child in the classroom along the following continuum, Maslow would be more in favor of an increasing emphasis on internal control.

| EXTERNAL CONTROL (Use of social rewards and punishment) | INTERNAL CONTROL (Use of inherent and internal reward) |

A child in this school would not be motivated so overwhelmingly with gold stars, grades, or threats, but would learn to value his own feelings and evaluations of his behavior. When the child shows a picture he has drawn to the teacher and she states, "That's good," it is usually possible to observe disappointment on the child's face. Conversely, if the teacher asks a question about some detail of the work, the child brightens up and begins excitedly to talk about his own feelings about his product. By discussing his own feelings and ideas the student is sharing his own internal reward system. Inherent reward occurs when the child gets satisfaction from activity just because the activity itself is fun from the child's frame of reference. However, children differ in what is inherently rewarding. One child may prefer baseball, another art, and a third, music. The school psychologist can make the teacher aware of the different ways in which he can make learning rewarding, as opposed to the solitary use of external rewards. He can also point out how external reinforcement, unless it is internalized, is only successful to the extent that there is an adult around to dispense rewards. The purpose of the humanistic school is to teach children how to meet their own needs and find rewards and pleasures from life without a dependence on external sources.

SCHOOL PERSONNEL

Next in importance to the goals of an educational system is its staff. Maslow has suggested that the therapist's experience and whether or not he is a self-actualizer determines the quality of psychotherapists. Because children do learn greatly by imitation, a self-actualizing teacher is necessary for the proposed school. Maslow's fifteen characteristics of the self-actualized person can, within limits, be assessed, and the school psychologist, in the teacher selection process, would employ instruments that are ordinarily neglected in most selection batteries. For example, creativity might be tapped through use of one of a number of "creativity" tests, humor through employment of the Levine Mirth Response Test (Redlich, Leving, & Sohler, 1951), self-actualization via the Bonjean-Vance (1968) short-from measure of self-actualization or via Shostrom's (1965) Personal Orientation Inventory. Creativity, humor, problem-solving ability, etc., are not so ethereal or elusive that they can not be assessed with limits. They are facets of life that need systematic training and exposition if Maslow's theory is to be translated adequately.

The role of the teacher will be to facilitate the child's interactions with the curriculum and with other children by attempting to help the child interpret his own thoughts and feelings as they occur. As the children pursue various interests in depth the occasion will continually arise where the child will know more about a specific area than the teacher; this is one more reason for the necessity of a self-actualizing teacher who does not need to feel all-powerful as an expert. This often occurs in science, geography, or history, where a child, by the nature of his parents' occupation or background, has had more exposure to the subject area.

The school personnel will have their esteem needs met in a way that is beneficial to the group, and they will be treated by the children as feeling, unique persons. This will require a school administrator who believes in the goals of the humanistic school and who feels confident in the role of coordinator and facilitator, as opposed to supervisor or expert. The administrators will view themselves as resources for the staff members, students, and parents, and can provide a sense of perspective that the school is progressing in the desired direction.

THE CURRICULUM

Probably most of the content and subject areas of most present school systems will be available in the proposed school. Many new areas and courses will be included and will be taught from the perspective of B-cognition (B-Being). B-cognition is viewing the world and everything in it as it exists naturally, as opposed to D-cognition (D-Deficiency), where an individual looks at everything in the world from the viewpoint of what he can get out of it. Often when the child asks why he has to learn something, the teacher replies, "So you can get a job." Learning poetry because it is fun to hear words rhythmically crash through the air is an example of the B-cognition perspective. Preschool children are involved in this type of perspective when they repeatedly splash water or dig holes in the sand. They are innately curious about life and reality and they test it out in different ways to satisfy their curiosity. The instruction of B-cognition would appear especially valuable in a society that is increasingly providing more leisure time. It is also possible that as a result of instructing a child in the appreciation of knowledge for itself he will be able to value other people more for what they are than for what he can get from them. The entire curriculum will have another main overlay, the merging of the classroom and the real world that children occupy during nonschool hours. Examples, problems, and study units will be brought directly from actual day-to-day occurences in society. In effect, the whole world becomes a classroom.

What does this catchy cliche mean? An example can be provided that invokes technology to help solve problems. To concretize the highly abstract goals and problems involved in teaching empathy, altruism, respect for nature, etc., programs can be scheduled to permit the TV satellite to show what is going on *now* in the world. Live TV spots showing Peace Corp volunteers demonstrating to backward peasants in underdeveloped countries the use of better planting and sowing techniques *and* showing the results in before-after fashion demonstrates the meaning of abstractions like empathy and altruism. Other scenes may contrast reforestation efforts after a fire with a live forest of great beauty or persons receiving medical treatment in a country lacking such resources. If malnourished children are shown, for example, similar children should be shown on their way to recovery to dramatize the positive, altruistic nature of mature and thoughtful people toward the less fortunate. Examples of endangered plants and animals would further the objective of making ecology come alive through early, learned respect for our planet. As in the earlier example of the students' eating pomegranates, the teacher would provide foods, samples, and concrete proof that would invoke the various sensory modalities of the children.

The following course areas would be included, in addition to the usual areas found in the regular elementary school classrooms:

1. Values: In our effort to maintain separation of church and state, our society has implied that education should discourage discussion of too much information on values. However, it is especially important that children be taught the importance of beliefs and values and how to evaluate various values that are implicit as well as explicit in behavior, using as criteria their own feelings and ideals.

2. Needs: A course in needs would be beneficial in helping the child understand his own needs and how to fulfill them. Knowledge of human needs and their expression could help children understand and love others.

3. Epistemology: This area of study would deal with the different ways of knowing and acquiring knowledge and would include integration of the cognitive, sensory-motor, and affective areas of the child's personality. Such a course would be designed to discourage a total dependence of the child upon logical and analytical thinking which is limited. One component of this course would be teaching and improving phenomenological observation. Emphasis will be placed on the synthesis of the various subject areas of exposure.

4. Philosophy and Religion: Besides the usual introduction of philosophy and religion, the child will also learn to observe the relationship of the founder to his religion or philosophy and how it is a unique expression of himself.

5. Emotions: The children would be encouraged not only to control their emotions but would be taught how to learn from them and to express them in beneficial ways. They would learn that to control one's emotions does not necessarily mean to show no emotion at all, but that one can honestly express how he feels in a way that is not destructive. Children can also be taught how to experience positive emotions such as joy, mirth, empathy, and self-satisfaction more frequently. Just as the school can foster intellectual development, it can directly contribute to emotional development. Many emotions are expressed facially, and learning to read these nonverbal communications is a real communications skill. These emotions can be taught via pictures or movies of grief, sorrow,

happiness, etc., in order to increase the child's sensitivity to non-verbal communication. Because the world has frustrations, children should acquire frustration tolerance. In emotions class the children will learn how to deal with frustrations and how they teach them about their own limits and the nature of the world. This course will also deal with the fear of knowledge and the basis of this fear.

Throughout all of the courses the child will be encouraged to follow hunches and be creative. Maslow (1962) has specifically commented on this point:

> Pure spontaneity is not long possible because we live in a world which runs by its own, non-psychic laws. It is possible in dreams, fantasies, love, imagination, sex, the first stages of creativity, artistic work, intellectual play, free associations, etc. Pure control is not permanently possible, for then the psyche dies. Education must be directed both toward cultivation of controls and cultivation of spontaneity and expression. In our culture and at this point in history, it is necessary to redress the balance in favor of spontaneity, the ability to be expressive, passive, unwilled, trusting in processes other than will and control, unpremeditated, creative, etc. [p. 185].

Within almost every structured activity in the classroom the teacher can allow for spontaneous behavior. For example, certain art periods can be free periods where the child is allowed to express himself with the art materials in any way he wishes. During a writing class a child can be allowed to write about anything without topical or grammatical constraints.

DISCUSSION

This paper shows how the real goals of any educational system can be seen in its products. Because some question exists concerning the popularity and desirability of the present educational product, the authors have focused on a more humanistic alternative. With its departure from the goals of traditional education, some parents might conceivably reject the humanistic school, but there would be a chioce. Once humanistic educational programs such as the one suggested are implemented, parents and educators will have an opportunity to compare the results of the different approaches. The authors encourage such experimental effort and reiterate that the school psychologist can be an effective catalyst in the entire process.

REFERENCES

BONJEAN, C. M., & VANCE, G. C. A. A short-form measure of self-actualization. *Journal of Applied Behavioral Science,* 1968, *IV,* 229–312.

CLELAND, C. C., & SWARTZ, J. D. *Mental retardation: Approaches to institutional change.* New York: Grune and Stratton, 1969.

DAVIS, D. M. Self-selection of diet by newly weaned infants. *American Journal of Diseases of Children,* 1928, *36,* 651–679.

LYON, H. C. *Learning to feel—feeling to learn.* Columbus, Ohio: Charles E. Merrill, 1971.

MASLOW, A. H. *Motivation and personality.* New York: Harper and Row, 1954.

MASLOW, A. H. *Toward a psychology of being.* Princeton, N. J.: D. Van Nostrand Company, Inc., 1962.

REDL, F., & WINEMAN, D. *Controls from within.* Glencoe, Illinois: Free Press, 1952.

REDLICH, F. C., LEVINE, J., & SOHLER, T. P. A mirth response test: Preliminary report on a psychodiagnostic technique utilizing dynamics of humor. *American Journal of Orthopsychiatry,* 1951, *21,* 717–734.

ROGERS, C. R. *Freedom to learn.* Columbus, Ohio: Charles Merrill, 1969.

SHERIF, M., HARVEY, O. J., WHITE, B. J., HOOD, H. R., & SHERIF, C. W. *Experimental study of positive and negative intergroup attitudes between experimentally produced groups: Robber's cave study.* Norman: University of Oklahoma, 1954. (Multilithed)

SHOSTROM, E. A. A test for the measurement of self-actualization. *Educational and Psychological Measurement,* 1965, *24,* 207–218.

Free Expression
Through Movement

Edith A. Buchanan and
Deanna Stirling Hanson

The importance of a child's early years to his educational development has been given widespread attention. The focus of most of this interest, as reflected in the huge sums of money spent for projects such as Head Start, Sesame Street, and numerous research programs, has been on the development of academic competence—and more particularly on reading or the readiness for reading. Such an emphasis has neglected the role of feelings and self-concept in the child's learning and in his total development. This article describes a study designed to identify and modify the expressive or affective behavior of four-year-olds through moving, touching, and feeling.

We became aware of the need for such a study through our experiences over a period of years in the Early Childhood Unit of the University Elementary School, University of California at Los Angeles. Each year a few children were identified who had trouble expressing their feelings or who expressed seemingly inappropriate feelings. Such children denied hurt, fear, anger, and joy not only verbally—"It didn't hurt," "I'm not afraid," "I didn't want it anyway," or "What's so great about that?" —but by facial expreoison, stance, and other behaviors. There were those children who laughed when hurt, smiled when rejected, or denied the need for assistance in the face of obvious frustration.

Talking about feelings had little effect and year after year some of these children progressed to elementary school still denying and suppressing their feelings. As we monitored progress throughout the elementary years, we discovered that an inordinate number of these affect "problem" children manifested severe problems—either learning, social, or personal.

It was apparent that identifying those children who seemed to have difficulty expressing feelings appropriately was far easier than determining

Edith A. Buchanan and Deanna Stirling Hanson, "Free Expression Through Movement," *The National Elementary Principal,* October 1972, pp. 46–51.

a productive intervention. Teaching teams in the Early Childhood Unit generated suggestions, none of them new:

1. *Dramatic play.* Would a child who was fearful of his own feelings and unable to express them appropriately find release in expressing hostility and aggression as the big bad wolf who frightened Red Riding Hood or the spider who scared Miss Muffett?

2. *Rhythms.* Would a child feel less tense if he were allowed to run freely, hop energetically, and gallop like a pony?

3. *Small-fry encounter groups.* Would such groups provide the catalyst for change?

Each suggestion was dutifully initiated. Children were encouraged to express feelings with teachers who were warm, supportive, nurturing, and enthusiastic. As the days rolled on, it became obvious that the children were still unable to express affect. The teachers became acutely aware that there was no change in most of the children involved in the small group activities, and some of them seemed to show regressive behavior as the school year progressed.

It was at this point that one of the teachers investigated some research studies of movement behavior and its effect on the affective behavior of the individual, done by Valerie V. Hunt, director of the Movement Behavior Laboratory at the University of California at Los Angeles.[1] An invitation to Dr. Hunt followed, and as a result of her insightful presentation to the teachers of the Early Childhood Unit, a movement behavior program was developed that provided a variety of opportunities for the child to:

1. Touch or be touched on all exposed body surfaces by self, others, or objects; appropriately verbalize awareness of tactual experiences

2. Explore and label a wide variation of possible movements of each joint and the combined movement of many joints

3. Explore the space around him by moving the parts of his body in a variety of spatial orientations—up, down, backward forward, sideways—starting from different positions and at different heights

4. Tolerate confinement in restricted space alone or with others

5. Experience a change in orientation and relinquish control by allowing himself to be whirled in space, either by an adult or a mechanized device; let his weight fall freely and submit to gravity's pull by allowing his body to absorb impact; experience the tensions produced from rapid loss or gain of weight; extend

the absorption of impact as impetus to other movement; balance body weight and the weight of peers and objects, all in a variety of positions

6. Explore the weight of objects by a variety of movements and postures; push and pull with different parts of the body to overcome the resistance of the weight

7. Duplicate the nonstructured rhythms of the environment; perpetuate repetitive feedback of kinesthetic sensation within a focused activity, such as using a hula hoop or rocking

8. Move with a range of rhythmic flow patterns that broaden the repertoire of movement patterns

9. Challenge a number of obstacles by moving in new and varied ways to avoid touching them or by touching them only with certain body parts and changing the pressure of the touch and the speed of movement through the obstacles

10. Explore the areas of the environment, verbalizing the changes noted in texture, space, and temperature.

It soon became obvious that remarkable changes were occurring in a number of children involved in the movement behavior activities. Dorothy, who had scarcely uttered a sound and had not become involved with peers in activities during her year and a half in school, began to chatter to any classmate who was nearby. Alan, who continually returned to the security and comfort of the block corner to reconstruct impassively the same block structure each day, now began to contact classmates for the first time. He began to express interest as the block building became a cooperative venture with others, and he smiled frequently at the comments and jokes of his peers. Mike, who flitted about rapidly, a fixed smile on his face in spite of obviously painful and frustrating experiences, began to focus and started a thoughtful exchange of ideas with the teacher and the other children.

Teachers became enthusiastic. Not only were the children apparently involved during the sessions, but they seemed to be transferring their change in behavior to other school situations throughout the day.

Observations of the children's behavioral change led us to inquire into some possible explanations. What was the relationship between movement and the expression of feelings? For years man has attempted to describe and explain human beings by observing physical attributes, such as posture, body type, and facial expression. Handwriting and drawings have been studied as expressions of personality characteristics.[2] More recently individual responses to symbols, pictures, and inkblots have been used as indicators of emotional factors. Scholars have made serious attempts to describe and categorize systematically other nonverbal expressive behavior.[3] H. A. Witkin and his associates conducted important studies showing a relationship between the perceptual mode and certain other personality characteristics, such as independence.[4]

In brief, there is sufficient evidence to show that the way a person moves, including writing and drawing and perceiving his world, expresses cultural as well as personal attributes. We often judge a person by the way he walks—as if he hasn't a care in the world, or as if he has the weight of the world on his shoulders. Even if we accept the notion that movement may reflect the personality, how do we explain the changes that we observed as we altered the children's movement behavior? Perhaps it was a reflection of the intimate relationship between movement and emotion that was demonstrated by Paul Schilder [5] in studies with psychotics who had recovered. When they were forced to repeat their disturbed motor actions, their psychotic emotional state returned.

By allowing, encouraging, and teaching children to move in new ways and to experience their bodies in a variety of ways, could we alter their feelings and perhaps bring about changes in the way they view themselves and their relationship to the environment about them? We wanted to document that these changes did occur.

Consequently, a group of children was brought each day to a classroom where they removed their shoes and socks and were allowed to interact with equipment and each other for thirty minutes. From the beginning of these sessions, the children were encouraged to move in any way that would extend their movement repertoire. On the first day the children and the teacher sat in chairs arranged in a small circle on the rug. There were only six children in each group, so the teacher's bare feet reached approximately to the center, and it was inevitable that as the children shifted about on their chairs some of their feet would touch those of the teacher. The teacher commented that she had felt "someone's feet." Her tone conveyed to three or four of the children that they were in a gamelike situation, and they again placed their feet on the teacher's. The teacher began to describe the various feet she felt, encouraging the children to make observations as to which were warmer and colder.

One child held his feet under his chair and seemed uncomfortable in the activity. The teacher did not encourage his participation. After a few more minutes of exploration and comment about the feet they were feeling, the children began to make a tower with their feet. The teacher suggested that if one of them felt his feet on the bottom of the pile he should slip them out and put them on top. As each child became aware of the placement of his feet in relation to the others, he shifted them.

Gradually the tempo of the activity increased, and the feet began to move so rapidly that the order of placement was soon ignored by all.

Thus an activity that began as a tactual experience moved on to a kinesthetic one. By this time, the child who had held back from the activity was smiling and appeared to enjoy watching even though he refrained from joining in the game overtly. It was not until two days later that he hesitatingly placed his bare feet on those of the teacher.

This activity was repeated for two or three days until the children appeared to be comfortable enough to try something new. They were asked to move their chairs back to allow each one more space. The teacher asked each child to feel which parts of his body were touching the chair. She moved quickly around the circle of chairs, pressing gently against the children and drawing each child's attention to the pressure on that part of his body.

Following this activity the teacher asked the children if they could think of a way of getting on the chair so that some other part of the body could touch it. Several responded, and the teacher commented immediately on each new position, describing these changes to the rest of the children. As the children observed each other they began to imitate the various positions, and the teacher continued to give encouragement by verbalizing and smiling whenever a child changed posture or position.

The young learners soon realized that they were in a situation where they were not only allowed but encouraged to move without restraint and to interact with equipment in new ways. As this realization grew, each child sought an activity that appealed to him. For example, a few days after touching feet and exploring with chairs, the children entered the classroom one morning to find a long line of chairs set side by side across the room. While the children removed their shoes and socks, several of them made comments about the chair formation and began to plan what they would do. Teddy said, "That looks like a bridge; I'm going to walk on it." Dorothy said, "It's not a bridge, it's a tunnel!"

They quickly ran to the chairs, and Teddy began walking along the top, while Dorothy spread out face down and began snakelike movements through the confining space under the row of chairs. She was followed by others, many of whom were able to move underneath the entire row of chairs. Although some children found that movement through this confining space was uncomfortable and crawled out along the way, others returned to the tunnel entrance immediately and began the action all over again.

Children were observed returning again and again to a particular activity throughout the duration of the program. As a result, at any given time during a movement behavior session, a number of activities were being carried on simultaneously.

It should be noted that an important aspect of the teaching role involved allowing children to continue an activity long enough to approach perseveration. For every child there seemed to be a time when assimilation of the activity was complete, and he would then turn his interest to some other task. Another aspect of the teaching role was the need to create a strong foundation of trust and rapport before interaction could begin. Since at first the children were unfamiliar with the particular classroom and teacher, each child was allowed to respond to the interaction at his own pace. If he chose to wait awhile, he was not made to feel guilty, but was supported and encouraged to explore new movement patterns and extend the old patterns in terms of time, force, and space.

Research has validated the importance of language in the integration of experience,[6] and talking about movement experiences was therefore emphasized throughout the program. The teacher often made such comments as, "You were holding your arms way out from your sides when you jumped," or "Can you tell how the rug feels when you rub your face on it?"

Besides the ability to perceive movement patterns in children's activities, it is important for the teacher to demonstrate and model various physical activities. She also needs to understand the component parts of a movement activity so it can be adjusted to meet the child's ability. For example, when it became apparent that René could not jump from the countertop onto the mat, she was helped to jump from the less foreboding height of a small chair. To jump from the chair was as demanding for René as the countertop was for other children. When this activity became easy for René, she was able to accept the challenge of jumping from an adult size chair and finally from the thirty-two-inch countertop.

Most of the equipment used in the program is available to a typical classroom: tables and chairs, which can be arranged to provide interaction in a variety of ways; a resilient mat for jumping, rolling, and wrestling activities; a rope, at least fourteen feet in length, for pulling, encircling a group, tug-of-war, and so forth; hula hoops, which can also be used as jump ropes, hoops for diving and jumping through, and as a merry-go-round; inflatable rubber balls, eight and twelve inches in diameter; and large cardboard boxes. The teaching staff contributed additional items: an old fur coat, two discarded velvet evening coats, a hand vibrator, a feather duster, a plastic barrel, an old satin sheet, a cotton bedspread, a hot water bottle, and numerous other objects.

Some children continued with an activity over a comparatively long period of time; others were eager to explore something new. For this reason, the environment was rearranged frequently and new equipment added so that the child's interest was maintained and he could pursue the activity he seemed to need.

A project designed to test the effects of a movement behavior program must have some means for describing the subjects both before and after. In this case, we were interested in measuring their affective or expressive behavior. Since no standardized instruments suitable for four-year-olds were available, teacher observation ratings were developed. These observations, along with ratings made by a qualified observer, became the base line data. In addition, the Holtzmann Inkblot Technique was administered to each subject to substantiate the ratings. Four variables were scored: anxiety, barrier, movement, and hostility. Because of the unvalidated nature of the measures, the authors decided to record the movement behavior sessions on film to document any visible changes in affect.

After the ten-week program, teachers and observers rated the children and administered the Holtzmann Technique again. Although during the program teachers reported many changes in a particular child's behavior, this was not reflected in the rating instrument. On the other hand, the observer ratings indicated positive, significant changes for children in the movement behavior program. The differences in these two ratings may be explained by the fact that teachers continued to have daily contact with the children, thus decreasing the vividness of the changes that occurred.

The post measurement by the Holtzmann Inkblot Technique showed that in the experimental group anxiety was lowered (99 percent level of confidence), as was the barrier score (90 percent level of confidence).

The findings seemed to indicate that the movement behavior program, with its concentrated sensorimotor experiences, helped children to integrate and organize data about themselves and their relationship to the environment. As a result, children who had been incapable of expressing feelings learned to show them freely and appropriately. These changes are documented and recorded on film, and some are shown in *A Time to Move*.[7]

Although this study was undertaken for the specific purpose of helping children to express feelings appropriately, three educational implications emerged:

1. There is an apparent need for formulating objectives related to children's appropriate expression of feelings. How a child feels about his relationship to his learning experiences and their outcomes determines how he will integrate that learning within himself. Also, those children who have difficulty in accepting their own feelings are not as free to reach out to new experiences and may expend a great deal of energy in dealing with their own anxiety.

2. Instructional techniques that employ moving, touching, and feeling can be successful in changing inappropriate behavior and initiating new learning patterns. It is important to note that the

program was based on an instructional viewpoint rather than expensive equipment and materials and was conducted within the framework of the daily schedule within a typical classroom.

3. Learning that is integrated through multisensory experience is more effective for most learners. In spite of this, we find that the curriculum for young children is focused on academic tasks leading to sedentary activities such as paper and pencil tasks, workbooks, and programed or computer-assisted instruction. When we deny young children the opportunity to experience their bodies in dynamic interaction with an environment designed to provide multisensory feedback, we may be setting the stage for undesirable consequences that are far reaching and long lasting, not only in terms of learning skills, but also in terms of failure to provide a strong base for emotional well-being.

Through touching, tumbling, jumping, and other basic movements—all in interaction with other children and supportive adults—the participants demonstrated a significant decrease in anxiety and an increased capacity to reveal their feelings during and immediately after the experimental program. However, the long-term effects of the movement behavior program have not yet been demonstrated and would prove a fruitful area for further study and research.

FOOTNOTES

1. Hunt, Valerie V. "Movement Behavior: A Model for Action." *Quest Monograph II:* April 1964. (Tucson, Ariz.: National Association for Physical Education of College Women and National College Physical Education Association for Men.)

2. Anderson, H. H., and Anderson, Gladys L. *An Introduction to Projective Techniques.* Englewood Cliffs, N.J.: Prentice-Hall, 1951.

3. Allport, Gordon, and Vernon, Philip E. *Studies in Expressive Movement.* New York: Hafner Publishing Co., 1967; Birdwhistell, R. L. *Introduction to Kinetics.* Louisville, Ky.: Louisville University Press, 1952; and Reusch Jurgen, and Kees, Weldon. *Nonverbal Communication.* Berkeley, Calif.: University of California Press, 1966. See also footnote 1.

4. Witkin, H. A., and others. *Psychological Differentiation.* New York: John Wiley & Sons, 1962.

5. Schilder, Paul. *The Image and Appearance of the Human Body.* New York: International Universities Press, 1950.

6. Craig, Robert C. "Learning: 1. Understanding Transfer and Retention." *Review of Education Research* 28:445–58; December 1958.

7. *A Time to Move.* 30 min., b. & w., 16 mm. Early Childhood Production Co., P.O. Box 352, Chatsworth, Calif. 91311. 1970.

The Structure of Affect in the Art Curriculum

David W. Ecker

A few Sundays ago, while jotting down some ideas I wanted to discuss with you, I was also intermittently scanning *The New York Times*—a weekly ritual with five pounds of newsprint which can easily stretch well into the next week. The two activities—reading *The Times* and thinking about "the structure of affect"—suddenly merged when I got to the section on "Arts and Leisure." Across the top of one page in Boldface were the words "love, peace, music, grass," followed by the statement "No one who was there will ever be the same." It was part of an advertisement for *Woodstock,* the movie created out of footage taken last August at the three-day Music and Art Fair (widely referred to as a "tribal celebration") in which 400,000 young people participated. I wasn't there, but observers all agreed—whatever their age or political persuasion—that love, peace, music, and grass did indeed structure that fantastic event.

And it was a deeply moving experience to judge from the reports. Let me quote from just three who were there. According to Paul Williams (ex-editor of *Crawdaddy!*): *Woodstock felt like home. A place to take acid. A place to make love. Felt like a place we'd been to before, but hard to remember, like yesterday's vision, like last night's dream. But now it's all now, and it feels like we're never turning back.* And Joan Baez, when asked what matters to her when she sings, replied: *I don't care very much about where a song came from or why, or even what it says. All I care about is how it sounds and the feeling in it.* (She had plenty of feeling to put into her songs at Woodstock; she was a few weeks away from the birth of her first child, and her husband was in a Federal prison serving a three-year sentence for draft refusal.) Finally, Ellen Sander's response to it all: *Joy is alive and well in rock and roll. Everyone I know feels it. Myths are fading, minds in motion conjure joy and let it be, values come to resemble*

David W. Ecker, "The Structure of Affect in the Art Curriculum," *Art Education*, January 1971, pp. 26–29.

feelings more than things, there is new music and life at its best is its dance.

Now if these are typical of the lessons learned at Woodstock, and if by extension those who are celebrating their deeply felt responses to similar events "will never be the same" in some non-trivial sense, then the implication is clear: Art teachers and others interested in the education and well-being of young people must take much more seriously than they have what I shall call the "structure of affect"—the dynamic forms of feeling exhibited by youth today and, more broadly, the contours and direction and significance of the qualitative life they are learning to live. I emphasize the word "structure" here, because I believe we are dealing with the beginnings of a "counter-culture" which already has not only its own music and dress and morality but also its distinctive literature and history, its symbols and mythology, its art and politics—all rooted in the affective nature of man. And when I say that we must take this "structure of affect" seriously, I do not necessarily mean that we should incorporate into the public schools an arts curriculum made up of courses in the aesthetics of smoking pot, political revolution through art, rock and roll appreciation, or the communal "love-in" as an art form. Assuming that we can still exercise some measure of control over the life-styles now developing in and out of school, I am asking that we re-examine our art curriculum in terms of the relationship between the affective and cognitive structures now built into it and those structures our students display outside of school.

What I suspect, of course, is that the gulf between what we as professional art educators want youngsters to do in the art room and what they do on their own in the area of "arts and leisure" is widening. And because I believe this gulf—this escalating cultural confrontation—is dangerous for both young and old, I want to identify some curriculum innovations that promise to narrow the gap, reduce the confrontation, and build into the experience of formal schooling the integrity it now lacks. Before doing so, however, I think it would be useful to re-state the problem in more precise terms and review briefly what I take to be important research on affect and curriculum development.

II

One of the great puzzles in educational theory and practice is how thoughts, feelings, and actions are dynamically related to instructional objectives. Apparently a student may learn to dislike a subject he has mastered, while he learns to love another subject he finds difficult. More paradoxically, some students learn how to fail in school just as surely as others learn how to succeed. Partial explanations for such phenomena abound. For example, academic success (or failure) is widely viewed as a function of aptitude, native ability, intelligence, and other "cognitive variables"; however, a resurgence of professional interest in student emotions, attitudes, motivation, and self-esteem has led to alternative explanations of academic achievement. This interest in the "affective variables," amplified by social and political pressures, is, in turn, leading educators to a consideration of the kinds of curriculum reform that would reflect new empirical findings. Yet the movement for affective education grows in the absence of a comprehensive and workable theory of affective learning.

Everyone knows, of course, that man feels as well as thinks. He is seemingly capable of both feeling deeply and thinking profoundly about anything whatsoever, including his own thoughts and feelings. Moreover, his actions, unlike animal behavior, are not governed solely by instinct, maturation, and habitual response to the immediate environment; he learns from his experiences, which early in life come to include more than what is physically present. Characteristically human situations contain elements of the past and possible futures symbolically represented in the present. Human activity is given meaning and guided by the symbolic forms provided by myth, religion, language, history, science, and art. But man, also unlike other animals, is capable of sustained hatred, contempt, anxiety; of systematic torture, murder, suicide; of genocide and wars of annihilation. On the evidence, the learned responses of humans seem infinitely varied, for good or ill, and variable.

This being so, the kind of formal education received by the young can play a crucial role in shaping the quality and character of our society. Even when education fails in this role, the over-riding concerns of people soon become the urgent problems of the schools. *Sputnik* triggered our space-race with the Soviets, and the great reform of American education begun in the fifties is still underway. "Excellence" became the watchword. In terms of curricular objectives, this translated as intellectual achievements, particularly in mathematics, languages, and the sciences. In the sixties, however, public attention has riveted on more basic social problems. Race riots in the cities, the specter of the nation's poor in an affluent society, and radical protest by young people against the Establishment, threaten to trigger a second major reform movement in education. Cognitive objectives may well be subordinated to affective objectives in the seventies. If "relevance" becomes the new standard, and personal and social well-being a compelling goal, how might the curriculum be restructured?

If by "the curriculum" we mean all school activities designed to change student behavior toward explicit individual and social objectives, it would seem imperative that educators not only have some notion of what significant changes are *possible* with regard to academic achievement, attitudes and values, personality, and the like, but also have some idea as to the age or stage of development at which these changes can be maximized.

These are the concerns that underlie Bloom's book *Stability and Change in Human Characteristics* (1964). This study is based on a survey and analysis of a large amount of data from longitudinal research on the physical, emotional, mental, and social growth of humans reported over the past fifty years. A central thesis advanced is that "variations in the environment have greatest quantitative effect on the characteristic at its most rapid period of change and least effect on the characteristic during the least rapid period of change." (p. vii) Specifically, the evidence suggests that "as much development (of intelligence) takes place in the first 4 years of life as in the next 13 years." (p. 88) Also, "we may conclude from our results of general achievement, reading comprehension, and vocabulary development that by age 9 (grade 3) at least 50% of the general achievement pattern of age 18 (grade 12) has been developed, whereas at least 75% of the pattern has been developed by about age 13 (grade 7)." (p. 105)

What about affective characteristics? The evidence is much less clear because of the general lack of valid instruments for measuring the emotional or affective components of human development, and the lack of a unified view of the area. Instruments range from self-reporting devices, and sociometric ratings, to observational techniques. Nevertheless, on the basis of R. N. Sanford's curves (1962), representing the development of "ego maturity" and "impulse control," Bloom estimates that "one-third of the ego development at age 20 is likely to be attained by age 5." Bloom warns the reader that "in the personality area we have no scale for determining the amount reached by maturity. We are not even certain as to what an absolute scale of aggression, dependence, etc., would mean at a particular age . . . or that we are measuring comparable characteristics at each age." (p. 137) With regard to interests, attitudes, and personality, Bloom concludes that "the genetic and organic base must be relatively slight, while the direction and nature of these characteristics must be largely determined by the environment in which the individual develops." (p. 210) In other words, affect is largely learned.

The obvious significance of Bloom's study lies in the intriguing possibility of planning preschool and early elementary school experiences that would radically modify characteristics previously thought to be relatively constant; e.g., intelligence and personality. Unfortunately, Bloom can say little about which kind of environment will do what for children because (as he recognized), the longitudinal studies he analyzed were based upon data of individual differences with little attention to measurement of environmental differences. What is worse, the kind of information that would be of most use to curriculum-builders is least available: knowledge about learning gained by *controlling* the environment in truly experimental curricula.

An even more perplexing problem faced by researchers, educators, and others when dealing with such recurrent notions as "affective learning," "emotional maturity," and "attitude formation," is the lack of agreement on what they are talking about. To help resolve this difficulty, an operationally specific terminology is offered as part of a major effort by Krathwohl, Bloom, and Masia (1964) to establish a *Taxonomy of Educational Objectives: Affective Domain.* While noting that this domain has been variously characterized in terms of subject matters, areas of human experience, and aspects of the self, the taxonomy systematically classifies *types of human reaction* or *response,* as did the earlier taxonomy of the cognitive domain. Thus those feelings, modes of thinking, attitudes, and values typically identified in statements of affective educational objectives are reduced to what is believed to be their behavioral equivalent—the student's overt response being considered as verifiable evidence that the desired learning has occurred as a result of the instructional process.

The taxonomy does not provide explicit curriculum strategies for soliciting preferred affective responses, but curriculum-builders will find provocative materials which suggest both sequence and content for possible lessons, units, and courses. I'm sure many of you are familiar with the outline of the taxonomy, which arranges affective responses in a hierarchy of categories, from "lower" to "higher" behaviors: from Receiving, Responding, Valuing, and Organizing a Value System, through Characterization of a Value Complex. Elsewhere I have constructed a behavioral continuum in the areas of art education and also moral development to see just how the taxonomy might be applied.

It should be noted that many of the objectives in these sequences have an implied cognitive component. One could argue that all of them do. Indeed, while discussing the important interrelations of the affective and cognitive domains, the handbook emphasizes the holistic nature of human behavior and acknowledges its arbitrary division into three domains (the third domain being the psycho-motor with its taxonomy yet to be produced). Even with so-called cognitive objectives, where the measure of success is determined by the student's ability to perform a task upon request, the *implicit* affective goal is that the student become intrinsically motivated to use this ability away from the test situation. For example, a worthy cognitive achievement is certainly the ability to determine whether an argument is logically consistent; but when the student appreciates and employs valid arguments in appropriate life situations, he has internalized the value of rationality, a sign of emotional as well as intellectual maturity.

Now if every objective has both affective and cognitive aspects, it must be said that cognition has generally received lopsided attention in research and curriculum development. A key example, of course, is Bruner's report, *The Process of Education* in 1961. Its central proposition, that "the foundations of any subject may be taught to anybody at any age in some form," stressed the teaching and learning of the structure of the discipline. Intellectual excellence was to be achieved by stimulating the student's desire to grasp ideas intuitively in a "spiral curriculum," which would later re-present these ideas in analytical form. The burden of developing such curricula was placed primarily on scholars who created instructional materials and set curricular goals in mathematics, and the physical, biological, and social sciences, to name some of the areas revitalized in the nation's schools.

I remind you of the excessive cognitive approach of the early sixties in order to highlight a major attack on Bruner's approach which appeared in 1968. It is Richard Jones' book *Feeling and Fantasy in Education.* He deals only obliquely with the relation between art and academic achievement, but what he says, I believe, is highly instructive for those of us interested in the relation between affect and cognition Jones' critique grew out of his work as evaluator of one of Bruner's projects, an experimental fifth-grade social studies course. Jones builds upon psychodynamic principles and techniques for involving the child emotionally and imaginatively in subject matter. In sharp contrast to Bruner, motivation to learn is examined in terms of its affective base, and primary responsibility is placed not on the scholar but, rather, on the teacher. For it is only the teacher who is in a position to develop strategies which incorporate those spontaneous thoughts, feelings, and images generated by students in response to the films, texts, and other materials provided by scholars.

This fact became clear to Jones and the master teachers of the "new social studies" when they attempted to recapture lost opportunities for building upon the obvious emotional content of the vivid and authentic films of the Netsilik Eskimo. The teachers had initially focused exclusively on cognitive skills by having students draw analogies between Eskimo social organization and their own. But instructional materials alone did not help teachers or students come to terms with those feelings and images aroused in response to film sequences of the harshness of Arctic existence: men hunting and killing seals and eating raw and bloody meat; a naked male baby playing in an igloo, breast feeding, swallowing a fish eye, and so on. The students were also deeply impressed when they read that old people and female children are abandond to freeze on ice floes by the Netsilik when seal hunting goes badly. Students were asked such leading questions as: What do we do with our old people and with children that cannot be supported by their parents? But the full realization of the educational objective, "understanding of man as a species," required that the development of emotive and imaginative skills be kept apace with cognitive skills. Thus, the children were encouraged to express their emotions and relate their fantasies about violence and death through wide-ranging discussions and by composing stories, making drawings and collages, inventing myths, and creating interpretive dances, all as a means of mastering the subject matter. Jones's basic argument is that "the construction of knowledge, as distinct from the attainment of it, presumes freedom and skill in sharing and use of controlled emotion and imagery." (p. 26)

Jones views anxiety and creative thought as two poles of a continuum. Therefore, strategies are required to help children avoid anxiety by being less alone and less helpless with their imaginations. His primary concern is with learning rather than therapy; however, since human learning involves creative thought, reducing anxiety by increasing community and self-mastery of feelings and imagination became a pervasive objective in the lessons he and the master teachers evolved. Jones shows, through sensitive analyses of classroom interactions, that subject matter becomes relevant only when children make "the lessons their own, are aroused, excited, interested, original, inventive." In his estimation, Bruner slights the processes of invention while championing the processes of discovery. More broadly, Jones challenges the current emphasis on cognitive achievement when it is sought independently from a full understanding of that achievement. How to cultivate aroused imaginations (only the first step in creative learning) must be demonstrated in any comprehensive theory of instruction.

Now I have outlined Jones' critique and his positive recommendations because I believe he offers educators a bridge between affect and cognition, between invention and discovery. And by implication he shows how the drive for "excellence" in school innovations of the sixties may be made "relevant" in the seventies. But you will remember that Jones views art activities as primarily in the service of academic achievement, fantasy and feeling as a means to cognitive learning. What about the reverse? Surely we as art educators would be interested in how other subjects in the school can be taught so as to enhance the student's achievement in the arts. And we are interested in making our art program relevant to the concerns and emerging lifestyles of our students. We, more so than non-art teachers, must build on and skillfully work with the fantasies and feelings, the imaginations and emotions of our students in response to the materials we present and the activities we encourage.

III

I don't have the time to review the merits of those innovations associated with the label of affective education. I do want to mention them, however, because I think we can learn something from them, especially how to re-vitalize some of our own art activities. Outstanding is the project initiated in 1968 by Norman Newberg and Terry Borton in the Philadelphia Public Schools. Activities involving dramatic improvization, role-playing, self-expression, exploration of the senses, fantasizing, etc., are designed to make the student more conscious of his humanity—of who he is and what his needs and concerns are. Other projects include the Harvard Achievement Motivation Development, the San Diego-based Human Development Training Institute, and the Eastern Institute Project at Santa Barbara. All deal directly in various ways with the feelings, attitudes, and values of students.

In art education, the Pittsburgh Public Schools conduct an experimental fine arts program that does avoid the loosely organized activities and vague objectives of conventional art instruction. Selected staff-members from the schools and from Carnegie-Mellon University offer five hours of instruction per week over a five year period for intellectually able students (grades 8-12), beginning with multisensory experiences with the "raw material of art" (line, color, texture, pitch, intensity, movement, etc.) and advancing to an understanding of how the artist communicates his ideas and feelings in visual, aural, tactile, and kinetic form. The program, called *The Arts: Structure and Purpose,* emphasizes the interrelations of the arts by means of team teaching, a diversity of curriculum materials and teaching strategies, and a sequence of concepts which guide college-bound students from perceptual and aesthetic to cognitive activities.

In contrast, the relatively unstructured program offered in the Art Action Centers of Rochester, New York, located in six inner city schools and one parochial school, was established to help culturally deprived students who were finding difficulties in their academic work because of inadequate reading skills. Through flexible scheduling, students are encouraged to work during the school day with pottery wheels, kilns, and tools and equipment for weaving and sculpture. They make their own artistic decisions, working independently as much as possible. Apparently the reading levels of most students improve, some considerably. The idea behind the program is that the sense of accomplishment in non-verbal communication and expression will reduce frustrations and anti-social tendencies and enhance self-esteem. This outcome, it should be noted, is consistent with one of the findings of Coleman's report *Equality of Educational Opportunity;* namely, that students' self-concepts and attitudes are highly correlated with academic achievement.

Studio-oriented programs continue to dominate art education, but, increasingly, programs are appearing that cite as their objective the teaching of art appreciation. The model of the art student as appreciator and critic is supplementing the traditional model of student as creator and artist. A pilot program to test techniques for the direct teaching of visual awareness and the making of aesthetic judgments is being conducted with sixth-graders in the Public Schools of Newton, Massachusetts, under the direction of Al Hurwitz. The children work with specially made slide tapes, original works of art, and reproductions; there are trips to local studios, galleries, and museums; and discussion is the primary activity although some studio work is included. Stress is placed on the process of criticism and student progress is recorded by pre- and post tests incorporating Wilson's Aspective Instrument and Eisner's Art Information Inventory.

Despite the great diversity of the innovations I've described and the seemingly boundless range of ideas to which curriculum reformers have appealed, a common element stands out: the belief that "affect" is not so much a domain as a dimension of human experience, and more generally that affective and cognitive learnings are so inextricably tied together that the educational neglect of either will adversely modify or limit the development of the other.

IV

I would like to conclude my remarks by offering some guidelines for building an art curriculum for the seventies, a curriculum that would build upon those positive advances in the educational thought and practice of the sixties but that would also constitute a sensitive response to the explosive nature of those social and cultural conflicts now very much a part of our times.

First, it seems clear to me that we must make a major effort to understand the *characteristic* attitudes, feelings, values, and beliefs of the young—especially in the expressive forms they take in music, art, and social behavior. We must acknowledge their widespread indifference or outright hostility to traditional culture and what we call "fine" art, whether modern or contemporary. To "start where they are," it will be necessary to learn more about the "life-styles" of students through sociological research of our own and by means of a synthesis of findings of research already carried out.

Second, a knowledge of today's youth should not only be *reflected* in teaching strategies in the art room; the *discovery* of each individual's beliefs, attitudes, and feelings—including those of the teacher—should be a formal objective of art instruction. The teacher and students should talk about what they like and dislike, value and reject, in the realm of the arts and aesthetic experience in a free exchange. Art activities must be included not only to reveal aptitudes in art but also to reveal attitudes toward these very activities.

Third, the art curriculum should not be construed as a series of assigned tasks to be mastered, but rather as a means for suggesting potential problems for inquiry. In other words, any sequence of activities organized before instruction is to be viewed as open and hypothetical—subject to change as artistic and aesthetic inquiry proceeds. And the natural outcome of genuine artistic inquiry is creative art work; the outcome of aesthetic inquiry is knowledge about art and a finer perception, discrimination, and judgment of individual aesthetic experiences.

Finally, and most important, artistic activities and aesthetic concepts should be so related that the consummatory value of experience is emphasized. That is, experience should be valued for its own sake. Deeply felt experiences both of the creative process and the aesthetic response to art should be the overall objective of art education for the seventies. Only a truly aesthetic education, I believe, will bridge the gap between cognition and affect, connect the drive for excellence in the sixties with the demand for relevance in the seventies. Only an aesthetic education can restore the integrity of individual and social experience so out of balance today.

Humanism:

Capstone of an Educated Person

Stephen N. Stivers, L. Gerald Buchan,
C. Robert Dettloff, and Donald C. Orlich

For all society's attempts to utilize formal education to assist its members to become better people, that is, more acceptable to themselves and their fellow men, it is apparent that something has been omitted from the educational process. Student riots, the violent physical activities representing the anguish of the black people, political apathy, and the intolerable dominance of television over the leisure hours of man are but a few manifestations of this apparency of omission. What formal education must do is create within its process, by incorporating within its curricular activities, experiences particularly designed to assist in the linking of man's knowing the subject matter to relating with the actual, relevant ability to relate.

Philosophy, as a course of study, generally gives a history of western thought, for example. Concurrently, experiences must be given which not only assist students in the art of philosophizing but, more importantly, allow them to develop into *practicing* philosophers whereby their behavior reflects both the study of the subject and their ability to translate a means of thinking into a manner of acting. The ability to become a philosopher of account is possible for any human mind if given the opportunity to progress toward this end. Philosophy is used here as merely a point of illustration and in that context does not mean to preclude the viewing of all other subject matter in the same vein of pragmatic examination.

The problem, then, is one of adding to the curricular activities of the schools those experiences which will *utilize knowledge, be internalized by students, and become change agents of behavior for those participating.* Two such activities are Role Playing and Human Relations training. While these activities are acknowledged to be functions of knowledge

Stephen N. Stivers, L. Gerald Buchan, C. Robert Dettloff, and Donald C. Orlich, "Humanism: Capstone of an Educated Person," *The Clearing House,* May 1972, pp. 556–60.

utilization rather than subjects themselves, the thesis of this article is that such functions are as important as the subject matter. Implicit is that a pragmatic view of the learning of knowledge is the sensible approach to the meaningful utilization of knowledge. This meaningful utilization manifests itself in an improved ability of humans to relate with humans through the use of the educational process and an implied advantage toward constructing a better society.

In considering the advantages of including role playing experiences and involvement in human relations training in the formal educational activities of students, this article addresses itself to two questions:

(1) How can role playing activities and experience in human relations training be incorporated into the educational process as curricular activities?

(2) What are the benefits which will accrue to the students because of their involvement in role playing and human relations training with respect to their improved ability to interrelate with their fellow men?

ROLE PLAYING

In developing a method in which a student can translate his accrued knowledge into an actualized state, role playing becomes one form which the educator can utilize. Role playing not only utilizes the dimensions of thinking, but feeling and acting become important concepts as the student and teacher become involved in the learning process. The essence of role playing is generally understood as that of "making believe" that a situation is real or acting in a spontaneous manner. Traditionally formal education frequently utilizes the thinking dimension and students are not able to become actionally involved. This noninvolvement limits their potentiality and reduces the effectiveness of the teaching-learning process.

Knowledge acquired without a goal in mind is not meaningful learning. For decades knowledge has been dispensed by learned men and women, yet the acquisition and implementation of knowledge in a meaningful manner has seldom been accomplished. To build a better society, one where people can learn to relate to one another, make meaningful decisions, and learn to gain respect for human dignity, the previously mentioned dimensions of thinking, feeling, and acting must become an important part of the curriculum. The role playing model can successfully fill the "gap" in developing more meaningful interaction between students and teachers.

A child growing up in our society learns through the process of imitation and an insidious kind of process called developmental meta-morphosis, which is an ingesting of ideas, values, and actions, usually in a random manner. This approach has been successful with a segment of our society; however, with increased technology programmed efforts must be made to develop techniques and methodologies whereby more inter-action and relating between people will be evidenced. George Meade has expressed the idea that social intelligence is the ability of a person to take a role of another; it is our contention that in this computer age, developing functional social intelligence is a highly important task for all educators.

Curricular activities in school will obviously be placed in a more significant position when considering role playing experiences. Rather than considering the content of a book per se, it will be necessary for the teacher to relate the material in the book to human experiences dealing with people, developing decision-making skills rather than serving pri-marily as a purveyor of knowledge.

Social studies is an area which can utilize role playing; considering, for instance, history, economics, government, sociology and psychology. These particular subjects can become alive with the assistance of role playing techniques. The student who is able to take on the role of George Washington, Abraham Lincoln, Dr. Martin Luther King will begin to ex-perience greater empathy for others. The role playing process then be-comes the instructional means to educating students.

The question is asked, "How do you incorporate role playing into a subject area such as mathematics?" With an increased technology in this computer age only a small fraction of the population will be involved in advanced mathematics due to the increased use of machines and com-puters. Perhaps the populus will need to gain meaningful understanding of the history and development of mathematics, portraying the early mathematicians and how they derived formulas. Setting up situations with the assistance of unfinished scripts, one technique of role playing, teachers can assist students to assume the roles of famous mathematicians. In the field of economics the student can portray a character such as Malthus and his concept of the impact of an expanding population upon the world's economic climate. In sociology the student can take on the customs of a particular group of people, contrasting this with his own customs.

With each situation the student is then provided an opportunity to make decisions and derive values from role playing. These experiences become a part of the learning process versus having a teacher relate the information in lecture form. Role playing techniques as viewed in this paper utilize the concept of "discovery." This means that when situations are planned or spontaneously developed and regardless of the subject covered, the most efficacious manner to instruct is to leave the situations open-ended or unfinished. This allows the student to derive meaning from the experiences in his own way rather than how the "expert" teacher may view them.

The curriculum which utilizes role playing concepts in a consistent, systematic manner will evidence student growth in many ways. Two immediately apparent results will derive. First, increased verbal ability will be noted even among students that are considered shy and withdrawn. Second, increased decision-making ability will be evidenced, especially if the teacher indicates that there are not good or bad decisions per se, but recognizes that at the time that the student is engaged in decision making the process was based upon the best information available to the student at the time.

Role playing techniques should commence at the kindergarten level and must be a regular part of the curriculum. Teachers should utilize this particular activity several times daily or weekly, depending on the subject covered and appropriateness of the related activities.

HUMAN RELATIONS

Assuming our introductory statements as valid analysis, it seems apparent that school and society are paying dearly, and will doubtless pay more dearly, for their "learn from the past for use in the future" approach to education. As the demand for more years of education continues, students progressively experience less relationship between their education and their personal lives. They feel that they are in danger of becoming "thinking machines" or, perhaps more accurately, "think rejecting machines." Increasingly they are compelled to live for the future. A common mode of behavior becomes rebellion, whether it be active or passive. In our opinion the student movement toward drug and rebellion experiences are evidences of self-defeating and destructice attempts to gain a modicum of self-experience and self-direction in an immediate sense.

The emergence of T-Group, sensitivity training, and human relations training account for a hope that these conditions might be ameliorated. There is hope in this new movement because it offers means and methods of focusing on the "here and now." Very importantly, these methods are drugless, yet they will assist student in exploring their sensory, subjective world. Further, our position endorses the legitimate use of these techniques for positive building of self-concepts and unalterably opposes the "cultish," self-destructive quacks who have capitalized on insecure individuals.

Assuming that the reader has at least a passing acquaintance with the above groups, we will present what seems to be the benefits which might accrue to students and faculty as a result of using human relations training in schools. Broadly speaking, two major benefits would emerge:

(1) Establishment of an emphasis on interpersonal relationships as a function of formal education.

(2) Establishment of an emphasis on intrapersonal experience, or subjectivity, as a function of formal education.

These two benefits would comprise two goals which have been almost totally lacking in education.

In the area of interpersonal relationships, human relations training would very likely promote more effective communication between students and among students, faculty, and administration. Development of a "here and how" emphasis through interpersonal relationships and sensory awareness would make it possible for students to see school days as living, or alive, days. Relationships with peers and teachers would take on a present urgency and meaning. Subject matter would be dealt with not only in terms of future utilization, or for appreciation of the past, but it would also be responded to in terms of present needs, ideas, and feelings.

Further, students would be free to feel and think about how the subject matter is presented to them. There would likely emerge a trust between teacher and student, student and student, administration and student, because students would have been allowed to express freely their honest opinions about rules and regulations. Administration and faculty would better be able to hear what students are trying to say than they previously had; thus they would likely be more able to implement student ideas.

Through such training students would be able to become aware of themselves to a greater extent than they would have through typical educational means. They would likely use all their senses more fully than they would have without the training. They would probably be more creative and open to new experience, more experimental in their approach, more individual yet better able to cooperate. Once again, students would experience more aliveness.

Human relations training could be incorporated into the curriculum in a number of ways. But, in order for this to be accomplished, teachers and administrators should be provided in-service training in the technique and they should be provided experienced psychologists for consultation relative to psychological problems that might arise.

Art, music, English, and physical education classes could be expanded to include sensory awareness training. The "whole person" educational cliché could approximate a reality. Overdependence on vision, for example, could be dealt with by role playing a blind person. Students in art classes could become more fully aware of texture, form, and mass by blind role playing. Composition classes could assist in developing the senses by special exercises emphasizing concrete, present reality. Students could be helped to perceive more clearly and creatively by writing poetry and essays describing people and objects. Speech and English classes could assist communication in a more real sense by promoting T-Group techniques which will be described later. Music classes could involve much more intense listening experiences by using relaxation techniques and instruction, or exercises, on "tuning in." Perhaps less emphasis on technique and more on feeling would produce more "soul" in white music. Physical education classes could make use of yoga and promote more aliveness in the body using some of the intrapersonal touch techniques now being developed.

Psychology and sociology classes could well be devoted, or at least partially devoted, to the direct experience of understanding others and revealing self through group techniques. The concept of feedback is central here. Using feedback techniques, student A informs B how he "receives" student B. Other students in the group would be expected to share their perceptions along the same line. These experiences provide students with invaluable data relative to the effectiveness of their behavior. New behaviors may be tried if desired. Students in college have typically indicated that they learned more about others and themselves through these techniques than they did in formal class work. Student government, student clubs, and faculty-student committees could profitably incorporate T-Group techniques. Business and industry have been using these techniques for a number of years now.

Obviously only a few of the many possibilities for incorporating group techniques in schools have been identified here. We strongly encourage readers to explore these techniques by attending workshops, promoting in-service training in their school, and by reading the numerous books and articles currently available on the subject.

SUMMARY

The foregoing discussions of role playing and sensitivity training stress the vital importance which an educational system must place upon interhuman relationships. Equally of consequence to the discussions was the enhancement and expansion of the dimension of intrapersonal perceptions due to curricular activities involving these techniques. The dual consequences, then, are evidenced in a more healthy society which is so maintained by the ability of its members to relate to each other and the accompanying aspect of healthy individuals, capable of knowing themselves and acknowledging their value as individuals. A natural inference is that a healthy society will be populated by healthy individuals.

The meaningful utilization of subject matter is also considered. Subject matter, when utilized as suggested, remains not only a cardinal factor in the curriculum but also achieves its basic educational purpose, that of assisting in the behavioral changes which occur in the students. No longer is there a need for defending subject matter for its own sake, it would become an integral part of the educational process whereby experience and subject matter are allied to produce the desired results of a truly human society.

Role playing and human relations training are two vital means of producing activities which will make the educational process in the public schools more attuned with the social needs of society. These social needs appear to be of paramount importance at any time but most certainly in the present age. Role playing and human relations training appear to be those activities which will help the individual establish his positive self-image, enhance the general welfare of society by developing skills in interpersonal relationships, and make subject matter a meaningful part of the students' experiences by their ability to relate it to their needs.

Society could ask much less of an educational system and has. It is evident, however, that society must now enlist its educational system to help cure society's ills and to develop some preventive medicine for future use. It is in this manner that the educational system can then assume its proper function with respect to society.

7 / We Learn Through Experience and Experiencing

We learn through experience and experiencing, and no one teaches us anything.

If the environment permits it, anyone can learn what he chooses to learn; and if the individual permits it, the environment will teach him everything it has to teach. . . . It is highly possible that what is called talented behavior is simply a greater individual capacity for experiencing.

—Viola Spolin

Self-Science Education:
The Trumpet

Gerald Weinstein

It seems ironic that most, if not all, of our formal education is geared to processing those areas most distant from our everyday living experience while those areas closest to our daily experience—our relations with ourselves and others—are left to chance. We have been quite willing to train for scientific skills and attitudes toward the world "out there," while inner-world transactions tend to be ignored. Our educational institutions devote most of their efforts toward having learners think and respond more carefully and rationally to such areas as history, science, math, and so on, but rarely do they give that kind of attention to having learners acquire the skills, atttiudes, and explicit processes by which they might more carefully and effectively negotiate their self-to-self and self-to-other experiences.

> Lacking the necessary skills for seeking and processing information about themselves, is it any wonder that few of us can construct relatively clear and unambiguous accounts of our goals, aspirations, values, traits, and abilities? And in the absence of learned skills necessary to the understanding of interpersonal interaction, is it any wonder that many individuals are confused about their relations with others [Sechrest & Wallace 1967, p. 223]?

It is in response to this issue that a number of us at the University of Massachusetts are attempting to devise educational strategies and approaches that would help learners become their own self-scientists.

Science seeks to give us a more accurate and consistent picture of our reality. It is basically a systematic way of gaining knowledge. This systematic approach is usually referred to as the scientific method, and it involves such activities as careful observation, hypothesizing, further observation, experiments, and evaluations. If this is science, then what might self-science be?

Gerald Weinstein, "Self-Science Education: The Trumpet," *Personnel and Guidance Journal,* May 1973, pp. 600–606.

373

One characteristic of a scientific approach is the activity of creating hypotheses. Hypotheses are generalizations, explanations, or predictions. Throughout our everyday lives we are constantly creating hypotheses. We hypothesize about the weather ("I think it's going to rain"), about each other ("You don't like me, or you wouldn't be talking to me that way"), about ourselves ("I'm shy because I'm afraid of making a mistake"). One's self-concept is a cluster of hypotheses one has about oneself. A quality that makes scientific hypothesizing different from the everyday variety is that the former consciously concedes that the speculation *is* a speculation and therefore tentative. In addition, a person with a scientific perspective seeks to check out, or affirm more accurately, whether or not a particular hypothesis has a greater or lesser degree of congruence with reality.

In contrast, many of us operate as if the ideas, notions, or hypotheses we have about ourselves and others are established truths, and they therefore become the absolute maxims by which we conduct our lives. We may think, "I am a failure; nothing I do seems to turn out right" or "Whenever I start to feel close to someone, I know I'm going to get hurt, so I keep my distance." Those who hold such beliefs probably have never been very careful or deliberate in determining how much of each of those beliefs is fact and how much fiction. Since such beliefs are rarely regarded as hypotheses, as tentative, they remain unchecked.

Self-science education involves programs for training learners in those skills, concepts, and attitudes that will expand their self-knowledge concerning their own unique style for being in this world. We hypothesize that, by training learners to perceive more accurately their relation to themselves, others, and the world and to anticipate more accurately the phenomena of their personal experience, their intentionality, or power to choose their own ways of being, will be increased.

THE TRUMPET: HOW IT WORKS

Just as in any formal discipline, in self-science education there are clusters of appropriate tools, skills, and methodologies that the self-scientist acquires. We are just beginning to formulate and explicate those process tools with learners in a variety of classrooms in order to evaluate their potential for facilitating personal inquiry.

One such process tool we call the Trumpet (Weinstein & Fantani 1970). It is similar to stages in a problem solving sequence often described in educational literature. The Trumpet attempts to provide the self-scientist with a cognitive map or sequence in working through a set of personal observations (see Figure 1, p. 375). It does not provide

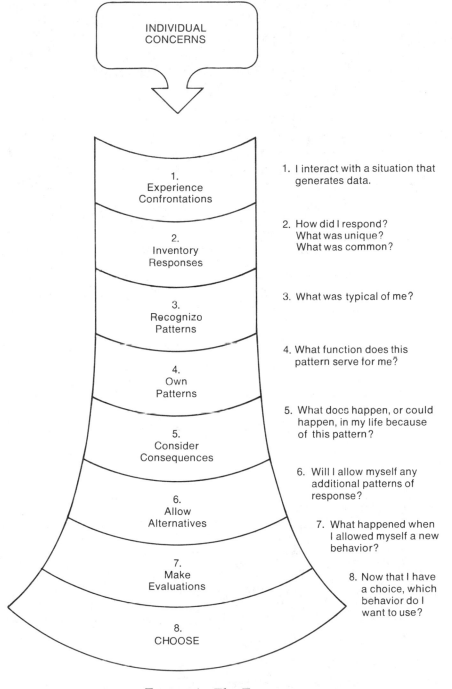

1. I interact with a situation that generates data.

2. How did I respond? What was unique? What was common?

3. What was typical of me?

4. What function does this pattern serve for me?

5. What does happen, or could happen, in my life because of this pattern?

6. Will I allow myself any additional patterns of response?

7. What happened when I allowed myself a new behavior?

8. Now that I have a choice, which behavior do I want to use?

FIGURE 1. *The Trumpet*

solutions but is an aid in setting direction for the inquiry. It systematizes introspection by providing models of the kinds of questions one might ask at each phase of personal exploration.

In our experimental self-science education classes, learners are taught the language and skills for proceeding through the Trumpet—pattern clarification, self-inventory, pattern function, and so forth. A variety of personal situations and themes of the learners are then processed. We usually move from relatively simple concerns such as "Why I rarely volunteer" to more complex issues such as "Why I feel so distrustful of others." In other cases we focus on the student's responses to selected, preplanned exercises as the major content for processing. (For an example of how the Trumpet is used in a 16-week college course entitled "Education of the Self," see Weinstein 1971.)

To illustrate the Trumpet process, following is a counseling situation with a sample set of responses. The process begins after the student has had a confrontation. In this sample, C is the counselor and S is student.

Inventory Responses

S: The teacher called on me today in class to explain something we had for homework.
C (*Inventorying*): What happened?
S: I got so nervous I could hardly answer.
C (*Inventorying feelings*): What were your feelings like?
S: I was scared as hell.
C (*Inventorying body feelings*): Where in your body were you feeling the fear?
S: In my throat; it got so tight it was hard for me to talk. My hands were trembling and sweaty.
C (*Inventorying actions*): What did you do?
S: I mumbled a few words, stopped, then stammered a few more. Nothing made sense.
C (*Inventorying actions*): Where were your eyes looking?
S: First I looked at the teacher for a second or two, then the rest of the time I stared down at the floor.
C (*Inventorying thoughts*): Do you remember what sentences you were saying to yourself at the time?
S: I was thinking about what a fool I was making out of myself in front of everybody in the class, that I was going to say something so dumb everyone would laugh, and how I wished I were someplace else.

Recognize Patterns

C: Has this ever happened to you before?
S: I'll say.

C: In what kinds of situations?

S: Whenever I have to say something in front of a group of people.

C: Is it only in school that this happens?

S: No. Sometimes at home, when we have a lot of company, I kind of stay in the background and hope that nobody asks me anything.

C: If you wanted to teach me your pattern of responding to situations like this, what kind of directions would you give me?

S: Well, first of all, I'd tell you to start imagining things the night before the day you might be called on.

C: What kinds of things?

S: Oh, imagine the teacher calls on you and you say something so stupid the whole class breaks up and starts whispering to each other about how stupid you are. Then imagine the teacher putting you down for giving such a dumb answer and then giving you a lousy mark.

C: What else would I have to do?

S: Do just what I did. When you get called on, get nervous as anything. Mumble, look down, and finally give up and don't say anything.

Own Patterns

C: Can you tell me any way that your pattern helps you? What might it help you avoid or get? Try finishing this sentence: "By reacting this way in those situations, I avoid—"

S: Well, I guess I avoid giving the wrong answers.

C: How is avoiding giving the answers useful to you?

S: If I don't give the answers, I can't make a mistake.

C: And if you can't make a mistake?

S: Then I won't do anything stupid.

C: So you use the pattern to protect you from feeling dumb?

S: Yeah, I guess so.

C: Do you feel less stupid when you use the pattern?

S: No. In fact, I think I feel more stupid.

C: So your pattern isn't too effective in helping you get what you want?

S: I guess not.

C: What do you want?

S: To feel smarter. To not feel so darn scared anytime I have to say something in front of people.

Allow Alternatives

C: Would you be willing to try some experiments with yourself to see if you can find anything that works a little better for you?

S: Maybe. What kinds of experiments?

At this point the counselor and the student would brainstorm a set of possible alternative ways to negotiate these feelings and responses. One set of possibilities might involve getting some reverse sentences, such as: "Whenever I'm about to speak before a group, before speaking I will tell myself, 'I am smart, even if I make a mistake,' or 'Even if they laugh at me, I'm still a very worthwhile person,' or 'I will no longer give you the power to make me feel stupid.'" Other alternatives might include: "If I don't know an answer to a question, I will say, 'I don't know the answer,' and I will say it with confidence, or each time I have an opportunity to say something before a group, I will practice making at least one contribution, such as telling whose opinion I agree with."

After a list of alternative experiments is compiled by the counselor and the student, the student decides which alternative to experiment with for the next two weeks or so. As they are carried out, the experiments are reported to the counselor at mutually arranged times, and they are then evaluated and/or revised.

The example given is highly condensed and simplified. Since every individual will be at a different comfort and skill level of self-disclosure, this level will affect the ease and depth with which the sequence will proceed.

IMPLICATIONS OF THE TRUMPET

If the Trumpet process were to be used solely for helping someone solve a specific problem or concern, the entire thrust and basic assumptions of self-science education would be lost. (Self-science education is oriented primarily toward developmental and constructive skills rather than symptom removal.) Thus the key training strategy is to have the learners become their own processors. In order to achieve this they must learn the skills and cognitive maps that until now have been solely in the possession of the professional helper. In this case learners would be trained to use the Trumpet processing skills and procedures on their own.

In operational terms, a training sequence might have the following phases:

1. Someone with experience and expertise would help a learner through the Trumpet process, as in the example given.
2. The Trumpet and processing guide would be explicitly taught to the learner.
3. The learner would then be trained to help another person through the Trumpet process.

4. Under supervision, peer co-counseling pairs would continue with further training in processing.

While most of the Trumpet processing in our own work has been with individual concerns, it is possible for the same procedures to be applied to many different social units, such as couples, families, staffs, and even total communities. When used in this fashion, the dyad, group, or institutional members examine their own patterns of communication, styles of problem solving, and typical methods of completing a task. Such patterns could then be taken through the group using the remaining Trumpet steps. Hopefully, the outcome is learners (individuals, groups, and communities) capable of facilitating the expansion of each other's self-knowledge as well as their own, which is the ultimate goal of self-science education.

REFERENCES

SECHREST, I., & WALLACE, J. *Psychology and human problems.* Columbus, Ohio: Charles E. Merrill, 1967.

WEINSTEIN, G. The Trumpet: A guide to humanistic curriculum. *Theory into Practice,* 1971, *10,* 196–203.

WEINSTEIN, G., & FANTANI, M. *Toward humanistic education.* New York: Praeger, 1970.

TRUMPET PROCESSING GUIDE

Following are some processing ideas (in addition to the ones found in the article) for each phase of the sequence.

Confrontation and Inventorying Responses

1. What happened? What did you do? What specific actions did you take?
2. What were you paying most attention to?
3. At which points in the situation did you feel most comfortable? Most uncomfortable?
4. Can you describe any of the feelings you had?
5. Where in your body were the feelings being experienced?
6. What sentences were you saying to yourself? What was your internal monologue or dialogue?
7. Can you write down, as if it were a script, what some of the different voices in your head were saying?
8. How many of the sentences involved "shoulds" or "shouldn'ts"? What were they?
9. If you felt like doing something else, what stopped you or allowed you to do it?
10. Were you affected by the responses of others? How?
11. How were your responses to the situation the same as or different from others' in the situation?

Recognizing and Clarifying Patterns

1. How is your response typical of you?
2. In what kinds of situations do you usually respond that way? (When, where, under what conditions?)
3. If you were going to train someone to respond as you do in those situations, what would you train them to do? Be as detailed as possible.
4. Can you remember the first time you responded this way? Describe the situation as if it were happening right now.
5. What response would be the exact opposite of yours? Describe it in detail.
6. Fill in the following blanks in regard to your pattern: Whenever I'm in a situation where _____, I usually experience feelings of _____. I tell myself _____, and what I do is _____.

Owning Pattern by Clarifying Function

1. Imagine that your pattern is a servant you hired. What is that servant supposed to do for you? Can you write a job description?

2. Put your pattern in an empty chair opposite you. Now get into that chair and become your pattern talking to you. Begin your statements like this: "(Your name), if it weren't for me . . ." (Let the pattern brag about how useful it is to you.)

3. What does your pattern get for you?

4. What does it help you avoid? From what and how does it protect you?

5. Suppose you wanted to sell your pattern to others. Make up a powerful advertisement that would make others want it.

Considering Consequences

1. Is your pattern getting you what you want?

2. Where is it falling down on the job?

3. Are there some effects your pattern is having that you don't particularly like?

4. What price are you paying for your pattern?

5. What part of your pattern annoys you?

6. Suppose you could never do anything different with your response. What might happen?

7. Are you missing out on anything by responding this way? What?

8. What precautions would you give somebody who was going to use your pattern?

Allowing Alternatives

Imagine that you have discovered the "perfect solution" and have found a way to respond that doesn't cost you as much as your original pattern. Picture yourself with this new response pattern (a) in your classroom, (b) at home, and (c) at a social occasion. (Use any appropriate situation.)

Answer the following questions for each of the above situations:

1. What are some of the specific new behaviors you would be exhibiting?

2. What differences in you would those who know you best be most likely to notice? What would they say? How would you respond?

3. What new feelings would you have about yourself?

4. How would these feelings affect your appearance? Would you walk, talk, look different? How?

Brainstorm all the possible experiments that might serve to get you started in the direction you want to go. Pick one or two that seem to be achievable. For each one answer the following questions:

1. What within you will attempt to sabotage your experience?

2. What within you will allow you to try the experiment?

After deciding on some strategies, outline the specific actions you will take. What are they? In what situations are they to be tried? With whom? How often? How can you reward yourself for your efforts? Let at least one other person know of your experimental design, and decide how and when you will report your progress to that person.

Making Evaluations

1. What happened with your experiments?

2. What were some of the thoughts, feelings, and action consequences that resulted?

3. Did your strategy seem adequate, or does it need some revision?

4. If what you tried was given a fair trial and didn't seem satisfactory, what else might you try from your list of alternatives?

Choosing

After running these experiments wtih yourself, what decision are you ready to make about your original pattern and alternative "try on" behaviors? A person who had successfully internalized the Trumpet process would be adept at filling in the blanks of the following passage for most intrapersonal or interpersonal situations: Whenever I _____ (confrontation), I anticipate that _____ (thought), so I usually _____ (feelings, behaviors, typical reaction). I react that way in order to get and/or avoid _____ (function), but in the process _____ (consequences, price paid). So what I would really prefer is _____ (ideal, end state). The last time I found myself in that situation I tried _____, _____, and _____ (experiments). I liked what happened when I tried _____ (specific experiment), so from now on I am going to _____ (choice).

Human Development
in the Classroom

Uvaldo H. Palomares and Terri Rubini

"Elephant," declared a curly-haired six-year-old.

"Elephant," repeated his teacher after a pause. "Would you like to tell us something about it?"

"It has a long nose and it's big." David smiled toothlessly as he stood up and stretched his arms wide apart to illustrate.

His teacher nodded. "Yes, it *is* big. Thank you for telling us about your word, David."

As he returned to his seat, Lisa wiggled impatiently. "I have a word —hot wheels! It goes fast and makes a big noise. RRRRmmmm." Several of her classmates repeated the "RRRRmmmm," and the teacher praised her for contributing to the group.

In this first grade classroom, eight children and their teacher were seated in a circle, telling words that they knew and explaining something that they knew about the words. They were working on a "mastery in language" task in this session of their daily Magic Circle. After the circle session, the school counselor, who was observing, spoke supportively to the teacher, reinforcing the communication skill the teacher had used when she asked an open ended question to help David describe his word. As a consultant to the teacher, the counselor continued his encouragement of the active listening skills the teacher had learned during the training session the counselor had led at the beginning of the school year. "David beamed when you repeated part of his description. I could see that he was not only showing you and his classmates his power, but also himself. You really supported his feeling."

Later in the same day the counselor demonstrated a circle session to a fourth grade teacher who had asked for help on a problem. This teacher had begun using the magic circle with his class and was having difficulty

Uvaldo H. Palomares and Terri Rubini, "Human Development in the Classroom," *Personnel and Guidance Journal*, May 1973, pp. 653–57.

383

with some disruptive behavior. He began a unit on "awareness," and the class was discussing pleasant and unpleasant feelings. During a discussion of bad feelings, some of the children began acting out in the circle. The teacher remembered that he had learned in the training session that an atmosphere of acceptance should prevail in the circle, so he was hesitant to discipline those who were misbehaving. Before beginning the demonstration, the counselor explained to the teacher that the feeling is always accepted but that disruptive behavior is not condoned.

During the circle session, with the counselor as facilitator, the children talked about something that made them feel bad. One of the boys told about how someone had made him angry during recess. A classmate had taken his baseball and thrown it on the roof. The boy still felt very bad, so he tried to kick the girl sitting next to him in the circle. The counselor stopped him and said, "I can see that you are angry, and I can understand that, but you may not kick Diane." The counselor modeled acceptance of the child's feelings while discouraging the hostile behavior.

Both of the above situations are examples of the Human Development Program implemented in a public school with the school counselor acting as a teacher trainer and consultant. The magic circle is the process by which the teacher and students explore their thoughts, feelings, and behaviors on a daily basis. The teacher is trained to act as the group facilitator, making sure that every child is invited to share and is listened to. The teacher introduces the task as suggested in the lesson guide and models active listening and positive behaviors. In time the teacher will turn the leadership over to the students so that they will also be given practice in positive behavior patterns. Because these behaviors are repeated on a daily basis and the tasks are sequential in nature, the child develops positive patterns of behavior. As a curricular approach to preventive mental health, the Human Development Program focuses on a developmental model to promote social and emotional growth in children. It teaches little people to get in touch with themselves so that they can become more responsible for their choices and their actions.

The counselor's role in training, critiquing, coaching, and follow-up in the Human Development Program is further discussed later in this article. Although this article stresses elementary classroom uses, the same concepts have validity for older students and adults.

AWARENESS, MASTERY, AND SOCIAL INTERACTION

The Human Development Program focuses on three main themes: (a) awareness (knowing our feelings, thoughts, and actions); (b) mastery (self-confidence); and (c) social interaction (knowing other people). As children grow older, they begin to bury their feelings and thoughts, unconsciously distorting their expressions and actions. They start to feel that they are different, inferior, socially unacceptable. This feeling of negative uniqueness has been created in our society by a conspiracy of silence. Nobody talks about fantasies, dreams, wild thoughts, feelings of helplessness, loneliness, feelings of worthlessness. Children are educated away from validating their own feelings. When they are afraid, they are told that there is nothing to be afraid of. When they feel pain, they are told to be brave and smile. They conclude at an early age that what is going on inside of them is unique, suspect, and unsayable.

In the magic circle, children are given an opportunity to develop an awareness of their positive *and negative* feelings, positive *and negative* thoughts, and constructive *and destructive* behaviors. They discuss the discrimination between real and fantasy, their ambivalence and fears, and the issues involved in making commitments, all of which help to dispel the delusion of uniqueness. For instance, a kindergarten student ran home from school, bubbling with excitement over that day's circle session. "Guess what, Mom? Lanny's afraid of the dark; Kathy's afraid of the dark; and Paul's afraid of the dark too! I'm not so silly after all!" This child had learned that his classmates were very much like him. Awareness topics such as "I had a very scary dream," "One way I wish I could be different," or "Something I wish for that is impossible" help children realize that actually we are much more like each other than we are different from each other.

Schools haven't capitalized on the sense of mastery—the motivation that put human beings on the moon. Mastery is what motivates a child to balance himself on a railroad track when it is easier to walk along the side. It is the reason people jeopardize their lives to climb a mountain. It feels so good to say, "I did that, and it was hard." Mastery activities are designed to enhance children's feelings about themselves and their control of their environment. In a preschool mastery circle, children can feel their power when they do the task "I can relax," making their bodies limp like a rag doll's, and their teacher recognizes it: "You can really relax."

Another factor that has been built into the concept of mastery in the Human Development Program is that of responsible competence, or developing capabilities with a deep sense of responsibility to one's fellowman. Self-confidence and competence are not enough in themselves. Adolf Hitler was a very competent man, but at other people's expense. Responsible competence deals with the value of all human beings. We all can be winners by bettering ourselves while respecting the lives of others: I build a paper mill, but I don't dump all my waste products in the river. In the magic circle, each child can talk about "Something I can do well" or "A promise that I made and kept." There need not be losers for all to be winners.

In the social interaction topics of the Human Development Program, we help children understand the element of causality in human relationships. "Something that I can do can make you feel good or bad." "Something that you can do can make me feel good or bad." In the magic circle, children explore their effects on others. They can have a harmful effect on people as well as a caring effect on them. They can learn how to be winners with other people by seeing that what works is being nice. "Nice" is a vacuous word to adults, but it means something important to children. When asked what they want to see in a friend, children generally answer, "I want a friend who is nice to me." The circle gives children an opportunity to share their worth and to learn how to become winners with others.

In general, the Human Development Program helps children learn to be better listeners. They become more involved with each other and their teacher. Group cohesiveness is strengthened. Their motivation to learn increases as they experience successes. There is less absenteeism, and there are fewer discipline problems. They learn to verbalize their thoughts and feelings and to understand their behaviors. They learn the dynamics of interpersonal relationships. In the circle, children who have undesirable behaviors or exhibit some abnormality will talk about it. Problems that already exist will come to the surface, thus enabling earlier referrals to be made by the teacher and preventing more severe problems in later years. Teachers also learn to evaluate changes in teaching procedures and classroom techniques.

APPLICATIONS OF THE PROGRAM

The Human Development Program has been adapted to all levels of education. It has also been used by social workers, mental health personnel, governmental agencies, and correctional institutions. There is a set of materials that helps the teacher or other group leader implement the program (Bessell 1970, 1969–72; Bessell & Palomares 1971; Palomares 1971, 1972), but *the most important factor in the success of the program is the process by which the group leader manages the magic circle,* and this is often difficult to learn. It requires training, practice, support, and guidance. Once learned, however, this set of skills, processes, and procedures can provide a new and significant role for school counselors and psychologists.

Although many teachers have been provided with special training in the Human Development Program, we have found that success cannot be completely guaranteed unless supportive and guiding personnel give continuing reassurance and follow-up. The counselor, as an expert in human development, not only can serve as a teacher trainer but also can assure supportive guidance in the use of the program. Even more important, counselors can help teachers get in touch with their own personal dynamics by continually reminding them that they *can* lead circle sessions because they care about their students. Further, by developing inservice programs for teachers in these positive techniques, the counselor can reduce the amount of energy spent in remediation.

To date, most school counselors touch the lives of only a very small percentage of the student body. The counselor's position is often the first to go when the budget gets tight and monies are cut back, because the counseling program is not operating on a wide scope of influence. Aside from test administration, scheduling, and vocational guidance, counselors concentrate most of their time on remediation. Only those students referred by their teachers as severe problems are being reached. Students avoid seeing counselors because they view counselors as the disciplinarians. Too often when students display disruptive behavior in the classroom, they are sent to the counselor.

Counselors can widen their scope of influence and take on a more dynamic role if they begin to shift their emphasis to preventive guidance, teaching social-emotional curriculums to students in groups and acting as consultants to teachers in developmental programs such as the Human Development Program. They can increase communication between students and teachers by supplying new communication skills that can be used daily within the classroom. The counselor's role, then, takes on a new significance: that of the liaison person serving at the heart of the communication system in affective education.

REFERENCES

BESSELL, H. *Methods in human development: Theory manual.* El Cajon, Calif.: Human Development Training Institute, 1970.

BESSELL, H. *Human Development Program: Activity guides—Levels B I, II, III, IV.* El Cajon, Calif.: Human Development Training Institute, 1969–1972.

BESSELL, H., & PALOMARES, U. *Human Development Program for institutionalized teenagers.* El Cajon, Calif.: Human Development Training Institute, 1971.

PALOMARES, U. A place to come from. In J. Ballard (Ed.), *Dare to care/dare to act: Racism and education.* Washington, D.C.: Association for Supervision and Curriculum Development, 1971. Pp. 11–17.

PALOMARES, U. Communication begins with attitude. In the Joint Committee on Educational Goals and Evaluation (Ed.), *Education for the people.* Sacramento, Calif.: California State Education Department, 1972. Pp. 36–38.

Value Clarification

Sidney Simon and Sara Massey

Have you ever been on an archaeology expedition?

Learning about one's self is very similar to an archaeology "dig." An archaeologist finds a clue which leads him to suspect something interesting exists in an area. He focuses his attention on the covered area and begins the uncovering process in his search for the treasure.

The initial digging which removes large amounts of superficial rocks and dirt may be rough and crude. Yet as the archaeologist feels the nearness of the desired objects, the uncovering process becomes one of removing tiny trowels of dirt and a gentle brushing, in the care not to damage the anticipated treasure. This may be a long ongoing process which is not easily abandoned because of the hoped-for reward. To gain knowledge about one's self is like that.

A person gets a clue of himself that is enticing, and he begins the uncovering process. Once under way he begins to use many processes and techniques. One helpful tool he may use is the process of value clarification. The process of value clarification allows him to learn about himself and what he values. It does not give him values; rather, it permits the discovery of his own values.

The basic questions that he will ask to arrive at his values revolve around the following areas:

1. *Prizing:* What do I prize and cherish? What am I willing to affirm publicly?

2. *Choosing:* What alternatives do I have? What are the consequences of the alternatives? Am I free to choose?

3. *Acting:* Do I act on my beliefs? Do I act with a pattern, a consistency, a repetition?

Sidney Simon and Sara Massey, "Value Clarification," *Educational Leadership,* May 1973, pp. 738–39.

For information about current values clarification materials or a series of nation-wide training workshops, contact Values Associates, Box 43, Amherst, Mass. 01002.

There are numerous strategies that can be used in the process of valuing.[1] Each strategy, though, is designed to clarify responses to the aforementioned questions. A person does not really have a value if these questions cannot be answered positively regarding a specific behavior or belief.

One helpful strategy that can be used is called "Are you someone who . . . ?" Each question is answered yes, no, or maybe.

A	B	C	Are you someone who:
			1. Likes to break the curve on an exam?
			2. Likes to stay up all night when friends visit?
			3. Will stop the car to look at a sunset?
			4. Puts things off?
			5. Will publicly show affection for another person?
			6. Will do it yourself when you feel something needs doing?
			7. Will order a new dish in a restaurant?
			8. Could accept your own sexual impotence?
			9. Could be satisfied without a college degree?
			10. Could be part of a mercy killing?
			11. Is afraid alone in the dark in a strange place?
			12. Is willing to participate in a T-group?
			13. Eats when you are worried?
			14. Can receive a gift easily?
			15. Would steal apples from an orchard?
			16. Is apt to judge someone by his or her appearance?
			17. Would let your child drink or smoke pot?
			18. Watches television soap operas?
			19. Could kill in self-defense?
			20. Needs to be alone?

Another thing we have often done with the list of "Are you someone who . . ." is to set up vertical columns, A, B, and C. After someone codes the list for himself, we ask that person to fold back his answers and give

[1] Sidney Simon, Leland Howe, and Howard Kirschenbaum. *Value Clarification: A Handbook of Practical Strategies for Teachers and Students.* New York: Hart Publishing Company, Inc., 1972.

the sheet to someone who knows him pretty well. That person fills in column B, trying to guess at the answers the first person made. Column C could be used for a third person to guess. Then, they could do this for each other and finally sit and talk about the messages we send and how these are received by others. Some students have learned a great deal about openness, about congruency, about self-concept from sharing in this way.

This strategy allows a person to consider more thoughtfully what he values, what he wants of life, and what type of person he is.

The 20 items are only some of the hundreds of possibilities. Students can brainstorm 20 sets of 20, quite easily, and they are fun. Set up trios and get the students to dream up a list. Give them a chance to try their list out on another trio and vice versa. Eventually, get a master list dittoed for students to try out on other groups in the school. (Your class could start a whole school thinking about value clarification.)

This exercise can be followed by "I am someone who . . ." sentences.

I am someone who:

1. Blushes at a compliment.

2. Talks loudly when nervous.

3. Has faced death.

4. Enjoys intimacy with another person.

There are other variations on the strategy too. A student who is in love could make up a list of "I care deeply for someone who is . . ." and give it to the person he or she loves. Or it could be, "I am looking for someone who is. . . ." Or at a later date, a list of, "I am not looking for someone who is. . . ." Other creative variations will occur to the teacher who begins to see the spinoffs from this simple strategy. We might even ask, "Are you someone who will try it with your students?"

The search for self, the "Who am I?" of life as a conscious act, is a continual ongoing process. As a person works and plays, this self-adventure becomes a touchstone for living. From knowing one's self, behaviors, patterns, etc., a new confidence, an internal security, a sense of potency emerge which are life-giving. Too often in our lives we search outside ourselves for meaning and become preoccupied with assigning blame and trying to change others. A life of meaning lies within each of us by discovering and cultivating what we are right now. Know what you prize and cherish and act on it as you live fully each day of your life.

Depth Unfoldment Experience

Herbert A. Otto

Depth unfoldment experience is a new small-group technique for helping people to break down interpersonal estrangement in order to facilitate communication and participation. It is also a method designed to help people "get to know each other." More than an "ice-breaker" or superficial "get-acquainted" device, the DUE Method gives participants an opportunity to share emotionally significant experiences and incidents with the group—thus establishing "open" communication between group members at the earliest possible time. This DUE Method was first tried in a laboratory group of the Human Potentialities Research Project at the University of Utah in the fall of 1964.

This research project represents a small-group approach to discovering and utilizing the human potential and has been in existence at the University of Utah since 1960. An underlying hypothesis of this research is that the average "healthy" human being is functioning at a fraction of his potential. A number of contemporary behavioral scientists in the United States (Gardner Murphy,[1] Abraham Maslow,[2] Erich Fromm,[3] Carl Rogers,[4] Margaret Mead,[5] among others) subscribe to this hypothesis. Work in the area of human potentialities at the University of Utah is essentially in the nature of pilot research projects and focuses on the development of theory and methods designed to help non-patient populations to function more optimally. This research with healthy or normal groups has been described in details elsewhere.[6, 7, 8, 9]

PERSONAL POTENTIAL

Much of the human potentialities research has been conducted within the framework of a University of Utah course entitled Adult Edu-

Herbert A. Otto, "Depth Unfoldment Experience: A Method for Creating Interpersonal Closeness," *Adult Education*, Winter 1967, pp. 78–84.

391

cation 31, "Developing Your Personal Potential," which is offered every quarter by the Division of Continuing Education. The non-credit course is open to anyone who wishes to enroll and is described in the catalog of the Division of Continuing Education as follows: "This program is designed to help to discover capacities, strengths, talents, and abilities which you have but which you may not be aware of or using fully. Emphasis is on discovering your potentialities and developing them, leading to more vital, creative, satisfying living and productivity." The class meets for two hours once a week throughout the quarter, for an average of ten sessions. (Beginning in the fall of 1966, this class was offered in Los Angeles by the University of California Extension Division.)

It has been our observation (and this was supported by an analysis of tape recordings) that prior to the use of the Depth Unfoldment Experience, hereafter referred to as the DUE Method, groups had spent between five and six meetings "getting acquainted" and attaining that level of interpersonal closeness which enabled them to communicate with the minimum intrusion of "social masks." Formerly it was only after the fifth or sixth meeting that most group members really began to be involved with each other. This meant that *a significant portion of the group life was spent essentially on the "get acquainted process" in an effort to achieve interpersonal closeness*. During this period both the level of communication and class participation was affected. Therefore, it became important to develop a method which would help people get to know each other intimately and closely in a relatively short space of time.

PURPOSES AND AIMS

The purposes and aims of the DUE method are as follows:

1. To foster interpersonal involvement of group members on an emotional level and to create an atmosphere distinguished by the sharing of self leading to interpersonal closeness early in the group life.
2. To provide a means of helping people who are strangers in a group to "get acquainted" within a relatively short space of time.
3. To facilitate meaningful communication between group members and to maximize frank and "open" communications and participation in class activities as early as possible.
4. To provide group members with an experience which can develop increased self understanding and self awareness.
5. Through the sharing of emotionally significant experiences and

incidents to offer participants an opportunity for empathy and sensitive understanding of fellow group members.

PROCEDURES

The DUE method utilizes a three-minute egg timer of the hourglass variety (obtainable in most variety stores). Each person has six minutes for the process of sharing of himself. Five of the six minutes are to be devoted to sharing with the group key experiences and key incidents beginning early in childhood which the person believes have been deeply formative in relation to the development of his personality. Usually the following or similar words are used in this connection: "We want each person to share those important experiences throughout his lifetime—beginning early in childhood—which he considers to be of importance in the sense of leaving a strong impression on his personality. In other words, we want you to share with us those experiences you consider formative—that you believe have exerted a strong influence in the growth of your personality. We do *not* want you to share only chronology such as dates and places, but we *do* want you to share incidents and experiences you consider important in your life—beginning early in childhood and bringing us up to date. *Now we want you to take five minutes sharing with us these important experiences in your life which you believe have a lot to do with the person you are now.* The last minute of your six minutes we want you to tell us *what you consider the happiest moment in your life.*"

It is pointed out that the person in charge will begin the process by sharing of himself for the first six minutes. Then a coin will be flipped; if it lands "heads," the egg timer will be passed to the person on the right who will be next. If "tails" comes up, the one next in line for the DUE experience will be the person sitting on the left of the person in charge. At this time it is also made clear to the group *that if a person does not use up his full six minutes, the class is expected to ask personal questions of him in an effort to get to know him better.* This is done until the full six minutes are used up.

THE LEADER'S SHARING

We have found that *the leader's way of sharing himself sets the tone and establishes the depth of the experience.* If the person in charge remains on a superficial level and does not share deeply of himself, the subsequent self-presentations by members will be superficial. The deeper the level of sharing by the person in charge when he begins the process, the deeper, as a rule, will be the sharing of self by group members. Usually it is best when the person in charge can share one or two incidents in early childhood, one or two in later childhood and adolescence, and another one or two in later life. However, this has to be "played by ear"; and the quality of the sharing (the level of emotional giving which is in a measure the re-living of the experience) is more important than the total number of incidents communicated. The group leader should, however, strive to retain some semblance of chronology by using connective summary sentences between incidents so that group members will get a general overview of how his life developed.

Repeated use of the method by a number of group leaders has revealed a tendency on their part to search out new meaningful experiences to share with the group. If group leaders repeat experiences which have been shared with a previous group, the affective involvement in most instances continues to be strong and vital despite the element of repetition.

EMOTIONAL INVOLVEMENT

It is important to limit the DUE process to about six or seven persons at one session. We have found that the emotional involvement of participants around this experience is so strong that after the seventh person has shared himself the group usually displays symptoms of fatigue. "I am all wrung out—you really get in there with them," and "you feel so much—it wears you out," are remarks commonly heard. The person in charge usually interrupts the process after the sixth or seventh person has presented himself to ask if the class wishes to go on or finish the process during the first part of the next group meeting.

TIMING

Participants in the experience who are sharing of themselves during their six-minute period usually become so involved that they forget to turn over the egg timer at the end of three minutes. The person in charge through motions and gestures can usually indicate to the individual sitting next to the person making the self-presentation to turn over the egg timer. When approximately one minute remains, it is well for the person in charge to interrupt gently: "You have about one minute left to share the happiest moment in your life." If a person does not use up his full six minutes and the group members do not address any questions to him, the group leader should take considerable initiative by asking personal questions in an effort to help the group get to know the presenting person better. (The types of questions to be asked suggest themselves by the nature of the self-presentation and often involve gaps in the presentation or things left out or unclear.) In addition, *the group leader should vigorously encourage the group to ask questions*—"Now is the time to ask some personal questions of Mary in our effort to get to know her better. We have about two and a half minutes for this." Again, this process has to be "played by ear" as it is sometimes best to exceed the six minute time limit if the interaction is especially vital and meaningful. Use of the method appears to be especially effective if name tags are affixed prior to the DUE experience and if the class can agree on using first names on name tags.

VERBAL, NON-VERBAL SUPPORT

Occasionally, members have burst into tears when sharing an especially meaningful incident. At such times it has been our experience that the non-verbal as well as the verbal support which the class brings to bear has very quickly helped to re-establish the person's equilibrium. In only one instance in the course of two years has it been necessary to postpone a self-presentation until the next meeting. In this instance, a middle-aged professional woman began to share some of her deep feelings of grief surrounding a particular incident with her father which occurred during her adolescence. As she told about this incident, she began to weep, was shaken by deep sobs, and seemed to have difficulty in regaining her composure. It was then that the person in charge suggested she finish her presentation at the next meeting.

The effect of this incident on the group was to create a greater feeling of "we-ness" or closeness. Several group members remarked that "It took a lot of courage to share this with all of us." Subsequent self-presentations seemed to be on a deeper level. It has been our observation that the use of the DUE method fosters increased freedom in communication between class members and also seems to trigger "affinity relationships." For example, there have been many instances of class members at a later point in the life of the group making comments such as the following: "When Mary told all these things about herself, I felt I really understood her as I had had a similar experience. I talked to her afterwards about this, and we are now good friends."

EFFORT COUNTS

We have also noticed that although some class members are able to share only superficial aspects of themselves, *effort counts;* and that if the group feels the person is *really trying* to share himself, this appears to have considerable impact. The content of the experience shared often seems to be less important to the group than the feeling tone or emotional investment which accompanies the sharing of an experience. Generally, the more sensitive and responsive the group, the more sensitive and searching the questions addressed to the person who does not use up his full six minutes.

Immediately following the DUE Method we now use an "empathy-building technique" which further facilitates communication and deepens relationships. The following instructions are given: "We will now have a touch experience which is also an exercise in strengthening the will. We ask you to hold the hands of the neighbor on each side of you so that everyone in the group will be holding hands forming a circle. We then want you to close your eyes. Do not talk, and have loving thoughts and loving feelings about everyone in the group and have loving thoughts and loving feelings about yourself. We ask you to do this for five minutes. I will call out the time." The instructions are then repeated slowly to initiate the experience.

The person in charge enters into the experience, and at the end of five minutes the comment is made, "Now what is your reaction to this experience?" Although the technique seems deceptively simple, responses by participants indicate a high level of involvement and deepening of relationships. This empathy-building technique with its attendant discussion furnishes an excellent closure for the DUE Method.

FINDINGS

In spring, 1964, a study was conducted by Neva Wise [10] under the direction of the writer. Tape recordings of six classes covering a two-year period from 1964 through March, 1966, were analyzed. It was found that Depth Unfoldment Experiences related by class members could be classified into thirteen categories ranging from Experiences with School and Education to Experiences with Family in Early Childhood, and with Nature and Beauty. The eighty-six enrollees from the six classes shared a total of 398 Depth Experiences. Of this number, the largest number of Depth Experiences fell into the category of Experiences with Family (21%). This category included experiences of class members with parents, siblings, grandparents, aunts, uncles, cousins, and their own children, as well as experiences of close or distant family relationships. The next largest number of Depth Experiences (15% of the total) were in relation to School and Education. Included here were both positive and negative experiences about school from elementary school through graduate school and experiences with dropping out of school. Depth Experiences from these two categories accounted for 36 per cent of all experiences shared. The third largest category (8%) was Experiences with Nature and Beauty, including those with out-of-doors, nature, and beauty and with sports and pets. The categories of Moving and Travel, Work, Marriage, Illness, and Early Childhood accounted for another thirty-five per cent with each accounting for seven per cent of the total.

COMPARISON

A comparison of the Depth Experiences shared by males and females showed no significant differences in the number of experiences shared. Males shared an average of 4.84 Depth Experiences, and females 4.78. Men and women showed a slight difference in their distribution of shared experiences. Both sexes had their largest clusterings in the categories Family and Experiences with Schools, which accounted for 46 per cent of the total male experiences and 32 per cent of the female experiences.

SUMMARY OF STATEMENTS

Analysis of the tape recordings revealed that aside from Depth Experiences, so-called *summary statements* could be distinguished. Summary statements are defined as "statements of fact describing a happening in the life of the individual which is devoid of emotional involvement, usually only one or two sentences in length and a part of the chronological information." Class members in the six groups shared a total of 366 summary statements as contrasted with 398 Depth Experiences. There was no significant difference in the number and ratio of summary statements to Depth Experiences shared by men and women.

There were seven different categories of experiences for the Happiest Moment. The category of child birth was the one most frequently shared. Twenty-five class members (30%) shared an experience in this category. Achievement and success were shared by fourteen participants (17%), and eleven class members (13%) shared in the category of marriage. Travel and recovery from illness accounted for twenty-one per cent of the total number of happiest moments shared. Women cited child birth as their happiest moment (30%), whereas men most often chose achievement and success (24%). There appear to be two reasons for the large number of experiences in the category of child birth: (1) the total sample was composed of a considerably larger number of women (58) than men (25), and (2) the leader almost always chose the birth of his first child as his happiest moment. Typical comments were: "It really works fast." "It does put you under pressure, but we really know each other now," and "I know everyone and feel much freer to talk."

CONCLUSIONS

The following conclusions emerged from a study of the use of the DUE method over a period of two years:

A. Communication and class discussion are greatly facilitated by use of the method. Members feel freer to talk with each other, and communication in depth is facilitated.

B. Participation in class activities, assignments, etc., is facilitated through use of the method. Class members appear to become more involved in the class and develop a higher level of commitment to aims, goals, and purposes of the course.

C. Use of the method encourages formation of friendship ties and affinity relationships early in the group life. These relationships in most instances persist over and beyond the duration of the class.

D. The quality of the initial sharing by the leader influences and determines the quality of the Depth Experiences shared by members. The experiences shared by the leader seem to exert some influence on the choice of the happiest moments but do not influence the content of the Depth Experiences.

In summary, the method has been used in adult education classes as well as educational and training programs. The DUE Method is effective in breaking down the barriers of estrangement and isolation among class members, facilitating communication as well as increased involvement and participation in the class.

FOOTNOTES

1. Gardner Murphy, *Human Potentialities.* New York: Basic Books, Inc., 1961.
2. Abraham H. Maslow, *Motivation and Personality.* New York: Harper & Bros., 1954.
3. Erich Fromm, *Man for Himself.* New York: Holt, Rinehart, and Winston, 1960.
4. Carl R. Rogers, *On Becoming a Person.* Boston: Houghton Mifflin Co., 1961.
5. Margaret Mead, "Culture and Personality Development: Human Capacities." *Explorations in Human Potentialities,* Springfield, Illinois: Charles C. Thomas, Publisher, Fall, 1966.

6. Herbert A. Otto, "The Personal and Family Resource Development Programs —A Preliminary Report." *International Journal of Social Psychiatry,* 1962, 8, No. 3, pp. 185–195.

7. Herbert A. Otto, and Kenneth A. Griffiths, "A New Approach to Developing the Student's Strengths." *Social Casework,* 1963, 45, No. 3, pp. 119–124.

8. Herbert A. Otto, "Personal and Family Strength Research and Spontaneity Training." *Group Psychotherapy Journal,* 1964, 17, No. 2–3, pp. 143–149.

9. Herbert A. Otto, "The Personal and Family Strength Research Projects—Some Implications for the Therapist." *Mental Hygiene,* 1964, 48, No. 3, pp. 439–450.

10. Neva Rae Wise, "Human Potentiality Groups, University of Utah, 1966." Unpublished master's thesis, Graduate School of Social Work, University of Utah, 1966.

How to Help Students Learn to Think . . . About Themselves

Merrill Harmin and Sidney B. Simon

Everyone is for thinking, but not much of it goes on inside our schools. Or outside of schools, for that matter. Life for most of us is essentially mindless. We buy what advertisers tell us we need. We give the power of government to smooth-talking personalities. We handle our family conflicts with the savvy of a spoiled child. And we kill people unfortunate enough to be outside our tribe with the empathy of a rock. Mindless. A thinking man would have difficulty defending any of it.

Is the remedy to teach children how to think? That would certainly help, if it were successful. But it might not be enough. For even a thinking man can use his mind for purposes irrelevant to human dignity. Witness the scheming slum landlord, the poison gas scientist, the creative advertising writer, and the successful businessman with the miserable life. We would want students not only to learn how to think, but to learn how to think about life itself, especially themselves.

This article elaborates what we mean by that and how we suggest it might be managed in the classroom. Clearly, we believe that the most critical and the most relevant thinking that must be taught is thinking about life decisions and about personal values. In a sense we want students to learn how to become self-scientists, to use Gerald Weinstein's term. We want students to learn how to look more searchingly and deliberately at themselves and the people around them, to discern why they do what they do, how they might do things differently, and what is to be done about it all. The classroom activities discussed below are concerned with those goals. They are based on a theory discussed in *Values and Teaching,** a book we co-authored with Louis E. Raths.

* Columbus, Ohio: Charles E. Merrill Books, 1966.

Merrill Harmin and Sidney B. Simon, "How to Help Students Learn to Think . . . About Themselves," *The High School Journal,* March 1972, pp. 256–64.

Activity 1. *I Urge Telegrams*

We ask our students to think of someone in their real lives to whom they need to send an "I Urge Telegram." Such a telegram must be sent to a real person, preferably a significant other in their lives. They might ask the person to change something, to start doing something, or to quit doing something. These are heavy telegrams. The telegrams come out like this:

"This is going to a good friend of mine, T. K. 'I urge you to get your head together and see that life won't get sweeter if you keep numbing it with alcohol.' Signed your pal, Joe Sanders."

"I'm sending mine to my mother. 'I urge you to take it easy. You work to hard.' Signed your #2 son."

"To my sister. 'I urge you to quit getting me in trouble with your lies and fake crying.' Your brother, Bill.'

We ask our students to send at least six "I Urge Telegrams" over a period of several months. Each gets put into a folder after an opportunity to share telegrams with other classmates. After the sixth "I Urge Telegram" has been "sent," they are all taken out of the folder and spread across the student's desk to be examined. This is a "self-scientist" at work on fascinating data. He might ask himself: How important are these issues in my real life? Is there a pattern to my telegrams? What have I done lately to try to solve any problem indicated? Who can help me? When?

Activity 2. *I Learned Sentences*

With the telegrams spread out on the desks, we make use of another strategy which gets students thinking about their own lives and the direction those lives are taking.

Each student is asked to examine the data and to come up with several complete sentences beginning with such phrases as these:

I learned that I . . .

I re-learned that I . . .

I was pleased to see that I . . .

I was disappointed to notice that I . . .

I see that I need to . . .

I'm aware that it's o.k. for me to . . .

Teachers will note that these "I learned's" always contain the pronoun "I" in them. These "learnings" are not about the standard subject matter of the school. They are "I learned's" about the "self," and thus become part of the inquiry into what makes us tick.

There is no right answer to an "I learned . . ." statement. The wise teacher plays the very model of Carl Rogers and accepts, accepts. (The wise teacher also makes his own "I learneds.")

Here are some examples of "I learned" statements made after study of one's own "I Urge Telegrams":

"I learned that I have one telegram I really, really must send tonight."

"I learned that I have done something about all of my telegrams and I feel pretty good about that."

"I see that I need to face this friend of mine. I've sent him three telegrams, but none of them face to face."

Activity 3. *Weekly Reaction Sheet*

A systematic, weekly inventory of one's responses is a most useful technique for getting students to continue to play self-anthropologists.

The teacher prepares six identical ditto sheets for each student. The students are asked to complete one every week for six weeks. Included are such questions as these. (The reader would do well to ponder how he or she would answer each of these questions.)

1. What was the high point of the week for you?
2. With whom were you in emphatic agreement or disagreement this week?
3. Did you make any plans for some future happening? (Make any dates, or order any tickets, invite anyone to join you, etc.?)
4. What did you procrastinate about this week?
5. In what ways could the week have been better?
6. With whom do you have any unfinished business this week?
7. Open comment on the week.

Students can share what they have written in small groups. (We quickly establish semi-permanent support groups in classes and students learn to turn to these groups for assistance in processing the data generated by these values-clarifying strategies.)

Activity 4. *Thought-Feeling Sheets*

At regular intervals often right in the middle of the class, the teacher asks students to get out a piece of paper. On one side they write the word, THOUGHTS and on the other the word, FEELINGS. In the few minutes given, each student tries to get in touch with the thoughts running through his head and the feelings beating in his guts and writes samples of each on his sheet.

Students learn, after a while, how to monitor what is going on inside of them. This then becomes another tool for the self-scientist to use as he investigates what responses he has to the world swirling around him.

Thought-Feeling sheets are read aloud by volunteers, and everyone is urged to keep them in self journals or folders. For the teacher, thought-feeling sheets are a way to sample quickly the mood of the class and, for students, it is a way to know what is going on inside others.

Activity 5. *Here and Now Wheels*

We are indebted to Gerald Weinstein of the University of Massachusetts for introducing us to this strategy.

Students are asked to draw a large wheel with four spokes. In each section, they are asked to capture what they are experiencing, immediately, right in the here and now, at the instant the assignment is given. Then the students are asked to expand one of their words by two sentences. This takes them deeper into one idea and helps them push ahead in the process of finding out what is going on as they live their lives.

The wheels are then timed and dated and filed for future reference.

Here and Now Wheel

I am eager to find out if she thinks like me.
Eager to just talk with Len, actually.

Perhaps twice a week for the first few weeks of the semester, the teacher asks for a Here and Now Wheel. The students are urged not to censor, but to capture just what they are experiencing, in the here and now.   After a while, students don't need the mechanical device of the wheel.   They are becoming scientists who can monitor, almost instantly, what is going on within that complex laboratory of their selves.

Activity 6. *Twenty Things You Love To Do*

One of the most tender and most moving of the strategies we recommend involves making a list of what you love to do in life.   The students are asked to number from 1 to 20 on a piece of paper.   Then they are requested to list any 20 things they truly love to do in life.   Any 20 at all.   These lists are not to be shared, so one can list just what one loves to do, regardless of what it might be.   In any order.   Just as fast as one can think of them.

The room gets very quiet.   Thinking goes on as it never does during examination time.   People are looking into their own lives and pondering what they love to do with that life.

After everyone has listed 20 things, we ask students to code their lists in various ways:

1. Put a $ sign next to every item which requires an expenditure of at least $3 every time you do it.
2. Write A or P indicating whether you prefer to do each item *alone* or with *people*.
3. Put an R next to every item which has an element of *risk* to it. It can be physical risk or emotional risk or intellectual risk.
4. Place the number 5 next to any item which probably won't be on your list 5 years from now.
5. Use an * to show which items are your favorites.
6. Think of someone you love.   Place an X in front of every item which you would hope would appear on his list, if he made a list of the 20 things he loves to do.
7. Date each item to indicate when you did it last.

The teacher will think of other interesting codes.   This list can be done several times during the semester.   And after each time, ask the students to say aloud some "I learned that I . . ." statements.   Get them to write more of these "I learneds" into their journals.

If our aim is to have our students think about their lives as self-scientists, what better way than to look at what is in the great banquet of things we love to do.   It is at the core of what we value.

Activity 7. *Rank Orders*

Rank orders help a student think through his priorities. They put values into conflict with other values. Rank orders thus promote a thinking skill which every child needs to develop. Look at these few examples:

The teacher says, "Imagine your mother coming out on Thanksgiving morning and saying, 'We have these three options for Thanksgiving. Which is your first, second and third choice?' "

———"No traditional Thanksgiving. We'll just send out for a Pizza and that will be it."

———"I'm tired of cooking. I don't even want to eat. Look, here's $10 for each of you. Go to a nice restaurant and movie and just let me alone."

———"The whole family is to eat the giant Turkey with trimmings in 12½ minutes and then rush in to watch a football game, leaving Mom to clean up the congealed gravy."

A rank order generates lively discussion. We recommend the use of small groups and the chance to talk about this choice with people who disagree with you. It is guaranteed to make for a spirited class.

Here is another rank order. Which of these three jobs would be the dullest for you? Say the three in order of undesirability; worst first.

———To be a toll collector at a toll bridge or toll highway.

———To be a pickle inspector at a pickle bottling factory.

———To be a wiper at a car wash.

Students can be asked to think of a fourth, fifth and sixth job which would be pretty bad for them. When the teacher gets three new items, he has a new rank order.

Here is a rank order our students generated once from the toll collector rank order:

Which of these three jobs would you feel would be most *unfulfilling?*

———To be an airline pilot who flies only between Philadelphia and Rochester, New York.

———To go around from door to door trying to collect money from people who have not made their insurance or rent payments.

———To be a psychiatrist whose patients are all rich, old women who are bored with life.

The skill developed by rank ordering is useful in our lives in many ways. It is useful, in fact, whenever one has to make a choice and the alternatives confuse us or paralyze us. As we learn to rank alternatives in terms of our values and needs, we learn to deal with life.

Activity 8. *Value Sheets*

Here we make use of a duplicated sheet. No teacher-time is necessary on this one other than to prepare the sheet. The student picks up one of these, and there are hundreds of variations of them, takes it to his desk or home, and finishes it in his own rhythm and in his own way. We think the exercise speaks for itself.

HAPPY OR NOT

"Pat, are you a good person?"

"Yes, I guess I am. I try to be good to others. Most people probably would consider me a good person."

"I know you have a family and friends, Pat, and a decent income. Have you the basic things you want from life?"

"Hmm. I suppose so. At least there is nothing substantial that I really feel I need."

"Tell me then, Pat, how come you're not happy?"

1. Play with that dialogue a bit. Pretend that you are Pat. Write a response you might make to that last question.

2. Are *you* a good person?

3. Have you the basic things you want from life?

4. Are you happy? Why or why not?

When all the students have done the "Happy or Not" sheet, it would be very useful to have large group time on "I learneds . . ." As we teach this process of thinking, we need to provide lots of opportunities for students to check out their thinking with the thinking of others in the class, always supported by a teacher who views himself as a facilitator in the Carl Rogers model.

One last and very simple activity.

Activity 9. *Small Group Discussion Issues*

As stated earlier, we make abundant use of small group discussions. We like to form a class into trios or quartets and give groups a brief time to share thinking on a provocative topic. The small size allows everyone to get his two cents in.   Often we rotate group members to in-crease diversity of ideas and appreciation of new persons.

Here are a few topics which we found useful for small group dis-cussions:

1. Share a series of *highpoints* in your life.   What was the highpoint of Christmas at your house?   What was the highpoint of your 6th grade year in elementary school?   What was the highpoint of your learning how to dance?   What was the highpoint of the first time you fell in love? etc.

2. What are some of the things you believe in with all of your might?

3. What are some things you hate to do?

4. When have you come closest to death?

5. Where do you stand on population control?

6. Who are your heroes?

7. When do you cry in movies?

8. Would you provide your own children with sex education?

9. How do you resist keeping up with the Joneses?

*   *   *

Our point has probably been made.   We believe that students need to learn to think and especially need to learn to think about themselves. The preceding examples provide just one set of means toward that end. See *Values and Teaching* for many other examples in the same style.   Used now and again, a little at a time, these activities generate their own evi-dence of success.

The classroom climate is, of course, a critical factor in opening up students' minds to this kind of thinking.   That climate must be kindly, and as supportive of revelations of personal confusions as of strengths and suc-cesses.   Occasionally the teacher will have to be firm in limiting discussions that are moving toward potential hurt for someone, but experienced teach-ers have always done this.   Risk is certainly higher in such teaching, but so is excitement and growth.

Our commitment to these ideas runs deep.   We see students more and more ready to turn away from intelligence and from education, con-vinced that neither has served mankind very well.   So long as we have students doing their thinking about non-human issues, or about real issues in an abstract, this-doesn't-involve-me fashion, we invite the growth of this anti-intellectualism.

We are alarmed about a society which has lost its way.   We see students in deep pain, and we see them turning to drugs or to drag racing on the local streets to drown out unhappiness in frenzied and desperate attempts to find meaning for themselves, or escape. The schools cannot stand by and conduct business as usual. Just listen sometime to a group of students sending "I Urge Telegrams." The experience argues forceably against the way we now kill time in our schools. Our students need to learn to think. There is no better way than to get them to begin to look at their own lives. We could paraphrase Socrates and say, "The school which doesn't help its students examine their lives isn't worth going to."

Sociodrama in the Classroom—
A Different Approach to Learning

T. J. Michels and Nolan C. Hatcher

Imagine that you are a visitor in a classroom where pupils are discussing the problems of cheating in schools. The instructor stops the discussion and initiates a unique classroom drama with the students playing the following roles: the teacher, the student caught cheating, the accessory student, the "tattle-tale" student, the principal, and the mother of the cheating student. After about three minutes of dramatic action, the students are asked to swap roles with one another and other students in the class are inserted into the spontaneously improvised playlet. There are no scripts and no rehearsals. Before a logical conclusion is reached, the instructor rings down the imaginary curtain and asks the class for its reaction to the emotional involvement that has just been experienced. This is sociodrama.

Sociodrama is becoming more appropriate in our schools today, because recently there appears to be a significant movement of youth who are posing basic challenges to existing values and traditional approaches to learning. These young people appear to be attempting to create new life styles in order to preserve their individual identities. In addition, there are increasing demands for all persons to participate more actively in social, cultural, and political programs designed to improve the quality of American life.

Traditional methods of classroom learning are felt by today's youth to be out of step with their real world. The present-day student does not accept many of the past routine learning methods. Social scientists have been telling us for years that this is the case; and yet, until recently educators have persisted in ignoring the changes in youth and have held to the lock-step, rote learning approach by which they were taught. We are addressing this paper to those educators who are willing to try new and different methods to replace the time-worn teaching methods being re-

T. J. Michels and Nolan C. Hatcher, "Sociodrama in the Classroom—A Different Approach to Learning," *The High School Journal,* January 1972, 151–56.

jected by youth. It is the thesis of this paper that sociodrama can fill an important role and serve the useful purpose of helping to solve current educational problems and promote educational objectives.

Sociodrama, the teaching method we are espousing, is a technique whereby situations are acted out by a group. Its purpose is to give a clearer picture of a problem by living the situation. The situation can then be analyzed on the basis of a common experience. Thus, in a sociodrama, the students act the parts of the characters in the problem situation. J. L. Moreno, in his book, *International Handbook of Group Psychotherapy,* states that the exploratory value of sociodrama is only half of its contribution. The second, and even more important part is that a sociodrama can change attitudes as well as provide the vehicle for studying them.

Sociodrama permits the presentation and analysis of situations outside their natural settings and allows the creative meaning of the situations to be investigated. In doing so, it is action oriented instead of being purely verbal or cognitive. Further, it encourages the spontaneous learning process to occur in the here-and-now of the life context of the classroom.

Both sociodrama and psychodrama were developed by J. L. Moreno in the 1930's, but until very recently were applied as techniques in psychotherapy only. Both have been tried recently by far-sighted educators; however, the sociodrama appears to be less threatening to teachers and appears to be more flexible and adaptable to the classroom situation. (Students, on the other hand, have warmly accepted both innovations.) Inasmuch as sociodrama appears to have the greater appeal and broader application to educators, our focus will be on this mode of facilitating learning.

At the outset, we stress the point that no great amount of training or special skills are required of teachers to incorporate sociodrama as a learning method. As a case in point, these writers have learned this approach and incorporated it in their work solely from their own inservice, trial-and-error efforts. Of course, the theoretical concepts were learned in the context of psychotherapy. In the process of learning to use sociodrama in classroom teaching, we have concluded that the theoretical rationale is not a prerequisite for successful adaptation of sociodrama to teaching, and that any teacher who will invest a brief period of time and has the courage to give it a try will find his class taking on a new aura of excitement. For the teacher, the experience will be most rewarding.

TECHNIQUE AND APPLICATION

There appear to be three basic prerequisites to the successful use of sociodrama in the classroom: 1) the class should have a cooperative group feeling, being concerned about the accurate portrayal and understanding of the issue at hand; 2) the students who participate should have some knowledge of the situation and the person they are to represent (knowledge and feel); and 3) the sociodrama should be used as a supplementary technique rather than as an end in itself.

Basically, a sociodrama is an interpersonal situation coupled with role playing. From the role-playing context, sociodrama depends for its success on spontaneity, with no rehearsals, no scripts, and no props. This application of role playing is one in which an individual assumes an identity in a specific moment when he reacts to a specific situation involving other people and their interaction. An example for a class that is studying a unit on the coming of the atomic age might be: The class is given the instructions, "Suppose you are Dr. Robert Oppenheimer, working in a laboratory beneath a football stadium in Chicago, and you are nearing a scientific break-through. You know that you are about to deliver to the world some awesome power never before known to man. What are the thoughts in the minds of yourself and your colleagues?"

Having presented the situation and locale to the class, and with no further instructions, a student is designated to be Dr. Oppenheimer and others his colleagues. They are brought to the front of the class and told to interject their own reactions and values as they assume their designated roles. The teacher's role here would be, perhaps, to inject controversial ideas or issues that may have been actual in the past or have some current application.

An alternative example for a class studying a unit on race relations would be as follows: The students will have previously been assigned specific readings on the subject, and the teacher introduces the sociodrama by illustrating a situation with the following words: "You are a white homeowner in a middle-class suburban community composed of whites only. Your neighbor on the west side is ultraconservative and outspoken in his belief and value judgments (most of his conversation is about conserving racial segregation). The house just to the east of yours has recently been purchased by a middle-class Negro family with whom you have become quite friendly. You are also a friend of your conservative neighbor on the west. The locale for the sociodrama could be your backyard, where you and your white neighbor are having a friendly chat. Your Negro neighbor strolls up and joints the conversation." The teacher of the class, having set the stage, designates the characters and has them carry on with the spontaneous enactment. This example of sociodrama gives the teacher an excellent opportunity to try role reversals and, also to involve a great many students taking the three basic roles involved.

Role reversal, in this case, is done in the following manner: The student in the Negro role is asked to assume that of the white segregationist and vice versa. Students are then asked to continue the discussions as if there had been no interruption and to inject their own, newly reversed feelings.

As the sociodrama continues, other members of the class may be encouraged to go up and stand behind the key characters and whisper their own thoughts and ideas for incorporation into the dialogue.

A key value of the sociodrama is the follow-up or ensuing discussion at its conclusion. The teacher may introduce the discussion period with such open-ended questions as, "What were your feelings or reactions to this situation and to the characters as the drama developed?" or "What key points have you thought of that were apparently overlooked in this drama?"

As may be seen from the above examples, the topics for use in sociodrama are limitless, and may be on the subject of any aspect of social, vocational, and educational problems. Some additional suggestions would be: 1) social skills (rehearsal for a first date, sexual expectations, or boy-girl etiquette); 2) applying for a job; 3) parent-student argument; 4) student-teacher situations; 5) intercultural situations; and 6) actual classroom lessons.

CONDUCTING A SOCIODRAMA

1) *Selection of the Situation.* The situation should be as simple as possible and should involve personalities. The issues should be those that arise from human desires, beliefs, hopes, anxieties and aspirations or problems that occur because people do not understand each other's points of view. These writers have discovered that the sociodrama works best when there are between four and eight persons taking part. The teacher, in planning the sociodrama, should identify approximately three basic roles to be taken. At the same time, he should remain open to the emergence of other roles which may enter the situation as it moves through the drama. Some of the most interesting, thought-provoking outcomes arise from the emergence of spontaneous roles initiated by the students themselves.

2) *Choosing Participants.* When first trying out sociodrama, the teacher should select students who are fairly well informed on the issue to be presented and who are imaginative and articulate. In the early sociodramas, let the shy and retiring persons take minor roles. As the teacher and the class become more proficient and accepting of the technique, effort should be made to bring out the shy types by letting them play the major roles. It is often

surprising to note the depth of feeling and ability of such students when they are placed in the more aggressive, assertive roles. Dramatics training is not necessary and may even be found to be detrimental because sociodrama draws upon the individual's own resources. It is helpful to know the background of students so that they can be placed in situations that will most benefit them. For instance, if the problem is one of prejudice, those with marked prejudice could unobtrusively be cast in roles to demonstrate the issues. Inasmuch as the sociodrama is an excellent vehicle for revealing personalities, this technique may have an additional bonus effect for the teacher in that it will help him to know his students better.

3) *Setting the Stage.* There are a variety of approaches to this component of sociodrama. We have found that breaking the class into small groups (four or five in each) and allowing each group to plan the scene serves to involve more individual participation. Having allowed the groups five to ten minutes for private discussions, the teacher calls on one of the groups to perform its sociodrama. An alternative approach is to select the roles and allow these students to leave the room and briefly talk through their method of presentation.

4) *Preparing the Audience.* Each class member should observe the sociodrama as if each one were an active participant. Each member of the audience should be encouraged to ask himself, "Is this the way one would feel in real life?" The teacher should emphasize that in sociodrama no finished product is to be expected.

5) *Acting Out the Situation.* The teacher's role is a blend between being the director and a member of the audience. He should remind students of their roles, if they slip out, and, if the sociodrama appears at a stand-still or impasse, he can either add to or cut short the situation. He should keep emphasizing the students' freedom of expression and allow for an appropriate mixture of reality and creativity. After the drama has developed for about five minutes, the teacher could do a role reversal or substitute new roles or place different students in current roles. These writers have found that their most insightful sociodramas last from five to twenty minutes. When a sociodrama appears to drag, an interesting technique is for the teacher to ask the cast to reenact the scenes as if they occurred at a different place or point in time. For example, the teacher could shift time backward and have a current sociopolitical sociodrama enacted as if Hitler were just ascending to power.

6) *Follow-up*. The sociodrama should be interrupted or stopped prior to a logical conclusion. The teacher thus should find that the class is quite eager for comment. The focus should be on how the class members felt toward the situation and the roles being depicted, why they acted as they did, and what new ideas could have been incorporated with different actors. Many times the teacher and students will feel new knowledge is needed; this tends to stimulate further research before reenactment of the situation. Finally, the participants should be requested to report on how they felt in their respective roles.

The teacher should assure the class that no one is expected to do a perfect job of acting. He should express pleasant surprise at how well the students succeeded in the task. Sociodrama can, in this manner, be a very effective learning device providing both the teacher and the students with an exciting opportunity for joint creative learning experiences.

REFERENCE

MORENO, J. L. (Ed.) The International Handbook of Group Psychotherapy. New York: Philosophical Library Inc., 1966.

Developing Sexual Awareness:
A Humanistic Approach

Donald A. Read

Within the last few years there has been considerable controversy concerning sensitivity training, especially as it relates to education. But with the need for greater student involvement and understanding has come a shift from the traditional substantive content and skills to affective learning.

By whatever term one wishes to use, however, sensitivity training holds tremendous potential for improving education by creating an environment in which both student and teacher become agents in learning-with boundaries amebically changing, rebuilding, disappearing, reawakening. It implies teacher as student, student as teacher, group as leaders, searching and sharing together. In short, it implies that education is much more than the frenzied acquisition of knowledge for knowledge sake.

IMPLICATIONS FOR SEX EDUCATION

Traditionally, it seems that sex education has followed this knowledge for knowledge sake approach. That is, it has been approached from a point or points outside of the individual. Beginning with labels in an anatomical illustration, the instructor moves from anatomy to the fertilization process, conception, pregnancy, birth, child development, the American social-sexual system, and then for added depth and/or stimulation to a history of sexual mores in our culture and others. My approach differs from that conceptualized plane, horizontal chronology in that I use a vertical, dimensional paradigm. In this, the first focus is upon each student and where he finds himself emotionally in his stage of sexual development and awareness. Instead of first defining terms and "relevant" words, the students attempt to define themselves as sexual persons, their

Donald A. Read, "Developing Sexual Awareness: A Humanistic Approach," *The Journal of School Health*, June 1972, pp. 330–33.

415

values, sexual roles, parental, peer, and self-expectations. In my classes, motivation at once begins to be the responsibility of the individual and comes from within, rather than being external. You will notice that the individual-in-a-society and the students' involvement as experiencing human beings come first. This seems logical in sex education. The students themselves as sexual beings are partially the results of their biology, but are handled first, in a reverse chronology. This approach differs from the chronology of biological facts to conception, etc. *Effects first, causes later*.

It would seem that such a personal subject as sex and sexuality should never become an unemotional human experience. (Rollo May calls attention to this need for emotion and feeling in his book *Love and Will*.) [1] The teacher's as well as the learners' feelings should become an integral part of the learning experience—to be aired, to be shared, within the context of a mutually trusting relationship.

Humanistic education, which is "the integration of cognitive learning with affective learning," [2] lends itself beautifully to this sharing process because it advocates an integration of the intellectual atmosphere with feelings in the learning environment. It is the process of people getting together as people to share their feelings, however emotionally charged or resistant they may be.

APPLYING HUMANISTIC TECHNIQUES TO HUMAN SEXUALITY

It should be made clear that the techniques that are described below are not meant to be taken as "the method." Unlike curriculum guides, they depend on a wide range of factors, foremost of which is the level of real human feelings that are present within one's own teaching-learning situation. In short, don't take a "traditional" class and expect them to respond to this humanistic approach overnight.

An important ingredient in the humanistic approach to teaching is trust and confidence. This trust has three directions. They are: (1) that each student trust himself—what he feels, what he values, how he acts and responds in various situations. In short, that he not feel constrained or threatened by self or others; (2) that each person develop this same degree of trust in others that he has in himself; and (3) that the teacher share in this trusting—that he trusts and is trusted. [3]

It goes without saying that when someone feels unable to express his own true feelings about certain issues that may be raised, then the goal of self discovery is blocked to some degree. This is because there is a considerable amount of "risk taking" which becomes an integral part of the class. It is quite different, for example, for a student to say "I personally feel that the research available does not prove that homosexuality is a sickness" and "*I* am a homosexual, and *I* do not think that I am sick."

Basically, trust is an internal feeling. To say "I trust you and feel I can be my true self with you" comes from within. But there are certain external factors that can help in accomplishing a sense of trust within the group. For example, a blind walk to build up a sense of trust on a "one-to-one" basis can achieve a certain degree of trust. One student is blindfolded and another takes him on a walk—around the room, outside, feeling, sensing—without any verbal messages. This takes about a half hour. When they are done and have had a chance to share feelings, they switch blindfolds. Upon everyone's return, we again form our circle and share our various reactions to the experience.

Another trust exercise is to have the group do a levitation. One person lies on the floor (either on his back or on his stomach) and a group of six or more people lift him into the air very slowly all the time rocking him to-and-fro. Once the group senses that the person is relaxed (trusting of them) they slowly let him down to the floor again. After a brief moment, there is a sharing of feelings.

On a verbal level, students are asked to lie on their backs in a circle, with arms interlocked, and share their sexual fantasies one at a time within the confines of a dark room. It is a threatening situation for some, but they generally get into the sharing mood quickly. The experience generally is able to show most of those who are threatened that their sexual fantasies (however bizarre) are often shared and accepted by others.

TECHNIQUES

I begin my class by developing "support groups" which are usually made up of six people—three males and three females.

These groups are self-selecting. That is, after the students have had a short period of time to get acquainted with one another they make the choice as to who they would like to be with in their support groups.

These support groups are important because students often find it difficult to relate to twenty-eight other people (the usual size of my class). Relating seems to come much easier in small groups. (I would like to make note here that we all pull together for a sharing of feelings at the end of each class.)

A "Mini" Encounter. Once the initial support groups are formed we usually start out with a "mini" encounter just to loosen up our feelings much as an athlete loosens up before competition. We just do a little "jogging of the mind."

Students are asked to pair up (within their support groups) and face one another. They are told that they have five minutes to get to know one another. At the end of five minutes they reverse roles. That is, they become the person they were facing. In their new role they are asked to tell the group all they can about themselves.

Once done they are asked to remain in their groups, sit in a circle, and consider and respond to these questions:

1. Give a one sentence *virtue* of yourself.
2. Tell the group about something that happened to you as a child. (What was your feeling at that time?)
3. Relate a peak-experience (truly a high plateau-experience) in your life. (Maslow, 1970)
4. Tell how *you* view yourself as a sexual person.
5. Tell how you would *like* to view yourself as a sexual person.
6. Tell how you think *others* view you as a sexual person.
7. Express how you would like to change some aspect of your physical self in some way.
8. Respond, non-verbally, to the group, (i.e. share your feelings with them without talking.)
9. Move around, one at a time, and tell each member of your group what you have learned and now feel about them.
10. Pull in very close and share one last thought (feeling) about the group. (It may be verbal, nonverbal, or both.)
11. Meet in one large group and share feelings.
12. Do a group levitation.
13. Say farewell.

Feeling With Words. Words are the prime tool of our age (perhaps of many other ages as well, but I cannot speak for them). In this session students are asked to associate feelings with certain words. For example, in one class I hand out a sheet of paper on which are written certain words. I ask the students to find a place in the room, get comfortable, and respond as spontaneously and openly as possible. Below is just a sample of some of the words to which they are asked to respond:

In loving . . .
I feel sexually . . .
Masturbation . . .
Sexually . . .
Sex is wrong . . .
Premarital sex . . .

Once done, students are asked to get into their support groups. Here the students take turns sharing their responses.

This is always a plus night. We conclude with a "total" group experience. As an example, we may do a "Gunther Hero Sandwich." [4]

Role Playing. Role playing is an excellent technique for allowing individuals to play themselves or "play act" someone else *if* they so desire. The choice is theirs. We usually role play three different scenes in one night. I will relate just two to you.

I usually start out with a warm-up exercise by having the support groups play out a situation in which they find themselves in an airplane which has developed engine trouble and crashes into the ocean. They have one raft which will hold five people (remember there are six people in each support group). They are given five minutes to decide who will get into the raft and which individual will have to stay behind. (The one who stays behind will certainly perish as the situation is impossible for him to do otherwise.) This situation tells the groups much about one another, and it helps me learn about each group as a whole. From here the class goes into a second role playing situation, and then we pull together to play out a single scene.

What will follow now is an imaginary scene involving eight people (four females—four males) who usually volunteer to act.

Scene: A group of eight people are seated in a circle. (The rest of the class is seated around them and are asked to remain silent.) The group of eight is asked to pair-up. That is they are asked to choose someone who they could imagine to be their spouse. They are then asked to imagine that they have been invited to a party and have come to realize that it is a "swinging party" and they have been informed by the host that they have fifteen minutes to determine whether any of them want to stay. (For those who may not know the terminology a "swinging party" means a party in which couples have sexual intercourse with one another.)

The actors do not take much time getting into the scene. They usually begin by making a flat statement. "I'm not going to stay even if my spouse wants to." "I think I would like to try it, how about you honey?" "I'll stay if my spouse wants to." And so the discussion goes.

Two important techniques that go along with role playing are *role reversal* and *doubling.*[5]

What this situation does is to confront each of the actors with their own personal feelings concerning husband-wife relationships, extramarital relationships, sexual insecurity, jealousy, etc.

Once the play is over (the length varies), I ask the actors not to talk and to let the audience have a chance to share their feelings about the play and individual actors. Comments such as "I think so-and-so was play acting (not being his real self)" or "I just knew that Tom would be all for it" come out. Once the observers have talked I suggest that the actors share their feelings, taking into consideration what has been said by the audience.

We may do a sociogram by having all group members put their left hand on the shoulder of that person they could most relate to in terms of how they played out their role. It lends insight into self and others.

The class concludes with a group experience.

EVALUATION

Harold Lyon said in his book, *Learning to Feel—Feeling to Learn,* that one must begin to accept students as "human beings who have feelings—feelings which directly influence their intellectual growth."

Through the humanistic approach to teaching in sex and sexuality, students are more able to relate their *subjective* responses regarding how they feel about themselves as sexual persons. Additionally, a greater emphasis can be placed on feelingful emotions rather than on an intellectualization of subject matter, and on examining alternatives for the achievement of a more comfortable and satisfying sexual self-concept. The teacher quickly finds that the classroom becomes a forum for group learning, sharing, experiencing, and "This is the power that can unlock in their (the teacher's) students self love and the ability to feel and learn which accompanies that love." [2]

REFERENCES

1. MAY, ROLLO, *Love and Will,* New York: W. W. Norton & Co., Inc., 1969.

2. LYON, HAROLD C., *Learning to Feel—Feeling to Learn,* Columbus, Ohio: Charles E. Merrill Pub., Co., 1971.

3. ROGERS, CARL, *On Encounter Groups,* New York: Harper & Row, Pub., 1970.

4. GUNTHER, BERNARD, *Sense Relaxation Below Your Mind,* New York: Collier Books, 1968.

5. BLAND, LEONARD, G. B. GOTSEGEN, and M. G. GOTTSEGEN (eds.), *Confrontation: Encounters in Self and Interpersonal Awareness,* New York: Macmillan, 1971.

Role Playing
in the Classroom

Mark Chesler and Robert Fox

During their recent studies dealing with the process of identification and diffusion of innovative teaching practices, the authors discovered many classroom teachers experimenting with role playing. They were using it as a method for teaching children to look at themselves, to look at the actions and behaviors of others, and to look at social life in general. They were using it to help in the diagnosis and treatment of classroom interpersonal problems, for teaching lessons in interpersonal relations, and to give feedback and insights to particular individuals. They were using it to dramatize and illustrate subject matter in courses such as history and English. They were using it, in short, as a means of making the classroom a real-life laboratory for social and academic learning.

ROLE PLAYING AND LEARNING

Role playing has a tremendous potential for the average elementary and secondary school classroom.

First, by taking on the role of another person and by pretending to feel like, think like, and act like another person, students can act out their true feelings without the risk of sanctions or reprisals. They know they are only acting, and can thus express feelings ordinarily kept hidden. This experience can give rise to greater individual spontaneity and creativity in previously repressed or inhibited children.

Second, students can examine and discuss relatively private issues and problems without anxiety. These problems are not focused on the self; they are attributed to a given role or stereotype. Thus children can avoid the normal anxiety accompanying the presentation of personal matters that may violate rules and regulations. This experience may result in greater individual insights into behavior and a better understanding of the place of rules and behavioral standards. Such learning can best be accomplished in a nonjudgmental situation where "correct" solutions are not the goal.

Third, by placing themselves in the role of another, students can identify with the real worlds and the imaginations of other children and adults. In this manner they may begin to understand the effects of their behavior on others, and they may gain significant information about the motivations for their own and other people's behaviors. By sympathizing with the scapegoat, many a bully may understand how it feels to be picked on; by sympathizing with the bully, many a scapegoat may understand why his behavior is a red flag to the bully. When both roles are examined and discussed by the entire class, both bully and scapegoat may understand how their behavior looks to others, what some of their needs or motivations are, and what other forms of action might be appropriate. Students can begin to develop an elementary but systematic understanding of the science of human relations from repeated experiences and discussions of this sort.

Fourth, this increased opportunity for understanding oneself and others paves the way for behavioral change. Achieving systematic insights into self, into others, and into motivations for various actions can aid students in clarifying their own values and in effectively directing or changing their own behavior. By practicing a variety of behaviors in a series of role-playing exercises and by discussing the effects of each, students may be able to make more realistic choices for their actions than before. The supportive atmosphere may also legitimize in the students' eyes the peer-helping process in the classroom, encouraging them to give and receive insights, suggestions, and help.

Fifth, role playing may also be used to demonstrate less personal but pervasive problems between and among people and groups. Social problems, to the extent that they reflect conflict between man and man, can be dramatized fruitfully in the classroom. For instance, classroom portrayals of problems of prejudice may lead to greater understanding of the dynamics of this phenomenon and some clarification of ways of dealing with its occurrence. Such understanding need not be purely abstract, on the theoretical or moralistic level; it can include the alternative behaviors that are available when one is a witness to an act or feeling of racial, religious, or economic bias. Further, small-scale examples of political events, instances of political decision making, or dilemmas facing criminals and courts of law can be examined in the classroom. These portrayals may help make the student aware of selected social problems and the human meaning for those involved. They may help him to examine thoughtfully different ways of resolving social and personal conflict and to identify the advantages and disadvantages of each path. The exercises may not reduce conflict, but they may give the student skills to deal with his world more effectively. He may come to see the ways in which some of these universal social issues are reflected in his own relations with other individuals and groups and how they bear upon the decision he must make in his own life.

Sixth, role playing that helps individuals to understand their own and others' behaviors can free them to utilize their intellectual potential more fully. Substantial research has shown that interpersonal relations and feelings of high or low self-esteem affect a student's academic performance. Thus role playing directed toward understanding and changing interpersonal situations may lead indirectly to a higher level of academic performance. But it may also be used to present academic materials. Historical or contemporary events can be acted out in class to dramatize the feelings and conflicts of the participants in pivotal situations. After a brief introduction to the plot and characters, students can role-play a story, a novel, or a play in English class. The comparison between the student's portrayal and the author's presentation may stimulate thoughtful discussions about the author's style and point of view, the historical context and traditions, and similar topics. The technique of role playing can bring to the study of academic materials the dramatic import, the immediacy, and the student involvement that may otherwise be lacking in the classroom.

Seventh, role playing may prove to be an instructional technique particularly useful with nonverbal, acting-out students. The typical middle-class child is apt to be satisfied with intellectual talk about a problem but reluctant to express the feelings and emotions necessary to a full understanding of the dynamics of the problem situation, or hesitant to carry his talk into action. Lower-class students, on the other hand, often reject the verbalism and abstraction of many school activities, but delight in giving their more visceral responses. Through the acting-out technique of role playing, lower-class students can have a chance to experience success by making a valued contribution to the class activity in a way that is within their range of skills, and they can thereby become more highly involved in the total learning activity. Middle-class students, through the confrontation with feelings and action provided by role playing, may learn to express concretely their intellectual understandings.

A final and unique advantage of role playing as an instructional technique is its active nature. Participants and audiences do not merely discuss theoretical problems of behavior and alternative ways of acting; they observe and practice new ways of behaving. Thus there is a stress on active participation in learning that enhances the learning itself. The necessary connection is made between knowing a principle and acting upon that knowledge. The mere addition of information neither solves classroom interpersonal problems nor teaches new social relations: interpersonal issues are resolved only as students or teachers begin to behave differently. New behavior is the testimony of new information; it changes the effects one person has upon other persons. The shy child who can intellectually appreciate the importance of taking the initiative in beginning a conversation may practice this insight through role playing. With successful dramatic experience under his belt, he may be better able to introduce these new behaviors into the real-life situation. Similarly, the bully who has come to understand himself and the scapegoat through observation and discussion has an opportunity to practice alternative ways of dealing with his aggressive feelings.

Skill practice in role playing is only one step in this change process, but through such understanding and practice and with decreased anxiety and isolation, a student may become willing and able to take the additional steps to change. He may still require a great deal of practice and reinforcement before he can apply these lessons to his own experience and actually perform more effectively.

Thus role playing can be seen as one technique in an educational procedure that is directed toward the scientific improvement of classroom learning and social behavior. Such a procedure assumes that learning needs to be more than "studying about" and more than mere activity or "real-life experiences." The classroom can provide the opportunities for relating ideas to action, theory to practice. It can become a laboratory for problem identification, for experience and analysis, for drawing conclusions, for formulating and reality-testing new behaviors, and for learning to generalize and behave differently in other situations.

THE BOUNDARIES OF CLASSROOM
ROLE PLAYING

The preceding chapter discussed different uses of role playing—industrial and psychotherapeutic as well as educational. There are also several depths or levels at which role playing can be used within a single program. The uses with students range from classroom instruction and portrayal of literary or historical events, through examination of individual and group problems in social skill development, to intensive personal or group psychotherapy with disturbed students.

The classroom teacher need not be a psychologist to use role playing at the instructional and interpersonal levels. In general, the kinds of problems he chooses to work with can and should be dealt with as "sociodramas": that is, with emphasis on typical roles, problems, or situations that children usually face. For example, the teacher may wish to portray such stereotypes as the "shy child," the child "dealing with aggression" or "learning how to use the resources of adults." These are conditions in which students must learn appropriate and effective roles. As such, they are excellent examples of topics for role playing.

The teacher can avoid too direct a confrontation of any individual student by concentrating on such roles, or typical behavior patterns. The application of general problems to a specific student's abilities or inabilities should be initiated primarily by the student as a result of whatever insights he has developed. A respect for the student's ability to deal effectively with new information is a help at this point. The teacher should not engage in depth probing, nor should he publicly air a reluctant individual's problems. A basic rule is that the teacher should be cautious of involving himself and his students in portrayals and interpretations that seriously impinge upon their psychological privacy or security. Psychodrama and other intensive and individualized forms of role playing are ordinarily used for therapeutic purposes and should be attempted only by the trained therapist. The potential dangers of an overzealous confrontation of a disturbed or even a seemingly healthy child by an untrained technician are well worth these precautions and limitations.

Within these limitations, however, even the relatively inexperienced teacher can learn to use role playing effectively. Starting with a simple charade, a short problem story, or other relatively "safe" topics, a teacher can experiment with increasingly complex and meaningful issues dependent upon his own skill, confidence, and specialized training. As the students and teacher continue to practice, classroom rapport and acceptance are likely to grow. Within such a supportive atmosphere individual students are likely to become more comfortable about discussing their insights, accepting suggestions, and changing their behaviors.

Increased freedom of emotional expression, involvement in and portrayal of a role that is not one's own, and the dramatic presentation of lifelike events are as much a part of the role-playing technique as they are of acting and creative dramatics. Role playing, however, does not regard the development of dramatic skills as ends in themselves. It seeks to utilize whatever abilities a child may have in these areas as tools with which to influence his social and academic growth. The improvisation and public discussion of dramatic presentations are strategies for leading the classroom group toward greater learning and change.

CLASSROOM NEEDS AND ROLE-PLAYING STRATEGIES

The role-playing technique should not be used as an isolated classroom event or experience. Like any good educational tool, it is best used as part of a larger instructional plan. Any particular role-playing situation must be selected and adapted on the basis of the teacher's professional judgment as he diagnoses and assesses the educational needs of his classroom. The teacher's decision as to how and when to use this technique is crucial to effective learning.*

The issue or problem to be enacted in class may be a real-life situation or a fictitious example of a real situation. Role-playing situations may develop from interpersonal problems in the classroom, from outside issues facing young people, or from the desire to present subject matter more forcefully and dramatically. In any case, the problem situation should be concrete and real enough for students to understand its relevance to their daily lives.

One way of getting relevance is to provide for student involvement and participation in planning the role-playing exercises. The teacher might simply ask the class to suggest personal or general problems that they think can be studied. Alternatively, he might take a problem census by asking his students to list some common problem situations they have experienced. After his students have some experience with the technique, the teacher will generally find them eagerly suggesting new situations or events with which to role-play. The teacher who has clarified his own learning goals, and who has carefully diagnosed and interpreted the social situation in his classroom, is in an advantageous position to construct a drama designed to deal with those issues especially relevant to his students.

Once a diagnosis is made and a problem situation selected, some other guidelines are important. The topic or problem should be clear, specific, and not too complex. It should be a topic that can be handled, solved, or investigated by the group members without making them feel inadequate. Both teacher and students will improve in their role-playing skill as they have common positive experiences, but too much should not be tried too early. Tense and emotionally threatening situations should not be used initially with a class new to reflecting on its own behavior with the role-playing technique. At some point threatening issues are necessary and important to deal with, since they often represent the areas of greatest growth potential. But comfort with this content and learning style develops gradually, and episodes that are threatening to the teacher or his students should be avoided until the class has developed positive ways of handling feelings.

---

* For a discussion of the importance of this diagnostic process in solving classroom problems, see Schmuck, Chesler, and Lippitt, *Problem Solving to Improve Classroom Learning* (Chicago: Science Research Associates, 1966). Detailed examples of tools for diagnosing many types of classroom problems, including instructions for their selection, administration, and interpretation, are presented in Fox, Luszki, and Schmuck, *Diagnosing Classroom Learning Environment* (Chicago: Science Research Associates, 1966).

A decision to use role playing for dealing with controversial problems in which parents and the community, as well as the students, are deeply involved requires careful consideration and evaluation. Race relations, sex, religion, moral values, politics, cultural conflicts, parent-child relations —these areas may provide educational topics of impelling urgency and relevance. Through role playing, young people can examine some of their true feelings in a nonthreatening atmosphere, explore possible consequences of alternative actions, and derive some help in facing these problems constructively. The degree to which the student can and should be exposed to these problems will vary with each classroom.

Controversial problems can be dealt with at several levels of abstraction or immediacy. One approach avoids facing such issues directly, but offers the student opportunities to experience, observe, and think about different ways of reacting to situations pertinent to his life as a student and a human being in a social context. Role playing allows the student to experience success in such general areas as interpersonal communication and to try out ways of dealing with problems of human relationships. The gratification, confidence, and insight into motives that the student gains from acting out roles with his peers can open up new alternatives and provide new skills for dealing with more controversial situations as they arise outside the classroom. Many teachers who have been working conscientiously with the problems of disadvantaged youth and minority groups are convinced that the most fruitful results are obtained by giving these students some experience with success, rather than a further reflection of the constant demoralization and defeat they face in their lives out of school.

Another approach faces controversial problems more directly but presents them in a generalized form: "What do you say when your dad refuses to let you have the car for a date at the drive-in movie?" "How can a girl respond graciously to a compliment from a boy?" "What can your class do when a new child from a minority group joins the class and some of your classmates are making things difficult for him?" This approach remains impersonal, does not single out particular individuals or groups, and is relatively nonthreatening. Many children may not yet have had personal experience with interracial, religious, or intimate interpersonal situations. Role playing helps them anticipate some of these problems in more meaningful ways than would mere discussion. It also provides a chance for those students who have realistic contacts with such situations to bring to bear their information and insights as resources rather than as evidence of personal difficulties. Opportunities like this are going to be increasingly needed if youth living in the somewhat restricted environment provided by each community (no matter how "privileged" it may be) are to become alert to, and learn to deal at last in an elementary way with the human-relations problems of a complex urban society.

A more direct approach may be made to specific incidents or problems in interpersonal relations as they arise. As the teacher and class become skilled and comfortable with role playing, this is perhaps the most rewarding technique of all. If used with nonthreatening problems, such as testing how a new child is to be greeted by the others, or how to appreciate a new passage in English literature, the teacher can have the class play an actual incident by assigning roles quickly and informally. Much greater care needs to be exercised in more sensitive situations such as race relations or sexual behavior. The teacher needs to have an established rapport with parents, a supportive working relationship with his principal, and, most important of all, the confidence of his stdents. Given such conditions, role playing is a means for students to deal with difficult issues, which are *already a vital part of their living,* in an accepting and educationally planned atmosphere, guided by an understanding and expert adult.

Another issue in role-playing strategy involves the length of a program or session. Very young children usually enjoy a session of not longer than fifteen to twenty minutes. Older elementary school children may stay highly involved for twenty to thirty minutes; junior and senior high school students forty-five minutes or more. These times include, of course, the relevant preparation, discussion, and evaluation activities. The actual role-playing improvisations are likely to last only a few minutes before they are cut for analysis, discussion, and reenactment.

Finally, it may be pointed out that a well-planned curriculum unit for interpersonal learning frees the teacher from complete dependence on incidental or accidental problem situations, which might cause overwhelming strategic and organizational problems. However, too rigorous advance planning may overlook the learning potential in immediate events or problems. A good balance of planned and spontaneous activities, oriented to meeting educational goals, may be the best strategy for the teacher. Some teachers set aside a regular weekly period that the class comes to anticipate as the time to consider a variety of topics and problems for role playing. Other teachers utilize role playing when the opportunity presents itself as a part of the continuing class activity, rather than on any regular basis. With either strategy, role playing is most effective when used in conjunction with specifically planned educational goals and procedures.

THE TEACHER'S SELF-PREPARATION

The effective use of an instructional tool depends upon the teacher's knowledge of it and his assurance in using it. The first time he threads a motion picture projector, even after reading the directions carefully, he may be awkward and slow. Since this is embarrassing with a class impatient to see the picture, most teachers practice a bit in private or have the projector threaded and ready to go before the pupils come into the room.

It is not so simple to prepare oneself for role playing. Practice cannot be accomplished in private; interaction with other persons is needed to develop skills and confidence in the technique. Many teachers might be reluctant to try role playing without a clear conception of what their specific job is and without a series of practice runs. As one teacher put it:

> "I've read some material about role playing. I'm interested in the possibilities it might hold for my classroom. But what do I do? How can I keep from falling flat on my face and having my class in chaos? How do I get started?"

It is understandable that there may be some initial fear or reluctance to introducing role playing into the classroom. Many teachers fear that spontaneity in the classroom will lead to a loss of control or chaos, and many attempt to avoid all show of emotion in the class for this reason. Teachers subject to such fears are apt to be those unfamiliar with the technique, new teachers without an instructional plan, or experienced teachers who are relatively set in their ways. However, emotional factors do influence learning and a temporary loss of unilateral teacher control may not mean chaos or permanent loss of influence. Several suggestions for meeting the initial problems of getting started may be helpful.

A first step might be practicing or exploring the technique with a few other people—with friends, family, or colleagues. Perhaps several other teachers in a school would also like to get the feel of role playing and would agree to meet after school or in the evening. Some of the situations suggested in the Appendix could be tried, with each teacher taking turns at being the director and playing the various roles. It would be ideal, of course, to secure the consultant help of some teacher who has used role playing and is willing to share some of his experience. Failing this, or in addition, the advice of recognized experts or other resource persons might be sought.

In one instance the authors set up an actual session to instruct teachers in the administration of role playing to their classes. It focused on a common teacher problem—teacher interaction. The report of this session states:

> "The next training session, on role playing, was most successful. The locale of the role-play situation was designated as the teachers' lunchroom where several teachers had gathered and one teacher was to present ideas for a new curriculum outline to the others. In the design we included a hostile colleague, a pair of close friends, a 'principal worrier,'

a discussion blocker, and two teachers who would immediately support the ideas. Some teachers were a little anxious from the beginning and did not wish to participate; they were made observers whose job it was to report objectively on what happened.

"We went ahead and got thoroughly embroiled—the hostile colleague, in particular, doing a good job. We noted, during the play, a previously hidden staff resentment of the principal's role and some antagonistic staff alignments. The participants recognized some of these issues and accepted them as problems of role relationships, not as problems of individual personalities or abilities. They will probably be able to understand and improve staff relations as a result. After the role play was completed, we moved to a discussion of how this technique might be used to deal with students' feelings in the classroom."

In this adult session the role-playing exercise was most helpful in bringing previously hidden problems to the surface, in allowing teachers to understand how it feels to innovate or to suggest innovation in a crowded lunchroom, and in giving the participants some skill in planning and administering role playing.

A second step in self-preparation might be to interest a small group of students in staying after school to try out some "creative dramatics." These few class members can be taken into the teacher's confidence, and learning this new technique can be made a cooperative project in which the teacher admits that he has not used it with a class before and is experimenting. The students can help by trying out some role-playing episodes as well as suggesting what can be done in class to improve the sessions. In class the teacher and his helpers can explain their collaboration in the development of this teaching-learning technique.

As suggested earlier, the teacher using role playing for the first time should start with very simple situations that are familiar to the students and in which the action is clear-cut—for instance, "Your best friend, Jane, asks you to her birthday party when you have a date. What do you say?" Other simple examples are listed in the early parts of the Appendix. Later the students and teacher can move to more difficult problems. The early periods should be brief and should be stopped while student interest is still high. It is not necessary for every student to be an actor in the first role-playing session.

In preparing for a role-playing session, the teacher may find it helpful to write out briefing sheets to give or read to each participant in the improvisation. Examples of these instructions are shown in Chapter Five. He may also feel more secure at first by writing out ahead of time a detailed description of the situation and of the instructions to the audience. As he becomes sufficiently confident to introduce on-the-spot improvisations, he will become more facile in extemporizing the situations and instructions.

As a general rule, and particularly in the early sessions, the teacher and the students should talk over how each session went. The teacher should solicit student help in searching for reasons why the role playing did not work as well as it might have. Such student involvement results in more effective learning and focuses responsibility for improvement of role playing on the class and teacher together, rather than on the teacher alone.

STEPS IN THE ROLE-PLAYING SEQUENCE

Role playing in the classroom works best when there is an attempt to follow a definite sequence of steps. The sequence outlined below allows for a logical ordering and development of the role-playing session. It has been tested successfully by teachers.

Preparation and instruction, the first stage, covers problem selection, warm-up, and general and specific instructions to participants and audience. It involves the selection by the teacher, with or without class help, of an issue or problem to be worked on. After selecting the problem, the teacher needs to warm up or relax the students and give them practice and security in public performance and expression. The explanation of the general problem situation should make clear the educational purposes of the drama and the relevance of the issue or problem for the entire class. The teacher is now ready to brief the actors, to explain in detail the exact role each of them will play. The final step in this stage is to delineate the roles of the audience, the students who are not acting out the dramatic roles. These students can observe the general interaction of actors, or they can be charged to watch for specific actors or for specific events.

Dramatic action and discussion, the second major stage, covers both the role playing itself and the subsequent discussion and interpretation of the action. Sufficient time should be allowed during the improvisation for students to become thoroughly immersed in the problem situation, so that they can take full advantage of the situation's promise for discovering and practicing alternative ways of acting. At the conclusion of the drama it is important to bring the class back to everyday reality, to dissociate the actors clearly from the role they played. This is important so that critics and other students can concentrate on the role behavior and not on the actions or person of the actors. The post-role-playing discussion may take several forms and involve several different students or groups of students. The role players or the audience, or both, may contribute to an analysis of the dramatic session. A final important focus of this learning experience should be the student's ability to apply the examples and lessons of this new role behavior to his own interpersonal experiences.

Evaluation, the final stage, must follow the enactment and discussion of the role-playing situation. In this stage the teacher and pupils review the successes and failures of their role-playing experience. The purposes, procedures, and effects of such a learning experience should be analyzed so that teacher and class can make decisions about the need for additional role playing or reenactment of the scene. The teacher will certainly want to make a further personal evaluation of the experience in the light of his original diagnosis and goals; he will want to consider what verbal and behavioral evidence there is to show that the students have learned from the experience.

The Come Alive Classroom:
Personal Approaches to
Good Teaching in Health

Donald A. Read

In our general elective health course at Worcester State College we attempt to teach students processes or skills they will need to guide their lives and successfully deal with issues of "identity, connectedness and power." [1] Values clarification is one such approach, emphasizing the process of prizing, choosing, and acting which lead to the development of affective responses. [2] Human relations training (in many forms) is another example. It focuses on teaching the processes of listening, giving and receiving feedback, handling conflict, etc. Transactional analysis [3] is yet another process approach, dealing with discovering and fostering awareness, self-responsibility, and genuineness. [4] Transactional analysis is also concerned with the *here and now* (as is also true of Gestalt therapy as interpreted by Dr. Frederick Perls). [5]

In our particular course, all the above mentioned techniques are used either individually or in combination. Their use depends to a great extent upon the teacher, the student(s), and the unique situation in which one is working. The key is in being able to integrate both the intellectual (cognitive) with the feelings (affective) in one's classroom situation.

One important aspect of this type of teaching is that one begin to accept students as real, feeling, worthy, responsible and valuable members of the teaching-learning environment. This requires that the teacher begin to relinquish his/her role as authority figure and begin to assume the role of facilitator. [6] That teacher and student begin to work in a sort of collaborative effort. This ". . . advocates that we begin to look upon people (students) as whole human beings who have feelings—feelings which directly influence their intellectual growth." [7]

Donald A. Read, "The Come Alive Classroom: Personal Approaches to Good Teaching in Health," *The Journal of School Health,* April 1974, pp. 225–27.

433

Conceding that personal (feelingful) concrete experiences often provide a more realistic and functional perspective, how can we, in health education, assist the student to move toward a greater awareness of, and appreciation for, what is going on within himself or to assist him in developing a greater openness to experiences and to develop a greater confidence in what he values? [8]   Listed are but a few of the techniques we use:

Learn to accept students as they truly are.   Don't aim to "change" students.   If a group of your students smoke, don't try to get them to stop. They only become targets for your anti-smoking campaign.   Instead, attempt to provide them with "alternative solutions" and let them make the choice.   Better yet, have the class come up with alternative solutions.

One way of dealing with issues which lend themselves to alternative solutions is through the process of "reality testing," [9] which is the process of checking out what is real.   It involves separating fact from fantasy, healthy from unhealthy.   An exercise that deals very well with this concept is:

EXERCISE: Want Ads

PURPOSE: Diagnose student concerns and develop alternative solutions to student concerns

PROCEDURE: Give each student a 3x5 card.   Have them anonymously place a "want ad" listing a particular behavior pattern they feel is unhealthy and that they feel they would like to change.   Example: "I want to exercise more than I do," or "I want to stop smoking."   They may wish to elaborate on these "I wants" to some extent.   Collect the cards, shuffle them and give each student one.   Allow students a few days in which to come up with some possible solutions to the want ads.

ANALYSIS: Allow students class time to share their alternative solutions.   Discuss, *nonjudgmentally,* the plausibility of the solutions.

Another exercise that can be used in touching on alternative solutions is:

EXERCISE: Fishbowl

PURPOSE: To examine group decision making processes

PROCEDURE: Use the fishbowl design for a discussion.   Pick six participants to sit in the center of a circle of observers.   Engage the six in the following discussion:

A friend of yours is using drugs extensively. He would like to quit but he does not have the strength or reason to. This is the last time you six will have to talk to him as he plans to move away. He will be coming by in about 15 minutes to say his goodbye's. Can you come up with some good alternatives to his drug use? In other words—how can you help him to help himself in 15 minutes?

ANALYSIS: Stop the exercise after 15 minutes and have everyone do a "Here and Now Wheel." That is, with the participants sitting silently, ask the observers what they saw and heard. Were the alternatives realistic? Which sounded most plausible? Which could be put into action quickly? Then check out the comments of the observers with the inner group.

Work towards the building up of self-concept in students.[10] A second suggestion is that we provide students with experiences that will help them find their own strengths and build on them. Instead of dealing with the negative aspects of health, allow students to search out the positive aspects and to relate them to one another. Each student has something he does do well and which benefits his well being. Let him relate it to the class. One exercise which can lend itself to building up self-confidence in students is:

EXERCISE: Strength Bombardment

PURPOSE: Development of positive self-concept

ANALYSIS: Have the class break into groups of six. Focusing on one person at a time, each group member is to "bombard" him with all of the strengths and values that they see in him. The person being bombarded should remain silent until the group has finished. One member of the group should act as recorder, listing the strengths and giving them to the person when the group has finished.

PROCEDURE: Have students share "I learned . . ." statements. That is, allow students to share their feelings with the class concerning what they have learned due to this exercise. This should be voluntary—not required.

Suspend judgment and encourage individual differences. There are so many ways to do one thing—just lots of ways. Thus it is important that we, as teachers, allow students the opportunity to clarify their values from time to time. In this way they begin to see, and feel, the importance of thinking and doing for themselves and standing up for it. It gives them something to believe in—themselves. An exercise dealing with individual differences is:

EXERCISE: Either/Or

PURPOSE: To help students in making (and sticking by) value decisions.

PROCEDURE: Place a line (masking tape is always good) down the middle of the classroom. Have students stand up, and push their chairs aside. Have students respond to differing value choices by standing on one side of the line or the other. Example: Pointing to one side of the line say "Are you more athletic than . . ." Pointing to the other side say "Unathletic." Give students a chance to choose and move. Other examples of value choices could include:

healthy	than	unhealthy
reckless	than	safety conscious
happy	than	sad
fighter	than	appeaser
heavy	than	light
yellow	than	black

ANALYSIS: Have students respond (voluntarily) to such questions as: "Were you swayed to choose by others?" "Did you feel comfortable in your choice?" "Would you change certain choices now that you think about them?"

Allow for a variety of values and life styles. It is one thing for the teacher to allow personal values to be voiced in the classroom, still another to be nonjudgmental. By allowing all values to be aired and shared and not criticized lends itself to greater openness in the classroom. One exercise that gets at a variety of values is:

EXERCISE: Know Yourself

PURPOSE: To show that people have different values and to show that value choices may differ between the sexes

PROCEDURE: Have students get into groups of six or less. Write on the blackboard (or hand out ditto sheets) these various value choices. Do one at a time. Have students rank order them in terms of most to least acceptable to them. (Number 1 is most acceptable and 3 is least acceptable.)

Rank order what you would do.

———— give money to a friend who needs an abortion

_____ make yourself available to talk to a friend who has a sexual problem

_____ visibly support a friend whose sexual practices have been maligned by others in school

What kind of husband/wife would you prefer?

_____ one with no prior sexual experience

_____ one with very limited sexual experience

_____ one with considerable sexual experience

Which would be most to least acceptable to you?

_____ to become (or get someone) pregnant

_____ to be dependent upon hard drugs

_____ to date someone from another race

ANALYSIS: In groups of six or less have students share responses to items. Allow for discussion. Have students write one "I learned . . ." statement and allow them to share in large group if they want.

Another exercise that can be used is:

EXERCISE: Abortion Continuum

PURPOSE: To determine whether a difference does exist between male and female students concerning abortion.

PROCEDURE: Place a piece of masking tape down the middle of the classroom. Have students push chairs aside and stand up. State that on one end of the continuum are those people who believe strongly in "ABORTION ON DE-MAND." You may wish to elaborate a bit on this. The other end of the continuum represents the "RIGHT TO LIFE" people. Also elaborate on this. The middle represents those people who cannot arrive at a decision.

ANALYSIS: Ask about six students, one at a time, to place themselves on the continuum. As each does ask him what his individual feelings are concerning abortion and why he placed himself where he did. Finally ask the entire class to place themselves on the continuum. As a few to express their feelings. Have the class note where their fellow classmates are standing. Do they see a difference between male and female students? Share some "I learned . . ." statements.

IMPLICATIONS

The goal of humanistic education is for long-term life changes, not short-term gains in mastery. Through the humanistic approach to teaching in health, students are able to increase long-term operant behavior as well as respondent behavior.

In a field such as health, where there is no one critical mass of common values necessary to the health and vigor of a society, humanistic education can provide us with the tools and techniques necessary for a more creative teaching-learning environment. Additionally, humanistic education allows for a greater emphasis to be placed on examining alternatives for the achievement of a more satisfying self-concept, respect for one's body and one's well being. In the words of Jerry Rubin "To love your body, to accept yourself, to know your own personal rhythm, to go inward, gives you better control of your own life . . ."

REFERENCES

1. FANTINI M, WEINSTEIN G: Making Urban Schools Work. New York, Hole, Rinehart and Winston, 1968.

2. RATHS LE, HARMIN M, SIMON SB: Values and Teaching: Working With Values in the Classroom. Columbus, Ohio, Charles E. Merrill, 1966.

3. BERNE E: Principles of Group Treatment. New York, Oxford University Press, 1964.

4. JAMES M, JONGEWARD D: Born to Win: Transactional Analysis with Gestalt Experiments. Reading, Mass., Addison-Wesley Publishers, 1971.

5. PERLS FS: Gestalt Therapy Verbatim. Lafayette, Calif., Real People Press, 1969.

6. POSTMAN N, WEIGARTNER C: The School Book. New York, Delacorte Press, 1973.

7. LYON HC: Learning to Feel—Feeling to Learn. Columbus, Ohio, Charles E. Merrill, 1971, p. 5.

8. ROGERS CR, STEVENS B: Person to Person: The Problem of Being Human. Lafayette, Calif., Real People Press, 1967.

9. JAMES M, JONGEWARD D: Born to Win. Reading, Mass., Addison-Wesley Publishers, 1971.

10. PURKEY, WW: Self Concept and School Achievement. Englewood Cliffs, New Jersey, Prentice-Hall, 1970.

11. RUBIN J: From the streets to the body. Psychol Today (Sept) 1973, p 71.

Let's Be an Ice Cream Machine!
Creative Dramatics

Gary A. Davis, Charles J. Helfert, and
Gloria R. Shapiro

Around mid-year, the janitor, secretary, and principal cornered you in the cloakroom as you were about to pile the last boot of the day in the lost-and-found. With carefully picked words the principle spoke first, "Many are called, but few are chosen. YOU have the honor of teaching the first creative dramatics course at Central. This honor is yours because of your genuine ability as a geography teacher, your homeroom victory in the clothing drive, and because you are the only teacher free from 3:30 to 4:30 on Monday, Wednesday, and Friday."

The secretary was next. With script in hand, she began reciting the role expectations of every new teacher. The janitor and principal reinforced her speech with a smiling round of applause.

The janitor was last to step forward. "You can use the Girl's Gym. Take off your shoes and don't leave a mess! The Union sez I don't hafta clean the Gym twice in one day." The trio turned and paraded out.

WHAT IS CREATIVE DRAMATICS?

Stunned, you sat yourself on the lost-and-found box, looked desperately at that last boot and quietly screamed, "HELP!" Creative Dramatics is indeed a strange school subject. There are no agreed-upon goals nor any standard course content. There are almost no published workbooks, no achievement tests, and no behavioral objectives. Rows of desks and memorizing will just get in the way. While creative dramatics is not one of your standard subjects, it can do things which no amount of traditional classwork can accomplish.

Gary A. Davis, Charles J. Helfert, and Gloria R. Shapiro, "Let's Be an Ice Cream Machine!" *The Journal of Creative Behavior*, 1973, pp. 37–48, 53. Copyright © 1973 by Gary A. Davis.

439

In a sense, creative dramatics is the education of the whole person by experience. For example, you can tell students how important the human senses are, or you can let them feel, hear, see, smell, and taste. You can teach concepts like *trust* or *faith* with a dictionary-type description, or you can ask some students to shut their eyes and let unknown others lead them around the room or even across a busy street.

There are many ways to stimulate thinking, problem solving, and imagination (Davis, 1972), but one of the best is creative dramatics. There are *not* many well-known methods for increasing awareness and concentration, for developing control of the physical self, for sharpening the senses, for learning to discover and control emotion, for developing pride in individuality, and for strengthening self-confidence in speaking and performing. Creative dramatics helps with these too.

It is important to note that creative dramatics is not "children's theatre" or "acting." However, creative dramatics experience is guaranteed to improve any amateur theatrical performance, and we highly recommend it for the classroom teacher seeking to loosen up her memorize-your-line thespians. As a rule of thumb however, "theatre" is concerned with communication between actors and an audience; "drama" deals with the unique experiences of participants (Way, 1967)). More simply, theatre develops actors, creative dramatics develops people. In fact, the demands of formal stage play might well damage the self-confidence which creative dramatics is trying to strengthen. Further, the presence of an audience only interferes with the imaginative, sensitive involvement of successful creative drama. Few children are natural actors, but everyone can be 100% successful in creative drama.

THE LEADER

An *ideal* (read: non-existent) creative dramatic leader would be highly skilled in guiding creative thinking. She would possess a large working knowledge pertaining to physiological and psychological development, dramatic structure, and children's literature. She also would be skilled in dancing, acting, and instrumental music. But more importantly, and more realistically, the leader must have or adopt a particular personality.

First of all, it helps to love kids, and we don't mean the old turn-it-on, turn-it-off variety that shows one face at parent conferences and the real one in the teachers' lounge. Can you pay compliments when none have been earned? How would you feel about a 7:30 Saturday morning door-bell ring, which suddenly reminds you of a casual promise to show the boys where the muskrats live? Do you often bring along an extra peanut butter and banana sandwich or two for the kids with thin lunch bags?

If love is no problem, the next hurdle is *energy*. A creative dramatics leader must be able to show, not merely to tell her people what to do. She not only needs to keep up with the kids, but occasionally must out-energize them. The best teachers are usually eight jumps and a bushel of ideas ahead of their students. Can you survive swinging through the jungle like a monkey, wading through a field of flypaper, crossing a burning desert in a bouncing box, swimming in a tank of jello, being anchor man in an imaginary tug of war—and still provide the horsepower for a giant people machine?

If you have the love and energy, the last ingredient is a good sense of humor. It may seem strange that a key ingredient for anything is funniness; but for creative dramatics high quality silliness—with all its laughs, freedom, joy and spontaneity—is essential. We are speaking now of a creative atmosphere, an atmosphere of freedom of expression and acceptance of the whole child. There is no wrong and there is minimal direction as to *how* a student should perform. Each person invents and discovers the "how" for himself. He does his own imaginative thing in his own unique way, and this is creative dramatics.

AGE DIFFERENCES

The Older You Are, the More You Need It

So far, we have said little about student age differences. Creative dramatics is a valuable experience for all ages. The first author, Davis, teaches undergraduate and graduate college courses in creative thinking and problem solving. The highlight of a given course is always the creative dramatics session. As a totally new experience, these adults (some in their thirties and forties) involve their bodies in creative exercises and activities. They bend and twist in dozens of forms. They beep, chug and twirl their limbs as a people machine grinding out chocolate ice cream. They stare at a fellow student, almost a total stranger, mimicking his every move. They melt to the floor as ice cubes on a stove; and there in total silence listen intently—to fast steps in the hall above, the buzz of fluorescent tubes, a noisy bird, some laughing, a diesel-engined bus. Then these proper adults pick themselves up like rag-doll puppets with strings fixed on noses and elbows. With eyes shut, they feel the face of a fellow student—for the first time in their educational lives gathering information so they can later pick him from the class.

How do adults react to such an experience? They might take the class over before the hour is out—"Let's make another machine—do whatever you want!" "Everyone balance on one leg in an awkward position and hold on to everybody else to keep from falling over!" It is a day of true creative regression that they do not soon forget and they likely will share their experiences with their own future students.

Naturally, the teacher must gear the activities to the age of the class. The graduate students won't feel too silly tugging on an imaginary rope or holding up a sinking ceiling, but they might be embarrassed at prancing like circus ponies or role-playing the Three Bears. Also, if creative dramatics activities are to continue for a long period, you as the leader will need a couple of books for new ideas. While we especially recommend Way (1967), several helpful volumes are listed in our bibliography.

If you do lead a session, remember that creative activities will at first be strange and unfamiliar. Be sure that directions are clear and that everyone understands what to do. Examples may help, so long as the examples are not copied. How to perform is the student's creative task. Also while you will have certain activities planned, be ready to get off-course at any instant.

SOME ACTIVITIES

For organizational purposes, we have subdivided this section into three parts, movement exercises, sensory and body awareness activites, and pantomime and playmaking. In practice, movement exercises and sensory/body awareness activities will be interwoven—for example, creative listening is a great relaxer following a robot-walk through a butterscotch swamp. Also, if you include playmaking in your session, some preliminary movement and sensory exercises will loosen up mind and body.

Movement Exercises

1. *Holding up the roof.* All participants strain to hold up the roof; slowly let it down (to one knee), then push it back up. Strenuous.

2. *Circles.* Students stand in large circle. Each participant, in turn, thinks of a way to make a circle using his body. All other students make the same circle. The circles can be made with part of the body or all of the body, it can be a fixed circle (e.g., a halo) or a moving circle e.g., a circular motion of the foot or rolling eyeballs). Names add to the fun, e.g., "This is a *halo circle,*" "This is an *eyeball circle.*"

3. *Tug-of-war.* Pick two five-man teams for imaginary tug-of-war.

Leader narrates, e.g., "This side seems to be winning; Look out! The rope broke!" Students will fall in two heaps without coaching.

4. *Mirrors.* Form two lines facing each other; each person needs a partner. Each individual in one row becomes a mirror that mimics the movement of his partner, who might be brushing his teeth, pulling faces, or putting on clown make-up.

5. *Puppets.* Several variations. Leader can narrate as all rag-doll marionettes are lifted from floor by strings attached to nose and elbow— then dropped! Or, with children in pairs, one is marionette and other is string-pulling puppeteer.

6. *People machine.* Infinite variations. Students can create ice cream (or donut or environmental clean-up) machine, with or without humms, buzzes, beeps and boops. Students can spontaneously join action, or join systematically one by one. All can move, or else every other one can make a noise to match his neighbor's movement. Slow it down, speed it up. One of the best is a people machine which makes people on an imaginary assembly belt.

7. *Invisible balls.* Form subgroups of 4–6 students. Each student makes up an invisible ball which, one at a time, is tossed, floated, hauled, etc., around the circle. In one variation each person in a large circle describes the new form of the ball as he passes it to his neighbor ("Now it's heavy"—or hot, gooey, slinky, etc.).

8. *Ice cubes.* Everyone is an ice cube which melts; different effects if melted by sun or by stove. A variation is to be sand bags which leak.

9. *Statues.* According to "Go" and "Stop" signals, or beginning and ending of leader's drum beat, students freeze in ugliest positions imaginable. Student observers or statues themselves describe what they are. (See Way, 1967, Ch. 5, for many extensions and variations.)

10. *Biggest thing.* Participants physically expand themselves into the biggest thing they can be. Follow with *Smallest Thing.* Variations include lightest, heaviest, stiffest, angriest, happiest, most frightful, most fearless, etc. Transition from one form to its opposite may be in slow motion.

11. *Circus.* Each child becomes a different circus performer or animal. Variations include the leader directing what *everyone* should be, e.g., tightrope walkers, trained elephants, lion tamers, jugglers, etc.

12. *Obstacles.* With chalk, draw "start" and "finish" lines about eight feet apart on the floor. One at a time, each student makes up

imaginary obstacle, which he must climb over, dodge, past, wade through, overcome, etc., to get from start to finish. Observers guess the obstacle.

13. *Gym work-out.* Participants pantomime activities as if they were in an imaginary gym. They run in place, lift weights, roll a medicine ball, climb a rope, etc.

14. *Leader Game.* Students form a large circle. One person goes outside the room until called. Another person is selected to start some motion which the other children follow. The first person is brought back into the center of the circle and tries to guess who the leader is. The leader changes the motion when the observer is not watching.

15. *Robot walk.* Each person is a robot with a sound. Whenever one robot touches another robot, both stop, sit down, and begin again to rise, with a new sound and a new walk.

16. *Awkward hold up.* Students balance on one leg in awkward position, holding onto the arms and ankles of others to keep from falling.

17. *Balloon burst.* All students are on the floor as *one* deflated balloon. The leader begins to blow the balloon up and the students must work together to expand and create a shape. Variations of balloon bursting: Let the air out slowly, pop with a pin, or blow the balloon so full of air that it bursts.

18. *Making letters.* Have two people at a time make any alphabet letter with ther bodies. Others guess the letter. Or have larger group spell ENVIRONMENT or word of their choice.

19. *Nature's shapes.* Children shape their bodies to become a tree, stone, leaf, growing flower, rain, sun, etc.

20. *Sticky floor.* Have students glue a portion of their bodies (e.g., elbow) to the floor. Discover movements they can make while glued.

21. *Creative locomotion.* Have children walk like a Crooked Man, Jolly Green Giant, Raggedy Ann, Robot; run like a mouse or Miss Muffet frightened by a spider, the fattest lady in the world running for a bus; jump like a kangaroo, pop-corn, or plow horse. Music such as Sibelius' *Peer Gynt Suite* or Moussorgsky's *Pictures at an Exhibition* is a good movement stimulus.

Sensory and Body Awareness Exercises

1. *Body movement.* Children discover moving parts by teacher asking them to move their fingers, then hands, wrists, elbows, shoulders,

neck (head rolling), face (chew, make faces, bat eyelashes), back, hips, legs, ankles, feet and toes. Variations: Ask students for more ideas (e.g., eyeballs, tongue, stomach muscles); ask students to keep *all* parts moving as more are added.

2. *Waking up the body.* Have children lie on the floor in any position with eyes closed and body parts relaxed. With slow, quiet music have the children begin waking up the various parts of their bodies one at a time until they are on their feet.

3. *Stretching.* Beginning at their heads and working down, have the children stretch the various parts of their bodies.

4. *Swinging.* Let the group discover all of the ways a body can be made to swing—head, arms, legs, waist, etc.

5. *Warm-up at different speeds.* Have children run in place in slow motion, speed up until children are moving very fast. Variations include jumping, skipping, hopping.

6. *Rag doll-tin man.* Have children perform simple warm-up exercises as limp as a rag-doll; as stiffened tin men let them discover how their movements change.

7. *Paper exploration.* Give each child a piece of 9 x 12 construction paper. Have them balance the paper on different parts of the body (especially the foot); run with the paper on the palms of their hands.

8. *Exploring an orange.* Give everyone an orange to examine closely. How does it feel, smell, taste? What is unique about *your* orange; could you pick it out from a crowd of oranges? Take it apart and look at it, taste, touch, and smell the inside. Eat it.

9. *Blind man.* Divide participants into pairs. Member with eyes shut (or blindfolded) is led around room, under tables and chairs, and allowed to identify objects by touch, smell, or sound. Variation: go outside. Can lead to discussion of blindness and replacement senses.

10. *Observation test.* Cover some article of apparel, such as earrings or necktie, and ask what the object looks like. Variations: Ask a particular person to close his eyes and describe what the person next to him is wearing. Ask students to shut their eyes. How many windows and lights are there? What color are the walls? Are the maps down?

11. *Focusing.* Ask students to see only things which are very close; middle distance, very far. What do they see?

12. *Empathic vision.* Ask students to inspect the room through the

eyes of an artist, fire inspector, lighting engineer, a termite. Look at to-day's weather from the point of view of a duck, a skier, a field mouse, smoke jumpers. Who else?

13. *Listening.* Have students sit (or lie) silently, listening for whatever they can hear. Encourage concentration, letting sounds evoke associated images and memories. Variations: Listen only for close sounds or far sounds. With *all* eyes shut, have students describe source of sound with hands, communicating without words.

14. *Imaginary sounds.* Ask students to suggest sounds found in particular places—a factory, zoo, railroad station, department store, gas station, police station, etc.

15. *Touching.* Have students touch many surfaces, concentrating fully on the feel. Use strange things (e.g., a piece of coral) and familiar things.

16. *Imaginary touching.* Have children imagine the feel of different objects and surfaces, e.g., warm sand between the toes, a hot sidewalk, a wet paw and a lick on the face, ice cream, a Twinkie, mud, and so on.

17. *Body contacts.* Have participants concentrate on contacts of body places with, e.g., soles of shoes, shirt collars, chair seats, contacts between fingers. Can they feel the shirt or blouse in the middle of the back? Can they feel heart beats, stomach, lungs?

18. *Texture walk.* Have group walk through imaginary substances, e.g., jello, flypaper, deep sand, chocolate pudding, tacks, swamp, etc., with leader and members calling out new substances and surfaces.

19. *Smelling.* Indoors and outdoors, have students shut eyes and sniff. Can they identify individual smells?

20. Have students imagine good smells. What are they? Can every-one imagine them? Have them imagine the smell of, e.g., tulips, his mother, a bus, a barn, a hamburger, etc.

21. *Tasting.* Encourage students to be aware of and to concentrate upon different tastes of foods. Imaginary tastes can be suggested; per-haps some new taste experiences can be shared, with reasonable sanitary precautions.

Pantomine and Playmaking

Playmaking involves acting out stories and scenes without a script. In fact, you can even do it without lines. When a child is asked to pantomime an action, full attention may be given to the elements which compose it. He creates the proper shape and movements of his body and even intently fixes his eyes upon objects in his imaginary environment. With encouragement, he can use his face, hands and body to display sadness, glee, love or fear. If this same child were allowed to speak, he might very well dismiss all bodily and facial expression and let only his words convey the message. Some suggestions for pantomime exercises are as follows. Throughout, encourage students to "show me, don't tell me."

1. *Animal pantomimes.* Have the children imitate the way a particular animal moves. In turn, each child can come into the center of the circle to pantomime his animal. The rest of the group can guess the animal, perhaps by moving into the center to feed it. For variety, two or three animals can act out a simple plot, for example: (a) a cat sneaking up on a mouse, (b) a bear looking for honey, but finding bees, (c) a bloodhound tracking down a possum, (d) a bull spotting some picnickers, or (e) a fox sneaking up on a chicken.

2. *Alice's potion.* Have two bottles filled with magic potions. One makes people very small and the other makes them very tall.

3. *Upside down.* If the world turned upside down and your group remained right-side up, what difficulties might you encounter? Pantomime activities like walking on your hands (or the sky), pouring drinks, or changing clothes.

4. *Hats.* Create a hat shop, real or imagined, in which various kinds of workers come in to select a hat fitting their job, e.g., baseball player, policeman, fireman, Indian chief, cowboy, movie star, milkman, etc. With hat in place, each child pantomimes the behavior matching his hat.

5. *Picnic.* The children decide what kind of person they would like to be at a picnic. It is helpful to suggest that they give their character a quality which makes him more readily identifiable, such as a slight limp, a brisk walk, a burly strut, or a skipping or dancing motion. Of course, their faces should match the motion. When they have decided, let them walk around together until they are in character. As leader, you become the bus driver that loads up the group and takes them to the picnic. Once there, they are ready to apply their characterization to improvised situations: They can organize sports, a food table, feeding animals, dodging the local bull, swatting ants and flies, opening the pop, etc. When the players decide to leave, reload the bus and drive off.

6. *Inside out.* Many pantomimic activities can be explored from the inside out. Children become fish in a tank and others look in. Zoo animals in cages are good sources for this activity. You may wish to move

into empathic abstraction by having a child's mirror describe what it's like to be looked into all day; likewise for a book's pages, a TV set, a road map.

7. *Add-ons.* An add-on, much like a people machine, is an environment created by the group. For example, one child begins rolling a bowling ball down a lane. Another becomes the ball, a pin, the scorecard, a drinking fountain, and whatever else they can think of until the picture is complete. If available, sound effects records are helpful. Other worthwhile subjects are fishing, croquet, baseball, hanging clothes on the line, a circus, an orchestra, marine fish and animals (octopi, star fish, crabs, lobster), zoo animals, farm animals, etc.

8. *Miscellaneous pantomime.* Many brief sketches may teach characterization, for example, a jolly drugstore clerk making an ice cream soda, a fussy lady trying on hats, a scared mountain climber scaling a cliff, tired pirates digging for treasure, giggly kids watching a funny movie, a grouchy cab driver fighting 5:00 traffic, a nervous, sneaky thief entering a candy store, an awkward cook flipping pancakes. You and your students can think of more.

Playmaking as a form of creative drama can take many forms other than pantomime activities. With one straightforward strategy, students are given a simple scene or plot, characterization and then turned loose. In some examples from Way (1967, pp. 107-109), one group of three students could be the three stooges robbing a bank. They're so half-witted they do everything wrong, backwards, or both. Other groups of the same idiots can act as a surgery team performing a heart-transplant ("Gimme a knife and a blood bucket!"); perform as a musical quartet for trombone, drum, nose harp and garbage can; erect a tent on a windy, rocky hill, or paint and wallpaper a kitchen.

Note that by giving students a perfectly logical reason for being silly, they are helped in overcoming feelings of self-consciousness. Fear of failure is removed and confidence built (Way, 1967).

But mini-plays need not always be silly. Way (1967, pp. 83–84) suggests that groups can be miners working against time to reinforce a mine about to cave in; slow-moving astronauts assembling something on the moon; toyshop toys (or museum displays) coming alive at the stroke of midnight; or witches cooking up a magic brew. Historical events also present possibilities: Columbus discovering America, Boston tea party, Pilgrims landing at Plymouth Rock, and others.

A more involved playmaking strategy runs as follows. After a few warm-up exercises, the leader tells a story. Then she and the students review the sequence of events—what happened first? second? The group then discusses characterization, considering physical, emotional and intellectual qualities (nervous, calm, slow-witted, happy, angry, excited, scientific-minded, beautiful, quick-stepping, limping, stuck-up etc.). The play typically is broken into scenes and worked out scene by scene. The group may first act out a scene without dialogue to explore the physical possibilities and believability of the characters and the overall effect. After the group thinks of ways to make the scene better, it is replayed with improvised dialogue. A given scene may be played many times with different students experiencing various roles. This general strategy may be adapted for use with such familiar tales as Goldilocks or Peter Cottontail for small children, Cinderella for third graders, and Pandora's Box or Electra for the sixth grade. Generally, fairy tales, nursery rhymes, myths, folklore, historical material, and animal stories provide fine literature sources.

Direct questioning may add to the educational experience. Ask such questions as, "Why did Electra hate her mother? Could you hate your mother?" "Why are Cinderella's ugly sisters so mean?" Questions such as "How would you feel if . . . ?" and "What would happen if . . . ?" also will stretch the creative, empathic imagination.

SUMMARY

Creative dramatics clearly is different in purposes, activities, and results from every other school subject. Apart from the fun—which increases appreciation of school—creative dramatics activities build confidence in speaking, behaving, and being oneself in a group. They sharpen a child's observation, listening, and other sensory skills and increase body awareness and control. Creative dramatics also provides a non-threatening atmosphere which allows stretching the creative imagination and solving unusual problems. Students learn to empathize with humans in other roles and with other interests, needs, and problems. While creative dramatics is not the same as children's theatre, the use of creative dramatics as warm-up activities will lead to more flexible, confident and involved acting. Creative dramatics indeed is a valuable creative experience for children and adults of all ages.

REFERENCES

ALINGTON, A. F. *Drama and education.* Oxford, England: Blackwell, 1961.

BROWN, C. *Creative drama in the lower school.* NYC: Appleton-Century-Crofts, 1929.

BURGER, I. *Creative play acting.* Cranbury, NJ: Barnes, 1950.

CROSSCUP, R. *Children and dramatics.* NYC: Scribner, 1966.

DAVIS, G. A. *It's your imagination: Theory and training of problem solving.* NYC: Basic Books, 1972.

HUTSON, N. B. *Stage—A handbook of ideas for creative dramatics.* Educational Service Inc., Michigan, 1968.

KASE, C. R. *Stories for creative acting.* NYC: French, 1961.

LEASE, R. & SIKS, G. B. *Creative dramatics in home, school, and community.* NYC: Harper, 1952.

McCASLIN, N. *Creative dramatics in the classroom.* NYC: McKay, 1968.

OLFSON, L. *You can act.* NYC: Sterling, 1970.

SIKS, G. B. *Children's literature for dramatization: An anthology.* NYC: Harper, 1964.

SPOLIN, V. *Improvisation for the theater.* Evanston, IL: Northwestern University Press, 1963.

WALKER, P. *Seven steps to creative children's drama.* NYC: Hill & Wang, 1957.

WARD, W. *Playmaking with children.* NYC: Appleton-Century-Crofts, 1957.

WAY, B. *Development through drama.* London, England: Longman, 1967.

Simulation Games as Method

Virginia M. Rogers and Audrey H. Goodloe

If a student wants to determine the genealogy of his family, find out about Abraham Lincoln's views on a certain political issue, or trace the history of space travel, he can do so by consulting books, printed records, and other primary or secondary sources. If, however, a middle class student wants to experience the feelings of defeat that ghetto people have in trying to improve their circumstances, if an urban student wants to gain some understanding of the economic pressures influencing farmers, if a youngster totally uninvolved in politics wants to better understand forces influencing political decisions, if a student wants a more realistic basis for learning about budgeting, or if he wants to make worthy decisions about a host of events which influence his life, he must become more directly and personally involved with the problems, possibly experimenting with several alternatives.

Teachers often talk about the importance of developing empathy for others, the desirability of sound economic practices, making responsible ecological decisions, developing a more responsive government, alleviating traffic congestion, and a range of other problems about which most students have little basis for developing feelings, making decisions, or suggesting alternative actions. Largely because of their lack of personal concrete involvement in these problem situations, they can be so objective as to be unrealistic and insensitive in their suggestions for solutions.

Conceding that personal concrete experiences provide a more realistic and functional perspective, how can such experiences be provided in a school setting? Because it is impossible to experience some situations directly without physical or emotional danger to the student, or because it is economically or politically not feasible, some alternative mechanism that provides reasonably personal concrete experiences must be utilized. Simulation can provide such a mechanism.

There is a concomitant and possibly even more important rationale for using simulation games in a classroom. It is to develop one's inquiry skills. Hopefully, schools no longer view their sole responsibility as requiring all students to acquire a specific body of information. Rather, the schools in contemporary society should help students develop social awareness, understanding of self and others, as well as logical thinking or reality testing skills.

Using the terms of Transactional Analysis,[1] schools should help students develop their Adult, to learn to gather information, process it, analyze it along with data already stored in the individual, and make logical decisions. Of course, after a decision that seems logical is made, the person will hopefully be open to reconsidering his decision as new data are acquired. Compare this process with making decisions based on stored prejudices (Parent) or solely on an emotional level (Child).

To develop inquiry skills using simulation, teachers must free students to learn; that is, the teacher must become a guide and resource rather than the primary source and direct conveyor of knowledge. Teachers must be willing to accept activity outcomes and students' attitudes with an open mind. By their actions, including nonverbal actions, they must value student judgment.

The use of simulation games implies that the teacher values the unique needs of individual students. It implies that learning is an active process rather than a passive one. It underscores the importance of students' examining their values and the values of others. And it means the instructor values the goal of learning to live with ambiguity, that two ideas may not be consistent although both seem to have validity.

COMMERCIAL GAMES

Teachers considering the use of simulation games should be cognizant of what simulation games can and cannot be expected to do. Instructors who have no previous experience using simulation games will find it helpful to use commercial games until they have developed confidence in using simulation games in their classrooms. When the teacher has developed security in the mechanics of the games, he can begin to be more creative in adapting games to meet specific needs, in developing games himself, and in guiding a class to develop a game. Games such as Dangerous Parallel (Scott Foresman), Ghetto (Western Publishing Com-

[1] Thomas A. Harris, *I'm OK—You're OK*. New York: Harper & Row, Publishers, 1969.

pany), and Star Power (Western Behavioral Sciences Institute) are excellent for novice gamers, and fit well into many curricula.

STUDENT-MADE GAMES

After playing one or more games, class members may be able to use the format as a basis for developing their own games. The development by students of simulation games can be a tool, just like note taking or committee work, to organize data collection and help solve a problem. The students then play the games to test their hypotheses, simulate a situation for further research, and generally broaden their perspective of the problem.

A list of elements generally included in simulation games follows. Teachers or students with teacher leadership can use this skeleton to develop games themselves after a problem has been identified.

Roles

What roles are involved in the simulation? What is the status (economic, political, etc.) of various roles, and how are persons in each role affected by the problem situation? As an example, suppose the problem situation being simulated involves pollution. The roles might include conservationists, industrialists, concerned citizens, farmers, politicians, or fishermen. Depending on the geographic location and the specific type of pollution, the roles might vary.

Goals

What are the goals of the individuals and groups in the simulation? If the problem is one on international conflict, the goals will vary according to political affiliation and economic circumstances. Whatever the problem, all goals will not be the same for each individual or role in the game. It is important for students to realize that goals differ and that they change with the situation over time.

Simulation games should allow players to set some of their own goals, using data they have collected and the framework of the game to guide them. They should also be given the opportunity to reevaluate and change these goals as the game proceeds.

Alternatives

What alternatives do various individuals or groups have in trying to achieve their goals? An important but often difficult step in the decision-making process is identifying reasonable alternatives. Rational decisions can seldom be made unless these alternatives can be identified, analyzed, and evaluated.

Simulation games should provide an opportunity for the players to consider the consequences of alternatives.

"Chance" Element

A very real part of life is the "chance" element, those things over which one has little or no control. Some chance elements can be anticipated, while others give no advance warning. What are the chance elements that may affect the individuals and groups involved in the simulated problem?

If one role in a game is that of a miner, chance elements might include an accident, a mine shutdown, a strike, and a better job becoming available. If the role involves a wage earner in any job, chance cards may include a hospital bill, the need to buy a new appliance, an increase in rent or insurance, and a wage increase or bonus. When rewards in the game are in the form of image points, as in Sunshine (Interact), the chance element might give a person of a specific race or economic level a high honor, which would increase the image points of all similar roles.

Focus on Interaction

There are various formats for simulation games and various reasons for choosing one over another. The problem or situation being simulated should of course influence the focus of interaction students choose. For example, the purpose of Generation Gap (Western Publishing Company) is for young people to think through some of the problems of communicating with their parents and other authority figures. The interaction is, therefore, player vs. player.

Some games may begin with each individual having separate goals and working independently with the option to form groups as it seems advantageous. For example, the Seal Hunt game (Education Development Center) has five or six individual roles. However, the option is open for the hunters to cooperate and share if they so choose. In Dangerous Parallel, students play the roles of leaders in six different countries (group vs. group); however, groups often form alliances as in the real world of politics.

Some games focus on interaction of student or group against the game or system, rather than competing against each other. For example, if the purpose of a game is to help students learn something about budgeting and responsibilities of wage earners, there might be no competition between the players in the game. In fact, the competition might be between the players and the system, that is, the economic system. The goal of each student might relate to budgeting his monthly earnings and getting ahead economically with the action of other players influencing him very little or not at all.

Most simulation games do not end with a "winner" or "loser," as in traditional games such as Monopoly, basketball, or Yahtzee. If the reason for developing and playing a specific game is to gain empathy for other individuals, a winner could scarcely be determined by the number of points gained. While evaluation of final outcomes must be the responsibility of the players who must decide for themselves how well they have achieved their goals, points or chips might be used as a source of pressure or incentive or to measure accomplishments or advancement within the game. In Ghetto, points represent money earned and increase in self-image. The immediate goal in Star Power is to increase points; the parallel in reality is the goal of people to gain power, status, and financial security.

Debriefing

The debriefing session of a game is that time when students talk about and examine what happened during the game, including their feelings, actions, and reactions. The situation simulated should be related to reality as the students know it. The debriefing should be used as a time of evaluation by the students and teacher, and it should also be a springboard to motivate further investigation and experimentation with alternatives, understandings, and feelings.

The debriefing emphasizes the necessity of keeping an open mind and making tentative decisions based on the data at hand, while being receptive to new data. Values are reexamined in the light of experiences in the game and related to reality. Open-ended questions and acceptance of all seriously given answers should be the rule during the debriefing.

Student-made games often demonstrate creativity but are seldom finished products. Even so, several worthwhile learning objectives can be achieved in the process of developing a simulation game. When students ask questions such as, "What data do we need to make the game more realistic?" and when they seek this information, they are developing research skills far beyond that which is typically expected from reading a chapter in a book.

In developing descriptions and background data for roles or in describing a scenario, students typically delve deeper and with far more enthusiasm than one finds where traditional methods are employed. Facts are still acquired; concepts are still being developed. More important, feelings and values are examined with a better understanding of self and others.

Simulation is suggested as a method for students to learn to empathize and develop inquiry skills. The use of commercially available simulation games is proposed for teachers and students to become familiar with the mechanics and potential of simulation. Upon gaining that perspective, it is suggested that a class (or convenient subgroup) of students develop a simulation game based on some problem situation they have identified, and that they then play the game. To aid in the development, elements of simulation games, possible formats, and other characteristics were briefly considered. The teacher's attitude and questioning techniques are judged to be especially crucial.

Communication Grows
in a "Magic Circle"

William Lefkowitz

A dozen children and a teacher sitting in a circle using simple group dynamics techniques to create an intricate communication exchange—that's a "magic circle." Devised by two California educators and psychologists, the magic circle helps to promote personal growth of pupils in the classroom—growth in awareness, in the mastery of skills, and in the ability to interact with peers and adults.

Dr. Harold Bessell and Dr. Uvaldo Palomares recognized that learning in academic areas (cognitive learning) can be greatly enhanced by continued personal growth (affective learning). Feeling that such personal growth was too important to leave to chance, the two men designed the Human Development Program for grades K–6. The program's teaching guides present a series of cumulative, sequential activities that classroom teachers can direct.

Subject matter for the daily 20-minute talk sessions is the children's own experiences. Their words and feelings are the learning medium. What the children learn is how to be more effective, why people are sometimes happy or unhappy, how to feel good about themselves, and how to get along well with others.

The teacher serves as leader until pupils are ready to assume that role. A leader makes sure that relevant information gets expressed and that the information expressed gets shaped, correlated, and refined by continuous feedback. For example:

> *Teacher:* The subject for today's magic circle is "I felt good when . . ." Who'd like to start?
>
> *John:* I felt good when my dad took me fishing.
>
> *Teacher:* How good did you feel, John?
>
> *John:* I felt happy . . . and proud. Happy 'cause I like to fish.

William Lefkowitz, "Communication Grows In A 'Magic Circle,'" *Teacher's Edition: My Weekly Reader,* April 5, 1972.

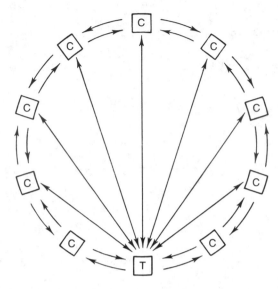

The *mandala* is oldest magical symbol known to mankind. Used as an art form by modern children, the mandala suggests the "sun" of a nuclear family in an expanding social universe. The diagram shows the various lines of communication possible in a magic circle.

And proud 'cause I felt grown-up.

Amy: John, I heard you say that when your father took you fishing you felt happy 'cause you like to fish, and proud 'cause you felt grown-up.

Teacher: Thank you, Amy, for listening so well. And thank you, John, for sharing your feelings with us. Who else would like to tell about a time they . . . ?

If you'd like to try some magic circles in your classroom, here are some suggestions:

GETTING STARTED

Split the class into groups of 7 to 12 children, with a nearly equal number of boys and girls in each group. As one group meets in a circle, other pupils may observe or engage in quiet activities. Establish these rules:

1. Anyone who wants to speak gets a chance to do so.

2. To get a chance to speak, a pupil must raise his hand and wait to be called upon by the leader.
3. Everyone is to listen and be able to show that he or she has listened by repeating what has been said.

LEADING THE CIRCLE

Introduce and explain the topic for discussion. Demonstrate what is expected by going first. Call upon volunteers to feed back information to the speaker.

Be accepting. Show an interest in what children say, but do not indicate approval or disapproval.

Invite shy children to participate, but *don't insist* that anyone speak who doesn't want to.

Limit sessions to about 20 minutes.

Don't be afraid of silence. Children may just be thinking. Should interest wane, end the session.

Thank each child for his or her contribution and for observing the rules. Thank the observers and others outside the magic circle if they have behaved well.

After every third or fourth speaker, ask someone to review what has been said. Before closing the session, help children review and summarize what was learned.

TOPICS TO START WITH

Start with positive topics; then try the negatives.

I felt good (bad) when . . .

A pleasant (unpleasant) thought I have is . . .

Something I can (wish I could) do is . . .

I made somebody feel good (bad) when I . . .

Somebody made me feel good (bad) when he . . .

Ask pupils for things they'd like to talk about.

For information and/or teaching guides write to: Warren Timmermann, Institute for Personal Effectiveness in Children, P.O. Box 796, Amherst, MA 01002.

Self-Concept: A Critical Dimension in Teaching and Learning

John T. Canfield and Harold C. Wells

"... *the most important ideas any man ever has are the ideas he has about himself.*"—Robert Bills

I am happy. I am sick. I am good. I am beautiful. I'm a loser.
I'm okay. I am bad. I am clumsy. I'm a gossip. I'm neurotic.
I am a bore. I'm a mess. I'm cool. I am successful. I'm a failure.
I'm loveable. I am sexy. I'm sad. I'm a good teacher. I am smart.
I am a good person. I'm a slow learner. I'm not okay.

Which of these sentences describe you? Go back and draw an imaginary or actual circle around each sentence that expresses how you feel most of the time. Go ahead and actually do it now.

How many of your circled sentences please you? There are twenty-six sentences: thirteen are essentially "positive" and thirteen "negative." When you look at your responses in this light, what kind of picture do you get of yourself? That picture is a little glimpse of a tiny part of your self-concept.

Your self-concept is composed of all the beliefs and attitudes you have about yourself. They actually determine who you are! They also determine what you think you are, what you do, and what you can become!

It's amazing to think that these internal beliefs and attitudes you hold about yourself are that powerful, but they are! In fact, in a very functional sense, they are your *self!*

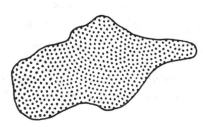

Imagine the above "glob" as a representation of your self. You are an entity that hangs together in an organized, consistent, reasonably firm and permanent state, yet you also have the quality of fluidity—something like a strong jellyfish. The dots shown in your self represent the thousands of beliefs you hold about yourself. These beliefs are neither random nor contradictory. They fit together in a meaningful pattern or "system," each complementing the others so that they form an integrated whole.

HOW IS THE SELF FORMED?

It is evident that the self is learned. It is not inherited. From our earliest moments of life we begin to accumulate data about ourselves and our world. New impressions flood in upon us. We soon learn what eases pain and what makes us comfortable, what satisfies our hunger, what it takes to get attention, and so on. As our experiences multiply, our developing self becomes a perceptual screen through which subsequent impressions must pass. For example, if we've been fed at the breast for weeks, we'll not be satisfied if someone puts a brick to our mouth! Our perceptual screen rejects the brick as too hard, rough and cold, and we scream for the object we *know* is right.

In the same manner we gradually formulate impressions and attitudes about ourselves. A crawling baby reaches out to grasp a figurine on a low coffee table. His mother says, "No, no, no! Mustn't touch. Bad boy!" Repeated exposure to such responses teach the child: "I do things wrong. Things are more important that I am, and I'm bad." This, of course, is not at all what the parent wanted to impart, but it is nevertheless precisely the message that many youngsters receive in such situations.

YOUR SELF IS CONSISTENT

Let's return to your "glob" floating through life. Any new experience you have is interpreted in light of all the beliefs and attitudes you've accumulated as little dots in your self. If the new experience is consistent with what you believe, it is enveloped by your "glob" and your self becomes a little larger. On the other hand, if the new experience is not consistent with your self (concept), it is ignored or rejected. Your "glob" simply bends a little where the new experience hits and moves right on past it, filling itself in as though nothing had occurred. This is a wonderful protective quality, actually; it keeps us together. It has some problems, however. It makes change in self-concept extremely difficult because to *significantly change anything* in this "self full of dots" requires modification of the whole "system" in order for it to remain a consistent self. Here is an illustration of this concept:

> Jack is a good kid. He's a typical boy so he sometimes gets in little scrapes but never anything too bad. However on this occasion Jack is playing with some other boys and they decide to steal some cigarettes and hide somewhere and smoke them. Jack is scared, but excited, too. The boys go ahead with their escapade. In the end Jack's little brother hears about what happened and tells their father who just raises the roof with poor Jack. What does Jack say? What does he *really* believe about this incident? "I didn't want to steal but . . . well, the gang kind of . . . you know. Besides *I* didn't steal the cigarettes. Charley did! I only smoked one and I hated it. It was a good lesson. I'll never smoke those awful things."

Sounds like a lot of kids you know, doesn't it? Now why did Jack respond like this? It's simple, really. Jack, *just as every other human being alive, has got to protect his self-esteem—his feelings about himself.* He did that in this instance by rationalizing about being kind of "forced" into the situation and by figuring what a great lesson it was. He may, in time, actually come to believe he did it as an experiment; a lesson to himself on how bad cigarettes taste so he'll never be tempted by the habit. See how smart that makes him, and how good he can feel about himself? So, two things have happened. First, Jack's image of himself as a "good kid" is retained. He has taken an objectively "bad" incident and filtered it through his Self system in such a way as to maintain this consistency of his concept of himself as a "good kid." Secondly, and this is closely related, he has maintained or increased his self-esteem. This is the prime motivation for all behavior. It is perhaps our highest value. We must, in spite of everything, be able to see ourselves as worthy people. The strangest, most bizarre, and often most hideous behavior can be accounted for by the motivation of the individual to maintain and enhance his *self in his own eyes.*

It is difficult for others to see how some behavior can possibly be self-maintaining—but it is. We need to be inside the skin of the other person to fully comprehend his point of view, which of course we can't do; but we can keep this idea in mind and try to probe for data that will help us understand his rationale, no matter how distorted it may seem in *our* eyes.

SELF-CONCEPT AND LEARNING

By the time a child reaches school age his self-concept is quite well formed and his reactions to learning, to school failure and success, and to the physical, social, and emotional climate of the classroom will be determined by the beliefs and attitudes he has about himself. There is considerable evidence to support this view. Perhaps the most dramatic is that of Wattenberg and Clifford [1] who studied kindergarden youngsters in an attempt to see if self-concept was predictive of reading success two and a half years later. It was. In fact it was a better predictor than IQ! Children with low (poor) self-concepts did not learn to read or did not read as well as children with high (good) self-concepts.

Other studies affirm the position that self-concept is related to achievement in school, that the relationship is particularly strong in boys, that it begins to evidence itself as early as the first grade, and that early school difficulties in learning persist.

We have developed a theory to explain this phenomenon which we call the "poker chip theory of learning." We see all learning as the result of a risk-taking situation somewhat akin to a poker game (or any other gambling situation, for that matter). In any potential learning situation, the student is asked to take a risk: to write a paper that will be evaluated, to make a recitation which may be laughed at, to do board work that may be wrong, to create an object of art that might be judged, etc. In each situation he is risking error, judgment, disapproval, censure, rejection, and, in extreme cases, even punishment. At a deeper level the student is risking his or her self-concept.

Imagine that each student's self-concept is a stack of poker chips. Some students start the learning game, as it were, with a lot of poker chips; others with very few. The students with the higher number of chips have a great advantage. To continue the poker analogy, the student with one hundred chips can sustain twenty losses of five chips each. The student with only fifteen chips can only sustain three losses of five chips each. The latter student will be much more cautious and reticent about stepping into the arena. This kind of student manifests a variety of behaviors indicating his reluctance to risk learning. They range from "This is stupid, I don't want to do it." (translation: "I am stupid; I'm afraid I can't do it.") and withdrawn silence on one extreme to mischievous acting-out on the other.

The student who has had a good deal of success in the past will be likely to risk success again. If perchance he should fail, his self-concept can "afford" it. A student with a history predominated by failures will be reluctant to risk failure again.

His depleted self-concept cannot afford it. Similar to someone living on welfare, he will shop cautiously and look for bargains. One obvious recommendation in this situation is to make each learning step small

---

[1] W. W. Wattenberg and C. Clifford, *Relationship of Self-Concept to Beginning Achievement in Reading,* U.S. Office of Education, Cooperative Research Project No. 377. (Detroit: Wayne State University, 1962).

enough so that the student is asked to only risk one chip at a time, instead of five. But even more obvious, to our eyes, is the need to build up the student's supply of poker chips so that he can begin to have a surplus of chips to risk.

If a student starts out, metaphorically speaking, with twenty chips and he gains fifteen more through the exercises contained in this book, then, even if he loses ten in a reading class, he is still five ahead of the game. But if he loses ten from a starting position of twenty he is now down to ten and in a very precarious psychological position. Viewed in this way one can see self-concept building as a sort of pump priming to the academic learning process.

WHAT CAN YOU DO ABOUT STUDENTS' SELF-CONCEPTS?

As you can tell from what we have written above, we are convinced that one of the major challenges to teachers is the creation of a positive and self-enhancing learning environment. Theory is helpful, but the heart of the matter is how to translate it into specific classroom activities and behavior. Some special people seem to do this quite naturally out of their own authentic being and their commitment to others. Most of us, however, benefit from specific useable suggestions that help us toward that end. With that in mind we offer you the following classroom activities. For ninety-four more we refer you to our book *100 Ways to Enhance Self-Concept in the Classroom* (Prentice-Hall, 1974).

THE NAME GAME

This two-part exercise has several learning goals. It can be used to help one learn others' names, and to establish positive feelings towards oneself and his classmates. In the event that the students are already well-acquainted start with part B.

A. Have the class sit in a circle. Start by saying, "I am Miss (Mr., Mrs.) Jones." The first student to her right says, "I am Billy and that's Miss Jones." Continue this process around the circle until the last person has repeated everybody's name.

B. The second time around in addition to their name, each person must add something he is good at. For example, "I am singing Miss Jones." "I am basketball-playing Billy, and that's singing Miss Jones." "I am cookie-baking Sally, and that's basketball-playing Billy, and that's singing Miss Jones," and so on around the circle.

AUTOBIOGRAPHICAL SHARING

In order for the child's self-concept to grow he needs to be in an environment of trust and rapport so that he can feel secure enough to take risks. One of the best methods for developing an environment of trust is mutual self-disclosure.

Ask the students to sit in a circle. Tell them that each student will have one (two or three) minutes to share with the group an autobiographical sketch of his life. Appoint one student with a second hand on his watch to be the timer. If you're working with elementary students, you may have to supply the watch. When working with a small group of eight to ten students, you may wish to use a three-minute egg timer.

Ask the students to share those important experiences throughout their lives, beginning with early childhood, which they consider of importance in the sense of leaving a strong impression on their personalites.

In this type of exercise it is a good idea for you to be the first one to share in order to model the behavior you are after with the students. Your going first also creates an environment of less risk.

SUCCESS SHARING

Another way to help students focus upon the positive aspects of themselves is to have them publicly share their accomplishments with the group.

In small groups of five or six, or with the entire class, ask the students to share with their group a success, accomplishment or achievement they had before they were ten years old. Next ask them to share a success they had between the ages of ten and fifteen; then between the ages of fifteen to the present time. Obviously, these age ranges wiil need to be revised depending on the ages of the students in your class.

At first some students may have difficulty remembering some of their earlier successes, but as others share theirs, it will trigger their minds. Children with extremely low self-concepts often report that they haven't had any successes. If this happens, you will need to help prod the students with questions such as:

"Well, you've been taking care of your younger brothers and sisters for two years; I consider that an accomplishment, don't you?" "Can you remember when you learned to ride your bicycle? Did you feel good about that achievement?"

PRIDE LINE

Pride is related to self-concept. People enjoy expressing pride in something they've done that might have otherwise gone unrecognized. Our culture does not encourage such expressions and it is sometimes difficult for people to actually say, "I'm proud that I . . ."

Ask the students to make a statement about a specific item, beginning with "I'm proud that I . . ." For example, you might say, "I'd like you to mention something about your *letter writing* that you'd be proud of. Please begin your response with "I am proud that I . . ." Students may say "I pass" if they wish.

Below are some suggested items for use in the Pride Line.

1. Things you've done for your parents.
2. Things you've done for a friend.
3. Work in school.
4. How you spend your free time.
5. About your religious belief.
6. How you've gotten some money.
7. Something you've bought recently.
8. How you usually spend your money.
9. Habits you have.
10. Something you do often.

SUCCESS-A-DAY

At the end of each day, have the students briefly share with the rest of the class the successes they have experienced during that day.

Some students will find this difficult at first, but as others begin to share, they too will realize they have had some of the same successes. It has also been our experience that if a student says he has had no success, that some of his classmates will chime in with successes they have seen him accomplish. The sensitive teacher will also look for successes to be pointed out to the child with extremely low self-esteem.

SUCCESS SYMBOLS

All of us have symbols of success, things which remind us of our past successes. We have photographs, medals, certificates, dried-up corsages, dance books, ticket stubs, autographed baseballs, newspaper clippings, bronzed shoes, mounted golf balls, fish and antlers, trophies, plaques, and ribbons. Most of us save these objects because they remind us of our abilities and competences and our likability and popularity.

Have the students bring to class five tangible objects that recall or symbolize some past successes or accomplishments they have had.

During the next class period have each student share one or more of his "success symbols" with the rest of the class. Instruct the students to share the feelings and meaning connected with the specific object as well as the success it symbolizes.

STRENGTH BOMBARDMENT

Have the students break into groups of five or six students each. Focusing on one person at a time the group is to bombard him with all the strengths they see in him. The person being bombarded should remain silent until the group has finished. One member of the group should act as recorder, listing the strengths and giving them to the person when the group has finished.

The students should be instructed to list at least fifteen strengths for each student. They should also be cautioned that no "put-down" statements are allowed. Only positive assets are to be mentioned.

WISHING

Dreams and wishes range from the simple to the fantastic. One may simply desire a new toy or he may imagine himself walking on the moon. A child can easily imagine himself to be anything or anyone he chooses. While wishes may often seem impossible and farfetched, they are very often expressions of real needs—such as the common need to be accepted by one's peers. Once wishes are expressed and recognized as normal, they can be used as a motivating force behind action. With the use of goal setting a child can begin to realize that, with action, a wish may be attained.

Genies and magic fairies often grant people three wishes. Ask the children to imagine they had three wishes. What would they be? Ask them to imagine they had three wishes for someone else whom they liked very much. What would they wish for them?

If they could relive the previous day, what would they wish to have been different? To have been the same?

Did you ever wish to be someone else? Who? Why? Do you think someone might wish to be you? Why would he want to be you?

Did you ever have a wish come true? Tell about it. Is there anything you can do, besides just wishing, to help you get your wish?

THE GOAL POST

Decorate a bulletin board in the form a football goal post. Each day, as the kids come into class, ask them to set a goal for that day or for that night at home. Record the goal on a 3 x 5 index card and post it on the bulletin board below the cross bars of the goal post.

At the end of the day, or the following day, ask all those who completed their goals to move their index card above the cross bar. If you are working in a group situation, ask the kids to share their goal and how they completed it with the group. This provides the goal achievers with the attention of their peers as a reinforcement of their successful action.

These are just a few of the exercises we have completed and developed. All of them work. They have been used successfully in hundreds of classrooms with teachers reporting back tremendous differences in the tone of their classes as well as in the behavior of individual students. We hope you too will try them, adapt them, invent new ones, and experience the joy of seeing your students grow to believe in themselves and their ability to achieve their individual goals. It's a very rewarding feeling.

Directory of Organizations
and Periodicals
on Alternative Education

Gary F. Render, Charles E. Moon, and
Donald J. Treffinger

Controversy is not unusual in the history of American public education. Even so, the last decade has been marked by unusual activity; there have been many critical analyses and a number of strong pressures toward change. Consequently, the number of organizations and periodicals devoted to critical analysis and new alternatives has grown so rapidly that any attempt to catalog them is destined to have some errors and omissions before it can be printed. Since interest in the development of new alternatives is very high, however, and many sources are difficult to obtain without some direction, a survey of some of the organizations and periodicals may have value for many readers.

The purpose of this bibliography is to provide an overview of the resources that the compilers have been able to identify in our efforts to study this field; it is concerned with education in general, although no attempt has been made to incorporate the literature pertaining to higher education. Although books are not included in the present bibliography, a listing of books may be obtained from Dr. Treffinger. The compilers would be happy to hear from readers concerning changes or new resources which may be available.

ORGANIZATIONS

Adirondack Mountain Humanistic Education Center, Upper Jay, New York 12987. A group that works with faculties and school systems through workshops as outside change agents. Emphasis on alternatives to grading.

Gary F. Render, Charles E. Moon and Donald J. Treffinger, "Directory of Organizations and Periodicals on Alternative Education," *The Journal of Creative Behavior*, 1973, pp. 54–65.

469

African-American Teachers' Association, Inc., 1064 Fulton Street, Brooklyn, New York 11238. An organization of black teachers working to raise political consciousness of blacks. Publication: *Forum,* 10 times per year.

American Friends Service Committee, 319 E. 25th Street, Baltimore, Maryland 21218. Publishes the *New School Switchboard,* and list of resources for getting into alternative education.

Bay Area Radical Teachers' Organizing Collective, 1445 Stockton Street, San Francisco, California 94133. Tries to make political sense of what happens in the schools. Publication: *No More Teachers' Dirty Looks.*

Boston Vocations for Social Change, 48 Inman Street, Cambridge, Massachusetts 02139. Publishes *Peoples' Yellow Pages,* area free schools list, and other information on education.

Center for Educational Reform, 2115 S. Street NW, Washington, DC 20008. Clearinghouse for information on educational change and radical alternatives in and out of the system. Publishes *Edcentric* and many reprints and publications (Center Publication Series).

Center for Intercultural Documentation (CIDOC), APDO 479, Cuernavaca, Mexico. Holds seminars on education and publishes papers on many subjects including education.

Chicago Teacher Center, 852 W. Belmont, Room #2, Chicago, Illinois 60657. Sponsors a variety of work projects, activities and services for radical school teachers.

Consortium for Humanizing Education, c/o Jim Clatworthy, New College, Oakland University, Rochester, Michigan 48063. To help schools create environments response to individual needs of students and facilitate growth and change in schools.

Counter-Culture Law Project, 360 E. Superior Street, Chicago, Illinois 60611. Publishes a *Legal Manual for Alternative Schools* directed specifically to Illinois but may be helpful in other states.

East Bay Education Switchboard, 1744 University Avenue, Berkeley, California 94703. A group helping people get together who are interested in alternative schools.

Education Action Fund, Inc., Box 27, Essex Station, Boston, Massachusetts 02112. An organization collecting and distributing information about free schools.

The Education Center, 57 Hayes Street, Cambridge, Massachusetts 02139. Information clearinghouse for the new schools in the New England area. Publication: a newsletter, *Centerpeace.*

Education Exploration Center, 3104 16th Avenue South, Minneapolis, Minnesota. Publishes a monthly newsletter, book reviews, job openings, articles of interest to teachers.

Free Peoples' Exchange, Arrakis, R. F. D. 1, Jeffersonville, New York 12748. Clearinghouse to help people in the northeastern United States who are exploring alternative life-styles, free schools, etc.

Free School Press, Box 22, Saturna Island, British Columbia, Canada. List of publications available and publishes *Free School: The Journal of Change in Education.*

Free School Switchboard, Box 635, Baltimore, Maryland 21203. Medium for communication and exchange among Baltimore area people involved or interested in the new schools movement and in improving education.

Gemini Institute, 8160 Sycamore Rd., Indianapolis, Indiana 46240. Supports the free school movement in the U.S. Lending library of new school literature.

Holt Associates, Inc., 308 Boyleston St., Boston, Massachusetts 02116. A group of speakers available for various aspects of education. Also available, reprints of articles, bibliographies and information list and much information about schools.

Intentional Education (formerly EDAL), 106 Morningside Drive, Apt. 65, New York, N.Y. 10027. Published Report from EDAL conference, *Alternatives in Education: What Next?* Helpful to those establishing Radical Educational Conferences.

Learning Center, c/o Exploring Family School, Box 1442, El Cajon, California 92021. Regional clearinghouse for southern California community schools, teacher organizing projects, help with starting schools.

Movement Speakers' Bureau, Room 602, 917 15th Street NW, Washington, D.C. 20005. Speakers available from the counterculture and Far Left.

National Association for Community Schools, 1707 N. Street NW, Washington, D.C. 20036. A resource group for community schools.

New Directions Community School, 445 10th Street, Richmond, California 94801. Needs lots of money and resources.
Publication: *New Schools Manual* ($2.00).

New England Free Press, 791 Tremont Street, Boston, Massachusetts 02118. Publishers of an assortment of radical literature.
List available on request.

New Jersey Alternative Schools, Terry Ripmaster, 271 Leonia Ave., Leonia, New Jersey 07605. A clearinghouse for materials concerned with free schools. Publishes a list of New Jersey free schools and assists existing free schools.

New Life Environmental Designs Institute, P.O. Box 648, Kalamazoo, Michigan 49005. Publishes the *Access Catalog,* information about designing., building and maintaining self-supporting environments with a small education section; subscription $8.00/year.

New Nation Seed Fund, Box 4026, Philadelphia, Pennsylvania 19118. An organization requesting small contributions to help new free schools get started and keep existing ones alive.

The New School Movement, 117 Madrone Place E., Seattle, Washington 98102. Planning and organizing activities in support of humanistic objectives and goals in education.

New Schools Network, 3039 Deakin Street, Berkeley, California 94705. Publishes a newsletter dealing with free schools; $2.00/year.

New University Conference, 852 W. Belmont, Room 2, Chicago, Illinois 60657. Publishes the *Radical Teacher,* quarterly. Articles dealing with alternatives to traditional education.

New York Summerhill Society, 339 Lafayette Street, New York, N.Y. 10012. Prints a bulletin six times a year ($.50 each); lists schools who claim to be following the Summerhill approach ($.50 each) and sends out names of people who wish to get in touch with others about projects related to Summerhill ($.50 each). The movie, "Summerhill" is available for rent.

Radical Education Project, Box 625, Ann Arbor, Michigan 48107. Publishes the newsletter, *Radicals in the Professions.*

Radical Educational Project, Box 561-A, Detroit, Michigan 48232. Publishes a literature list and bi-monthly magazine, *Something Else.*

Radical Teachers Group, c/o Green, 83 Chestnut Hill Avenue, Brighton, Massachusetts 02135. A collective of people working to change Boston-area education. Publishes the *Red Pencil* and *The Red Pencil Bulletin*.

Relational Education, 3053 Main Street, Buffalo, N.Y. 14214. A communications network for alternatives to present living and learning. Group has five centers as "university free schools" to strengthen the counter-culture.

Rio Grande Educational Association, P.O. Box 2241, Santa Fe, New Mexico 87501. A group that serves as an educational network for the southwestern U.S. Its goal is to aid non-coercive education.

The San Francisco Education Switchboard, 1380 Howard St., San Francisco, California 94103. Catalyst for alternative education and humanizing education by virtue of workshops, meetings, resources, and information.

Southwest Educational Reform Center, 3505 South Main, Houston, Texas 77002. An organization that will assist in setting up free universities and colleges in the southwest.

Student Rights Project, New York Civil Liberties Union, 84 Fifth Avenue, New York, N.Y. 10011. Publishes the *Student Rights Handbook for New York City*.

Summerhill Collective, 137A West 14th Street, New York, N.Y. 10011. A group of adults committed to children's liberation. Publishes a magazine called the *Summerhill Bulletin*. Offers teacher training programs and list of schools.

Summerhill Society of California, 1778 S. Holt Avenue, Los Angeles, California 90035. Monthly bulletin, conducts workshops; List of Summerhill-type schools; has the film "Summerhill" available.

Teacher Drop-Out Center, Box 521, Amherst, Massachusetts 01002. An organization to help alternative schools find teachers and teachers find alternative schools. $17.00/year for directory of schools, description of schools, and listings of job openings.

The Teachers, Inc., 2700 Broadway, New York, N.Y. 10012. A non-profit teacher-training organization developing programs that are related to the specific needs of children and their communities.

Teacher Organizing Project, New University Conference, 852 West Belmont, Room 2, Chicago, Illinois 60657. A project of the New University Conference. A group of educators in Chicago who believe in schools which liberate the potential of students and teachers and in a society based on human dignity and equality. Has available a pamphlet series for teachers including, *Classes and Schools* and *Down the Up Staircase.*

Teacher Works, Inc., 2738 N. E. 24th, Portland, Oregon 97403. A non-profit corporation of Portland teachers has started a teacher drop-in center for meeting and working with other teachers.

Teachers & Writers Collaborative, c/o P. S. 3, 490 Hudson Street, New York, N.Y. 10014. Brings together writers, teachers, and students to create a curriculum relevant to the lives of children today, and can make language a living process. Publishes a newsletter 4 times/year.

Vocations for Social Change, Box 13, Canyon, California 94516. A clearinghouse for information and ideas pertaining to institutional change. Seeking alternatives to present institutions. Publishes the *Vocations for Social Change,* a bimonthly journal.

Washington Area Free School Clearinghouse, 1609 19th Street N.W., Washington, D.C. 20009. Central resource of information for people interested in alternatives in education, free schools, or reforms in the public schools in the Washington area; tries to publish a newsletter regularly.

Whole Earth Truck Store, 558 Santa Cruz Avenue, Menlo Park, California 94025. Source for book, *De-Schooling—De-Conditioning* based on Ivan Illich's ideas on de-schooling society. Mail-order house for items from Whole Earth Catalog.

The World Future Society, An Association for the Study of Alternative Futures, P. O. Box 19285, Twentieth Street Station, Washington, D.C. 20036. Publishes *The Futurist* bi-monthly. A clearinghouse for different views about the future that does not take official positions of what the future will or should be like.

PUBLICATIONS

Access Catalog
New Life Environmental Design Institute, Box 648, Kalamazoo, Michigan 49005. Diversity of alternatives is the subject matter of the catalog that will hopefully serve as a tool to create awareness of the possibilities for the future; 12 issues/$6.

Alternate Society
47 Riverside Drive, Welland, Ontario, Canada. Publication dealing with alternate life styles, collectives, communes, etc.

Alternatives for Education
P. O. Box 1028, San Pedro, California 90733. Publishes educational alternatives newsletter: Alternative job listings, book reviews, new school openings, resources, etc.; $5/year, 50¢/ issue.

Big Rock Candy Mountain
1115 Merrill Street, Menlo Park, California 94025. A learning-to-learn catalog designed to lead people to sources that aid in personal education. Published quarterly; $8/year.

Centerpeace
The Education Center, 57 Hayes Street, Cambridge, Massachusetts 02139. Publication of the Education Center.

Change—The Washington Area Newsletter on Alternatives
7403 Holly Avenue, Takoma Park, Maryland 20012. A free newsletter to help people get in touch with new ideas, people, and places in the Washington area.

Edcentric
2115 S. Street N.W., Washington, D.C. 20008. Publication of the Center for Educational Reform. Published 8 times a year; $5/year.

Forum
African-American Teachers' Association, Inc., 1064 Fulton Street, Brooklyn, N.Y. 11238. Articles and comments on the struggle of blacks; $5/year, 10 issues/year.

Freedom
Anarchist Weekly, Freedom Press, 84b Whitechapel High Street, London, England 1. This is a weekly newspaper dealing with a variety of topics including education and schools.

Free School: The Journal of Change in Education
Free School Press, Box 22, Saturna Island, British Columbia, Canada. Publication of the Free School Press; on educational alternatives.

From the Canyon Collective
Box 77, Canyon, California 94516. A "survival" newspaper dealing with many topics including education, the draft, women's liberation, etc.

The Futurist
P.O. Box 19285, Twentieth Street Station, Washington, D.C. 20036. Bi-monthly magazine of the World Future Society; $7.50/year.

The Green Revolution
School of Living, Freeland, M.D. 21053. Monthly publication dealing with alternative life styles.

The Horripilator
315 Voltz Road, Northbrook, Illinois 60062. A newsletter for the exchange of ideas on individualizing and humanizing educational experiences.

Interchange: A Journal of Educational Studies
Ontario Institute for Studies in Education, 252 Bloor Street W., Toronto 5, Ontario, Canada. A quarterly journal concerned with relationships among theoretical perspectives, empirical research and educational practice; $3/year—students.

KOA Newsletter
c/o Arrakis, R. F. D. 1, Jeffersonville, N.Y. 12748. Communications on alternatives; $5/year.

Media Mix
Box 5139, Chicago, Illinois 60680. Ideas and resources for educational change published 8 times a year; $5/year.

Mother Earth News
P.O. Box 38, Madison, Ohio 44057. Bi-monthly magazine that stresses alternative life styles, ecology, working with nature and doing more with less; Subscription—$5/year.

New Directions in Teaching
Department of Education, Bowling Green State University, Bowling Green, Ohio 43403. A non-journal dedicated to improving undergraduate teaching and learning.

New Jersey School Magazine
16 Crestwood Avenue, Glen Rock, New Jersey 07452. Communication network for people starting new schools in New Jersey area: $3/year.

New School of Education Journal
4304 Tolman Hall, University of California, Berkeley, California 94720. A forum for the exchange of radical and creative ideas in education; $5/year —individuals, $6/year—institutions.

New Schools Exchange Newsletter
701B Anacapa Street, Santa Barbara, California 93101. Central clearinghouse for people involved in experimental education. Newsletter and directory of schools is available; $10/year.

New Schools Manual
New Directions Community School, 445 10th Street, Richmond, California 94801. Publication of New Directions Community School.

New Voices in Education
Box 2456 Norman Hall, University of Florida, Gainesville, Florida 32601. Published by graduate students in education. A forum for student ideas and discussion; $3/year—students, $5/year—others.

New Ways in Education
1778 South Holt Avenue, Los Angeles, California 90035. A monthly newsletter covering alternative schools and innovative public schools in southern California; $5/year.

No More Teachers' Dirty Looks
Bay Area Radical Teachers' Organizing Collective, 1445 Stockton Street, San Francisco, California 94133. News of San Francisco area and writings of radicals on education; $2/year (4 issues).

Observations from the Treadmill
357 Hidden River Road, Narbeth, Pennsylvania 19072. Published periodically but no less than quarterly, dealing with education and other social issues. Price determined by each issue's worth to the reader.

Outside the Net
P.O. Box 184, Lansing, Michigan 48901. For those who seek a radical and humane alternative to the educational system. Spreads information about change in education; $4/2 years (Six issues and maybe 2 summer issues).

Peoples' Yellow Pages
48 Inman Street, Cambridge, Massachusetts 02139. Publication of the Boston Vocations for Social Change.

Radicals in the Professions
Box 625, Ann Arbor, Michigan 48107. Newsletter of the Radical Education Project.

Radical Teacher
New University Conference, 852 W. Belmont, Room 2, Chicago, Illinois 60657. Quarterly publication of the New University Conference; $1/copy.

The Red Pencil
c/o Green, 83 Chestnut Hill Avenue, Brighton, Massachusetts 02135. Publication of the Radical Teachers Group.

The Red Pencil Bulletin and Teacher Center News
c/o Green, 83 Chestnut Hill Avenue, Brighton, Massachusetts 02135. Publication of the Radical Teachers Group.

Rio Grande Educational Association News
P.O. Box 2241, Santa Fe, New Mexico 87501. Newsletter of the Rio Grande Educational Association; $5/year—includes membership in the organization.

Something Else
Box 561-A, Detroit, Michigan 48232. Bi-monthly magazine of the Radical Education Project.

Student Rights Handbook for New York City
84 Fifth Avenue, New York, N.Y. 10011. New York Civil Liberties Union publication from the Student Rights Project. A description of the laws that affect students in New York City; $.10 each—1 copy free.

Summerhill Bulletin
137A West 14th St., New York, N.Y. 10011. The publication of the Summerhill Collective.

Switched On
1380 Howard Street, San Francisco, California 94103. The occasional newsletter of the San Francisco Education Switchboard.

The Teacher Paper
3923 S. Main, Portland, Oregon 97214. Published quarterly and publishes only articles written by classroom teachers. Anything having to do with public school teachers' problems; $3/year (4 issues), 75¢/single copy.

Teachers and Writers Collaborative Newsletter
Pratt Center for Community Development, c/o P. S. 3, 490 Hudson Street, New York, N.Y. 10014. Works of kids and teachers; $3 for 4 issues.

This Magazine is About Schools
56 Esplanade Street, Suite 301, Toronto 215, Ontario, Canada. Quarterly journal devoted to educational alternatives and radical critique of schools; $4.50/year.

Toolkit
Southern Media Project. Available through Center for Educational Reform; a tabloid for the media freak-to-be.

Additional Readings

ASHTON-WARNER, SYLVIA. *Teacher.* New York: Bantam Books, 1963. A magnificent, personal story of an amazing woman and her inspiring method of teaching based on joy and love.

BORTON, TERRY. *Reach, Touch and Teach.* New York: McGraw-Hill, 1970. A readable, provocative, and informative introduction to process education for student concerns.

BROWN, GEORGE ISAAC. *Human Teaching for Human Learning.* New York: The Viking Press, 1971. This book encompasses a philosophy and a process of teaching in which the affective or emotional aspects of learning flow together with the cognitive or intellectual functions.

COMBS, ARTHUR (ed.). *Perceiving, Behaving and Becoming.* Washington, D.C.: Association for Supervision and Curriculum Development, 1962. This book presents a series of articles by the leading educational theorists in perception, self-concept and self-actualization.

FAIRFIELD, ROY P. (ed.). *Humanistic Frontiers in American Education.* Englewood Cliffs, N.J.: Prentice-Hall, Inc., 1971. This book offers new understanding of directions and goals, explores the forces shaping the future, and traces the birth of humanistic revolution to the impact John Dewey had upon education.

FAST, JULIUS. *Body Language.* New York: J. B. Lippincott Co., 1970. An entertaining survey of proxemics, kinesics, and non-verbal communication.

GOLEMBIEWSKI, ROBERT T., and ARTHUR BLUMBERG. *Sensitivity Training and the Laboratory Approach.* Itasca, Ill.: F. E. Peacock Publishers Inc., 1970. This book contains 37 selected articles and extensive editorial comments to provide a "stereophonic" view of the laboratory approach. The book illustrates basic T-group dynamics.

GREENBERG, HERBERT M. *Teaching with Feeling.* New York: The Macmillan Publishing Co., 1969. This book focuses on the inner life of the teacher rather than the emotions of the learner. The author stresses "honesty, spontaneity and variety" in teaching.

GOFFMAN, ERVING. *Encounters.* New York: The Bobbs-Merrill Co., Inc., 1961. A look at the encounter group movement including group psychotherapy and especially small-group analysis.

GUNTHER, BERNARD. *Sense Relaxation Below Your Mind.* New York: Collier Books, 1968. Gives exercises for individuals, partners, and groups to

479

achieve greater sensory awareness. Many of the exercises are adaptable to class or group use.

GUNTHER, BERNARD. *What to do Till the Messiah Comes.* New York: The Macmillan Publishing Co., 1971. This book demonstrates gestalt therapy, group encounter, verbal and non-verbal ways to work through "destructive behavior patterns and mind/body/energy blocks."

GUSTAITIS, RASA. *Turning On.* New York: The Macmillan Publishing Co., 1969. One woman's trip beyond LSD through awareness-expansion without the use of drugs. Included are discussion on truth-labs, gestalt therapy, meditation, zen, sensory awareness, hip communes, brain-wave control.

HAWLEY, ROBERT C. *Human Values in the Classroom.* Amherst, Mass.: Educational Research Associates, 1973. The author sets forth a basic approach to teaching and learning based on human needs and human values.

HAWLEY, ROBERT C., SIDNEY B. SIMON and D. D. BRITTON. *Composition for Personal Growth.* New York: Hart Publishing Co., Inc., 1973. This book contains a vast number and variety of specific suggestions and techniques to stimulate students to exchange ideas about themselves and each other.

HEATH, DOUGLAS H. *Humanizing Schools.* New York: Hayden Book Company, Inc., 1967. Through his analysis of a dropout's experience of personal estrangement, Heath develops a model of healthy maturing whereby he identifies the experiences young people need to become flexible, educable adults.

HOWARD, JANE. *Please Touch.* New York: McGraw-Hill Book Co., 1970. The author took part in over twenty different encounter groups—among them an interracial workshop, a nude marathon, a Synanon workshop, and a weekend of "aggressive dating."

JAMES, MURIEL and DOROTHY JONGEWARD. *Born To Win.* Reading, Mass.: Addison-Wesley Publishers, 1971. This book is primarily concerned with transactional analysis theory and its application to the daily life of the average person. Valuable to those in education, particularly the mental health fields.

JONES, RICHARD M. *Fantasy and Feeling in Education.* New York: New York University Press, 1968. One of the few books in humanistic education written from the viewpoint of a Freudian-oriented psychoanalyst.

LEDERMAN, JANET. *Anger and the Rocking Chair: Gestalt Awareness with Children.* New York: McGraw-Hill Book Co., 1969. This book is a dramatic, visual account of Gestalt methods with so-called "difficult" or "disturbed" children in elementary school.

LEONARD, GEORGE B. *Education and Ecstacy.* New York: A Delta Book, 1968. This book celebrates the joy, the unity, of learning and living-with practical suggestions on how to make this vision a reality in our schools.

LOWEN, ALEXANDER. *The Betrayal of the Body.* New York: Collier Books, 1967. This book charts a new course toward emotional fulfillment through body awareness and the recovery of a gratifying mind-body relationship.

LUFT, JOSEPH. *Group Processes.* Palo Alto, Calif.: National Press Books, 1970. Starting with the assumption that behavior is best understood in the context of interpersonal ties, the author establishes a basic framework within which components of the communication process may be viewed.

LYON, HAROLD C. *Learning to Feel—Feeling to Learn.* Columbus, Ohio: Charles E. Merrill Publishing Co., 1971. A factual, down-to-earth book, giving straight-forward accounts of the results experienced by the author as he tried out novel methods of bringing the "whole" student into the classroom, with the feeling aspects of himself, the intellectual aspects, and the capacity for self-responsibility.

MANN, JOHN. *Encounter: A Weekend with Intimate Strangers.* New York: Groseman Publishers, 1969. A book about a group of strangers who meet for a weekend encounter group and freely act and talk out their feelings.

MASLOW, ABRAHAM H. *Religions, Values, and Peak-Experiences.* New York: The Viking Press, 1970. Maslow articulates on one of his prominent theses: the "religious" experience is a rightful subject for scientific investigation and speculation and, conversely, the "scientific community" will see its work enhanced by acknowledging and studying the species wide need for spiritual expression which, in so many forms, is at the heart of "peak experiences" reached by healthy, fully functioning persons.

MONTAGU, ASHLEY. *Touching: The Human Significance of the Skin.* New York: Columbia University Press, 1971. Ashley Montagu presents a lively inquiry into the importance of tactile experience in the development of the person.

NYBERG, DAVID. *Tough and Tender Learning.* Palo Alto, Calif.: National Press Books, 1971. A view of the current climate of the classroom and a method of approach the author feels would greatly improve the learning environment.

OTTO, HERBERT and JOHN MANN. *Ways of Growth.* New York: The Viking Press, 1968. This book brings together authoritative descriptions of contemporary methods of self-development. These efforts seek to cultivate normal human functioning beyond the level of average performance—in the matters of sensory awakening, sex, family life, group living, the psychedelic experience, etc.

PETERSON, SEVERIN. *A Catalog of the Ways People Grow.* New York: Ballantine Books, Inc., 1971. A catalog which presents description, excerpts from principal sources, and an extensive directory of information for the ways some people have found to grow.

PFEIFFER, WILLIAM J. and JOHN E. JONES. *Structured Experiences for Human Relations Training.* Iowa City, Iowa: University Associates Press, 1969–71. Each of three volumes contains detailed descriptions of about 25 "structured experiences" often similar to those described in the first part of this book. Some of the experiences are easily adaptable to the general classroom.

PURKEY, WILLIAM W. *Self Concept and School Achievement*. Englewood Cliffs, N.J.: Prentice-Hall, Inc., 1970. This book introduces an exciting new happening in contemporary education. This is the growing emphasis placed on the student's subjective and personal evaluation of himself as a dominant influence on his success or failure in school.

RATHS, LOUIS E., MERRILL HARMIN, and SIDNEY B. SIMON. *Values and Teaching*. Columbus, Ohio: Charles E. Merrill Publishing Co., 1966. This book illustrates concrete examples of how a teacher may cultivate pupil skill in the process of valuing.

ROGERS, CARL and BARRY STEVENS. *Person to Person*. Lafayette, Calif.: Real People Press, 1967. Professional papers by Rogers and others—about therapy, experiencing and learning—are set in a matrix of personal response and the use that Barry Stevens has made of these papers in arriving at better understanding of herself, and her view of the problem of being human as she encountered it in her life.

RUBIN, THEODORE ISAAC. *The Angry Book*. New York: Macmillan Publishing Co., 1969. An easy-to-read essay encouraging readers to allow themselves to be constructively angry.

RUITENBEEK, HENDRIK M. *The New Group Therapies*. New York: Discuss Books, 1970. A guide to the dynamic effectiveness of the human growth potential experience.

SIMON, SIDNEY B., LELAND W. HOWE, and HOWARD KIRSCHENBAUM. *Values Clarification*. New York: Hart Publishing Company, Inc., 1972. A handbook of practical values-clarification strategies for teachers and students.

SIROKA, ROBERT W., W. K. SIROKA, and G. A. SCHLOSS. *Sensitivity Training and Group Encounter*. New York: Grosset's Universal Library, 1971. The book discusses new approaches to greater awareness and deeper perception of one's self and others through T-Groups, attack therapy, psychodrama, marathons, etc.

SPOLIN, VIOLA. *Improvisation for the Theater*. Evanston: Northwestern University Press, 1963. The book describes about 200 games that have been played with children and teens learning to act, games that involve emotional expression, sensory awareness, a sense of place, etc. The ideas are easily adaptable to personal-relations work and are fun.

THELEN, HERBERT A. *Education and the Human Quest*. Chicago: The University of Chicago Press, 1972. The author presents four learning experiences that he believes a child must have to become educated—personal inquiry, group investigation, reflection, and skill development.

WEINSTEIN, GERALD and MARIO D. FANTINI. *Toward Humanistic Education*. New York: Praeger Publishers, 1970. Based on a model that engages the child as a whole-hearted participant in the educational process by making that process "relevant" to him in the most profound sense.